Further acclaim for
Rubies in the Orchard

★(Starred Review)
"In a forest of dry marketing books, [Lynda] Resnick's animated debut stands out as its own hidden gem, filled with juicy real-life tales of marketing . . . The author charms with her winning wit and a self-deprecating tone as she distills the secrets of her extraordinary career . . . A must-read for anyone who aspires to Resnick's level of promotional genius, success, or commitment to environmental sustainability."

—*Publishers Weekly*

"Lynda Resnick is one of the great marketers of our time—who else, after all, could have rebranded and relaunched a food as troublesome as the pomegranate, a fruit formerly more trouble to eat than it was worth? Whether you're in the business of selling products or ideas, *Rubies in the Orchard* is full of indispensable advice. Even better, it manages to delight even as it instructs."

—MICHAEL POLLAN, author of
The Omnivore's Dilemma and *In Defense of Food*

"There are pearls of wisdom in *Rubies in the Orchard*—wisdom that marketing genius Lynda Resnick has gained through long experience, hard work, and dealing with many challenges on the road to her outstanding success. In sharing her personal life story she gives us very useful tips about discovering real value in the world around us and making best use of it. An inspiring book and a good read!"

—DR. ANDREW WEIL, MD, author of
Healthy Aging and *8 Weeks to Optimum Health*

"An inspiring story and an enthralling treatise by one of America's most imaginative and energetic entrepreneurs . . . Lynda Resnick, the POM Queen, shows each of us that it's possible to do well by doing good."
—ROBERT F. KENNEDY JR., award-winning author
and president of Waterkeeper Alliance

"Lynda Resnick understands popular culture, she reads it brilliantly and places her products in a context that uses popular energy to advance them."
—DAVID GEFFEN, founder, Asylum and Geffen Records;
co-founder, DreamWorks SKG

"Part marketing master class, part can't-put-it-down biography, *Rubies in the Orchard* is as refreshing as a cold bottle of FIJI Water on a hot day and as fortifying as a glass of POM juice. Read this witty and wise book to learn how to sell your brand . . . but, whatever you do, read it. It sparkles as brightly as the gem in its title."
—ARIANNA HUFFINGTON, editor in chief, The Huffington Post

"Exactly the spirit we need to deal with the gloom and doom of Wall Street. I read it cover to cover without stopping. I felt emboldened."
—FRANK GEHRY, architect

"*Rubies in the Orchard* is the can't-put-it-down, remember-every-word, must-read book of our era! Read it, enjoy it . . . and tell your friends everywhere to do the same!"
—KEVIN KLOSE, president, NPR

"Irving Berlin said of Fred Astaire that he was 'the purest talent' with whom he had ever worked. As to marketing and original creation, Lynda Resnick is the purest talent and her writing, irresistible."
—DAVID G. BRADLEY, chairman, Atlantic Media Group

"Lynda Resnick is one of America's great brand builders. *Rubies in the Orchard* is a strategic marketing primer wrapped in a witty narrative that celebrates the seller's honesty and the consumer's sense of value."
—MICHAEL MILKEN, chairman, Milken Institute

"If pomegranates are the rubies in the orchard, then this book is the diamond on the bookshelf. This book sparkles with Lynda Resnick's expertise in marketing and is flawless, a perfect gem on how to see the best in what is sometimes a rough stone."

—RITA WILSON, actor, producer

"*Rubies in the Orchard* talks about real experiences with products that are good for people, marketed in a conscientious way. Real-life stuff, involving balancing business and social concerns."

—CRAIG NEWMARK, founder and CEO, Craigslist

"Lynda Resnick has done Adam Smith one better: she has given the business world a much-needed face-lift and a sense of humor. *Rubies in the Orchard* is a twenty-first-century *Wealth of Nations* for every man and every woman who has ever dreamed of starting a business and marketing it effectively. Above all else, it is a charming memoir of one of the truly brilliant entrepreneurs of our time."

—DR. HENRY LOUIS GATES, JR.,
Alphonse Fletcher University Professor, Harvard University

"Lynda Resnick is a genius at marketing. In this wonderful new book, she reveals her potent secret: meeting the most powerful yet unmet human needs for integrity, quality, and sustainability as well as for love and community . . . *Rubies in the Orchard* is the new bible of marketing."

—DR. DEAN ORNISH, founder and president,
Preventive Medicine Research Institute

"A 'must-read' for anyone interested in selling or marketing. Lynda Resnick is a master marketer, and we can all learn from her."

—LEONARD LAUDER, chairman of the board,
The Estée Lauder Companies

"A candid and sharp analysis of today's world of product marketing. Lynda Resnick has generously offered the truth behind her success, which is a refreshing combination of authenticity, value, and transparency in marketing."

—ALICE WATERS, bestselling author,
founder, and co-owner, Chez Panisse

"Everybody playing and toiling and wanting to achieve success with a brand in our difficult economy should read this book to understand right from wrong, good from bad, quality from junk."

—MICHAEL EISNER, founder, Tornante Company, and former chairman and CEO, The Walt Disney Company

"Lynda Resnick humbly resists being called a marketing genius. Read her book at the risk of becoming one yourself."

—NORMAN LEAR , award-winning television and film writer, director, and producer

"This illuminating, captivating, and sassy book has it all—marketing savvy, life values, and a clear path to success no matter what your goal."

—BARBARA GOLDSMITH, bestselling author and historian

"Lynda Resnick is one dynamic, persuasive gal. She can talk anybody into anything, including getting me to write a blurb for this book. Now that's persuasive."

—LARRY DAVID, star of HBO's *Curb Your Enthusiasm*

"Lynda Resnick is a force of nature and a force for good. She is also a brilliant marketer. *Rubies in the Orchard* reveals the secret of her success—effective marketing is not about fooling people but respecting them."

—MICHAEL SANDEL, professor of government, Harvard University, and author of *Public Philosophy: Essays on Morality in Politics*

"With insight, elegance, and simplicity [Lynda Resnick] has become an icon in the world of marketing. We should be so lucky that a little of her magic might rub off on us all!"

—STEPHEN McPHERSON, president of ABC Entertainment

"Lynda Resnick is to branding what Warren Buffett is to investing: a master of honesty, common sense, and belief that one can do well while doing good."

—GLORIA STEINEM, bestselling author, feminist activist, and co-founder, *Ms.* and *New York* magazines

"A fascinating and instructive guide into the world of a marketing genius, told with a beguiling frankness and good humor."

—MICHAEL YORK, actor and author

"The single best piece of writing I have read in years by an active and successful CEO. Stop everything you're doing right now and take a swig of this honest and useful book."

—WARREN BENNIS, Distinguished Professor of Business Administration, University of Southern California, and author of *On Becoming a Leader*

"I recommend *Rubies in the Orchard* to marketers, business executives eager to unlearn bad lessons from business school, or anyone who has ever been sure they had a great idea but didn't have the confidence to get started."

—SETH SIEGEL co-founder and CEO, The Beanstalk Group

"Lynda Resnick is by far the absolute epicenter of future marketing where vision and language, form and appeal, attitude and personality, intelligence and spirit are all built into the product as to allow the Brand to speak and interact with the consumer . . . WOW!"

—PETER ARNELL, founder and CEO, The Arnell Group

"No one I know has more intuitive sense of consumer tastes and insight into what delights audiences more than Lynda Resnick. This wonderful book will be a catalyst to unlock the reader's strengths, skills, and abilities."

—BOBBY KOTICK, CEO, Activision

"From one Queen to another . . . Lynda Resnick, the POM Queen, has given us a crown jewel. *Rubies in the Orchard* is richly filled with insight from one of the cutting-edge marketers and entrepreneurs of our time."

—HER MAJESTY QUEEN NOOR OF JORDAN

"A captivating . . . read about visionary leadership and innovative marketing at its best."

—YORAM (JERRY) WIND, The Lauder Professor and professor of marketing, The Wharton School

"If there were one book that's a must-read for anyone trying to persuade people of the value of a product or to communicate to a mass audience why they should try something new, it is Lynda Resnick's fascinating, elegant, and succinct *Rubies in the Orchard*. Her wit, originality, and courage are infectious."
—LEON BOTSTEIN, president, Bard College, and music director and principal conductor, American Symphony Orchestra and Jerusalem Symphony Orchestra

"Lynda Resnick is smart, creative, and a doer. *Rubies in the Orchard* tells us how she thinks and how she makes great things happen in business . . . It's a good read authored by a good person."
—THE HONORABLE JON CORZINE, governor of New Jersey

"Highly entertaining and smartly funny . . . The marketing philosophy [Lynda Resnick] espouses in her book is so pure, powerful, deceptively simple, and easily adapted to any situation that it earns the ultimate marketing accolade . . . why didn't I think of that? *Rubies in the Orchard* should be required reading at every business school in the country."
—LEONARD GOLDBERG, television and motion picture executive and producer

"The Resnicks have a true talent for building successful brands by combining product with great marketing. Lynda's superb creative marketing skills and respect for the integrity of the brand and the consumer is the critical element to establishing brands and creating great value. *Rubies in the Orchard* offers a revealing insight into the process and is a road map for creating profit while being socially responsible."
—TERRY SEMEL, chairman, Windsor Media, and former chairman and CEO, Yahoo!

"Lynda [Resnick] proves that there is only so much you can learn in business school. The real world is where real learning happens. In *Rubies in the Orchard*, Lynda shows that it is not only great to produce the right results; it is also increasingly valuable to produce the right results the right way. Doing good is good for business. This is especially important in this demanding, informed, skeptical marketing world. Read it. Learn from it. And live it."

—LARRY LIGHT, chairman and CEO, Arcature LLC

"Lynda Resnick . . . weaves her magic through unmatched advertising campaigns, ingenious packaging, inspired product placements, inventive uses of the Internet, and surprising product extensions . . . a great story about a bold original, who inspires us to think differently."

—JUDY OLIAN, dean, UCLA Anderson School of Management

RUBIES
in the
ORCHARD

LYNDA RESNICK

with Francis Wilkinson

RUBIES
in the
ORCHARD

How to Uncover the
HIDDEN GEMS
in Your Business

DOUBLEDAY

New York · London · Toronto · Sydney · Auckland

ᴆᴅ

DOUBLEDAY

Copyright © 2009 by Lynda Rae Resnick

All Rights Reserved

Published in the United States by Doubleday,
an imprint of The Doubleday Publishing Group,
a division of Random House, Inc., New York.
www.doubleday.com

DOUBLEDAY is a registered trademark and the DD colophon is
a trademark of Random House, Inc.

All trademarks are the property of their respective companies.

Book design by Judith Stagnitto Abbate / Abbate Design

The illustration credits on pages 193–94 are an extension
of this copyright page.

Library of Congress Cataloging-in-Publication Data
Resnick, Lynda.
Rubies in the orchard : how to uncover the hidden gems in
your business / by Lynda Resnick with Francis Wilkinson.
—1st ed.
p. cm.
"The POM Queen's secrets to building brands and marketing
just about anything." Includes index.
(hc : alk. paper)
1. Marketing. 2. Advertising. 3. Value. 4. Business.
I. Wilkinson, Francis. II. Title.
HF5415.R462 2009
658.8—dc22
2008023167

ISBN 978-0-385-52578-7

PRINTED IN THE UNITED STATES OF AMERICA

1   3   5   7   9   10   8   6   4   2

First Edition

For Stewart

CONTENTS

PREFACE

I t was the kind of March day we sometimes get in Los Angeles: crystal blue skies, a few wispy white clouds, 72 and sunny. To celebrate her birthday, my friend Laurie David had invited a few friends to join her on a hike in the Santa Monica Mountains.

With so many business responsibilities to attend to, I don't get to spend as much girl time as I would like; my female relationships are usually relegated to the phone or double dates with their men and mine. But this day was different. I had set aside time to celebrate, and there was nothing pulling me back to the office.

We sat around an old picnic table, drank pink champagne through straws, and consumed a scrumptious lunch of soft cheeses and hard salami, French bread and olives. It was a magical day, one that would change my life.

The friends around the table were a stunningly accomplished bunch. Laurie David was one of the first activists I met in the green movement. In addition to helping open my eyes to environmental issues, she had just produced Al Gore's powerful documentary, *An Inconvenient Truth.* Never one to let the green grass grow under her feet, Laurie was now busy writing a book for children on the subject.

Rita Wilson was just about to appear as Roxie in the Broadway show *Chicago.* A brilliant actress, she was preparing to show the world that she could sing and dance, as well. She was nervous and excited, fulfilling a dream she had silently coveted for years.

Arianna Huffington's blog was growing by leaps, and she seemed to be everywhere at once, speaking out about domestic and foreign policy, our dependence on Middle East oil, and countless other topics, all while writing her eleventh book and raising two wonderful girls.

When it was my turn to discuss my plans, however, the conversation grew suddenly quiet. It seemed I didn't have any plans. Yes, I enjoyed my business. My family was doing well and my husband and I were happy together. But my dreams seemed to have stagnated. I had accomplished many goals; now I struggled to think up a new one.

"What's your dream, Lynda?" they all asked. "What do you want to do that you have never done?"

Suddenly, I blurted out, "I want to write a book."

"Well, why don't you?"

At that moment, I made a commitment to them—and to myself—that I would.

"Write what you know" is wise advice for authors. What I know best is marketing and branding. I have had a long and successful career. And over the years, I have educated myself with a bit of help from some very smart friends, mentors, and employees. I've worked hard and benefited from my share of luck. But through trial and error, I've also developed a formula for success. That day in the Santa Monica hills, I realized I could share with others what has taken me four decades to learn on my own.

Business in the twenty-first century is different from what it was when I started all those years ago. It gets tougher every day. Markets are unpredictable, the economy is unstable, the environment is a challenge, and the uncertainties of globalization and terrorism and energy supply don't make things any easier. But forty years of facing—and more often than not overcoming—market challenges have given me a useful perspective on business along with specific insights into a range of marketing issues. I have a system now. And if it's a marketing or branding challenge, chances are I've confronted it somewhere along the line and figured out how to prevail—or at least how to survive.

Experience is an invaluable asset, one gained through a life lived with passion, commitment, and energy. Your business career will be different from mine. But I hope this book helps you develop your own formula for success. At the very least, you can see not only how I approach marketing and branding, but why. Success isn't a matter of throwing something against the wall in the hope that it will stick. It's the sum of research, focus, discipline, and hard work. It flows from a systematic approach to uncovering value that others have overlooked (perhaps because they were busy throwing stuff against a wall to see what would stick) and learning how to communicate that value in clever, effective, truthful ways.

It's sometimes hard in the chaos of the moment to stay focused on what truly works. I hope that in following the trail of my experiences, and the methods (and occasional madness) I have laid out in this book, you'll see a road map for your own success. Take a hike with me. Follow your dreams.

CHAPTER 1

An 8,000-Year-Old Overnight Sensation

I had hit a personal low. I was out of work for the first time since I was seventeen. I had no job, a blank date book, and so much time on my hands I could lunch with the girls. Sure, I had money. But I was also a bit lost. The kids were grown and living their own lives. Without work, which had been central to my identity and my self-esteem for so many years, I was no longer sure who I was. I had been retired for two months, and already I was panicked.

My husband, Stewart, who was still very much in the thick of business and suffering none of my existential woes, invited me to attend a business meeting. He wanted me to serve as a sounding board for a new venture we had been working on for years. Maybe I would have something useful to say? Maybe. Maybe not.

Here was the situation: after having acquired more

than 100 acres of mature pomegranate trees in the San Joaquin Valley of California in 1987, Stewart had steadily planted hundreds of acres more throughout the 1990s. Like most crops, pomegranates were basically a commodity, albeit on a much smaller scale. But when the orchards were well managed, pomegranates could produce considerably better returns than the citrus, almonds, and pistachios that occupied most of our acreage. While the market for pomegranates was still tiny, it was growing.

The meeting wasn't about marketing pomegranates. It was about creating a market for pomegranate juice. There were several problems that made this unlikely. For starters, only about one in ten Americans said they were familiar with pomegranates, and fewer than half of that group said they had eaten one in the past year. So we weren't exactly responding to pent-up demand. We were talking about producing juice from a fruit that the overwhelming majority of Americans didn't know existed.

But we were responding to *something*. In 1996, we had begun funding medical research into the health properties of pomegranates, inspired, in part, by centuries of myth and folklore about the pomegranate's medicinal virtues. For centuries, different parts of the fruit—arils, rind, juice, bark—have been used to treat a wide range of ailments. In his *Natural History*, written in the first century, Pliny the Elder stated that "the branches of the pomegranate keep away snakes, the little buds . . . neutralize the stings of scorpions, and the fruit is in request for easing the nausea of women with child."

The Greek physician Dioscorides cited pomegranates as a treatment for ulcers, earaches, and, according to one early, unintentionally comic, translation, "griefs in ye nosthrills." The tenth-century Italian physician Shabbetai Donnolo recommended pomegranates not only for earaches but for laryngitis, as well.

Elsewhere, pomegranates were a symbol of fertility and wealth. In the *Odyssey*, Homer wrote of pomegranates in the gardens of the kings of Phrygia and Paecia. Maximilian I, the Holy Roman Emperor, adopted the pomegranate as his personal emblem and held one in his left hand as he sat for a 1519 portrait by Albrecht Dürer. Jewish folklore maintains there are 613 luscious ruby arils inside the pomegranate, one for each good deed to be accomplished in a lifetime.

The Koran advises against acting "extravagantly" when the pomegranate has borne fruit. In the Bible, the Song of Solomon identifies love with pomegranates in bloom. But the pomegranate was also used to animate less amorous passions. When Queen Isabella (the troublemaker who started the Inquisition) launched her conquest of the Muslim south of Spain, she vowed to take Andalusia like a ripe pomegranate—"one seed at a time."

While the fruit wasn't well known in the United States, it had clearly cut an impressive swath across much of the world, establishing an honored place in cultures as far away as India and China. We figured you didn't get a reputation like that—across different eras, lands, and cultures—unless there was at least a little bit of truth to the stories. Still, we had no idea what this bundle of myth, superstition, genuine folk medicine, and ancient wisdom would yield in terms of real health benefits. Was there anything here that could be documented by real science?

The early research, conducted at UCLA, UC Davis, Rutgers, the Technion Institute in Israel, and other leading institutions, was jaw-dropping. Among the first findings: pomegranate juice inhibits inflammation and pain. In addition, pomegranates turn out to be astonishingly rich in antioxidants, which inhibit oxidation in the body that can damage cells. Indeed, pomegranates are significantly richer in antioxidants than red wine, green tea, or just about anything else known to humankind. In addition, the fruit was shown to reduce arterial plaque and factors leading to atherosclerosis. Subsequent studies suggested that pomegranates have a powerful effect against prostate cancer.

In short, the news on the health benefits of pomegranates started off great. Then it proceeded to get better and then astound. One glitch: to get the full health benefits of this magnanimous fruit, you would have to eat it virtually by the pound—consuming two and a half whole pomegranates per day. Pomegranates are hard to open, and when they splatter—well, who has that many raincoats? It was all too impractical. Despite the emerging profile of the pomegranate as nature's great gift, folks would never be able to consume enough of them to get a daily dose. Unless, of course, they consumed pomegranates in the form of a juice. This might sound like a reasonable solution, but trying to get consistent, high-quality juice from a pomegranate crop is not easy.

We grow the Wonderful variety of pomegranates. When you combine Wonderfuls with the soil and climate of the San Joaquin Valley, you produce the tastiest, sweetest pomegranates in the world. But even under these ideal conditions, pomegranates are fickle. They have to be coaxed off the vine by hand. If the fruit is squeezed too hard, extracting the maximum juice, it bites back—producing a harsh, bitter aftertaste. If you don't squeeze enough juice, well, you'll pretty quickly go broke.

We literally spent years experimenting with juicers and applications. Eventually, we had to invent our own pressing technology. Then we had to figure out how to feed the presses more than a million pieces of fruit each day, which required a maze of conveyors and elevators operating with all the precision of a Broadway chorus line.

Even now, there are significant variations in sugar and acidity from one year's pomegranate crop to the next, and they even differ from orchard to orchard. Each season, we recalibrate the entire juicing process to accommodate the mood of the latest harvest.

I remember walking the orchards one hot afternoon in early fall. Using a jerry-rigged champagne press right there in the field, one of the farmers made a batch of fresh juice for me. When it's done right, pomegranate juice produces not merely a specific taste but a full sensory explosion in the mouth. It's tart yet sweet, heady with a robust, complex mouth feel. It has more in common with a fine Burgundy than with lesser juices like grape, pear, or apple.

The foundation of the juice business is essentially waste

management. (It's a lovely turn of phrase—makes you want to toast your health.) In practice, it makes a virtue of necessity. When grapes or apples are grown, for instance, there are always those unfortunate little specimens that just aren't pretty enough to pass the fresh-fruit threshold. What do you do with them? Squeeze them. Under that slightly bruised, discolored apple skin may be the sweetest, most delicious fruit of the tree. In the spirit of making lemonade from lemons, growers manage their unsightly "waste" by transforming it into juice.

IN THE CLUTTERED CHAOS of Stewart's conference room, the window ledges and conference table were strewn with various juice bottles, nearly three dozen in all, each labeled with its generally dubious contents. Around the long wooden table was a collection of cheerless marketing consultants and somber executives who no doubt wondered what I was doing in their midst. I had run into similar gentlemen (there was not a dame among them) in the past. I was familiar with their marketing gospel and commandments, their "thou musts" and "thou shalt nots."

The marketing gurus understood the challenge; in addition to the fact that few Americans had ever heard of a pomegranate, the fruit has a truncated harvest season (it begins in October and lasts less than three months) and a high retail price. A complicating factor was presumed to be a massive overproduction problem stemming from all the acreage my "crazy" husband had planted.

The team leader began with the confidence of a man who knows the one true path. "We will mix pomegranate juice with filler juices like white grape and pear and compete with those juices in the 'shelf-stable' aisles of the supermarket," he announced in what sounded to me like a eulogy for our unlaunched product. Visions of hideous, gasoline-type plastic jugs danced in my head.

He had already figured out the appropriate juice mix, saying "We won't be able to use more than ten percent pomegranate juice because it is too expensive. More would throw us out of our competitive advantage." I believe at this point I started to squirm.

The mention of "competitive advantage" was required by the setting. After all, we were contemplating launching a business. Without competitive advantage, there's no business. But pomegranate juice has only two such advantages, and they're very distinct. The first is its sensuous taste; the second, its remarkable health benefits. It seemed the plan was to dilute each of these powerful advantages by a full 90 percent. He was proposing to load diluted, adulterated pomegranate juice onto the nation's supermarket shelves next to similarly adulterated junk juice and simply hope for the best. While this well-meaning expert droned on, I imagined walking up the supermarket aisle in a rolling sea of red—from Hi-C to Welch's. The only way to stand out in that crowd would be to color our juice DayGlo lime— except Gatorade had already done that.

Summoning an inner strength usually reserved for saying "no" to pumpkin pie on Thanksgiving, I held my tongue through a couple hours of strategic marketing jargon as these gurus extolled the benefits of adding still more volume to the supermarket's red sea, despite an already perilously high tide. Then the tasting began.

Much of what America consumes when it buys prepackaged juices has misleading messaging. If the package says "Cranberry-Grape 100% Juice," chances are it's loaded with a little cranberry and lots of grape, pear, apple, and other content chosen solely for economy's sake. If the label says something like "Cranberry-Raspberry Drink," you might as well just pour yourself a Coca-Cola, because the main ingredients are almost certainly water and high-fructose corn syrup—a ubiquitous recipe that has done much to advance the cause of obesity over the past three decades.

Some people can sing. Some can draw. I can taste. I mean *really* taste. Stewart used to show me off at wine tastings, where, blindfolded, I could name the wine I was drinking and the year it was produced. I never imagined there would be a payoff to this particular talent—beyond the amusement of my husband and a few friends. My memory of that delicious taste of pomegranate juice in the orchard was still very fresh in my mind; I knew what pomegranate juice *should* taste like. The various forms of pomegranate pretenders that crossed my palate during this meeting could not have been more of an affront to that memory.

Various concoctions were pushed across the table, but their basic composition was the same: 10 percent pomegranate juice, 80 percent filler juices, and a 10 percent bonus of exotic flavoring. These included watermelon (delicious if you like Kool-Aid), lemon-lime (gag me), Hawaiian Tropical (whatever that means); they ran the dreadful gamut of phony fruit flavorings common in cheap candy and awful soda. The presentation proceeded with all the excitement of a chemistry final.

It was not my intention to insult the marketing team. And I doubt, given their supreme confidence, that I could have insulted them even if I had wanted to. But like most people in business, I had been in these types of meetings before, and I have seen people hold their tongues because they were intimidated by know-it-alls holding forth, because they didn't feel confident enough to challenge them or comfortable enough to upset the apple juice cart.

But I also knew that Stewart would soon turn to me and pose a question. And when he did, I told him the truth.

"What do you think?" he asked.

"I think you're crazy," I said.

"Yeah, I know," he countered. "But what about the pomegranate marketing strategy?"

There are always several different ways to make the same point. Whether the discussion is corporate or marital (or in this case a little of both), it's usually better to take a delicate path, one of constructive criticism delivered in a polite, gentle, and supportive framework. Someday, I promise, I will honor that universal truth. On this day, I dropped the velvet glove and picked up the sledgehammer.

"It's wrong," I said. "Just plain wrong."

"This is the real deal," I said to Stewart, "a gift from God—perhaps the healthiest natural product on the planet. If you water it down with filler juices, you water down its effectiveness. And if you do that, what do you have left?"

This was greeted with the raised eyebrows and sideways glances that welcome the loud and inebriated to an art lecture. The marketing team was not amused, but I had been asked to give my opinion, and I was not going to coat it in sugar—or corn syrup. Sometimes I think I know something and feel an annoying little quiver in my gut that tells me that maybe it isn't so. This was not one of those times. Despite all the challenges involved in creating this product—and at this point, I knew only a fraction of them—I wasn't burdened by self-doubt. My confidence never wavered. Why? Because I knew these were rubies in the orchard; pomegranates had real value.

Pure and unadulterated, this juice was not only delicious; it had the power to help heal people. It was health in a bottle. People needed pomegranate juice in their lives (even if they didn't know it yet), and I knew they would pay what it was worth.

Of course, there would be marketing challenges; but marketing is all about overcoming those challenges. If you have a product with intrinsic value, you can find a way to prevail. Besides, the fact that Starbucks could charge nearly $4.00 for a latte bolstered my resolve. A daily dose of pomegranate juice would cost less than that—and instead of giving you the three o'clock jitters, it would give you health.

"We know that pomegranates are very expensive to grow and harvest, and we know that hardly anyone knows what a pomegranate is," I agreed. "But I don't consider those reasons to go the way of all packaged goods. I see those reasons as the inspiration to create a new category of food."

I wrote **POM** on a piece of paper and passed it to Stewart. "Here is the name of your product. The heart will immediately tell them it's heart-healthy. We'll sell it in the refrigerated section of the produce department, and I'll design a bottle for you that will embody the spirit of this new food category."

I had made my case. It was time to sit back and wait for the usual chorus of naysaying to begin. I wasn't disappointed. Although, in the end, it was less a chorus and more like variations on the theme of *Mission: Impossible*. The meeting ended inconclusively, with the various junk-juice concoctions still littered about the room.

That evening, Stewart told me he understood what I had been saying in the conference room. What's more, he was willing to believe it might work. Then, with the same tone he uses when he asks, "What's for dinner?" he said, "Why don't you take over the business? You seem to have a vision for it."

When will I learn to keep my mouth shut?

———

I HAVE ALWAYS BEEN the marketer in the family. Stewart runs the shop, figures out the financing and margins, and hires the core executive team. I work on building the brands. A few people have very kindly called me a marketing genius. Naturally, I never tire of hearing that, but it isn't true.

I know what and who I am—and I am not a genius. I am, however, smart, disciplined, and hardworking. So far, that has proved to be enough to create a life in marketing that has often been thrilling. I have learned over and over, however, that good marketing for bad products inevitably leads to a dead end. I have been down that road myself, and I've watched others travel it. But I've also seen good products languish because they were poorly positioned, misunderstood by the very people responsible for promoting them.

For me, every marketing campaign begins with the same question: What is the intrinsic value of the product or service? When I talk about "rubies in the orchard," that's what I mean. Where does the value reside? And how can we coax it out and communicate it to consumers in a creative and cost-effective way?

> Every marketing campaign begins with the same question:
> What is the intrinsic value of the product or service?

Before you are able to convince consumers of the value of something, you have to be able to convince yourself. If it's not immediately apparent to you, it won't be to them either. That's where research comes in. Before we squeezed our first pomegranate into a bottle, I wanted to know everything there was to know about this fruit—and then some. I studied scientific data and interviewed doctors who were conducting tests. I delved into history, art, and literature. And I ate more pomegranates in more ways than you can imagine.

It wasn't enough for *me* to be passionate about the product I intended to bring to market. Just because you own a company (or an idea) doesn't mean your colleagues or employees (or spouse!) will follow you blindly into the marketplace. You must market ideas to your team before you can market them to the public. A lack of faith is deadly. Everyone needs to be a believer.

For me, the hardest sell is usually Stewart. He always plays devil's advocate against both sides of every argument. Grrrr! But in the case of 100 percent pure pomegranate juice, he saw the same great promise I did and was on board from the start. My first COO, however, wasn't quite so enthused. He was extremely capable and uniquely qualified to run the business with me, but he spent the better portion of his working day hunched over his computer, analyzing financial models that proved beyond doubt that there was just no way this juice business was going to work.

Business is often viewed as the realm of science and industry, of logistics, numbers, and cold, hard, irreducible facts. But like every other part of life, it's also a matter of faith. We see the proof of this every day, all around us. Talented people who lack faith in themselves or their mission fail, while people with less talent and more faith succeed. Bill Gates turned his back on a bright future the day he dropped out of Harvard. Ted Turner borrowed irresponsibly to buy the underperforming Atlanta television station that he built into CNN.

We all know these as great business stories. But more often, they're not business stories at all. That college dropout from Seattle didn't have a business. He had faith. The cowboy entrepreneur with a plan for a twenty-four-hour news channel didn't have a financial plan that any sober executive would find compelling (his competitors thought it was a joke). What he had was faith.

Business . . . is a matter of faith.

Building brands is, first and foremost, not about numbers. It is about value and people. If, on the marketing side, you have people with faith in the value of the brand, you can communicate and extend that faith to consumers. If even a small core of consumers begins to have faith in your product, you've got the building blocks of a winner.

In the beginning, I was having a hard time building a team and getting the business off the ground. Without the COO's emotional investment in the project, it was hard to get emotional investment from others. Every time we tried to take flight, something, some nagging doubt, some form of disbelief, would drag us back down to Earth.

We had so many other hurdles to overcome—operations problems, computer issues, and, two years running, a smaller crop than we had anticipated. (Demand outdistanced our supply by 300 percent, which may sound like good news, but, I can assure you, it was not.)

Gaining traction for a new brand is hard enough under the best circumstances. Without the level of emotional investment you get when people really believe in something, it's just about impossible. So before you spend a nickel to convince a consumer of anything, make sure you've convinced yourself and the people in your own office.

A month after that meeting in the conference room, as I prepared to show my marketing plan to Stewart and his sales force, I still had faith, although the facts of my particular situation were not all that encouraging. I was driving my brilliant designer, Bryan Honkawa, crazy.

I wanted something that would make POM's bottle as distinctive as its content. I didn't know what it was, but I was pretty sure I would recognize it when I saw it. Knowing how important it was to me, Bryan was in the process of producing about 100 different designs, hoping one of them would be "it."

There are many points in business when you need to compromise—either with your colleagues or with a stubborn reality. There are also a few areas that are so critically important that compromise is fatal. To me, the design of the POM bottle belonged in the latter category.

Why did the POM bottle have to stand out? If you've ever walked the aisles of a supermarket, you already know the answer. The run-of-the-mill American supermarket is

50,000 square feet of visual noise featuring nearly 50,000 SKUs (stock keeping units)—about one SKU for every square foot. It's an eye-popping cacophony of bold, bright colors and logos—all screaming for attention. Junk cereals and snack foods clamor to catch your child's wandering eye. Soft drinks scream out in bold reds, blazing oranges, and bright greens, high-fructose heralds of the artificial sweet life.

Many of these products benefit from marketing budgets in the tens of millions. How could we compete with them and distinguish our product from theirs if we all looked alike and they had all the advertising money? We couldn't.

We had come this far by focusing on the fundamentals, going deeper and deeper inside our product to understand its intrinsic value. Everything we needed to know was there inside the pomegranate. We had to resist the temptation to "think outside the box."

I know that's become a fashionable cliché in recent years, but it's just about always wrong. The answers are not outside the box—they're inside. They're inherent in whatever task you've undertaken, whatever product you want to market.

When I walked in to review the bottle designs, the answer was immediately apparent. It was so obvious, in fact, that I would have had the same instant response if Bryan had offered me 10,000 designs to choose from. The solution, of course, was fundamental, intrinsic to the pomegranate itself, inherent in the product we were bringing to market. Among the many choices was a shape that resembled one pomegranate on top of another. The bottle was derived from the juice's natural container. How perfect.

> The answers are not outside the box—they're inside.

There was just one little problem. Every packaging engineer said this bottle couldn't be manufactured in plastic (our first choice) and it was near to impossible in glass. Sure, an artisan glassblower could easily make *one*, but we needed millions. Bottle manufacturers are used to creating simple, cylindrical shapes at very high speeds. Shaping molten glass into a delicate pomegranate crown while spitting out thousands of units per minute simply wasn't in their repertoire.

The unique shape of the POM bottle also made printing on it difficult. It took a number of painful adjustments to figure that one out. Finally, filling the bottles with juice in a high-speed filling facility proved to be a shattering experience—a bit like industrialized bumper cars. Bottles constantly collided. With typical, straight-walled bottles, this bumping isn't a big deal. We solved the problem of our crashing bottles by creating a barely perceptible straight edge on the outside of each sphere.

At each hurdle, it might have made sense to throw up our hands, admit defeat, and do what so many experts were telling us to do: get a normal bottle. The only catch to that "follow the rule" consensus was that we weren't going to spend tens of millions of dollars to market our product. That beautiful, distinct bottle was going to have to carry part of the marketing load. It was integral to the product and too important to the brand to simply let it go.

We climbed—and sometimes crawled—over the obstacles. When I finally made my presentation to Stewart and his group, the marketing gang had the gung ho spirit of children forced to eat Brussels sprouts.

- "No one will ever pay $3.50 for a bottle of juice."
- "No one wants a glass bottle."
- "Men won't buy POM with a heart on it."

Oh, well. At least Stewart continued to stand by my vision. We may have been sailing on a sea of doubt, but there was still plenty of faith aboard ship.

CHAPTER 2

Selling Ice Sculptures
to Eskimos

I didn't start out focused on value. I'm not sure I would have seen the rubies in the orchard at the beginning of my career or understood why it was so important to nurture them. I was a product of the time and place into which I was born. Generally speaking, that meant the burgeoning consumer landscape of mid-twentieth century America. More particularly, it meant the household of one natural-born Philadelphia huckster.

My father, Jack Harris, was always selling. He couldn't help himself. He was a movie distributor on the East Coast with high hopes of realizing a Hollywood dream of his own. The 1950s were a tough time for distributors. Movie houses were closing across the country, felled by that rectangular miracle that was swiftly conquering the American living room. As a distributor, he sold movies before they were seen, even by him, which required an ability to paint a lively picture not only of the riveting drama-to-be on-screen, but of the crowds that would leave their televisions behind to line up outside the cinema. Dad sold an idea.

And me? I was Daddy's little girl. Little was the operative word: at the age of four, I wore a size one. I talked my way onto a regular role on *The Horn & Hardart Children's Hour*, a live weekly television show sponsored by the king of the automat—essentially a wall of vending machine boxlets from which your food was dispensed. I couldn't sing or dance, but at the audition I took command of the stage and talked. Man, did I talk. They liked me. I was the littlest stand-up comedienne they'd ever seen—so short they thought I was sitting down.

I liked the feeling of power—and the boost to my four-year-old ego—derived from owning center stage. My father, who had encouraged my television career over my mother's objections, coached me on my skit every Thursday, and come Sunday morning I went into the studio and delivered.

One week, my father didn't get back from a business trip in time to go over the routine with me. When the show began that weekend, I was unprepared. I fumbled my lines and began to cry—on live television. When I got back to my house, the neighborhood kids added insult to televised injury by taunting me about my very public tears, an opportunity for which they had been waiting months. A lesson was seared into my very young consciousness: I would never again be unprepared for a presentation. Never.

That era in America was a time of unprecedented

plenty. The consumer society that had begun to take root at the turn of the century had stalled in the Depression and been diverted to military ends during the world wars. But in the wide-open economic expansion that followed World War II, not even a lengthy war in Korea could stop American consumerism from roaring forward.

Harvard historian Lizabeth Cohen, who documented this land of plenty in A Consumer's Republic, noted that between 1946 and 1956, the national output of goods and services doubled. New-car sales quadrupled during the same period, and the percentage of American families that owned a refrigerator rose from 44 percent in 1940 to 80 percent by 1950. Before the end of the 1950s, John Kenneth Galbraith would publish The Affluent Society, analyzing (sometimes tartly) the unprecedented riches of a nation in which mechanical conveniences—and television, too!—were suddenly commonplace.

Consumption became culture in America, a vast machinery of marketing and salesmanship geared up to meet growing consumer appetites as well as to inspire desires, in Galbraith's words, "that previously did not exist." Personal credit expanded to accommodate the new American Way of easy monthly payments. Keeping up with the Joneses grew to rival baseball as the great American pastime. Feeding—and creating—consumer appetites became a huge business.

I threw my lot in with this Great American Selling Machine when I was still in my teens. My father had recently produced a horror movie destined to become a B-movie classic: *The Blob*. He wasted no time in moving us to southern California, where he adopted a lifestyle befitting a newly minted Hollywood mogul. We quickly had two Rolls-Royces in the driveway and a more or less permanent sense that we should enjoy the good times while they lasted, because financial doom was probably just around the next corner. My father is charming, gregarious, and loads of fun, and he *loved* to spend money—at least on *some* things.

Having long dreamed of being an artist, I was delighted when, after graduating from high school, I was accepted by the best art school in Los Angeles. Unfortunately, my father adamantly refused to pay the tuition. With a house in Beverly Hills and a pair of Rolls-Royces in the drive, I couldn't exactly plead poverty and beg the college for financial assistance. So for a year I ended up at a city college, where I was bored and frustrated.

My dreams of being a fine artist were all too easily dashed. The real artists I knew would do whatever they had to do, including living in poverty, to pursue their art. Even at a young age, I wanted the security and independence that I knew money could bring. I gave up on art and got a job at a dress shop instead. For the next forty years, I would never bother with long-range planning again. What was the point? Instead, I learned to go with whatever flow life provided, including the occasional rip tide.

I also learned quickly that, like the backslapping, gladhanding kings of sales, I, too, could "sell ice to Eskimos." Selling was like breathing to me; it came so naturally I didn't have to think much about it. Eventually, I discovered it was even better to sell the Eskimos ice *sculptures*—and charge a premium for the value added. But in the beginning, I sold dresses to women with closets already chock full of them, and I sold them like mad. They were frequently returned by customers who were also mad. After checking their new purchases in their mirrors at home, without the musical accompaniment of my sales spiel, they discovered they had made a big mistake.

Returned merchandise doesn't make for a very strong foundation in retailing. The shop owners complained constantly about the lack of business. To help them out, I drew enchanting little female characters that embodied the mode of the times. Then I worked up headlines and text to accompany my illustrations. The owners placed these homespun ads in the local papers.

It worked. Customers came in talking about the charming advertising and wanting to see what we had to offer. The owners were only too happy to take me off the merry-go-round of sales-followed-by-returns and keep me in the back room creating advertising instead. I was happier, too. I had found something that made use of both my natural design sense and my precocious marketing savvy. I was no longer a salesgirl; I was in the early stages of becoming a marketer.

Local newspaper reps taught me how to size an ad and set type. That's when I first learned a lesson that would be crucial throughout my career: you get a lot further in life by showing what you *don't* know and asking for help than you do by pretending to know it all. I have seen very accomplished people make big mistakes by succumbing to their insecurities and not asking questions when they should have.

> You get a lot further in life by showing what you don't know and asking for help than you do pretending you know it all.

I soon left the dress shop for a job at Sunset House, a mail-order company that sold a wide array of what might charitably be called useless gadgets. The Sunset House catalog offered one-stop shopping for everything you didn't need and likely would never use: automatic back scratchers, Sea-Monkeys, fallout shelter supplies, tie-dye kits. Sure, it was junk, but I was happy to work for its in-house ad agency. The experience, like most early experience, proved to be extremely valuable.

Sunset House ads consisted of far too little information about far too many products crammed into far too small a space. The magazine ads appeared on a grid, usually divided into nine boxes. Compressed inside each box was a tiny picture of a product, a headline, and some body copy. Success depended almost entirely on the allure of the headline, which offered the only, albeit slim, chance of grabbing a reader's attention. A production artist taught me how to lay out an ad and how to write headlines and copy that were attention-grabbing, yet sufficiently concise to fit the space.

On the side, I started freelancing for local shops, taking my growing portfolio from store to store. Eventually, I acquired enough freelance work to leave Sunset House and open my own little agency, Lynda Limited. I was nineteen. Around the same time, I got married.

I had no particular philosophy (let alone vision) about what I was doing in life or in business. I just loved advertising—I still do—and I was going with the flow. I can still recall the brilliant ads for Volkswagen and Alka-Seltzer and the now-defunct Braniff Airways. Braniff paired artist Andy Warhol and boxer Sonny Liston in one ad. The combination was so thoroughly bizarre that you couldn't take your eyes off them. I thrilled to the cutting-edge ad work of Mary Wells and Doyle Dane Bernbach. At that age, I loved everything about advertising—even the deceit. I had a lot to learn.

The turning point for my business was a direct-mail piece I developed for a charming potpourri of a shop in the San Fernando Valley called The Store. I had a ridiculously low budget for the job, so I got on the phone with the printing house to price paper. After every price quote I would respond, "Too expensive. What do you have that's cheaper?"

As it turned out, their cheapest paper cost more than my entire budget.

"Isn't there any kind of paper cheaper than that?" I pleaded. "Even if you don't carry it?"

The only thing the printer could think of was brown kraft paper—the kind supermarkets use to pack your groceries. "No photos," the printer advised, "and any color of ink as long as it's black."

I made do. Since typesetting was too expensive, I hand-lettered the entire thing and drew all the illustrations. On the outside of the self-mailer (I couldn't afford envelopes), a pair of eyes peered through antique wire-framed glasses. The headline read, "Look inside and be stupefied."

Believe it or not, that was a breakthrough. The piece went out to a list of names collected from friends, acquaintances, and local shoppers. Then I left for the East Coast to show my grandparents my new baby boy. When I returned, my husband handed me a long list of messages from potential new clients.

While other kids my age were smoking pot, discovering sex (as if no one ever had before), and grumbling about the establishment, I was a full-time working mother with a load of responsibilities both at home and at the office. By twenty-three, I had another baby boy and a growing business.

I developed offbeat approaches that would serve me well in later, larger businesses. I had a sense of humor, which was communicated in my work, some of which was not easily forgotten.

In one case, a young swimsuit manufacturer came to me with a real dilemma. He was hitting Market Week in New York for the first time. He was smart enough to realize that advertising in *Women's Wear Daily* would get him attention and help his business grow, but he was also worried about competitors getting an early look at his designs.

"You have complete creative license," he told us, a beautiful phrase that rang like a hymn in our ears, "as long as you don't show the swimsuits in the ads."

"You're kidding," I replied.

"No, this industry is vicious," he said. "If you show the product, by the time I land in New York, I'll see my designs in everyone else's showrooms."

He was a dream account, with the guts to really go for it. So we did. We created a jaw-dropping double page ad featuring the "Little Nothing" suit—consisting of a nude model in a Rubenesque pose with fruit nestled in all the right places. Our client got a front-page story in New York's *Daily News* during Market Week, his showroom was jammed and his ultimate dream came true; he sold his business to Jantzen a few years later.

My renamed agency, Lynda Sinay Advertising, had a dozen employees, a larger office, and some very nice clients. Then I did two things that jeopardized everything for which I had worked so hard.

There was a fellow who kept asking me out to lunch and suggesting that we merge our businesses. I reminded him that he was a freelancer—he *had* no business. He insisted that if we teamed up, he could bring in a big account. Besides, he was a pretty good creative director, certainly a better one than I could afford.

I had an uncomfortable feeling about this from the beginning. I didn't like the guy, but I convinced myself that

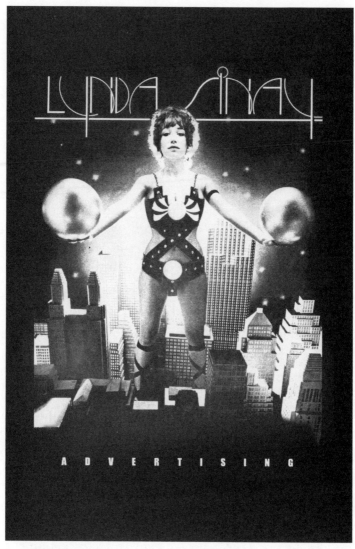

Lynda Sinay agency promotion poster from 1970.

it was business, not personal. After all, I wasn't *marrying* him. I suggested, "Let's work together for six months and see how it goes. If we like each other, we'll put your name on the door." He agreed.

There was a phrase making its way around feminist political circles in those days: "The personal is political." Well, guess what? Business is personal, too—and anyone who forgets that does so at her peril.

For the first six months, the relationship was lovely. He brought in the big account, and we staffed up to service it. Then, a few days after the six-month deadline, with his name now accompanying mine on our joint business cards, he started coming late to the office. As the weeks progressed, he took two-hour lunches, then whole days off to play golf.

Our office was not known for leisure; we were more sweatshop than country club. I worked at least six days a week and frequently seven. In that environment, his work ethic was an affront to everyone in the agency. Also, he had convinced himself that I found him wildly desirable, which led to an ugly late-night office encounter.

He quit and took the big account with him. The day he left was one of the longest of my life. First, there was a staff celebration—they disliked him as much as I did. Then my assistant and I closed the doors and ordered pizza and extra cigarettes. We analyzed all the accounts and what it would take for me to keep the shop open—and keep my newly expanded workforce in paychecks—while I hustled to replace the lost revenue. By 6:00 a.m., we had the answer: $20,000—that would be about $130,000 today.

I went home, got the kids ready for school, and then dressed to the nines. I met the manager of a local bank, who gave me the loan I needed to keep the business afloat. I repaid it in half the allotted time and soon welcomed back the big AWOL account. The client had quickly figured out who had really been doing the work and was eager to return.

But all was not well. I was twenty-four years old and looked forty-two. While my business was flourishing, my personal life was crumbling. My eldest child had been diagnosed with serious neurological problems, and I was in the midst of divorcing my husband, who decided to get back at me by withholding child support. Then came recession, and things began to unravel at work, too.

Between the Vietnam War, assassinations, radical violence, street crime, and racial, cultural, and generational clashes dividing the country, things weren't really going too well anywhere. I began doing some occasional work for the antiwar movement—creating posters and such. And my new boyfriend introduced me to his friend, a nice man named Daniel Ellsberg, who had previously worked at the Pentagon and at RAND, the government-funded think tank that did a vast amount of strategic analysis for the military. Dan, who had turned against the war, asked for a favor. Could he use my Xerox 812 photocopy machine on nights and weekends? I said sure. What could be the harm in that?

So at odd hours, Dan copied a trove of documents not very discreetly labeled "Top Secret." My favorites were the

Press from the Pentagon Papers trial: Time *magazine and (left to right)* L.A. Daily News, Chicago Tribune, New York Post, *and* Los Angeles Times.

carbon copies labeled "Eyes Only." Dan said the documents were so important they could stop the war in Vietnam. It seemed like a good idea at the time.

Like the country, I soon found myself in very deep trouble. I stopped dating Dan's friend, and Dan and his wife, Pat, moved back to Cambridge. Some months later, however, I read a story about the "Pentagon Papers" in the press. The whole thing had a familiar ring to it. Before long, Dan and my old boyfriend were implicated. A few days later, at 5:30 p.m. on a gloomy June afternoon in 1971, two FBI agents knocked at my door. They handed me a subpoena to appear before a grand jury the next day.

For the next two years, I was pursued by a very nasty prosecutor and my life was dominated by the Pentagon Papers case. I spiraled into debt and had to let all my employees go. Eventually, the case against Dan was dismissed and the cloud of potential prosecution lifted. I crawled out of a very dark place.

Not so the nation. The misery of Vietnam was soon compounded by the shock of Watergate. Together, they took the air out of the country's sails. The war ended and Watergate passed, but the cynicism lingered—a deeper, more abiding cynicism than America had ever known.

Toward the very end of my ad agency career, I did a great marketing campaign for a restaurant. I designed the space, planned the menu, even outfitted the staff. The client was delighted, and I was proud of the job I had done. There was only one catch: the food was awful. That was it for me. I could invent the advertising, create the marketing, and design the look, but what good was it if the product was junk?

> What good are advertising, marketing, and design if the product is junk?

I was tired of the game. I just didn't want to sell ice to Eskimos anymore. Maybe I could sell them heaters.

CHAPTER 3

Taking Root in the
Flower Business

Somewhere between my advertising firm spiraling down and the government hounding me for my tenuous connection to the Pentagon Papers, my personal life took a very sharp turn. After my divorce, I found myself a single mom with two small boys. Having married at nineteen, I was single essentially for the first time in my life. After my first out-of-the-box relationship (with the fellow who had introduced me to Dan Ellsberg) ended, a man who was on a board of directors with me kept telling me about a brilliant young businessman who wanted to meet me. He was in the janitorial business.

"Sounds thrilling," I thought (and may even have said).

When Stewart and I finally met—I went to his office because he was allegedly interested in my advertising skills—he made fun of my outfit. I thought he was cute but a bit of a jerk. He kept pursuing meetings, though, frequently after hours at my house. He was as brilliant as advertised, and he had great business insights. Besides, he was growing on me. When I asked him if he was ever going to give me the account, he responded, "I really want to have a meaningful relationship with you." I never got the account. But I sure got the business.

Stewart eventually sold that janitorial business to ITT for half stock and half cash. The stock doubled by the time he could divest it, and with that bankroll we began acquiring agricultural land. Over the years, we have bought many companies and sold a few. We discovered early on that we are operating people. We love running businesses and don't like selling them if they meet our expectations. We are in it for the long haul.

Whenever we make an acquisition, Stewart's mantra is always the same: "The management is good. I'll let them run the business and it won't take any time from me at all." (Notice he doesn't say, "It won't take any time from *you*.") The first few times I heard this, I actually believed him, but leaving well enough alone is not what entrepreneurs do, and every business has room for improvement. Some, of course, have more room than others—and ours seem to have more room for improvement than Britney Spears's mothering skills.

In late 1979, we purchased Teleflora, a struggling flower delivery service that was a ninety-eight-pound weakling in the market, overmatched by the brawnier FTD. Unfortunately, this was no time for business weaklings. The economy was sputtering, and the great oil shock of the late 1970s would soon produce record gasoline prices and long lines at service stations. FTD was actually a co-op owned by the florists themselves. When given a choice between using our delivery service or a service they owned themselves, there wasn't much doubt about which way they would turn.

Yet the florists were also the gatekeepers. Customers couldn't tell the difference between one floral wire delivery service and another; they just hoped the florist would complete the delivery across town or across the country. It was a leap of faith.

Teleflora's president came with the deal. He was a swell guy, an old-school, slap-on-the-back guy from the white-loafer set. He had come from a top job at one of the world's most successful companies and was part of the consortium that sold us the company. He wore a button that read "Assume Nothing." It was good advice, especially as it related to him. It seemed his idea was to take the job at Teleflora to semiretire, letting the company drift toward its inevitable fate while he endured lengthy rounds of golf. When he begged me to become head of marketing, it occurred to me that he might have asked me because an extended search to fill the post with an outside executive might have interfered with his tee time.

Within six months, Stewart had become the new president and I was executive vice president of marketing. A short time later, I would become president of Teleflora and enjoy one of the most rewarding work experiences of my life. Having at last moved to the client side of the business, I began to develop the principles of marketing and brand building that would serve me well for the next three decades.

But before I could implement any of my ideas, I first had to learn how to manage—in every sense of the word. I had about three hundred employees, roughly thirty times the maximum number of people I had managed in my small advertising firm. The challenges started soon after I came to Teleflora.

I had developed my first merchandising concept for our florists—a wedding guide and merchandising plan to help brides select flowers and arrangements for their big day. In my typical A-student fashion, the campaign was meticulously thought out, with no detail overlooked.

I presented the plan to Teleflora's field force, the roughly thirty salespeople who were our main points of contact with florists. These were the folks on the front line who sold our services and products to members. Every last one of them was male. Their response to my plan was unanimous—and vicious. In those days, you could be cruel in an office environment, especially to a woman, and this gang spared no contempt or vitriol in dismissing every aspect of my big idea.

I felt the same awful pain I had felt as a child when I was rejected by the Camp Fire Girls, and I responded in pretty much the same way. I retreated to my office, shut the door, and cried. I was rejected by the Camp Fire Girls for a reason I couldn't change: I am Jewish. But as the boss, there was sure something I could do about this.

I could have stoked my hurt and anger into a burning hot coal—then roared back at my insolent staff with all the hellfire I could muster. But rather than run them over, I knew I was going to have to *win* them over. First, you can't fire your entire sales force. Second, like it or not, I would need their support time and again in order to be successful.

So instead of allowing our antagonism to settle into a pattern of trench warfare, I worked hard to become their buddy. I courted my regional sales managers, cultivated their friendship, and worked for their respect. I made them part of my marketing team and part of management. It wasn't easy.

There were times when I wanted to kill one or another of them, but it was the only way. I was not going to play the victim, nor was I going to sacrifice the business in order to dominate a willful bunch of hard-drinking guys who would have resented every order delivered from on high. In time, I won them over—and in the process I made some good friends.

Listening to them was the key, and I learned a lot from it. They had their war stories, they knew the florists, and even though I eventually knew them too, I wasn't the one battling it out day after day against the giant FTD.

The Internet has drastically changed the wire service business. Back then, Teleflora was basically a clearinghouse handling transactions between one florist and another. Let's say you lived in New York and wanted to send flowers to your aunt in Des Moines. You would contact your local florist, tell them what you wanted, and they would find a florist in Des Moines to create the bouquet and make the delivery. The wire service billed the florist in New York (who had the customer's money) and paid the florist in Des Moines (who delivered the flowers). The two florists paid dues to belong to the service network.

Teleflora had about 7,000 member florists when we purchased the company. FTD had about 18,000. Some florists used both services. The only reason those florists needed two networks was to benefit from the "float" of money they needed to get by. If they overextended their credit with FTD, they could turn to Teleflora. It was like moving from one maxed-out credit card to another.

The florists paid Teleflora dues of $7.00 per month. To Stewart, that didn't sound like a lot of money.

"When is the last time you raised the dues?" Stewart asked the V.P. of sales.

"Three years ago," he replied. "We had so many complaints we never did it again."

"Really? How many is 'so many'?" Stewart wanted to know.

"At least fifty."

"Fifty complaints out of seven thousand members isn't that impressive," Stewart concluded.

Stewart was probably determined to raise the dues regardless. His first big success in business had been with an alarm company he had bought in the late 1960s. The business had taken off after he raised the monthly fee and improved the service. The increase in fees had allowed him to cover the cost of service improvements and still have extra profit left over.

Likewise, the most obvious way to increase profits at Teleflora was to raise dues. We needed to figure out how to add value and how to differentiate ourselves from FTD; without adding value for the extra dues, it was bound to be a short-term plan—possibly a *terminal* plan as far as Teleflora members were concerned. What we needed was that old, reliable pillar of marketing: the Unique Selling Proposition. And we needed it fast.

Since my college career had been measured in months and my interests were focused on art, I had never taken a marketing course. Everything I know about marketing I learned on the job. My lack of education would have stalled a career in nuclear physics, but it never hindered my career in marketing. You can't learn how to be a good marketer from a textbook.

Of course, there are advantages to graduating from a top MBA program, but the truth is that there is only so much you can learn in school. The most important lesson of all is self-taught. Ultimately, marketing is all about listening. If you don't listen and you don't care, you'll never be a good marketer. You want to be the equivalent of a good friend—someone who cares, someone who listens carefully, someone who tries to anticipate another's needs and to meet them or indeed exceed them. The rest—market research, statistical analysis, economics, and finance—are really important tools, but in the end, you have to use all that information to inform your own human instincts. That is where your own sound judgment and the empathy quotient come in; you might say it's where the art meets the science.

> Ultimately, marketing is all about listening. You want to
> be the equivalent of a good friend.

Though I didn't encounter it in a textbook, I was familiar with the concept of the Unique Selling Proposition, or USP. It was pioneered in the 1940s by Rosser Reeves, who was the chairman of Ted Bates & Company, one of the most successful firms in advertising history. I'm sure that marketing textbooks give a more comprehensive analysis, but here's how I gauge whether an attribute or marketing claim rises to the standard of a USP.

Unique Selling Propositions

1. Is it true? The honesty factor is essential.
2. Is it clear, concise, and easy to understand? Keep it simple.
3. Does its unique quality answer a need in the marketplace, whether consumers know it or not? That is your success barometer, because if consumers need it, chances are that you will succeed.

That's all. Pretty basic stuff. Yet it's amazing how often businesspeople forget it.

By the same token, we tend to notice—and reward—businesses that never forget to deliver a Unique Selling Proposition. Given the proliferation of coffee shops, consumers often have a local alternative to Starbucks. Starbucks' early success came from its understanding that it was delivering more than a cup of expensive coffee. It created a carefully calibrated social environment with meticulously selected music and a warm, friendly, and distinctively intelligent atmosphere. The coffee is premium. The experience is premium-plus. Recently Starbucks has lost its focus and become more like a large packaged goods company; growing too fast, slipping on its core values, and driving the business for quarterly earnings instead of long-term sustainability. Bringing the inspired founder, Howard Schultz, back to the helm should help steer the ship back to its course.

Similarly, Lexus has staked its brand on quality and, in the process, redefined quality by raising the bar several notches. What does it sound like when you close the door of a Lexus? Like you've just entered an airtight chamber. From the quiet yet powerful hush of the engine to the accoutrements—leather, wood, glass, and so on—every detail is engineered to join the chorus singing "This is quality."

Differentiating a brand by virtue of a Unique Selling Proposition is just as powerful today as it was in a bygone era. Remember Maxwell House coffee? In a pre-Starbucks era, it promised to purge the acidic, bitter taste that settled to the bottom of the coffee cup. Maxwell House, we were informed, was "good to the last drop."

At Teleflora, a USP was absolutely essential. In the pre-Internet era, consumers phoned or visited a neighborhood florist to make a selection for a gift, so the florist was the gatekeeper—and FTD was like a gated community. We had to figure out a way to pull florists away from their familiar home turf, get them outside the gates, and send orders through the Teleflora network instead of through FTD. Since florists had no incentive to alter their preference for FTD, we needed to give someone else an incentive to demand it: consumers.

In the early 1980s, the U.S. economy had still not recovered. In fact, 1982 ushered in a massive recession. Flowers, then as now, were a luxury, and they were a peculiar luxury—one that died. My research indicated that one reason people were afraid to send flowers was that they didn't know what would show up on the recipient's doorstep. I was desperate for a way not only to differentiate our service from FTD's but to give consumers added value that would inspire them to ask specifically for Teleflora flowers. Then I thought of the container the flowers came in.

Instead of simply sending flowers in a throwaway green glass vase, we could put the flowers in a gift. That way, when the flowers died, the recipients would still have the gift to remind them of the sentiment with which the flowers had been sent. For the price of flowers offered by our competitors, Teleflora would instead provide flowers in a keepsake watering can, a lovely tea cup, or a cookie jar. My concept gave wire customers peace of mind; they knew exactly what would arrive. Teleflora's Unique Selling Proposition was born.

Of course, the real trick was to figure out how to do this and still make a profit. Vendors wanted much more to produce what we called our "keepsakes" than we could afford to pay. Instead, we brought the design in-house, which set the pattern for the way we've done design and advertising work—and just about everything else—ever since. Then we went looking for a way to manufacture, seeking out factories in Far East jungles and remote places with names I can barely pronounce.

We hired a husband-and-wife team—let's call them Ted and Dolly. While not exactly the dream team of corporate etiquette, they turned out to be just what was needed to blaze new territory. Dolly was a whiz at product development ideas and using new materials to make products that looked like a million dollars but cost next to nothing. Ted was a burly guy, straight out of *The French Connection*— with a touch of larceny to drive home the resemblance.

When it came to Ted, you could never be too careful. He looked for every conceivable way to cut corners to get the best possible price. That, in turn, required me to inspect absolutely everything he did to ensure that his sense of thrift wouldn't result in customer complaints—or all of us being shipped off to the penitentiary.

Once, we were creating a "hand-painted" Jell-O mold that, when turned upside down, became a great floral container.

"Ted," I asked, "is this really hand-painted?"

"It sure is," he avowed.

"Well, the words that say 'hand-painted' were put on with a decal," I pointed out. "And it's upside down."

At first our member florists hated the whole idea of the keepsakes. "We are in the flower business, not the container business," they would tell me. They didn't want the added (albeit ever so reasonable) expense, and they didn't like being required to create a preconceived bouquet during holidays.

On one trip to Texas Retail, a huge floral show, I was separated from my team. A group of florists invited me to join them in their van on the way to the next event. It wasn't until after we had all piled in and they had locked the door that I started to sweat. "We want you to get out of the container business," they threatened. I brought out pictures of my soon-to-be-orphaned children and prayed the furious florists would spare me. In time, however, the florists came to an unavoidable conclusion: the keepsakes worked.

We advertised the "flowers in a gift" concept on television and in print and supplied our member florists with posters and direct-mail pieces to send to their customers. Even more important, we sent our design and marketing specialists around the country to teach member florists how to merchandise their shops for each holiday season. An old-fashioned Unique Selling Proposition was the focus of all of our advertising and marketing efforts.

The keepsakes turned the tide for our business. Suddenly, we were going *with* the flow instead of against it.

Business boomed (okay, bloomed). Since we were now adding enormous value to our members' businesses, we were able to grow our network and our profits. From a network of 7,000 florists each paying $7.00 per month we grew to be a network of 21,000 florists paying $140.00 per month. (You do the math.) Today, we are larger than FTD, the erstwhile floral Goliath in whose shadow we once toiled.

We had to transform the company to deliver value. Instead of an also-ran delivery service, we became a marketing and merchandising company for the flower industry. If the rubies are in service, don't go looking elsewhere to nurture value. Go to the essence of the business.

One of the vehicles we used to market to our own members was a magazine we inherited with the company, *The Teleflorist*, which was distributed to all our member florists. It was not a great asset; the art direction was hideous, and the content was meandering and dull. I decided to remake it.

First, I hired a new sales director. I found Diane, an experienced woman who had been working for a very profitable pornography magazine and was willing to take a big pay cut in order to go legit. Then I came up against my next management crucible: the "magazine ladies."

There were a half-dozen women who had run the magazine for years. When I described the changes I envisioned, they sat silently scowling, their arms tightly folded across their chests to form an impenetrable wall of editorial defiance. I wasn't getting anywhere with them, and they were making it abundantly clear that I never would.

My new sales director, late of the pornography industry, was not especially subtle. "If I were you," she said, "I'd fire their asses." She'd retained the colorful vernacular of her former job.

I realized I was going to have to do just that. Unlike my earlier experience with the field force, I was getting nowhere with the magazine ladies, who for some reason seemed to think that they had the power to do anything— or more often nothing at all.

Trouble was, I was not the firing kind. When my life was going down the rabbit hole of the Pentagon Papers case and my advertising business was falling apart, I had kept my staff on well beyond any reasonable point. I had gone into debt in order to continue paying their salaries, despite the fact that I didn't have enough work to keep them busy.

I am sure it was traumatic for them, but firing the magazine ladies didn't go over too well with me either. My back went out. My left shoulder and neck were in constant, throbbing pain. I was only in my thirties, but my body was a total wreck.

Eventually I learned how to fire people when it's absolutely necessary, but it never really gets easier. You just get tough enough as the years go by to handle it, realizing that if you don't get rid of the "deadwood" in your organization, you hurt the dedicated employees who are the future of your business.

I hired a great editor, Barbara Cady, who raised the magazine's standards and improved its quality. We went on to work with a top designer, Dugald Stermer from San Francisco, who gave the publication a modern, elegant look and feel. *The Teleflorist* was renamed *Flowers&*. It has thrived ever since.

I won an advertising award called the Gold Effie for the keepsake-with-flowers idea. Teleflora's Unique Selling Proposition remains our keepsakes, but the heart of our service is this: each and every bouquet we market has been designed by one of our 21,000 local floral shops and is hand-delivered to the recipient. The other wire services, such as 1-800-Flowers and FTD, do a lot of what we call "drop ship." The flowers are boxed in a warehouse and shipped to addressees. Then it is up to recipients to stop whatever they are doing in the middle of a busy day and arrange the flowers themselves. In addition, our competitors use their services to deliver everything from chocolates to lobsters. Teleflora, on the other hand, focuses only on our florist network, helping them deliver the joy of flowers. (Do I care about this? You bet I do.)

In 1999, the executive board of FTD, which was made up of florists, decided they would sell the co-op. I had come down with a terrible flu and high fever a few days before Stewart and I made the trip to Detroit to make our presentation to purchase the company. I should have stayed home.

In Detroit, the FTD board refused our offer, still viewing Teleflora as their sworn enemy. Instead, they sold FTD to a leveraged-buyout firm, which fired the staff and closed down its beautiful corporate headquarters. FTD is now a publicly traded company and has been led by many different teams of Wall Street management types. They still have plenty of brand equity due to that magical name recognition, but being under Wall Street's thumb is hardly an advantage.

Publicly traded companies throw lots of money into marketing because they want to see the stock price rise. To that end, they must show rapid growth to impress Wall Street. I won't go into my rant about the perils of managing a business for short-term stock price gains rather than the long-term health of the company and employees. Emphasis on the short term almost always comes at the expense of the long term. Just look at the financial quicksand that enveloped Fannie Mae, Freddie Mac, AIG, and most of Wall Street. Merrill Lynch, Lehman Brothers and the rest were riding high, quarter to quarter, on profit from shaky mortgage-backed securities. Denial is a powerful engine, but eventually it runs out of gas. When the fantasy ended, great companies with long and illustrious histories lay in shambles. The contagion spread to every financial capital of the world, destroying the weak and shaking the foundations of the strong. Even Goldman Sachs was forced to end its swashbuckling ways and submit to regulation as a bank holding company. Innocent taxpayers will be paying for the big boys' recklessness for years to come.

But sometimes forest fires are a good thing. Hopefully this debacle will clear out the toxic debris and in the long term bring citizens back to reality about living within their means. It might also give them a healthy skepticism toward the financial markets.

> Emphasis on the short term almost always comes at the expense of the long term.

I have been around long enough to have seen several incarnations of the new business model, the new economy, the new visionary geniuses who turn the old ways upside down and reinvent the world of business. "Nothing will ever be the same," we're told.

But it *is* the same. Economies, like societies, are dynamic. They change constantly, but the fundamentals do not. Value is rewarded, while the absence of value, sooner or later, is always exposed and penalized. Every economics lesson, from the tulip craze of the 1600s to the dot-com bubble of 2000, from the construction of the latest pyramid scheme to the collapse of Enron's new-wave energy trading, all confirm the primacy—and constancy—of value.

As you will see in the next chapter, value is real—even when the product itself is a certified, 100 percent fake.

> Value is rewarded, while the absence of value, sooner or later, is always exposed and penalized.

CHAPTER 4

The One True Copy of Jackie Kennedy's Real Fake Pearls

R unning Teleflora was a dream job. I was in charge of marketing and product development, and, of course, I supervised all my new friends in the sales force, which I had gradually shaped to fit my vision. The business was growing, and so were profits. I had reached a point where I could start delegating some of the work—provided I could let go of a certain nagging perfectionism (which today has a fancy name and a medication regime to go along with it).

My job was fulfilling, and my life with Stewart and the kids had hit a stretch of smooth sailing, about as close to domestic bliss as any family gets. For the first time in my life, things seemed comfortable and easy. With everything going so well, there was naturally only one thing left to do: shake it up.

In 1981, I hired a news clipping service to begin tracking a direct-response company called the Franklin Mint. There were similarities between the Mint and Teleflora. The Mint created unique products, just as we did, only without the flowers. In those days, its products were mostly coins and medallions, a few porcelain vases, and some miniature knickknacks worthy of display in a "free with purchase" vitrine. Unlike Teleflora, the Mint sold its collectibles through direct response, with no middleman between the company and its consumers. It was something I longed to do.

In an effort to replace myself as the New Products Creator at Teleflora, I was looking to hire the right person. The Franklin Mint was located in Philadelphia, where I was originally from. My best friend from childhood had grown up to be a hotshot recruiter, so I sent her into the Mint to find out who was creating their products. In no time at all, Stewart and I were sitting in our garden in California interviewing (or interrogating) the Mint's V.P. of product development. He told me the company was poorly managed and grossly dysfunctional. He also said the Mint might be for sale. We hired that fellow to come to Teleflora, and I went on to persuade Stewart that the Mint might be our next acquisition.

The company was owned by Warner Bros. It had been one of the last acquisitions made by legendary Warner CEO Steve Ross, who loved it. He saw the same potential we did. But he was ill at the time, and his top executives were too busy with their core businesses to pay much attention to this odd direct-marketing business that was miles away in the Pennsylvania countryside.

I had initially thought we might go into competition with the Mint. Stewart always says, "Start-ups are a bitch." Now, having a few in my history, I know he's right. We decided to look into buying it instead. Stewart heard from a Wall Street source that a sale prospectus of the Mint was making the rounds. Eventually, we paid a visit to the Mint's campus, about forty-five minutes outside Philadelphia on the Baltimore Pike. Perched high on a hill, the bucolic landscape included several sprawling buildings with eighty-five acres under roof. It was actually a little city unto itself: Franklin Mint, Pennsylvania.

"You know, the collectibles business is dead. What do you think you are going to bring to the party?" one of the executives asked in his Philadelphia twang. In this person's opinion, the current management was brilliant—and if *they* couldn't make the business work, well, the likes of Stewart and I certainly weren't going to get anywhere.

Steve Ross wasn't eager to sell, but his video business, Atari, was hemorrhaging money and the Warner board was pushing for a sale. In the end, Ross was forced to divest both Atari and the Franklin Mint. The company's sagging stock price had forced decisions based on short-term perceptions rather than long-term value—decisions that might never have been made by a privately held company. Imagine getting rid of the first video game business because "The Street" didn't believe in its long-term viability! It was a sad conclusion for a great business visionary. Steve died of prostate cancer in 1992.

We were more than happy to relieve Warner Bros. of its perceived burden. This would be the end of my brief patch of stress-free living. Stewart and I lived in Beverly Hills, where we've been in the same house for thirty years. That meant quite a commute to the new office in Pennsylvania. We ended up living in a hotel in Philadelphia. Stewart said, "Don't worry about this, we will turn the business around and be back in Beverly Hills in six months. You don't even have to give up your job at Teleflora." Right! For the first three months I almost believed him.

On my first day of work, I asked someone in the Mint's Female Collectibles department about a doll on her shelf.

"Oh, that's Scarlett O'Hara," she sighed, "in her green dress from the barbecue."

"Poor thing is all covered in dust. What happened?"

"Management doesn't believe in Hollywood—it's too riffraff. Conflicts with our image."

Wow. I suddenly knew exactly what I was bringing to the company barbecue.

Even through the dust, I could see that the doll was attractive, intriguing even, with fine features and an unmistakable aura of quality. I called a meeting of sales and sourcing, asking them how many of these little ladies they could produce for me—and how fast.

Overnight, we were in the high-end collectible doll business. Our dolls were based on characters that were both real and fictional, but they all had a built-in following. Our first run of Scarlett generated $35 million in sales. Despite the disdain of the previous management, you will probably not be shocked to discover that Hollywood was enormously popular with our collectors—and profitable.

We went on to do Scarlett in porcelain, in vinyl, in her burgundy Jezebel dress, in her bridal gown, in her widow's weeds, and even in the dress she wore when she delivered Melanie's baby. Our doll collectors knew every nuance of every dress worn in the film.

But our *Gone With the Wind* franchise didn't begin and end with Scarlett. We produced dolls of Mammy, Rhett, Melanie, Prissy, and just about every other character who had ever promenaded, strutted, or crawled across the set of one of the great films of all time. Scarlett O'Hara wasn't just a doll for us. She was an industry.

At the Mint, I learned how to predict and develop winning products. One of the first things I did was banish the word "customer" and replace it with "collector." By referring to the people who bought our products as collectors, we immediately elevated them in the minds of our employees. And we let our collectors know that we understood their passion and respected it.

We nurtured faith in the Franklin Mint brand among a following that eventually grew to eight million collectors worldwide. Our success depended on the interplay of two forces, both of which were at the heart of our value proposition. The first of these was the emotional connection our collectors felt with our products. Our dolls were too delicate and expensive for children because they were never intended for them. Our doll collectors were women in their thirties and forties, many of whom had been too poor in their childhoods to be able to play with fancy dolls. In effect, they had been waiting years to hold their Scarletts. We were meeting a demand that had been pent up for decades.

Similarly, we created die-cast cars for male collectors. These were the cars of their youth, the cars they would have proudly taken out on the boulevard on Saturday night and to the drive-in on Sunday—if only they'd had the money. Given the powerful emotions they evoked, it was all the more important that these products delivered quality and value. When you buy a cheap piece of junk and it breaks down, you get angry at yourself for being so stupid. But when you buy an expensive product that touches you emotionally and that product fails you, you experience that disappointment as betrayal. In addition to feeling used and hurt, you get angry. Our collectibles had to deliver both emotional satisfaction and high quality.

Our success depended on keen consumer insight. We conducted research and focus groups to understand our collectors' deepest motivations and desires. Then we set out to meet their highest hopes. I've always believed in giving people more than they expect. It compliments not only their taste but their awareness and intelligence.

> Give people more than they expect—it compliments their taste and their intelligence.

We staffed a research library that housed the artistic history of civilization. Through the efforts of our earnest librarians we could ensure that every detail of our products was authentic and true. I brought in decorative art scholars to educate the staff on everything from Gothic Revival and American Federal to French Rococo. When we copied a style, I wanted it to be accurate in every way. I hired prominent artists to sculpt the faces of our dolls. Their miniature clothes were meticulously tailored—right down to the fabric, the buttons, even the lace. Most of the dolls retailed for about $200, but some went as high as $500 and a few for more than $1,000.

Similarly, our cars were hand-assembled, die-cast, and built exactly—and I mean *exactly*—to scale with as many as 130 parts. They had baked-on enamel and doors that swung open, hoods that lifted, and steering wheels that turned. If the original automobile had leather seats, our model had leather seats. If it had spoke wheels, our model had spoke wheels. We sold them for as much as $145, but that was a small price to pay to own the car of your dreams. It wasn't long before one program, Cars of the Fifties, accounted for the biggest business the Franklin Mint had ever done, more than $125 million in sales.

To me, the Mint was all about the rubies. Precision, craftsmanship, and careful attention to detail were essential—and we were able to charge a very healthy markup for delivering them. Because we cared about the intrinsic value of everything we produced, we attracted a loyal base of collectors who knew they got their money's worth when they purchased from us. We understood that our products had emotional resonance. If you've always wanted a Rolls-

Royce Silver Shadow but could never afford one, that die-cast model is a lot more than just a shiny toy.

We had offices around the world and our staff and labor force was so large—it peaked at around 4,500—that we had huge expenses and overhead. But our profits justified the expense. In our first seven years, we took the business from $150 million a year in sales to nearly $1 billion. Given the volume of the Mint, it made sense to begin sourcing in Malaysia and China. We built our own factories, installed air-conditioning, and provided health care and hot meals to employees.

In order to keep the pipeline stocked with new products, I had a concept group whose sole task was to develop ideas: high-end dolls, collector plates, die-cast cars, male and female jewelry, bronzes, sculpture, porcelain figurines, coins, religious icons, doll houses, home decor, and on and on. We tested anywhere from 1,000 to 1,500 new product ideas a year. We gauged how in tune we were with the market by the percentage of ideas that stuck.

Our business was global. We had separate product lines for the United Kingdom, Germany, France, and Japan. Fifteen and twenty years ago, the world was less homogeneous, and individual markets were more distinct. Each had its own tastes.

Our licensing group was dedicated to acquiring the rights to old movies, beloved brands of bygone eras, plus stars such as Elvis Presley, Elizabeth Taylor, and John Wayne. We secured the rights to Marilyn Monroe directly from the estate of her acting teacher, Lee Strasberg. By the time I was finished teaching myself about her short, tumultuous life, I could tell you practically every line she had ever uttered in a movie and describe just about every costume she had ever worn.

To introduce our Marilyn doll collection (with Marilyn in the pink bow gown, of course), I needed a fine artist who could capture Marilyn's unique mixture of innocence and raw sex appeal. I chose Emily Kaufman, but unfortunately, she demurred. Eventually, I convinced her that when she created a singular work of art, only one person could own it. But if she created a Marilyn sculpture for the Franklin Mint, thousands of people could own, enjoy, and treasure her work.

Emily went on to create the entire line of Marilyn dolls for the Mint. Of course, there have been thousands of representations of Marilyn across every imaginable medium, but I don't think anyone ever captured the essence of Marilyn Monroe in quite the "art imitates life" way Emily did for the Franklin Mint.

Our licensing operation extended well beyond celebrities. In addition, we licensed Harley-Davidson along with practically every car company in the world, the Victoria and Albert Museum, the Louvre, and even the Vatican — in the first-ever licensing deal of its kind. We located an original member of the Fabergé family and licensed the name of the famous creators of Fabergé eggs. We were able to reproduce priceless museum pieces that you didn't have to be a tsar to collect.

All of our designs and illustrations were done in-house,

as was the advertising, which emphasized both the history behind a product and the Mint's fine attention to detail. In all our communications, we delivered the same message to collectors over and over again: We care.

Having earned our collectors' faith, we were able to take what might otherwise have seemed outrageous gambles—by spending millions on new product development. We licensed the right to produce our own Monopoly game. I figured that when you play Monopoly, you're playing at being a real estate mogul, buying and selling property. You're just like Donald Trump, right? So what kind of board would Donald Trump play on? A gorgeous, natural mahogany board with gold hotels and silver houses, that's what. That's the Monopoly board we designed and sold—at $550. The set grossed more than $150 million in revenue during its lifetime.

We did a great business in Japan when its economy was booming. We sold sake sets, scrolls, representations of Mount Fuji, coins, dolls, and much, much more. When the Japanese economy practically ground to a halt in the early 1990s, we shifted gears and did just as well.

I was a close student of Japanese culture and economics. I knew the good times were coming to an end; jobs would be tight, and expense accounts would all but disappear. Japanese men, who were used to going out every night after work, would be spending nights at home for the first time since the samurai returned from battle. So I bought the Japanese rights to Time-Life videos and did a great business in war documentaries, wild animal programs, and other videos targeted at these newly domesticated men.

If there is one venture that captured the essence of what was best about our business at the Mint, I think it would have to be the story of Jackie Kennedy's pearls. Nothing I've ever done is more illustrative of the search for intrinsic value than that. Nothing better captures the effort to locate the rubies in the orchard.

You know the pearls I'm talking about. Jacqueline Kennedy was so often photographed wearing those pearls that they seemed a natural extension of her—an integral piece of her legendary grace and charm. She wore them to state dinners. She wore them on trips to India, Greece, and Japan. She wore them when she greeted the high and mighty and when she was looking after the children. Believe me—you *know* those pearls! But what you may not know is that the pearls were fake. Jacqueline Bouvier purchased them at Bergdorf Goodman in the 1950s for about $35.00.

I worshiped Jackie Kennedy all my life. To me, she was the epitome of class; she managed to be beautiful and refined while still being refreshing, rather than stodgy or uptight. And I was certainly not alone in my admiration. For millions of American women, Jackie was the standard by which every woman on the public stage was judged. She was the closest we would have to American royalty.

In 1996, Sotheby's announced its "Auction of the Century" to sell the estate of Jacqueline Kennedy Onassis. I attacked the auction catalogs like a rabid librarian who had just been released from the gulag. Yet despite my affection for the subject and my appreciation of her belongings, I could find only one thing in the entire auction that I wanted: those pearls. My staff was shocked by my restraint.

The catalog listed the estimate on the pearls at $200 to $300. Shrewd as I was, I suspected they might go a bit higher. In the weeks before the auction, I realized—time and time again—what a truly naive notion that was. As I kept pace with the constantly revised estimate on the pearls, I did my best to keep Stewart up to date.

"Darling, I think we may have to go as high as five thousand dollars to get those pearls," I told him.

"They're fake, right?" he asked. "That's insane."

As the auction day neared, I gave Stewart the latest. "I think Jackie's pearls may go as high as twenty-five thousand dollars," I said.

"For a set of fake pearls? That's just nuts."

By this point, I had already talked myself into buying them. I wanted to convince Stewart that the investment— as crazy as it seemed—would be worthwhile. I spread photos across Stewart's desk—Jackie in the pearls here, Jackie in the pearls there, John-John on Jackie's lap pulling at those same pearls.

"She wore them in nearly every picture ever taken," I said. "They are the icon of the icon."

The day before the auction, the estimates were truly, undeniably insane—off the charts. I told Stewart the pearls might go for a ridiculous amount—maybe even $100,000.

He just stared with incomprehension. The next day, big, brave me handed the phone to Stewart. I knew he had the guts to go all the way, provided I had actually convinced him. I guess I had. The starting price was $5,000. By the time the hammer came down on our winning bid, we had agreed to a final price of $211,000. We now owned the most expensive strand of fake pearls in the entire world.

We were not the only ones astonished by our willing-ness to pay such an absurd price. *People* magazine ran a story on the pearls, as did most U.S. newspapers. Dewar's Scotch took out a full-page ad in *The Wall Street Journal* with the headline "Just pay $211,000.00 for a strand of fake pearls? You need a Dewar's."

We sent two guards from the Mint's private army (we stored large supplies of gold and silver because of our on-site minting operation) to New York to bring back the pearls. They delivered them to me directly at work. Every-one stood around and watched the unveiling. The pearls were still in their original silk-lined box from Bergdorf's. As I opened it, I caught a faint scent of Jackie's perfume. It was a chilling experience. My eyes welled up as I thought about what that divine creature had meant to me and my country.

We analyzed the 139 European glass faux pearls and made exact reproductions from a mold. The pearls were color-matched to the creamy originals, with the same seventeen coats of lacquer that the originals possessed. Then they were put on hand-knotted silken cords. The circle was closed by a silver art deco clasp featuring nine period-style rhinestones and bearing a Franklin Mint silver monogrammed emblem of authenticity. They were as close to the real fake Jackie pearls that any combination of art and technology could muster.

We put the original strand of pearls on a coast-to-coast tour before bringing them home and exhibiting them at the Franklin Mint Museum. A couple of years ago, we made a gift of them to the nation; they are permanently on view at the Smithsonian.

At $211,000, the pearls turned out to be a phenomenal bargain. We sold more than 130,000 copies at $200 a strand—for a gross of $26 million. Owning the original pearls gave us the credibility to sell the copies; it certified and rewarded our collectors' faith that they were getting as close to the real deal as anyone could. By wearing those iconic pearls, women everywhere could channel a bit of Jackie.

It mattered that we studied and analyzed the pearls. It mattered that our reproductions were made from exact molds of the originals. It mattered that we replicated the color, the cord, and every detail as faithfully as science would allow. In the end, it mattered that we cared about the pearls every bit as much as our collectors cared. That bond—that faith in the product and what it represented—is ultimately what transformed 139 spheres of ordinary glass into genuine rubies—with real and lasting intrinsic value.

Value is real, even when the product is 100 percent fake.

We included a Letter of Authenticity in every shipment of every product we created and marketed. It was more than a letter; it was a creed. Our dolls weren't just pretty ladies in frilly dresses, plucked randomly from some designer's fantasy. They had history and character. Our cars were painstakingly exact. And if we did our homework right, our collectors would see that we had been true to the history and character of the original—down to the smallest detail. It was Mies van der Rohe who said, "God is in the details." So is value. So is faith. Hey, so is life.

CHAPTER 5

Thinking Inside
the Pomegranate

In the early 1970s, General Foods, which was happily selling its Kool-Aid brand sugar powder by the ton, looked around for a way to sell a similar concoction that adults wouldn't be ashamed to drink. The company developed a lemon-flavored powder and conducted extensive research to determine how best to market it. They came up with the folksy name Country Time and sold it with the promise that, even though it was sold in canisters at the supermarket, once this powder was mixed with water it tasted just like "good, old-fashioned lemonade."

The product was hawked on TV by a "white-haired grandfather, suspenders and all, sitting on a sun-drenched porch on a sizzling summer day mixing up a pitcher of ice-cold lemonade."[1] Who could resist? It wasn't long before

---

[1]Allen P. Adamson, *BrandSimple*.

Country Time was selling big and Grandpa was snapping his suspenders to the tune of "I'm in the money."

At least until the day Minute Maid ran a negative ad that exposed Country Time for what it was: a fraud. As it happened, not a single lemon went into the creation of that "good, old-fashioned lemonade." Not one. The Minute Maid ad killed Country Time and took the whole powdered lemonade category down with it.

So what do you know?! It turns out people don't like being lied to and having their trust betrayed. It cost Minute Maid a pretty penny in advertising to make this point in the 1970s. Today, they could put up a virtually cost-free but no less devastating ad on YouTube, sit back, and enjoy the viral destruction of a competitor in a millisecond.

To me, the Country Time fiasco is the essence of "thinking outside the box." For years, we've been told that society's smartest, most creative, and biggest winners all think that way, and if we don't, we must be missing that special edge required for success. At management conferences and sales retreats, in business books and corporate seminars, we are exhorted by some guru or another to leave our foolish boxes behind.

Bear with me a moment as I pose a somewhat obvious question. How many successful people have you met in your entire life who can really, truly "think outside the box"? When was the last time you encountered someone who is able to conceptualize and create something that is truly new—something unlike anything that has come before?

Einstein could do that. For a contemporary business

example, I guess you could say Steve Jobs has done it, as did the brilliant technologists who devised the Internet. I've been privileged to meet some of the best business minds in the world, but I can count on one hand—maybe two—the number of people who really, truly "think outside the box."

One of them is my friend Michael Milken, who made a fortune with his invention of high-yield bonds. Mike has similarly built his Milken Family Foundation into an innovative force for good. Since 1982, he has invested in educational opportunity and saved hundreds of thousands of lives by directing medical research and health care outreach in pursuit of faster cures, particularly of prostate cancer.

Creative geniuses like Mike don't need business schools to inspire their ideas because they already view the world in a multidimensional context; it's a picture the rest of us, with our linear lines of sight, can't fully grasp. The vast majority of people, including those who are most successful in business, think inside the box.

This is not an incidental point, because it's easy to be awed by someone who comes up with a product or solution that you presume you never would have thought of yourself. It's easy to attribute their insight to a flash of genius that you don't share or to special talents you can't emulate. It's easy to assume that they achieve their success by thinking outside that box in which the rest of us spend our working hours. These flashes of genius, the subject of Malcolm Gladwell's *Blink: The Power of Thinking Without Thinking*, may seem to emerge out of the thinnest air.

More often, they are the product of years of experience and accumulated knowledge.

Art historian E. H. Gombrich said, "There's no such thing as the immaculate perception." He was right. New perceptions, just like new creations, are inevitably cobbled together from what has been experienced, perceived, or created before. Just as the first typewriter was derived from the telegraph transmitter and the first motorcycle from the bicycle, most breakthroughs are grounded in knowledge and experience. They don't descend from the ether. Every so often, an inventor takes a concept from one realm and applies it ingeniously to another. Reebok, for example, got the idea for its Pump sneaker from the inflatable insert used in a hospital IV bag.

Most of us are products of a society, culture, and educational system that have enormous influence in structuring the way we think. For every great idea that is generated outside those confines, there are thousands more that are the product of thinking inside the box—by people who have been working at solving a problem for a long time. As Thomas Edison said, "Genius is one percent inspiration and ninety-nine percent perspiration."

What we nongeniuses are apt to achieve when we think outside the box is something unhinged from reality, like good old-fashioned lemonade made without a single lemon. This is especially tempting to marketers trying to sell a brand that has no intrinsic value—in which case, reality doesn't give you a whole lot to work with.

Stewart and I have designed all of our companies to facilitate and encourage thinking inside the box, to allow us to go deeper and deeper into our brands to find more value there. The most obvious example of that is our preference for in-house work over outside consultants. I mentioned before that Bryan Honkawa developed our distinctive POM bottle. Bryan is our top in-house designer, but he is far more than that; he is a marketer, too. He and I have worked together for more than twenty years; he is there when ideas are born, and he attends most of the meetings where brands are created and developed. He knows his stuff—but he also knows our stuff. So when he creates a product, it is grounded in the brand and in all the knowledge of the brand that comes from being part of the team.

All of our advertising, media buying, public relations, and product design are created in-house, as well. Why? Well, one of the reasons I got out of advertising in the first place is that I started to feel that my efforts were mostly window dressing. My experiences with outside consultants have convinced me that, most of the time, their solutions tend to be both quick and shallow. That doesn't mean that from time to time I don't allow hope to triumph over experience, much like a second marriage. But I realize that consultants, too, are in business. Their mission is to maximize profit from the work they do—to get it in, get it done, and get it out in record time. That is how they are judged by their bosses. I'm not saying there isn't great talent out there; I just want that talent to work *with* us, as part of our team, rather than *for* us, as a consultant who has more than one client and agenda.

There are times, however, when we are faced with a

special project so big or so urgent or so far outside our comfort zone that we must rely on outside talent. In those instances, we *manage* the heck out of the process—even at the risk of becoming the clients from Hell. One thing we never do is leave our brand at the mercy of chance.

When I hire people full-time from the agency world, we reindoctrinate them and teach them our ways. I want creative solutions with no borrowed interest. The mission is straightforward: Get to know the brand you are working on, live with it day in and day out. Then create break-through advertising and programs born from the Unique Selling Proposition of the brand. At our companies, that is how we solve problems—and break new ground.

The one constant, whether the work comes from our own team or from guns for hire, is that the product is only as good as the brief that goes into it. I always say I want a marketing brief so tight that if the author were run over by a bus, anyone could pick up the project and complete it.

We take the same in-house approach to management consulting. Rather than hire McKinsey or Bain to help us sort through new ideas, potential acquisitions, and deals, we have created our own McKinsey in-house. Roll International, which is the umbrella company for all of our businesses, employs about twenty top-notch MBAs as a full-time, in-house consulting force. And just like our creative staff, our consultants become invested in the success of some part of our business and bring all of their talent and intelligence to bear on it. For example, they have been integral to helping us master the challenges of growth at POM, analyzing our operations and helping us design processes for juicing and bottling that maximize efficiency and minimize waste.

In any business, there are inevitably projects that deserve more attention than they receive. A project that's potentially crucial to long-term growth may not seem sufficiently urgent to capture the attention of managers immersed in day-to-day operations. Like many executives, our managers are often too busy to perform due diligence on every opportunity for new business creation or for the extension of an existing business. That's when our consulting team steps in. Since our in-house consultants are already part of our extended family, their advice is always valued. Just as important, we are able to evaluate it without fearing it stems from an ulterior business motive. Sadly, not everyone who hires an outside consulting firm can be so confident.

Our consulting team is also a phenomenal talent pool for management. POM president Matt Tupper came out of our consulting team, as did the presidents of FIJI Water and Teleflora. We had worked with them for a few years before they took over management responsibilities. We knew exactly what we were getting into—and so did they.

Another benefit we get from our in-house focus is hard to measure, but it's vitally important. We have a coherent business culture. Everyone is pulling in the same direction. Everyone understands our philosophy of searching for rubies in the orchard, digging deep to find value, and being truthful in communicating that value to consumers. We don't get a lot of people engaging in shady behavior—although when we've encountered this, it's almost always been instigated by an employee who joined us from a public company. In other words, someone who was accustomed to answering Wall Street's call of the wild.

At one of our companies, we hired a young fellow straight out of an investment banking firm to be our chief financial officer. He had a habit of making the financials look rosier than they actually were. We kept explaining to him that our company is privately held, that we needed to see a true picture in order to run our business, but the poor chap was so accustomed to manufacturing crooked numbers each quarter for "The Street" that he couldn't find his way back to the straight and narrow. If he had exhibited a drinking or substance abuse problem, we could have sent him to rehab, but where do you send a recidivist hooked on funny financials? We had to let him go.

You can't cook value any more than you can cook books. Sooner or later, it's bound to stink up the kitchen. POM's success is purely a consequence of avoiding the extrinsic and extraneous and instead going deeper inside the pomegranate, where the value resides.

We got into the pomegranate business with a helpful push from happenstance. In 1986, Stewart bought a large pistachio orchard and discovered that the sale included more than 100 acres of pomegranates. "Let's pull them and plant more nuts," one of Stewart's farmers advised. Stewart is successful not only because he's smart. He's successful in part because he keeps himself open to new opportunities. And he knows how to be patient. "Let's see how they do," he replied. Those five little words would create an industry.

Stewart soon learned that when the pomegranates did well, they could earn a better return than pistachios. He planted another 6,000 acres over the next decade. As pomegranates became a more significant business for us, we set out to learn more about them. That's when we began to discover the folklore and references in ancient texts about the fruit's remarkable healing powers.

In 1996, we began subjecting the health properties of the pomegranate to the proving ground of modern medicine. Stewart and our medical adviser, Dr. Leslie Dornfeld, met with Dr. Michael Aviram, an Israeli scientist who had done seminal research into the antioxidant powers of red wine. Stewart and Dr. Dornfeld asked him to begin research on the pomegranate, as well.

Antioxidants have increasingly been the subject of

POM Wonderful Antioxidant Potency Index.

medical research because they are capable of neutralizing free radicals, the unstable molecules that appear to damage cells and tissue and may be linked to disease and aging. Research by Dr. Aviram and others revealed that POM has 17 percent more polyphenol antioxidants than red wine and neutralizes 54 percent more free radicals. Prior to this discovery, red wine had been the antioxidant king, so the research findings were cause for a toast.

We went on to fund independent studies assessing the effects of pomegranate juice on cardiovascular disease, cancer—especially prostate cancer—and type 2 diabetes. Across the board, the findings ranged from propitious to downright startling. For example, a UCLA study revealed a significantly slower PSA doubling time for men who drank eight ounces of POM daily after having been treated for prostate cancer. (A slower doubling time may reflect slower progression of the disease.)

This research was costly; so far, we've spent nearly $25 million to explore the health benefits of POM, but it's been worth every penny because we now understand the value of these rubies in the orchard—and their enormous potential for good.

The pomegranate is a beautiful fruit, but there is also something a little weird about it. You can look up and down the fresh food aisle at the market and you won't encounter anything quite like it. That's because the pomegranate occupies its own branch on the evolutionary tree; it's an outlier with no direct relatives in the plant world, a Galápagos unto itself.

Having evolved in the highlands of Central Asia, the pomegranate found a cherished place in the packs of travelers and in the holds of ships. Over the course of months, while a pomegranate turns a dark, baked-brown color outside, the inside remains packed with sugar and other nutrients. In fact, its peel provides such an impervious coat of armor that the fruit can remain juicy for months after it has been picked.

So far, the research we've funded has yielded about two dozen published reports, which are available on the pom wonderful.com Web site. We have about thirty more studies in the works. Since the scientific standards on health claims are high, however, even some of the most promising research goes largely unheralded in our marketing.

Scientific data is not the only measure of POM's success, of course. Lots of people drink POM because it makes them *feel* healthier—data or no data—and that feeling has been a significant driver of our growth. Our fresh pomegranate sales went from 100,000 cartons in 2001 to 1.9 million cartons in 2007. Similarly, in just four years, POM has gone from zero to $165 million in sales—with an advertising budget that is a tiny fraction of what you would expect to launch a new product in the packaged goods industry.

Over the years, we've continued planting more acreage, growing more fruit, and building the market for both fresh pomegranates and our juice. Today we have more than 18,000 acres planted with pomegranates, and we keep expanding our orchards.

However, as we built up our juicing operations and our juice market, we faced two issues. Some POM drinkers were looking for a lighter drink that would still deliver the antioxidant power of POM. In fact, lots of POM drinkers had developed ritualistic ways of diluting POM, mixing it with seltzer or tea or lemonade or any number of other combinations to make it less like a weighty Burgundy and more like a light thirst quencher. Meanwhile, diabetics were eager to have a version of POM with less sugar.

It made sense for us to respond to this demand and offer consumers a light POM. That may sound easy, but when you're dealing with the world's most oddball fruit, things are seldom easy. If you dilute the unique sugars and phytochemicals in pomegranate juice—nutrients that occur nowhere else in nature—you undermine its anti-oxidant properties. Making a light version of POM simply wasn't possible without making the kind of compromises we are unwilling to make.

At the same time that we faced this quandary over light juice, we were trying to figure out what to do with tens of thousands of tons of discarded, mashed-up pome-granates left over from the juicing process. The pungent discards also possessed incredible nutritional value; the fruit's highest concentration of antioxidants is found in the peel, which has unique and powerful tannins. And the arils inside the pomegranate contain rare oil, stocked with unique compounds.

We had been selling this mash as cattle feed, all the time thinking "Wouldn't it be great if we could find some way to salvage the extraordinary health properties contained in this mound of reddish ooze?" I'm all for a happy Elsie but I would rather bring the powerful potion to people. The ideal would be a product more scalable than juice, something we could send around the world to meet the demand for health, but in a different way.

This innocent notion led to much consternation at POM. My marketing team and I were eager to learn if we could produce a pomegranate extract that could deliver the power of eight ounces of POM juice in a capsule. The operations team howled. We were asking too much. They had already performed a series of miracles to produce POM. Remember, pomegranates are as fickle as Goldilocks; as I explained in chapter 1, squeeze them too hard, and they produce bitter juice; squeeze them too little, and they will deny you both profit and health benefits. What's more, production of a pomegranate extract would necessitate a whole new round of science to determine whether it was safe and effective.

I've never been one to give up easily (or otherwise), so you may have guessed the outcome: Marketing won over Operations. We went to work developing a pomegranate extract. After a couple years of testing, we came up with an ultrapotent, 100 percent pure polyphenol antioxidant extract made from the same California pomegranates we use to make POM. We called it POMx. The mound of red ooze had delivered big time. But we still had one more hurdle.

The supplement market is a con man's Shangri-La,

crowded with dubious products hawked by fly-by-night marketers hailing from the sleazier precincts of the business world. Though virtually tone deaf, I feel more confident betting on the winner of *American Idol* than on the efficacy of a container of capsules at the local "nutrition" store. After years of investment, hard work, and testing—including the only safety review of a pomegranate supplement conducted by the Food and Drug Administration—I wasn't eager for POMx to keep company with the supplement crowd.

What to do? Distribution is everything in a new-product introduction. As brilliant, portable, shelf-stable, and pure as this supplement is, finding its market is our greatest challenge. In fact, putting the equivalent of eight ounces of juice into one little pill is nothing compared to finding the right direct-marketing campaign. At this writing, we are in a test phase, selling the pills online through the POM Web site and a dedicated site, PomPills.com. We are testing print ads in health, fitness, and general-interest magazines, and in media with broader reach, and we also have an online campaign.

> Distribution is everything in a new product introduction.

Yet we also realized that POMx is a fabulous ingredient that could enhance a wide range of products. While we were developing POMx, we were also thinking about how we might produce a tea that would meet the high standards established by POM. The tea seemed like a great idea, but it lacked the antioxidant punch that is integral to the POM brand. So we put the idea on a shelf, where it stayed for about a year.

POMx brought it back. With POMx in the mix, we could produce a tea replete with the remarkable antioxidant properties our consumers craved. We used hand-picked tea leaves and a brewing process not unlike that for sun tea. One result of our exceptionally gentle extraction process is a taste that's both delicate and delicious. Another result is that every flavor in the line has less than four milligrams of caffeine—an infant can drink it. With its lighter taste, fewer calories, and all-natural ingredients, POM Tea was the product we'd been searching for. After bottling our new brew inside a beautifully rendered keepsake glass, we went to market.

I don't want to give the impression that all this magically came together. It didn't. In fact, it was a struggle every step of the way. One problem with our tea was price; POMx is expensive to process in a form that lends itself to mixing with other liquids. In addition, most ready-to-drink teas on the market are made with powdered teas or low-end product. I wanted handpicked tea leaves brewed in a way that wouldn't cause the bitterness associated with other teas. I also refused to use high-fructose corn syrup, which is much cheaper than natural sugars.

Each time I put my foot down in the name of quality, the price soared. Then I made the problem worse by insisting on creating a keepsake glass. We didn't intend to use it forever, because eventually plastic is the way to go for both consumers and the environment. But I was searching for a way for POM Tea to stand out on the shelf while the brand was introduced. I wanted my consumer to know immediately that this wasn't your grandma's Snapple.

The money and time invested in POMx and POM Tea were money and time denied to other potential breakthroughs, and there was no guarantee of success. The path we followed was charted by our faith in our product and confidence that we could convince the marketplace to share our faith. In the end, POM Tea costs twice as much as—or more than—most of the competition, so we needed faith not only in the value of our product but in our ability to communicate that value and in consumers' ability to recognize it and embrace it. The success of POM Tea proved that our brand had enough equity and elasticity that we could afford to venture into new terrain.

I had always wanted to create a healthy energy drink. I was kept up at night fretting that half our hyperdriven society was imbibing the likes of bulls' adrenal glands in search of a liquid energy boost. Ugh. The ingredients in most energy drinks are more likely to be found in a chemistry lab than a farmer's market—this stuff isn't Popeye's spinach. I thought if we could come up with a natural energy drink packed with the antioxidant power of POMx, we would have another winner. We worked on it for several years, frequently banging our heads against the wall before shelving the idea. But of course, through near successes and total failures, we also learned a lot.

One of the things we learned was that POMx seemed to taste especially good with dairy products. In fact, Stewart had acquired a habit of mixing POMx in yogurt smoothies. So we decided to give it a try with coffee and milk.

One of the funny things about developing new food products is that you always know when you have a hit—and when you don't. If, after the presentation has been made, everyone gets up from the conference table and files out, leaving the test product in a half-consumed state on the table, you know you need to go back to the drawing board. If, on the other hand, the presentation ends and people seem to be lingering a little too long, availing themselves of another taste and eyeing the dregs in the containers, you know you've just passed the test.

Our chief food scientist had been experimenting with POMx and coffee. Among the few of us who had tasted this mixture, the enthusiasm—it was more like love—was overflowing. We needed a reality check. So we had a POM Coffee tasting at our house. When it was all over, we found people sneaking around our kitchen scrounging for leftovers. Something about this delicious combination of coffee and POMx just does that to people. As I write this, we're launching four flavors of POMx Coffee: chocolate, café au lait, caramel, and chai tea (yes, I know chai is not coffee, but it was so good we couldn't bear to leave it out of the lineup). We use ethically sourced, Rainforest Alliance Certified, premium Italian-roasted Arabica coffee beans, organic sugar, and milk from cows that aren't doped up with artificial hormones. And this drink really packs a wallop; a ten-ounce bottle has all the antioxidants, courtesy of POMx, of an eight-ounce glass of POM Juice.

Like all faith, brand faith is tested from time to time. In

2006, right when POM was really taking off as a brand, we faced a crisis. Demand had grown threefold in the prior two years. Supply had not. In fact, our crop yield that year was a major disappointment. That's one thing about agriculture—you can't simply keep the factory open round the clock to increase supply. Nature doesn't do business that way.

So at the moment when we should have been basking in our success, enjoying the huge spike in demand for our product, we were in a state of panic. Our stores were running out of POM, and we had none on hand to supply them. Our customers, big supermarkets and other retail establishments that we had worked very hard to cultivate, were extremely unhappy with us. Worse, our consumers, some of whom had grown accustomed to drinking POM every day, were traveling from store to store in a literally fruitless search for our juice. They wanted their POM fix, and they wanted it *now*.

We tried to explain. We hadn't expected so much success. There had been too much sun that year. The rains had come late. The bees hadn't been in the mood. All of these explanations were true, but to healthy juice addicts looking for their fix, frantically searching store shelves for an ever-dwindling supply, the truth was not very comforting.

As we scrambled to find some way to meet demand and keep our customers and consumers from deserting us, suddenly, on the horizon, it looked like our ship was coming in. Agents approached us with an offer of an enormous tanker full of Iranian pomegranate juice. It seemed like a godsend. After all, these agents were not the only ones who had noticed the huge, unmet demand for pomegranate juice. Everyone from small juice makers right up to Pepsi-Cola suddenly sensed a great opportunity to make inroads in a growing new market—at our expense. If we didn't buy the Iranian juice, someone else surely would—and they would use it to try to lure away our retail customers and consumers.

We were running so low on juice that we were cutting retail orders by 60 percent or more. As we debated what to do, we realized we really had no choice. The only responsible decision we could make was to resign ourselves to fate. We grow the Wonderful variety of pomegranates, and we grow them in our own way, on our own land, in our home state of California. My husband the farmer and his able staff run the best orchards in the world, where the science of modern agriculture meets the culture of old-world farming. The juicing plant is state of the art, our presses are so unique that they are a carefully protected trade secret, and we transport our product in refrigerated trucks to keep the juice fresh.

Let's assume, for the purposes of debate, that the Iranian shipment was truly 100 percent pomegranate juice. How did the farmers care for their fields? What kind of fertilizer or pesticides might they have used? How did they harvest the crop? How did they squeeze the pomegranates? We didn't know the answer to any of these questions, and we knew we wouldn't really be able to verify any of the answers we were given.

So how could we make the same claims about this Iranian juice—healthwise, tastewise, qualitywise—that we made about POM? The only way we could be sure would be to test the efficacy of the Iranian juice against POM's. That would take months, even years. Meantime, with all those question marks hanging in the air, if there was even one ounce of the Iranian juice in a POM bottle, it simply wasn't right to call it POM.

After analyzing the possibilities from every angle—believe me, we really wanted to meet the demand and make everyone happy—we circled back to where the company had started. Corporate mission statements can be awful things—full of false piety, hypocrisy, nonsense, garbled, strained language, and outright falsehoods. The worst of them are enough to make your skin crawl. When we formulated a mission statement for POM a few years before, we meant what we said:

> *Unique as the pomegranate itself—tough and protective on the outside, mythically beautiful on the inside—POM Wonderful is a global brand committed to creating an entrepreneurial legacy of innovation, profitability and wellness, by growing and marketing the highest quality pomegranates and pomegranate-based products that are healthy, honest and essential to the well-being of humankind.*

We knew that our own pomegranates and pomegranate-based products were of the highest quality; they were healthy, honest, and essential to the well-being of human-kind. They passed the test. We didn't know if the Iranian juice had been produced in a test tube on the dark side of the moon. If we meant what we said, we had no choice but to leave the Iranian stuff at sea, where it soon found another buyer.

The decision hurt us. In addition to losing money, we spent more time placating our retailers and answering customer service calls than we did running our business. But, as often happens when you opt to do the right thing, in the long run, it was probably good for business. It underscored our brand's integrity and the promise of freshness and quality, and it's certainly not the worst thing to have consumers angry and upset and yelling at the supermarket manager because they're craving your product and can't find it. Better that than a shrug of the shoulders! We posted an apology on our Web site, explaining that we simply didn't have enough supply to meet demand, and from grocery shelves that had formerly stocked POM, we dangled cards with the message: "Out of juice? So are we."

> As often happens when you opt to do the right thing, in the long run it is probably good for business.

The pomegranate shortage was a real threat to our business. Yet inside every threat is an opportunity. In fact, a great business consultant named Ichak Adizes, whom we worked with in the late 1980s, used to call these pivotal moments "oppor-threats," because like yin and yang, they always come in pairs. In this instance, the shortage prompted us to start thinking seriously about developing line extensions that would be less dependent on Mother Nature and the idiosyncrasies of our unique fruit. POMx and POM Tea were both products of crisis that catalyzed general talk into specific action. The way a business (or nation) handles oppor-threats goes a long way in determining its success or failure. For POM, the danger passed and the opportunity expanded.

Inside every threat is an opportunity.

The following year, our pomegranates came back strong with a bumper crop—a karma crop. This little parable of the juices has a lot to do with business honesty. It has a lot to do with understanding the upside of an oppor-threat. It also has to do with intrinsic value. We spent a lot of time and invested a lot of creative energy in devising the right name, packaging, and design for our brand. If we had believed that our iconic bottle or some other extrinsic element was the source of value, we could have put any old juice inside and called it POM, but we didn't—because we staked our value on the real thing inside, the juice.

We were able to recover from a shortage of POM on supermarket shelves. It's doubtful we could have recovered from betraying our own claims and the trust of our consumers. Does anyone believe a word that any cigarette maker has said in recent decades—about *anything*? Will parents simply forgive and forget that Mattel sold them tainted toys for their children to play with? I doubt it.

When prospective partners have proposed POM brand extensions, we've tried to keep in mind our mission and our understanding of value. Once you become successful, you have to be disciplined enough—and care deeply enough about your product—to leave money on the table from time to time. We've had offers to put POM in everything from candy to shampoo. But we're very protective of our brand equity. Any deal that might trivialize or dilute that equity is not in POM's long-term interest, regardless of how much revenue it might generate in the short term.

> In building a successful business, you have to be disciplined enough to leave money on the table.

Value and values have a similar root: authenticity. And when you damage one side of the equation, the other side just doesn't add up. Consider the example of a famous pizza chain. Instead of focusing on a value proposition—a modest pizza at an inexpensive price—Domino's hired the blond bombshell Jessica Simpson for its advertising campaign. The ads were served up extra hot, with Jessica's bodacious bod as the appetizer, main course, and dessert. A short time later, however, the pizza girl let it slip that she is allergic to wheat, tomatoes, and cheese, which is another way of saying she can't stand pizza. Domino's ended up looking like a fraud—and not a very clever one at that. How did a large, successful company get itself into such a mess? I think I know. Someone in marketing at Domino's was thinking outside the pizza box.

CHAPTER 6

Thinking Inside the Volcano

I t was a sunny summer day in Aspen. Stewart and I were on one of our Bataan Death Marches over the mountains. "We've been approached by a water company that's for sale," Stewart told me. I should have known by now how to detect another big job lurking behind his nonchalance, but my thirst for a challenge distracted me.

"Water?" I gasped. His timing was impeccable. My own water bottle was running low, and I was thirsty. "That's a really crowded category," I panted through parched lips, "and they all taste the same anyway." As it happened, I would later eat—or drink—those words.

To say the bottled water market is "crowded" doesn't really do justice to the colossal clutter of it all. There are more than six hundred brands of bottled water flooding the United States. There is filtered tap water gushing from that giant spigot known as Coca-Cola, which has a distribution network extending to every giant supermarket and corner bodega in the nation. There are countless local springs and wells—the water from which finds its way into regional bottled waters such as Adirondack in upstate New York and Calistoga in California. There are stylish European waters such as Voss and Acqua Panna. And there are hundreds of others that fall into one of those categories—or somewhere in between. Why would Stewart—or anyone—want to buy another bottled water company?

Back at the house, Stewart organized a blind tasting of about twenty bottles of water, including the top sellers. I performed my tasting trick—as he knew I would. "This one tastes better than the others," I said. A look of smug satisfaction crept over Stewart's face—a ridiculous, immature, and utterly annoying look known by every woman whose husband has just proved her wrong. He announced that the water I had singled out was FIJI brand. And he wanted to buy it.

This was all new to me. Up to that point, I had barely registered the existence of FIJI Water or even the island paradise that produces it. I never drank enough water. When I did, I usually spiked it with POM or something else to make it less boring. FIJI was different. I liked the taste, and I could drink it all day without doctoring it.

The brand had been around for only eight years. Still, it had made considerable progress in a very crowded field, especially in "on premise" work, meaning restaurants and hotels. "On premise" is a critical arena for beverages; it's where many consumers are first introduced to your brand

and where they develop associations between your brand and the experience (hopefully a superlative one) of fine dining or elegant leisure that a good restaurant, hotel, or spa induces. However, volume sales of water are built through grocery stores and mass retailers, not on premise. At the high end of the market, where it competed, FIJI was getting clobbered by Evian, the premium retail giant.

In spite of my misgivings, I knew Stewart's genius in spotting businesses with huge potential. To give you an idea of how good he is with numbers, he can actually help our granddaughter Scarlett do her fourth-grade math homework—and he has the patience to explain it well enough that she can do it herself the next time. Stewart also understands value—and he was certain FIJI had it.

We negotiated with FIJI founder David Gilmour, a wonderful character who combined the finesse of Fred Astaire with the grit of Gary Cooper. After making a fortune in land, gold mines, and who knows what, David bought his own island in Fiji. There, he fell in love with the precious water from an underground aquifer on a neighboring island. It wasn't long before I was packing a bathing suit and floppy hats.

To get the lay of the land, I took what was purported to be a forty-five-minute helicopter tour of the islands. Weather comes up rather unexpectedly in that part of the tropics, and our little flight extended to three and a half hours while we were stuck in a monsoon. In order to keep the interior of the vintage whirlybird from fogging up, the pilot kept the windows open throughout the storm. I got a

firsthand look at Fiji's 322 islands, including stunning wa-
terfalls and foliage. I emerged from the helicopter looking
like a hysterical middle-aged contestant in a wet T-shirt
contest, not the best way to make a great impression on
the plant employees who were on hand to get a first look
at me.

After months of negotiating—something for which
Stewart has the stomach but I don't—we finally bought
the company. My mission was to increase sales in every
channel. The first step, as always, was to think inside the
box—to look within the brand itself for creative solutions
to marketing challenges. I don't believe in makeovers for
the sake of makeovers, nor do I feel compelled to put my
personal stamp on every element of every brand. My staff
and I have enough to do already without creating busy
work. Before we made any moves with our new liquid asset, there was research to be done; we would need to learn
everything there was to know about water.

We assembled a great team of marketing and sales
professionals, and together we dipped into the well of information on the various sources of water and the ways
in which companies treated, packaged, and delivered it to
consumers. We wanted to understand the products and
the market, which provides America with more than eight
billion gallons a year.

Part of this rigor has to do with logistics. Unfortunately,
much of it has to do with health as well, because you can
no longer trust public or private water supplies. One of the
many downsides of a compromised ecosystem is that mi-
crobes, pesticides, and other contaminants have leached

into our groundwater. At the same time, airborne pollutants have contaminated the water that falls as rain—so water often gets spiked with pollution literally coming and going.

A 1999 test by the Natural Resources Defense Council found that hundreds of samples of bottled water contained bacterial or chemical contaminants, including carcinogens. According to *Reader's Digest*, even water from a well near a hazardous waste site was bottled and sold. As water shortages grow more serious in some parts of the country, local governments are adopting some truly drastic measures. Orange County, California, has built a $481 million plant to process and purify local sewage into drinking water. It doesn't get much scarier than that.

Making matters worse, many regions have aging water pipes leading from reservoirs and aqueducts to homes. Even New York City's tap water, once the pride of the Big Apple, has deteriorated in recent decades due to increased development in the Catskills region of upstate New York, from which the city draws its supply. I can remember the days when I first had enough money to visit New York and stay in style, instead of crashing on a friend's sofa. After taking a taxi from the airport to the Regency, I would rush up to my room, turn on the faucet, and, while standing over the sink, gulp down the delicious, cold, distinctly New York water. Sadly, as the quality of the water steadily declined, I took to drinking bottled water on my visits, forgoing a mouthful of increasingly chlorinated and sickly softened tap water.

In Europe, the infrastructure is even older and municipal water is even more dubious, which is why bottled water was introduced there before it developed a market here. Europeans live on bottled water—except for those who live on bottled wine.

In America, nearly half the bottled water is purified water that originates with municipal water systems. In other words, it's tap water. Aquafina, Dasani, and Smart Water are three of the most common brands. Basically, everything that occurs naturally in water—minerals and the like—is stripped away, and what's left is a kind of lifeless fluid without any discernible qualities. Some companies add back some of what they take out—but in a chemical, not naturally occurring, form. If not properly pH-balanced, it leaches salts, minerals, and bromides from your body, which is why you can actually overdose on it and go into shock. In a tragic case in California, a woman who had competed in a water-drinking contest actually died.

Nearly all the rest of the bottled water on the market is spring water. There was a time when spring water in America was uniformly pure and delicious, but not in this lifetime. Because springs generally lie just beneath the surface, ground pollutants can, and increasingly do, leach into the supply. Which brings us to the Unique Selling Proposition of FIJI Water.

FIJI Water isn't just a brand name; the water actually comes from a remote island in Fiji, thousands of miles from the nearest industrialized society. However, early research suggested that nobody believed it. We tried to have a little fun and educate consumers at the same time with a simple slogan: "The label says Fiji because it's not bottled in Cleveland." We should have known that the city of Cleveland would not find this humorous. We ruffled a few feathers and suffered a short boycott by the local newspapers for making fun of their fair city.

Our water is a renewable resource, supplied by the monsoon rains. It actually comes from an artesian aquifer on the edge of a Fijian rain forest, deep beneath the earth's surface. As the Environmental Protection Agency and others have pointed out, water from artesian aquifers is protected from contamination by confining layers of rock. Rainwater seeps through the rock over hundreds of years, but the rock acts as a barrier to pollutants. Consequently, water from artesian aquifers is purer than spring water. On this Fijian island, water from the aquifer is a whole different level of pure.

FIJI Water actually fell as rain hundreds of years ago, before the Industrial Revolution. The water filtered through the volcanic rock for two hundred years or so before settling into its ancient aquifer deep within the earth. This natural filtration system does more than protect FIJI Water from the evils of contamination; it adds tremendous benefits. As the water filters through the rock, it acquires mineral silica, which helps build strong bones, hair, skin, and connective tissue and gives FIJI Water its distinctive soft feel in the mouth. FIJI also has more naturally occurring fluoride than any other bottled water.

The aquifer is active—a moving liquid repository. We tap into it by boring deep inside the volcanic rock. The wa-

The source of FIJI's artesian water.

ter is siphoned through hermetically sealed pipes, which channel it directly into the bottle in a totally protected environment. There are no people present. This water comes from deep underground and is utterly untouched by man until you unscrew the cap.

Remember the old Stewart Resnick mantra? "The management is good. I'll let them run the business and it won't take any time from me at all." Right!

FIJI founder David Gilmour stayed on after the sale, as did the company president, but within a few months the old regime was gone. We moved the offices from lovely but inconvenient Aspen to Los Angeles, where we could take advantage of the various benefits of cohabitation with our other companies. Then, based on our new understanding of FIJI Water's Unique Selling Proposition, I set out to change the identity of the brand—while those who had created the original identity cringed.

I try not to be insensitive, but when you have invested $150 million in a company with the intent of taking it to the next level, a little insensitivity is sometimes hard to avoid. Seemingly unaware of FIJI Water's unique aquifer, the existing label on the bottle was a cartoon illustration of a waterfall. Yes, it was a picture of fresh, pristine water rushing over a dramatic cliff in the tropics. Yes, it evoked a sense of unspoiled nature and primitive beauty. Yes, it had a certain allure. But surface water? *Surface* water! Why would you want to suggest that FIJI came from surface water? The waterfall absolutely had to go.

In addition to the waterfall on the front of the label, the existing bottle had a back label that attempted to show where the islands of Fiji are located. The graphics were so weak that it was hard to understand what exactly was being communicated. In addition to these particular issues, there was a more general problem; the bottle was so discreet, so subtle, and so pale it just about disappeared on the supermarket shelf—it was indistinguishable from the background. In some refrigerated cases, which put a frost on the bottle, you couldn't find it with a magnifying glass and a bloodhound. It seemed we had just bought the *Where's Waldo?* of the packaging world.

One great lesson I've learned in retail is to take a mock-up of your product to the point of sale and look at it in its natural habitat—the jungle of competition. We photograph the tableau, take it back to the office, and study what the picture says. Your package at the point of sale is a minibillboard for your brand. You must use that space effectively to communicate your product's virtues, outshine your competitors, and reassure consumers that they are making the right choice when they select your product. I can't tell you how many times I have been surprised by those in situ photographs. Often, the package I loved at close range in the office wasn't the design that worked best on the shelf.

> Your package at the point of sale is a minibillboard for your brand.

We revised the front label of the FIJI bottle to make it clear that the water actually comes from Fiji. We used a photo of a lovely hibiscus, just like those that grow around our bottling plant, retaining the charming 3-D effect of the original bottle but replacing the waterfall with palm fronds.

The back labels became central to the marketing plan. There are now six different back labels, each supporting a different element of our Unique Selling Proposition, hopefully with a bit of charm. The first depicts and explains our artesian aquifer. The second places the Fiji islands in context—miles away from the nearest industrialized society. The third tells the story of our slogan: "Untouched by Man." The fourth explains how FIJI's unique mineral profile makes it the best-tasting water. The fifth and sixth labels explain our "green water" approach to sustainability.

As we had done with POM, we made FIJI available at happening parties, health events (like Race for the Cure), and corporate symposia while seeking a close association with movie stars, fashion models, political leaders, and the intelligentsia. But we never use a paid celebrity promoter or spokesperson. I'm thrilled to see a photograph of Nicole Kidman holding a bottle of FIJI or a *Los Angeles Times* photo of Oscar winners Tilda Swinton and Joel Coen clutching their FIJI bottles in one hand and their statues in the other—we all love glamorous movie stars. But we're not in the movie business. Our product is water—and we want the focus on our product.

There is an enormous difference between a product that celebrities love and a product that they are paid to *pretend* they love. Any marketer who thinks consumers are too dumb to notice that gap—and understand what it means—is fooling himself. (Yes, I'm talking to you, Domino's Pizza, but you've got plenty of company.) So why does Nike pay LeBron James a fortune to promote sneakers? Because LeBron James doesn't just get his picture taken with a pair of high-tops; he wears Nike sneakers to work each day—and he works in front of millions of people. Why did Smart Water pay Jennifer Aniston $10 million to hold a bottle of its water? I suspect the decision was made after a close examination of the intrinsic value of fortified tap water. Someone probably concluded it wasn't a very compelling proposition on its own.

After buying FIJI, we advertised on select billboards

and in vertical-interest (single subject) magazines, but a lot of our success was due to the events in which we participated—more than 1,500 a year—and we continue to do them. We are more focused on guerrilla and viral tactics than on advertising. It's hard to find an event where our target market is present and FIJI isn't. Just as important, our team works hard to make sure our brand appears in the kind of environments where we belong. We've benefited from a fair amount of product placement in movies, on television, and in magazines.

All of this has paid off. Since we purchased the company in November 2004, the sales of FIJI Water have increased by more than 300 percent, while the industry has grown by about 30 percent in the same period. In 2008, we surpassed Evian to become the leading premium bottled water in the United States. That wouldn't have been possible without a superior product, but it also wouldn't have been possible without smart marketing and sales.

For all its success, however, FIJI Water also illustrates a difficult communications challenge that is unique to this era. It's a challenge with broad implications, which I'll discuss later, but a number of issues are especially relevant to FIJI.

As I mentioned earlier, the market for bottled water owes much of its growth to environmental degradation. It seems to me that the bottled water industry has an even greater responsibility than others to be sensitive to the environment. As custodians of a little sliver of Fijian paradise, we strongly feel that responsibility. We've gone to considerable lengths to make sure we're fulfilling our obligations.

Fiji's reputation as an island paradise is well earned, and not just because the national food is ice cream. When you approach the atoll by air, you see hundreds of islands and the shallow reefs that surround them. The reefs are veritable forests of coral, in both soft and hard formations. Some formations resemble huge Frankenstein brains while others look like elegant Japanese fans dotted with tiny, brightly colored creatures. The tropical colors are magnificent, ranging from orange to green and deep violet.

These spectacular reefs are home to scorpion fish, ghost pipefish, blue-ribbon eels, mantas, hammerheads, and barracudas (not as stylish as the ones back home in L.A. but less hazardous to your health). If ever a quiet little corner of the earth cried out for preservation, Fiji is it.

FIJI Water has brought good jobs and an expanded tax base to the nation. However, given the fragile ecosystem there and the state of the globe in general, we felt we also needed to have a comprehensive environmental policy for our business.

The result is "FIJI Green," a multifaceted sustainability program with the goal of reducing our environmental impact, as well as the amount of carbon we produce. The program is based on ambitious goals and hard commitments to reach them. In 2008, FIJI Water became the first carbon-*negative* beverage on the market.

In addition, we will cut carbon emissions by 25 percent across our product life cycle by 2010. Working with our partner Conservation International, we will continue to invest in reforestation and other carbon reduction projects. These reductions will equal *at least* 120 percent of our carbon production each year. By 2010, 50 percent of our energy needs in Fiji will be derived from renewable sources such as wind and solar.

We are also working with the people of Fiji and Conservation International to protect and preserve the Sovi Basin, the largest lowland rain forest in Fiji. This effort alone will keep ten million tons of carbon out of the atmosphere in perpetuity. That's the equivalent of removing two million passenger cars from the roads for an entire year or planting 500,000 trees. We also contribute to more than one hundred water access projects in Fiji, ensuring that Fijians have access to their own clean water, especially in local schools.

Consumers rightly expect us to be not only environmentally conscious but environmentally *responsive.* The time for good intentions has passed. It's now time for *action.* As environmental issues grow more prominent—and the consequences of pollution more dire—this will become a larger priority for consumers worldwide. Right now, there is a small band of environmentalists in a sea of consumers. It won't be long, however, before the majority of consumers are environmentalists—and the majority of good companies, too.

CHAPTER 7

Eyeballs Ain't Enough

I n recent years, people who buy media have been obsessed with "eyeballs." How many eyeballs does that sitcom deliver? Whose Web site has the most desirable eyeballs? I'm fond of eyeballs myself. I use them regularly. But when I buy media to promote one of our brands, I'm not focused on eyeballs—that's a part of the anatomy that's easily distracted and often glazed over with consumer apathy. I want *hearts and minds.* So I need a message—and ways of using media—that can help us win them.

As it happens, I truly love media of all kinds, but that doesn't mean I like media indiscriminately, and it certainly doesn't mean I want to throw a lot of money at advertising and promotion in the vague hope that something sticks. I don't like media *that* much.

In POM's first four years, we spent a grand total of $14 million on marketing. That includes advertising, promotion, public relations—the works. I can't give you an exact figure detailing how much real communications value we purchased for that relatively small sum, but a conservative estimate is in the hundreds of millions. Every dollar we've invested in researching and understanding our brand has yielded many additional dollars' worth of media attention. I have several binders, all inches thick, filled with newspaper and magazine articles about Wonderful pomegranates and POM. They're the kind of credible, third-party endorsements that money can't buy. All of that priceless, positive buzz helped increase revenue and significantly enhanced our brand equity.

> I'm not focused on eyeballs—that's a part
> of the anatomy that's easily distracted and often
> glazed over with consumer apathy.

We follow the same approach with FIJI Water. If you asked me what the advertising-to-sales ratio is at FIJI Water, I wouldn't be able to tell you. We don't think in terms of set formulas, we instead think in terms of maximizing every investment dollar, doing the most with the least, and staying agile. At all of our companies, we maintain an entrepreneurial culture that enables us to move quickly to seize opportunities. We don't get locked into rigid routines or, worse, narrow mind-sets that limit creativity.

You rarely hear about Marshall McLuhan these days, but he was a brilliant and provocative thinker at least a couple decades ahead of his time. I grew up believing his famous aphorism—"The medium is the message"—only to discover through trial and error that the truth is a bit more complicated. The medium *shapes* the message, the medium *qualifies* the message, it can even *alter* the message—but the medium itself is not the message.

Messages are important, and, like most important things, it takes time to do them right. When I sit down with my team, our goal is to devise a message that is concise, direct, and immediately accessible. That doesn't mean I'm looking for a blunt instrument—more like a surgeon's scalpel. Above all, we're looking for a message that delivers on two distinct levels: we want it to be authentic, and we want it to register on the brain. The message has to be memorable.

Our POM campaign provides a number of excellent examples. We don't focus on extraneous plot lines or attributes. We treat our POM bottle as the hero of every ad. The iconic bottle is probably what catches your eye and draws you to the product in the first place; its organic form is an invitation to drop it into your shopping cart. In fact, the bottle has so much personality that we actually put a superhero cape on it and called it the "Antioxidant Superhero." Another POM example, perhaps our best known, likewise consisted of just two words: "Cheat Death." When you see that brave little bottle with a noose around its neck—a noose broken by the antioxidant power of POM—you identify with it just as you identify with a hero's triumph or last-minute escape from danger on the movie screen.

Empathy is a powerful social adhesive, so we try to elicit that natural feeling for our product/hero. When talking to our young female audience, we show the POM bottle under a hair dryer with the headline "Extreme Makeover." The audience understands that POM antioxidants make you over from the inside out. If we can make you chuckle, we have an opportunity to connect with a more serious message grounded in our brand's identity and intrinsic value. We can also go too far. When we used an image of a POM bottle in a bridal veil with the message "Outlive your spouse," it took only a few complaints posted on our message board for me to pull the campaign. I realized that for some people, it could never be funny.

Brevity is an essential principle of message creation. Remember Tom Peters's slogan from the late 1980s? "Keep it simple, stupid." Consumers didn't have the patience for a harangue then, and they have even less tolerance for one today. If your message is a paragraph long, you need to go back to the drawing board because you don't have a message—you have a paragraph. A concise, potent message travels well. You can publish it in a magazine and mount it on a billboard. You can put it on a Web site or embroider it on a baseball cap. The shorter the message, the more easily it adapts to different circumstances—and the more readily it travels between different media.

> If your message is a paragraph long, you don't have a message—you have a paragraph.

At best, most advertising skims the surface of our consciousness before we move right past it. That's hardly surprising. Estimates of the number of messages the average consumer confronts vary from about 250 to 5,000 a day. The low range is overwhelming; the high range is downright abusive. A recent report by the market research firm Yankelovich put a hard number on a common assumption: it found that 69 percent of Americans expressed interest "in ways to block, skip or opt out of being exposed to advertising."

Successful advertising makes us register the moment and take notice. If you can generate a reaction in consumers, you've already achieved a major goal; you've become a part of their life in that small but very critical moment. If you use that moment to land a solid message somewhere on the brain—a message grounded in your brand identity and value—then you've truly achieved a great deal.

Whatever you say in your ad and however you deliver the message, it had better be true. Don't put yourself—or your product—in the position of selling old-fashioned lemonade with no lemons in it.

If you're Ford or Procter & Gamble, I guess you see the benefit of spending tens of millions of dollars on thirty-second television spots, but the value of that approach has never been so obvious to me. According to Jeffrey Cole at the USC Annenberg School Center for the Digital Future, television viewers actually watch only between 5 and 10 percent of the commercials on TV. It's astounding but true.

More people than ever are watching TV; they just aren't watching commercials. I don't want to spend exorbitant sums to reach a television audience that has recorded a show on TiVo and is merrily skipping all the spots. It's pointless to shout at a consumer who just got up from the sofa to get a beer from the fridge or to put her child to bed. I don't want to try to interrupt a consumer who is talking to his spouse about paying the mortgage, and I'm not at all interested in reaching a video zombie who has been channel surfing for hours on end, zipping by dozens of commercials, all of which have begun to run together in the creature's increasingly mushy mind. We haven't given up on television altogether. We are running some outlandish thirty-second spots on late-night shows with some positive results.

The one place where television spots resonate sometimes even more than the content is on the Super Bowl. And at three million dollars for a thirty-second spot the creative better be outstanding and memorable. If consumers respond to your message these commercials can have a second life in traditional media where they become news and are shown over and over again on TV and the Internet. Three million dollars. At that price, it had better be a good one.

Billboards

Billboards may not be glamorous, but you can't TiVo your way through a billboard. In fact, the only way to miss a well-placed billboard is to drive with your eyes closed (much like the passengers in the backseat of my car). Of course, coming up with a memorable billboard ad isn't easy, but this isn't about easy—it's about effective.

> The only way to miss a well-placed billboard is to drive with your eyes closed.

Outdoor advertising is relatively cheap, although some locations are cheap for good reason. When you buy, keep in mind the old Reagan policy of "trust, but verify"—then throw out the "trust" part. We never buy sight unseen. Instead, we travel the city (*every* city) analyzing the best locations and making sure we're not buying a location with an obstructed view or some other undesirable attribute. We buy only premium locations, including cityscapes and wallscapes. We buy bulletins—large, illuminated, glowing boards that charge a big premium—whenever possible; they're the gold standard of outdoor advertising and are worth it. If we can get an extension on top so the image of our bottle literally rises above the city, we take it.

We keep our headlines simple and short—five words or less. One can absorb only a short burst of language at thirty-five miles per hour. We pay close attention to lighting. When we were introducing POM, I naively bought ad space in a bunch of telephone kiosks in Manhattan. Later, on a trip to the city, I kept looking for our ads but couldn't find them. Why? I hadn't bought illuminated kiosks, and by 4:00 p.m. on a winter day, they had disappeared into the darkness. It was a dumb mistake I never made again. Telephone kiosks are a great buy but only if you buy the Rolls-Royce of the line, the illuminated ones that glow through traffic 24/7.

There are some wild things you can do with outdoor advertising to cover a city for very little money. In introducing POM Coffee to Los Angeles and New York City, we wanted blanket coverage with a zany spirit reflective of the new brand. While transit postings and subway lines are a staple of ours, this time we experimented with mobile billboards, bus wraps, wild postings (numerous posters on deserted buildings, construction fences, etc.), taxi tops, sandwich boards, college kiosks and newspapers, bar coasters, and even posters placed on the wall above the toilets in select bars (talk about the concentration of your audience). The success of a launch in a big city can replicate itself as you roll out across the country, giving you a retail story to tell in each successive market.

There's nothing random about the way we buy. We want visibility in areas with high commuter density and in neighborhoods with a concentration of our target audience. Commuter rails and subway cars are a great way to get exposure in cities with large commuter populations. We may appear in only a few locations, but our target consumers see us everywhere: on their way to work, in the neighborhoods, where they live, where they shop, where they go out to dinner, where they meet their friends, creating different points of contact throughout the day. Despite limited resources and select locations, we still manage to achieve an effect of ubiquity. "I see your billboards everywhere," people tell me.

One of the many benefits of doing all our work in-house is that we're able to build the kind of relationships with vendors that are usually the exclusive province of ad agencies. And once in a while, we call in a favor. When Teleflora participated in a big campaign in which we donated 20 percent of sales on select bouquets to the fight against breast cancer, our key outdoor vendor helped us out with $500,000 worth of free billboards to support the campaign. Because our staff cares deeply about our mission—and about the charities we support—they take the time to convince others to care as well.

Newspapers

Print's heyday may have been the nineteenth and twentieth centuries, when newspapers and magazines proliferated, but I still adore the feel of the New York Times in my hands on a twenty-first century Sunday morning. No other medium is as tactile, portable, and immediate (and messy), allowing readers to linger over an article—or an ad—at their leisure, tear it out, and put it in their pocket for future reference.

When we owned the Franklin Mint, we had one of the largest magazine budgets in the advertising business, in excess of $300 million a year. We learned to negotiate directly with publications. Agencies, which get a commission on the total buy, have no incentive to negotiate lower rates, but we insist on getting value for our money—and vendors know we're willing to walk away if we don't get a fair price. When you add up what we save by avoiding agency fees and negotiating directly with vendors, it's a lot of money.

In the late 1980s and early '90s, the Franklin Mint was

the biggest advertiser in *Parade* magazine, the weekly delivered in Sunday newspapers. Because the Mint thrived on direct response, we needed a heavy and regular advertising presence. At the time, *Parade* had upward of 45 million readers and a weekly delivery schedule as sure as clockwork, making it an ideal vehicle for us. Learning the business through direct response was like running a research firm dedicated to measuring the effectiveness of print advertising. With direct response, you *know* if the publication is pulling in readers—you can count the coupons that accompany the checks. Alas, today *Parade* has a fraction of the pages it once had, and it no longer delivers the same response.

Today, the average reader of a big-city newspaper is sixty years old. When older readers die, they aren't being replaced. People simply get their news from too many other sources, including the Internet and TV. The average young consumer today doesn't have a relationship with a newspaper and doesn't seem to have the time or interest to develop one.

Nevertheless, in large metro Sunday papers, free-standing inserts (the coupons touting savings on everything from food to cleaning products and collector coins) are still a great deal. They aren't exactly sexy and they don't do much for your brand image, but they can entice consumers to give your brand a try. Without a trial, you don't get the second purchase that means so much. We use free-standing inserts for Teleflora holiday bouquets, with a discount coupon consumers can redeem online or at their local flower shop. POM, FIJI Water, and our Everybody's Nuts brand of pistachios are also frequent advertisers.

Despite their decline, I think that newspapers in small cities are still a viable medium. Millions of people rely on their local paper for everything from high school sports news to supermarket sales notices. There is a community spirit evident in a good local newspaper that can't be imitated by national media. Local news is always important news. I always read the local *Aspen Times* when I'm vacationing at our family home there. I like the sense of community it embodies, and I'm eager to know what's going on around town: movies, gossip, sales, and new restaurant openings. Local papers offer not only good value but real eyeballs that want to see what's being offered.

Magazines

Vertical-interest magazines remain an extremely valuable part of the media mix. Like newspapers, they're tactile, but they're also glossy and colorful, immersed in celebrity and pop culture. Women's magazines, health magazines, celebrity magazines such as *Shape, People, Us Weekly, OK,* and *In Touch* are all on our list. Sure, they've been running the same stories—"10 Minutes to Flatter Abs" and "Starlet Dates Bad Boy"—since the Neanderthals were a hot gossip item, but, hey, it seems to work. Also, when we see glossy photos of celebs holding FIJI Water, we know that's an environment in which we want to advertise.

Here again, our in-house operations give us an advantage. When we hear about a great remnant—which, like a carpet remnant, is always had at a discount—we move on it immediately without relying on the cumbersome machinery of an ad agency. Who knows if an agency would even bother to tell us about it?

Agencies are not conducive to speed. Is the account executive at the agency out to lunch? Making a pitch to a client? Who knows? Has the client's magazine budget already been spent? If it has, is the account exec going to pry new funds from the client to buy an unplanned ad at a discount? Not without a conference call and multiple deliberations. By the time a decision comes down, the ad space is long gone. I know, because I probably bought it.

When we are offered a quality magazine placement at a great rate, we take it. If a new expense is not in the budget, we change the budget to accommodate it.

We have a number of parameters that guide our magazine and ad buys:

1. We want the right-hand page, forward in the book.
2. No full-page ad opposite our ad.
3. No coupon on the back side of our ad.

For the right price, we'll give up all of those demands—except one. Our ad must appear on the right-hand page; that's the page that draws the eye even as the hand turns the page. No right hand, no business.

Radio

Radio is fundamentally a promotional medium. We don't advertise on radio, but we do promote there. I believe only in local radio—and only when we can work out a promotional campaign that's integrated into a show's content. We want listeners to hear about our product from the deejay they specifically tune in to hear. And we want to be included in the show's format—not outside it in the form of a "commercial break." We've had success working with top deejays, such as some of the Spanish-language radio stars in Miami, who have devoted followings and can introduce a brand with credibility and verve, generating excitement with contests and prizes. Today, it is all about content—and you want to be a part of it, not an add-on.

> **Radio is fundamentally a promotional medium.**

That's one of the reasons we love National Public Radio. NPR's *Morning Edition,* for instance, delivers an audience of 12.7 million people every day. These are civic-minded, influential citizens who vote, recycle, and care deeply about the planet, all qualities reflected in our brands. Now, you can't run a thirty- or sixty-second spot with a jingle, but I love to sponsor a segment because you become integrated with the content of the show. Your brand is gilded by association.

Product Placement

Similarly, we like to see our products in hit television shows and films. When someone on Wisteria Lane opens a refrigerator, you might see a bottle of POM or FIJI Water cooling on the shelf. Our products appear on *House, Heroes, Boston Legal, Scrubs, Friends with Money, CSI: Miami, Nip/Tuck,* and *Grey's Anatomy,* to name a few. This is hardly a new tactic. Back in the fifties, the Nelson family drank milk by the gallon on *The Adventures of Ozzie and Harriet,* which was sponsored by the American Dairy Association. We use product placement in part because it tips off our consumers—and target market—that they're "in the know." Getting great exposure for the cost of the product and a modest retainer paid to our product placement firm warms my heart and heats up the bottom line.

To make our mark at the cineplex, we worked our way into *Traveling,* a Jennifer Aniston film in which she plays a florist. We designed the bouquet her character arranges and then made it possible for our Teleflora florists to design and deliver the same bouquet. As the film business struggles and television viewership continues to fracture, producers realize that product placement is a viable revenue source and marketers like us still appreciate the rich combination of celebrity and seemingly organic environments. Most Sony films today include Sony electronics—stereos, televisions, computers—meticulously placed in select scenes. Characters may even pass ads for Sony products when they walk down the street. If the placement is handled poorly, it can look like a clumsy attempt at subliminal advertising, but when it is organic to context and setting, it works.

We've also been experimenting with running viral videos in art-house theaters. The spots have to be uniquely compelling—either charming or hysterically funny—for this gambit to succeed, but it's well worth a try.

Event Marketing and Promotion

Most of our marketing energy is focused not on advertising but on a wide range of viral activity. One of the most important lessons I've learned over the years is also one of the most counterintuitive: if you want to make money on a product, you have to learn how to give it away. FIJI Water is waiting at the finish line for the parched runner who has just completed a marathon. POM is in the gift bag at a high-profile celebrity event. We give thousands of Teleflora coupons away during the year.

Why give it away? You can't get a consumer to try your product twice if she hasn't had it once. We're all creatures of habit; some of us need a little extra incentive to try something new. Giving away your product shows you have confidence in it. It means you're convinced that if consumers try it once for free, they'll be willing to pay for it next time. That doesn't mean you give it away randomly. You need to choose the right events with the right consumers and the right atmosphere.

> If you want to make money on a product, you have to learn how to give it away.

We hired Dale DeGroff, the King of Cocktails, to develop a signature drink for the Academy Awards, Golden Globes, and Emmys, and the POMtini cocktail was born. It was such a hit that the Motion Picture Academy made it the official cocktail of the Oscars in 2003, 2004, and 2005. (In 2006, Coca-Cola, the 1,500-pound gorilla of the beverage industry, muscled into the show and everyone else was kicked out.)

We sent a team across the country to teach bartenders at top restaurants and bars how to make the POMtini. Great restaurants from coast to coast now feature pomegranate drinks on their bar menus. Consumers can find recipes for more than fifty drinks (with and sans alcohol) on our Web site.

Our efforts extend far beyond Hollywood. Each year, we send a gorgeous, hardbound coffee-table book on POM to editors and producers. The book, filled with history, recipes, and lush photography, is so expensive to produce it makes me shudder, but I also know that it conveys just how serious we are about our product. Last year, in an effort to advance our green initiative, we made a major push on the digital version of our press kit. (Look for the old press kits on eBay—they are true keepsakes.)

We make a point of sending POM to a long list of influential people, including doctors, celebrities, politicians, and media industry leaders. Years ago, I met Martha Stewart at a prostate cancer event. There was a workshop that day for the golf widows, who were kept busy making glass coasters. Martha taught us how. She was kind enough not to mention how disgraceful my handiwork was, but she did mention to me that she loved pomegranates. I paid attention. And each year at the beginning of our harvest, I send her a case of our Wonderful pomegranates with my compliments. I never expected anything to come of it, but was happy to nurture and encourage her enthusiasm for my favorite fruit. After all, she is Queen of Homemaking.

Some years later, Martha did a beautiful twelve-page spread on pomegranates in *Martha Stewart Living*. The following year, her television show filmed a segment featuring yours truly touring the orchards. In subsequent years, she has featured pomegranates when the season begins. Did my annual gift have anything to do with it? Probably not. By her own admission, Martha is crazy for pomegranates. But I know that at least once a year she is reminded of how much she likes them.

Of course, not everyone has the chance to meet Martha Stewart, but anyone can send a product to someone who is influential—whether it's the editor of a local newspaper or the head of the chamber of commerce. It probably won't result in an avalanche of sales, but you never know.

Having your product adopted by an influential person has its own rewards. After all, leaders have followers. In every city, there are charity events where you can have a coupon for your service or a sample of your product included in the goody bag that guests take home. I first discovered the mineral foundation makeup to which I have been faithful for five years now in a gift bag. So don't be stingy. Sharing your product shows confidence—and builds it, too.

Public Relations

Old media, new media—who cares? Just get mentioned in the media—that's what counts. Public relations is the unsung hero of marketing. There is nothing as effective in the entire world as getting someone else to say something good about your product or service—what we call "third-party endorsement." Of course, POM is newsworthy. First, the press loved us because the fruit was so new yet so old, and the health story was a revelation. As time went on, we became the darling of food editors when our fresh season started. We have new medical breakthroughs on a regular basis, so there is always something new and exciting to learn about POM.

Everything we've achieved has been done in-house, starting with one great public relations veteran. That was about five years ago. Today, we have public relations executives in each business dedicated to building our brands on TV and radio and in print. We have garnered hundreds of millions of dollars' worth of publicity through these efforts.

> Public relations is the unsung hero of marketing.

In addition to being featured on all the great cooking shows, we have become a staple on the morning news, with pomegranate recipes and decorating tips, but above all with medical breakthroughs from POM Wonderful. You can't beat that kind of exposure for brand building, with credible, third-party endorsements—no matter how much money you spend.

I'm going to discuss the WWW (that's either the World Wide Web or the Wild, Wild West) in the next chapter. I think the mysteries and minefields of the Internet merit a separate discussion all their own, but first, I want to briefly describe a kind of marketing test case, a campaign that integrated many of the strategies and tactics that I've just described in pursuit not of random eyeballs but of genuine hearts and minds.

TELEFLORA'S CONTEST TO CROWN America's Favorite Mom took more than a year of planning, multiple rounds of painstaking negotiation, seemingly endless hours of work, and millions of dollars of investment. But it was worth it.

"America's Favorite Mom" integrated television, Internet, print, and on-premises promotion in 21,000 florist shops to produce a marketing phenomenon tied to the hundredth anniversary of Mother's Day on May 11, 2008. The full name of the show was "Teleflora Presents America's Favorite Mom." Now, *that* is product placement—or, as I call it, Product Programming Integration.

Growing up in Hollywood as the daughter of a film producer, I was fully aware of the disappointment club that we call "the Industry." I never did want to be part of that ego-destroying affair. The reason I created "America's Favorite Mom" wasn't to become a TV executive, it was to make the Teleflora brand stronger with our target market and to sell beautifully arranged flowers in our keepsake container for the holiday. Most important, we wanted to communicate that Teleflora is the first name in flowers. To that end, we wanted to own the most important holiday in the floral industry: Mother's Day.

We started in April 2007, more than a year before the centenary, by traveling to a small West Virginia church. That's where Anna Jarvis first gave out flowers to the moms in the congregation in honor of her mother's memory. It was the nation's first celebration of Mother's Day.

We purchased the rights to tell the story of the founding and, for goodwill, helped out with a new organ for the church, because we wanted to include the church and its people in our celebration. But we also wanted the rights for another reason: because whether the subject is pomegranates, pearls, or Mother's Day, authenticity matters.

Having been around Hollywood so long, I knew that

striking the right television deal would require a lot of patience and persistence. Who was I kidding? I didn't know the half of it. After bringing in a first-rate producing partner, Reveille Productions, which is responsible for hits such as *The Office, Ugly Betty,* and *The Biggest Loser,* we proceeded to negotiate with NBC. Ben Silverman, the network's head of programming, immediately understood our vision for the special, but it took six long months to get the deal done through the network's legal department. It was excruciating at times, but we kept faith with our vision and eventually we had the makings of great television.

> Whether the subject is pomegranates, pearls, or Mother's Day, authenticity matters.

The premise of Teleflora's program was easily grasped: a celebration of American moms, all 82 million of us. But the number of moving parts was daunting. The campaign included: (1) our own dedicated and separate Web site (something the network rarely agrees to) for user-generated nominations for the title of America's Favorite Mom; (2) a five-day salute on NBC's top-rated *Today* show, with each of the five segments celebrating a different type of mom, such as single mom, working mom, or military mom (since *Today* is part of the network's news division and our special was entertainment, it required those two departments to work together); and (3) an hour-long, prime-time grand finale special on Mother's Day 2008, hosted by Donny and Marie Osmond, on which America's Favorite Mom was selected. (The eventual winner, Patty Patton-Bader, received $250,000, a new kitchen from GE, a family vacation in the Caribbean, flowers for a year from Teleflora, and a solid gold America's Favorite Mom pendant rimmed with brilliant diamonds.)

We developed a beautiful spring bouquet in a lustrous pink keepsake vase. The special bouquet was decorated with a lovely golden heart-shaped pendant attached, similar to the one America's Favorite Mom received. That way, everyone in America could purchase the bouquet and tell their mom that, in their eyes, she was their favorite.

We bought additional print advertising, created an outdoor ad campaign, did radio in select markets and made a huge PR push to be sure the maximum number of people knew about "America's Favorite Mom" and wanted to be a part of it.

On the Web, MySpace, which supports more than ninety million unique visits daily, was our social networking partner. Our site enabled video nominations of moms to be uploaded, viewed, and shared, along with testimonials and all manner of mom discussion. A special page was dedicated to essays on moms. We developed our own videos and seeded them on YouTube. Two of these videos—"Mom Simulator" and "Rock for Mom"—made it (organically) to YouTube's home page, the holy grail of viral media.

Most important, our 21,000 Teleflora member florists

were integral to the whole operation. In addition to selling the bouquets for the hundredth anniversary, they promoted the contest in their shops with special merchandising and an "America's Favorite Mom" marketing kit that we distributed. The florists themselves competed to produce the most eye-catching displays, with a winner in each state receiving about $1,000 in merchandise and a chance to enter a sweepstakes to win a new delivery van. Our florists processed "mominations" and delivered special "America's Favorite Mom" bouquets all across the country.

"America's Favorite Mom" was an enormously powerful marketing campaign, yet it cost us less than the price of an average television advertising buy. In fact, for what we spent on "America's Favorite Mom," we could not possibly have bought a TV advertising campaign that would have delivered real impact. Instead, we got a nationwide phenomenon that incorporated a full week of national network television, encompassing forty-five minutes of content on the top-rated morning show; a terrific interactive presence on the Web sites of MySpace, Teleflora, and "America's Favorite Mom" (the "America's Favorite Mom" Web site alone received 800,000 visits); promotional support from *Redbook*, one of America's most popular women's magazines; and a bricks-and-mortar promotion at 21,000 florist shops throughout the United States. It was integrated from top to bottom, and that doesn't even count all the press and public relations value generated as a result of this confluence of forces. What's more, we ran the whole operation with a small staff out of our offices in Los Angeles.

"Teleflora Presents America's Favorite Mom" was never intended to capture eyeballs. It went right for the heart of the matter. Does the English language contain a word more emotionally resonant than "mom"? Is there any group more deserving of celebration and reward than mothers?

Our moms got attention. Patricia Griffith, one of our Working Mom finalists, was approached by the Food Network about doing a show. Nora Leon, our Adopting Mom winner, saw interest in her work in Haiti increase dramatically. She was even contacted by musician Wyclef Jean about getting involved. Other featured moms attracted interest as well, suggesting that the programming really touched lives.

At every level, the "America's Favorite Mom" campaign met our criteria for marketing. It was grounded in authenticity. It targeted hearts and minds. It used multiple media and multiple platforms to support the campaign. It was a creative breakthrough that originated in-house and was achieved through promotion, PR, and innovative communications—not through expensive, wasteful thirty-second TV spots or generic national radio spots.

The results? We sold a record number of keepsake products. Sales of our "star" bouquet were up 90 percent over the previous year. And we rallied our florist network around a concept that benefited us all, paving the way for tighter collaboration in the future.

Marketers constantly say they are eager to "break through the clutter," to somehow get noticed amid the bombardment of commercial messages that assaults the average American consumer each and every day. But though everyone says they want to break through the clutter, many are afraid to do so; they feel more comfortable doing pretty much the same thing that everyone else is doing. In other words, they'd rather join the clutter than shatter it.

If you really want to break through, you first have to break out of decades of media habits that are no longer relevant. The old ways may still get you lots of eyeballs, but is that really all you want? Success in this environment requires a real connection to hearts and minds. Eyeballs ain't enough.

CHAPTER 8

Web of Wonder
(and Deceit)

1. The Internet is the greatest communications advance since Johannes Gutenberg invented movable type.
2. The Internet is a web of deception, half-truths, bias, spin, and pornography, both metaphoric and actual.

Which statement is true?

It's clear you could summon an army of evidence to support either view. But the two statements aren't mutually exclusive. The Internet *is* the greatest communications advance since the printing press, enabling rapid, inexpensive communication between individuals and groups around the world. It's also full of more lies and phony elixirs than a snake oil salesman's carnival wagon.

I have been working in cyberspace since the late 1990s, when I designed the first Franklin Mint Web site selling collectibles online. A few years later, Teleflora began selling direct to consumers over the Internet. Meanwhile, a subtle transformation had been taking shape all around me. I was unable to define exactly what was going on, but it felt a lot like the sand eroding beneath my feet on Malibu Beach. Everything I had learned about communications and marketing was shifting. The rules were changing, and I didn't have a firm grip on how to apply my knowledge to this new paradigm. Then it hit me. This was the first time since Julius Caesar addressed the people of Rome (slaves and women not included) that society could engage in a genuine two-way dialogue. Citizens were talking back—to government, to corporate America, and to each other, and they were doing it worldwide in real time. As *Time* put it in 2006, when "You" became the magazine's Person of the Year: "It's a chance for people to look at a computer screen and really, genuinely wonder who's out there looking back at them."

We all understand that the Internet is a transformational communications medium. But the old advertising ways, which easily morphed from print to radio to television as each new technology was introduced, have somehow stumbled with the onset of the Internet.

That's in part because it's not just new, it's different from its predecessors; a medium for a new world with new ways that are still being born. Advertisers that try to make the Internet conform to the old paradigms of television or print advertising are often confused and disappointed by the results.

With our brands, we quickly learned we had to adapt our marketing to the medium. As an advertising medium, the Internet is unique. We try to focus on its most compelling assets, which are social and informational.

We begin, not surprisingly, with a Web site. As Alexander King, a now-forgotten writer whom I adored when I was a kid, used to say, "What if the greatest snow skier in the world lived in deepest Africa—no one would ever know." Substitute "product" for "snow skier" and "Internet" for "Africa" and you have the gist of the challenge: How will they find you?

Ever since we first introduced POM, we have put our Web address on every product we sell. Putting your URL on your products is the cheapest and most effective ad spend you can make—because it's free.

Once our consumers locate our Web sites, they are pleasantly surprised by the huge trove of facts about our brands, their history and future, and our point of view on the planet. To give our consumers an easy way of talking back, we offer message boards and blogs that we constantly monitor in order to hear their voices. This enables us to react to issues quickly rather than wait for them to explode in the blogosphere.

One of the greatest time-saving, money-saving, and truth-telling capabilities of the Internet is its ability to generate accurate market research data. In the old days, market research was expensive and time-consuming. We used to conduct focus groups in different parts of the country to gauge reactions to a product. Then we'd follow up with field research by telephone or mail. It cost tens of thousands of dollars and took months to compile into meaningful data. By the time you finally received the executive summary of the survey, the information was often dated.

Now we hire a research firm that specializes in online lists, which are easily tailored to the needs of the moment. For a small fee, usually less than $5,000, the firm provides a list of our target audience of consumers. For example, we can request ready-to-drink coffee consumers to test our POMx Coffee or online floral buyers who fit Teleflora's demographic profile.

The results are ready in just days (not weeks or months) and I find them more reliable than the old research data. The time and money saved are considerable; the mistakes we avoid are priceless. But it's also important to remember that research is simply another information tool to help you make a decision. In the end, you still need to use your own instincts and common sense.

For example, when we were creating our campaign for POMx Coffee, research suggested that the phrase "Healthy Buzz" alienated some consumers, who associated the phrase with the drug culture. I listened. But in the end, I decided that the fact that those two words made people pause and think—even sometimes negatively—was okay. First, making people stop and think is the goal of good advertising. Second, no two words better describe what POMx Coffee delivers. We stuck with the language we knew was true.

We use banner ads around the holidays to promote traffic to our Teleflora site. For our other brands, we occasionally buy banners on sites that have a particular synergy with what we stand for. But we have not rushed headlong onto the Web with advertising dollars. In this, we're not alone. Advertising revenue on the Web is rising steadily. But as I write this, less than 10 percent of U.S. advertising is devoted to the Internet. We're at a crossroads of past and future. At the same time that culture and business are scrambling online, a surprising number of corporate executives still have their secretaries print their e-mails. But there is no question about which platforms the future will bless.

Internet users have gradually come to accept that exposure to ads on their favorite sites is the price to be paid for free content. Given that the amount of content on the Web is constantly approaching infinity, it's not a bad deal. But that doesn't mean they're eager to put up with any advertising that comes their way. Pop-ups, for example, are generally poison—although I suspect they may work better in certain contexts than many people think. Blunt, head-on tactics often do—but you won't find an argument for them in this book.

> Internet users have come to accept that exposure to ads on their favorite sites is the price to be paid for free content.

The department store magnate John Wanamaker's lament is perhaps the most famous axiom in the history of advertising. "Half the money I spend on advertising is wasted," he fretted. "The trouble is, I don't know which half." Wanamaker's complaint lingered for a century, vexing advertisers who could no more track the impact of mass advertising in print or on radio or television than Wanamaker could. Thanks to Google and the precision of search, we finally have an answer. If they click, it works. If they don't, it doesn't. We know which half is working.

Despite the relative precision of search, there will always be a bit of mystery to business. Back at the Franklin Mint, Stewart used to complain about the overhead cost of creating 1,500 new products a year. "You only need to roll out five hundred," he would say. Sure, Mr. Wanamaker, but which five hundred?

Teleflora's flowers-in-a-gift concept used to require a similar element of guesswork. Mall intercept studies are the least reliable research tool and very expensive to field, but in the old days that was all we had to test Teleflora's bouquet ideas. ("Madame, I know you have three shopping bags brimming with stuff and your kid is screaming for attention, but which of these bouquet concepts do you like the most?") Now we use the Internet to help us make decisions. Our in-house design team develops more than a hundred concepts for each holiday. We winnow those ideas down to a more manageable number for online testing, then let our consumers tell us which ones they would be most likely to buy.

Search and They Shall Find

T HERE ARE three forms of advertising on the Web that I find the most effective; organic search, paid search, and e-mail blasts. The last is self-explanatory: you build an e-mail list over time and regularly send communications to your customers. This form of advertising has a very low cost per order (CPO) and is extremely effective.

Search, however, can be confusing. To understand it, think back to the way some companies used to approach the Yellow Pages. Before that bulky, printed version of search first appeared, there weren't a lot of companies named AA Towing and Acme Lawn Care. But with the Yellow Pages guiding consumers to the goods and services they were seeking, entrepreneurs realized they might get a leg up if their company name appeared at the top of the alphabetical listings. As a result, names beginning in A or even AAA became popular. Internet search adapts the same kind of logic to a new medium.

Why Do We Care About Search Engine Marketing?

"Most online shoppers use search to research before buying," says a new study by Harris Interactive called "How America Searches." In fact, the study tells us that 88 percent of adult online shoppers conduct some form of online research before making a purchase on the Web. Internet search engines are used by 67 percent of these shoppers.

There are two types of **search engine marketing.** First, there is **search engine optimization (SEO),** which entails adapting your site to improve your chances of appearing more prominently in the organic results of your consumers' search queries. In other words, when someone searches for "pomegranates" on the Web, we want to be certain that POM is the top site they see as a result.

To do it right may take an armchair Einstein, but once you realize how important SEO is, you'll be motivated to find the right Einstein (you needn't have one in-house; such talents are readily outsourced).

Search engines (Google, Ask.com, etc.) **crawl** your Web site, as often as every hour if you are CNN.com or as infrequently as once a month if you are a small site with little traffic. They download your pages and store them, which is why nothing on the Web ever dies.

There are a number of techniques you can use to exploit search engine technology, including creating **meta-tags,** which is background coding on a site that's invisible to consumers; **changing site content** to be more relevant to key search terms; and securing **links to your site from other relevant source sites,** such as official sites in your field or industry (for instance, if you are a breeder of Cavalier King Charles spaniels, make sure you are listed on the American Kennel Club site).

Search engines **index** by extracting information from your site. **Content,** meaning the words on the page, is key. Images and Flash files are not interpreted as words, so they don't count as much, although you can get more out of them by utilizing alternative text for such elements. **Location of keywords is important, so make sure they appear early in page content. Weight** is the frequency with which words are used—so include important words often enough to improve page relevancy. **Links** register all the links included on the page.

By using an **algorithm,** software logic that can identify

and rate the most relevant Web pages, search engines rank information on their sites and determine what information is going to be first, second, or fifty-fourth on a given response to a search request. Sadly, there is no God—and certainly no fairness—governing this process. It is up to the advertiser to know how it works and how to take advantage of every nuance.

Let's say you go to Google and type in the words "dish towels," as I did recently after I realized the ones in my kitchen looked like they had been used to clean up after a pandemic. The clever sites that had seeded their home pages with dish towel information—information discovered by the search engine crawl—appeared higher up on the page. Long tails notwithstanding, most of us are not hunting for the obscure but look at the first few organic results that appear on the left (not the paid ones in the right column or at the top, which appear in a different color).

The second form of search engine marketing is **paid search,** which works as a kind of auction, with a marketer bidding on a list of search words/terms in order to have a site appear in the hierarchy of paid search sites. For instance, we would like Teleflora to come up first when someone types "flowers" in a search engine. However, so would every one of our competitors. So we bid for the honor.

In the doldrums of August, that is a rather inexpensive proposition. But in the days leading up to Mother's Day, it can cost thousands of dollars a day to win that **keyword.**

If we want to buy the key words "water from Fiji," there isn't much competition, so the expense is low. If, however, we want FIJI Water to come up first on the search for "bottled water," we have to bid against huge players like Pepsi and Coke. The narrower the definition of your keyword or phrases, the cheaper the buy; conversely, the more general the category, the more expensive.

At our company, we sometimes buy thousands of words for each brand. Here is a checklist of things to consider for your **keyword plan**:

Your product **category** (flowers for Mother's Day); your **product's name** (the Watering Can Bouquet); **attributes and accessories** (Flowers in a Gift); **manufacturer's** name (Teleflora); **advertiser's site functionally** (Florist Shop Locator); **lifestyle terms** (Holiday entertaining); **motivators** (Valentine's gift for my girlfriend); **corporate initiatives** (sustainability); **geographical terms** (Los Angeles Florists); and don't forget the all-important **typos** (misspelled words such as "Pomegranet" or "Fugi Water").

Getting to the top of the search engine requires a long-term investment of time and energy. It involves the efforts of your online and consumer marketing teams, designers, merchandisers, corporate communications and Web development people. Your search engine optimization strategy should be integral to your Web site development. It is the best return on investment you can get from Web advertising.

Community is the heart of the Web, and the advertisers that find a natural home there will prosper. What began as a virtual hangout for teens has become a place for all kinds of people and groups to meet: those who love Sharpeis (as though that were possible), retired NASA engineers, rugby fans, eco-moms.

> Community is the heart of the Web, and the advertisers that find a natural home there will prosper.

The Center for the Digital Future's 2007 study found that membership in online communities had more than doubled in just the past three years. Just as striking, more than half of online community members log on to their community daily, with 55 percent saying they feel as "strongly" about their online community as they do about their real-world community.

Facebook, MySpace, and other social networking sites are the metaphorical town squares of the twenty-first century. But they are expansive enough to include tens of millions of people in the discussion. Nearly one quarter of eighteen- to thirty-four-year-olds now keeps a personal blog.

We saw the impact of social networking profoundly in the 2008 presidential campaign. Barack Obama's youth-powered campaign acquired one million donors before the general election campaign even began. But in addition to using the Web to generate donations and spread viral campaign advertising via YouTube, as McCain also did aggressively, Obama's campaign used the Web to organize volunteers to an unprecedented degree. Despite the tens of millions spent on television by both campaigns, the Web was in some ways the more important technology, facilitating finance, communication, and organization—all at low cost.

We've nurtured a community of POM drinkers—Club POM—who enjoy having access to health studies and appreciate early notification of new products and announcements. Just as music fans enjoy talking about their favorite stars, members of Club Pom enjoy exchanging their favorite pomegranate recipes and personal health revelations, and just chatting about events in their area.

There's no reason to limit consumer participation to chat, however. Like other brands, we've also found it's exciting to put your fans to work—as your ad agency. With a grand prize of $3,000, a laptop, and a three-month supply of POM Tea—a sum that seemed awfully inexpensive even before we saw the high quality of work that contestants put in—we solicited video ads for POM Tea. Naturally, we had no idea what we would get. That's the whole idea—it's a free-for-all. Letting go is the nature of the interactive world. What we received was not just gratifying but astounding. As the ads began pouring in, posted on YouTube, I would wake in the morning, go online, and see what hilarious and imaginative new work had been posted in the past twenty-four hours—all for the love of POM Tea.

What could be better than engaging with consumers in a creative embrace of your brand? In the end, we received 148 submissions, with subject matter ranging from a backwoods survivalist hunting "free radicals" with his POM Tea to a hip-hop homage to POM Tea's thirst-quenching pleasures. On a dedicated site, visitors voted for their favorite POM Tea ad. The winner was a deeply felt romantic comedy of the POM Juice meets POM Tea genre produced by Griffin Hammond of Normal (no kidding), Illinois.

"Teleflora Presents America's Favorite Mom" also enlisted consumers, who produced video and written tributes to their mothers and posted them on the "America's

Favorite Mom" site. Nothing I've experienced in business compares to this creative collaboration. It's thrilling to see your consumers behaving like your partners rather than mere shoppers. And if you don't get inspired by their talent and enthusiasm, you're not paying attention.

Unfortunately, we're hardly alone in recognizing the Web's "creative" potential. The Web, of course, is essentially an open invitation to all manner of deception, ax grinding, and cheap shots.

After the popularity of POM inspired countless pomegranate juice imitators, we tried to enlist the government to battle the flimflammers and their false claims. We went to the FDA, presented conclusive evidence of fraud by companies slapping the "100% Pomegranate" label on junk juice mixtures of grape and apple and pear, and pleaded with the regulators to investigate them. Alas, the juice market is not a high priority for an overburdened, understaffed, and inadequately funded regulatory agency that is trying to protect us from potentially deadly drugs and other dangers. The government made it clear it was not going to police the junk juices, no matter how outrageous their claims. We were on our own.

In 2007, we decided to take a stand. We sued one of our competitors, Purely Juice, in federal court and laid out the case against their "100% Pomegranate" juice. It turned out to be a tough case to defend, owing to the fact that Purely Juice's definition of "100%" was actually "0%." We won that one. But there are plenty of other juice companies playing fast and loose out there.

As I said earlier, WWW stands for Wild, Wild West,

and if that means we have to don a badge and act like the sheriff, so be it. But we can't catch all the bad guys. Since 2003, roughly one thousand pomegranate products have been introduced to the marketplace. Not bad for a fruit hardly anyone had heard of six years ago. If imitation is the sincerest form of flattery, consider me flattered. At the beginning of 2008, we launched our pomegranatetruth.com site to give consumers a place to go for honest answers. Here's a sample of what we say:

> *Not every brand is as honest as POM Wonderful. Three independent labs tested ten other brands claiming to have 100% pomegranate juice and found that eight out of ten had added sugar, colorants and other low-grade fruit juices. So, other juices may be less expensive than ours, but you get what you pay for.*

Ideally, we wouldn't have to do this, but the marketplace has always had its dark corners, and just as the Web gives bad actors a terrific way to disseminate lies and misrepresentations, it also affords the opportunity to shine a light on their actions and expose them for the charlatans they really are. POM may be out in the forefront of using the Web to alert consumers to the frauds in our industry. But I think other honest companies in other industries will aggressively follow suit in the years ahead.

As it turns out, there are worse things on the Internet than fraud. In 2006, we came face-to-face with the Web's dark side. People for the Ethical Treatment of Animals

(PETA) began attacking POM for engaging in medical tests on animals. Using its Web site as a launchpad, they worked to organize a boycott of POM, including pressuring retailers not to stock it and consumers not to drink it. Their tactics were revolting. On their site, they featured an image of our POM heart logo being squeezed—with blood dripping down the bottle onto a dead rat. (Subtlety is not their thing.)

Not long ago, the standard approach in a case like this was to ignore the problem and hope it would fizzle out and, eventually, fade away. After all, boycotts were hard to organize and even harder to sustain. And why would anyone want to boycott POM? Our medical research had been conducted with the goal of improving human health. We were the good guys.

So initially we remained silent. Stewart (my own personal John Wayne) didn't want to "negotiate with terrorists." He chose the legal approach, fighting them in court. He felt if we just waited them out, PETA would get bored and move on to their next cause. That was a mistake. Apparently animal rights activists aren't easily bored.

The hundreds of thousands of people who visited their site couldn't understand why a juice company would be conducting tests using animals. What they didn't know was that we had invested millions in medical research to understand the efficacy of Wonderful pomegranates in treating a host of medical issues. Animal tests were necessary for the kind of rigorous, peer-reviewed science we were financing. Animal studies are generally a prerequisite for human studies and human studies are considered essential. (We didn't invent this protocol; but for the science to be considered sound, we had to follow it.) The news that we had done some animal tests struck many people as bizarre—as if we were engaged in gratuitous cruelty.

This was a fact that finally hit home with me when I was dining with News Corporation CEO Rupert Murdoch in the midst of the turmoil. Rupert is one of our most devoted customers. He keeps POM on his plane, in his office, and at his homes. He understands the medical advantages of drinking eight ounces a day. Rupert knew we were going through a hard time—he had read about it in Page 6 gossip in his own *New York Post.*

"Why do you have to do animal testing on your juice?" he asked. If someone as smart and committed to the juice as Rupert Murdoch was mystified, I realized, then plenty of other people were, too.

By retreating from the fight, we had ceded the field to our opponents. Misleading images and "facts" were soon disseminated over the Internet, including a video on the PETA Web site that implied that we had conducted research on dogs, cats, and primates. (Aside from one rabbit study exploring POM's positive effect on erectile dysfunction, all of the test subjects had been rats or mice.)

The PETA campaign was loaded with falsehoods, whether intentionally or simply as a result of the group's lackadaisical research. But what PETA's attack inspired was far worse. Animal rights extremists, some with their faces covered to avoid identification, began protesting outside our home. It was unnerving to drive each day past a group of screaming protesters who called us murderers and worse. Our grandchildren were scared to death whenever they visited. We felt like we were under house arrest.

Then the extremists descended on our employees. With bullhorns in their hands and bandannas over their cowardly faces, they confronted POM employees in their neighborhoods. The protesters were so proud of their intimidation raids that they videotaped them and uploaded the video—where else?—onto the Web. In one YouTube video, they can be seen hurling invective in front of modest homes in a modest neighborhood, against families with no protection.

They organized meetings through chat rooms and on MySpace and Craigslist. Our employees even endured death threats, some of them whispered through the windows of homes late at night. Meantime, at our headquarters, we received bomb threats. At one point, a group calling itself the Animal Rights Militia said it had poisoned five hundred bottles of POM in supermarkets on the East Coast. It turned out to be a terrible hoax.

Other strong-arm tactics were aimed at our retailers and consumers. Many of our retailers were determined not to give in to the threats. But as time went on and the protests continued, we could sense that some were beginning to cave. We tried every legal tool at our disposal, but nothing could stop the attacks. It was clear that the old ways simply didn't work in this new arena. Ironically, we had ceased animal testing on our juice six months before and had no plans to resume it in the future. So we adopted a two-part strategy to fight them in the same venue where we were being attacked—online.

We sent a detailed letter to our customers, which was also posted on our Web site, explaining everything—what research we had done and why—and refuting PETA's false claims. Then we posted a letter on our Web site and every relevant blog stating that we had stopped animal testing and had no plans to begin again.

The result? The Klan-like mob gatherings stopped. The boycott, which had lasted more than eight months, ended in three days.

But the experience revealed to me how much leverage a small, vocal, and relentless fringe can exert in the Internet Age. Mark Twain said, "One of the most striking differences between a cat and a lie is that a cat has only nine lives." On the Internet, you can drive a stake through the heart of a lie and watch it get up off the ground and race around the globe another time. I am unyielding in my support for the First Amendment. But the campaign of intimidation made me realize the price free speech can exact.

Despite the despicable tactics employed against us, I learned that even your worst enemies have something to teach you, if you listen carefully. We are more sensitive to the plight of lab animals now and more committed to doing all we can to protect their welfare. We contribute to a group seeking ways to advance the efficacy of test-tube science in the hope that, one day, medical tests on animals will no longer be necessary.

Even your worst enemies have something to teach you,
if you listen carefully.

The PETA campaign taught us other lessons, as well. Today we no longer wait for trouble to develop; we confront it head on. In 2007, at a panel discussion at the Aspen Ideas Festival, an annual event sponsored by the Aspen Institute, I heard the kernel of an attack with the potential to grow into a big problem. A young executive from Google was complaining about the environmental impact of bottled water. He cited an image he had recently created on a blog that showed a single bottle of our water three-fourths filled with crude oil. That, he claimed, was the amount of oil it took to bring our precious water from Fiji. He went on to urge that fresh water could be had—with no adverse effects—by simply turning on the tap. The moment was especially ironic because FIJI Water is a sponsor of the festival—our bottles were all over the dais. During his dissertation, the young critic was downing our water like a thirsty dog.

At the time, Al Gore's powerful film *An Inconvenient Truth* was igniting discussion of sustainability in living rooms and even boardrooms around the nation. The dialogue was long overdue—and it was expanding in all sorts of directions. For the first time, consumption patterns were coming under scrutiny.

Then Alice Waters, the famed owner of Chez Panisse in Berkeley, announced that she would no longer serve bottled water at her restaurant. It was one thing for a young guy on a panel to make noise. But Alice Waters is one of the most respected voices on food and sustainability in the world. If she said we had a problem, then we had a problem—and we had to deal with it.

As expected, the Chez Panisse news traveled all over the Internet, and what started as a trickle of criticism soon morphed into a gusher of dissent. With the credibility of Alice Waters behind it, the campaign was not limited to hard-core activists or extremists, as the PETA campaign had been. *Salon*, the online magazine, ran a column explaining how terrible bottled water is. The *New York Times* seemed to have an article about the issue every week. And my favorite newsman, Jim Lehrer, had a whole segment on his PBS show featuring San Francisco mayor Gavin Newsom holding his arms around a huge, imaginary ball, explaining the enormous amount of fuel required to transport a bottle of his "favorite" FIJI Water to his grocery store. As sometimes happens in the media, no one bothered to get the real facts or even to call us for our side of the story.

Fortunately, I had launched a hunt for the truth as soon as my alarm went off that day in Aspen. Our in-house consulting team was assigned to determine FIJI Water's actual carbon footprint. The claims being made about the amount of fuel required to ship it seemed impossible. For starters, if we were burning through that much oil, how could the business possibly survive, let alone make a profit?

Our team analyzed every detail in the production process and transportation of our water. They came up with a very different conclusion: our carbon footprint, including oil, accounted for just a tiny fraction of each bottle of FIJI Water. From the manufacture in China of preforms for our bottles until delivery of the finished product to the most distant retailer in the United States, a tablespoon of crude oil per bottle was consumed.

Because we use square bottles, we are able to pack them more tightly and ship them more efficiently. And because most of the miles we cover are nautical, rather than highway, we produce fewer emissions per ton carried and mile traveled. The container ships that transport our water from Fiji are seven times as environmentally efficient as trucks. Lately, we've been working to use rail transit on the mainland as much as possible. Trains are much better for the environment than trucks—and they reduce road congestion, too.

Armed with accurate data, we began to push back against the notion that bottled water presents an exaggerated threat to the environment. We used our FIJI Water Web site to make a comprehensive case for our FIJI Green initiative and lay out the facts about our energy policy and carbon footprint.

Because nothing ever dies on the Internet, however, you tend to have to fight the same battles over and over and over again, as new users pick up old data and arguments that were previously refuted or discredited. Keeping track of blogs and message boards helps keep you informed. We keep a close eye on Technorati, a free Web service that searches and organizes blogs as well as tagged social media (Facebook, Twitter, and others). Technorati tracks the links among these sources and indexes them according to relevance. That way we can check what the Web is saying about our brands.

It's important to keep your own Web site stocked with up-to-date information. We make sure our consumers have access to accurate information about the products they love. After all, they are the ultimate third-party endorsers and brand ambassadors. We make sure they can find the facts they need to argue our case.

But just as the fight against PETA alerted us to steps we could take to better protect animals, the controversy over bottled water got us thinking about how we could engineer our processes to do more for the environment—both in Fiji and elsewhere. In partnership with Conservation International, we accelerated our FIJI Green initiative.

It's not about spin. In order to be worthy of our consumers' affection, we had to go above and beyond expectations. By committing FIJI Water to a carbon-negative future, not decades from now but *today*, we took control of the issue and neutralized the attacks. We resolved to be defined by our actions—and our actions put us on the leading edge, the *greening* edge—of business ethics and corporate behavior in the world.

Now, in addition to stale complaints about bottled water, the Internet is buzzing with news and commentary about FIJI Water's leadership in tackling the environmental crisis of our time. In the raw and often crude marketplace of ideas that is the Internet, we're making our case—and we're winning.

For reasons I'll discuss in the following chapters, sustainability and business ethics are going to become more important, not less, in this new world. And partly because of the power of the Internet, the half-life of crooks and charlatans is going to shrink. In the old days, a huckster could take his medicine wagon from town to unsuspecting town, leaving a trail of victims in his wake. There is only one great big town now. If you're exposed once on the Internet, you're exposed for good.

On the other hand, if you're attacked unfairly, it's hard to remove the stain in cyberspace. There are plenty of reckless and irresponsible voices on the Web, as Andrew Keen documents in *The Cult of the Amateur: How Today's Internet Is Killing Our Culture*. But if the power of the Internet isn't always used responsibly, well . . . what power is?

CHAPTER 9

Green Is the New Black

General Electric and General Motors are two of the great industrial giants of the twentieth century. Unlike Microsoft, Google, and other Information Age behemoths, GE and GM run enormous factories where laborers churn out massive material goods—locomotives and turbines from GE, Hummers and Escalades from GM. Their products are forged steel, measured by the ton.

Now consider how these two aging titans have approached the twenty-first century. In 2002, when Enron was buried under the weight of its own fraud, GE purchased the company's wind energy business (yes, Enron apparently had a few assets other than greed) for nearly $400 million. Over the next several years, GE began investing heavily in alternative energy—photovoltaics, hydrogen fuel cells, and gasification equipment to increase the efficiency of coal-fired power plants and reduce their greenhouse gases.

In 2005, GE CEO Jeffrey Immelt launched the company's *ecomagination* initiative, promising to intensify the company's investment in green technologies while restraining GE's own greenhouse gas emissions. "We are launching ecomagination," Immelt said, "not because it is trendy or moral, but because it will accelerate our growth and make us more competitive."

Then there is GM. In recent years, the company has been eclipsed by more innovative competitors—Toyota and Honda in the first rank—selling cars that are better engineered, more reliable, and significantly more fuel-efficient. Even before the price of crude oil spiked, GM's gas-guzzling Hummer had become the symbol of wasteful, indulgent, and environmentally hazardous consumption.

The news of changing times somehow failed to get through to GM headquarters. In February 2008, the same month that the price of a barrel of oil burst through the $100 threshold, GM's vice chairman was quoted in the press calling global warming "a total crock of shit." What a charmer. This seems an apropos moment to mention that the company lost $38.7 *billion* in 2007.

Now, which of these companies founded in the era of heavy industry, GE or GM, do you suspect is more likely to navigate the challenges of the coming decades and live to see the start of another century? (You guessed right.)

Americans are very much aware of global warming and

other environmental challenges. But because public policy in the United States emanates from Washington, D.C., and since the White House and Congress have for years been almost criminally negligent in confronting these issues, we have not had the kind of public debate—let alone the sense of national mission—necessary to begin the transformation to a sustainable economy.

It wasn't long ago that Vice President Dick Cheney dismissed conservation as no more than "personal virtue" with absolutely no role to play in national energy policy. The comment was controversial at the time. But in retrospect, from the vantage point of a few more years of painfully high energy prices, increasingly shaky supplies, and the uninterrupted march of global warming, Mr. Cheney's remark appears not just cavalier but irredeemably stupid. It's the sort of thing that will find its way into history books a hundred years from now—provided we still have books and a civilization to read them—as evidence of ineptitude and ignorance at a pivotal moment in history.

While the Bush White House took its lackadaisical lead from the likes of General Motors, across the Atlantic, where energy use per capita is already half that in the United States, the future has been taking shape. In the United Kingdom, the public and private sectors have been busy constructing the institutional framework for managing a new environmental regime, including creation of the Carbon Trust, a government-funded company dedicated to helping industry and government lower carbon emissions.

Instead of wallowing in denial, Downing Street spent the past decade retooling to succeed in a difficult new environment. On a symbolic level alone, the differences are stark. British prime minister Gordon Brown has solar panels on his home in Scotland. Brown, of course, is the leader of the Labor Party, which you might expect to be more ardently green than the conservative opposition. But when it comes to leadership on the environment, Tory leader David Cameron is no Dick Cheney. The conservative leader has a wind turbine on the roof of *his* home and makes a point, when he can, of riding a bicycle to work.

Lest anyone miss the point, Cameron spelled it out in plain English. "There is no longer a rational case for business to fail to recognize the threat of climate change," he wrote. "Each company will have to play its part in reducing its own footprint; getting more value out of less resource; cutting energy and water usage; reducing packaging and waste; and becoming more efficient and profitable as a result."

In the absence of U.S. leadership on global warming and the environment, much of the world has moved forward regardless—including the business world. GE was hardly alone in recognizing the dawn of a new era.

In 2007, venture capitalists invested $2.2 billion in green technologies in the U.S. alone. Kleiner Perkins Caufield & Byers, the famed Silicon Valley venture investors, earmarked one third of the $1 billion the firm manages for green technology. Conferences on sustainability abound, where the corporate types talk about the environment and the environmentalists talk about sustainable business models. And it's no coincidence that the company that engineered and marketed the Prius automobile is among the most respected businesses and most valuable brands in the world.

States and localities have been stepping in to fill the void left by the federal government. California has adopted a broad range of measures to restrict greenhouse gases. New York City has pledged to reduce its carbon emissions by 30 percent by 2030. (According to *The New York Times*, because of the density of the city, New Yorkers already produce far less GHG than average—7.1 metric tons per person annually compared to 24.5 metric tons for the average American. Remember, they walk everywhere or take the subway.)

Even smaller cities and towns have joined the campaign. Nearly eight hundred towns have signed on to the U.S. Conference of Mayors' Climate Protection Agreement, which pledges to meet Kyoto standards for carbon emissions by 2012. Levittown, New York, that quintessential suburb of the 1950s, promised to stake its claim to the twenty-first century by reducing emissions by 10 percent in 2008.

Stewart and I recently attended a public lecture at Caltech where the professor said, "I don't know if the dire predictions of climate change will occur, but if there is a ten percent chance that they will, aren't we playing the most dangerous game of Russian roulette in the history of man?"

It's impossible to know precisely what the future holds. Maybe we'll get out of this mess—through the grace of nature or the technological ingenuity of humanity—without paying too dear a price. Then again, maybe we won't. In the face of potential disaster, common sense dictates a prudent course. Unfortunately, the prudent course right now is one of radical change. For any business, large or small, that means treating global warming like a deadly and imminent threat—and, of course, since we are in *business*, after all, also as a golden opportunity.

Regardless of whether or not the earth is on its way to being suffocated under a blanket of CO_2, the effects of global warming on the conduct of business will be enormous. In the past, no one really cared about the way we ran our businesses. Sure, if you cheated on your taxes or were one of those abusive executives exposed in the tabloids, you got some negative attention. But our operations were generally a private matter. And if our neighbors didn't care what we did, those on the other side of the planet cared even less.

Now my business and your business is *everybody's* business. If a factory in China is pumping gobs of CO_2 into the atmosphere and sending toxic effluents downstream to the fish farm that supplies my local supermarket, I have a vested interest in that factory's operations. In fact, a few billion people around the world might well conclude that they have a vested interest in that factory's operations. And they might decide it's in their collective interest for that factory to clean up its act or be shut down.

I must admit that "going green" to some extent has become a clever marketing ploy. But even when the motives are suspect, the change still helps us all in the end. A large water company recently took a fair amount of plastic out of its bottles. Now the bottles are so thin that if you grab them too firmly the water spouts out as soon as you open the top. But that's okay; if you don't mind a damp shirt, it works.

We are entering a new era in which stress on the planet, and on the humans and animals that inhabit it, is going to rise. Serious issues of production and consumption, energy use and waste, will be debated as never before. And the discussion will take place in front of a global audience of six billion people—perhaps rising to nine billion by midcentury—of which every single member has a profound personal stake in the outcome.

"Possessing an excessive carbon footprint is rapidly becoming the modern equivalent of wearing a scarlet letter," wrote Michael Specter in *The New Yorker*.

Business in the era of global warming will increasingly become public domain. When emissions from a factory in Topeka influence childhood asthma in Atlanta, crop yields in Uganda, and sea levels in Bangladesh, the notion that we're all connected has ceased to be a metaphor. If you can't justify your business operations and actions in that environment, you will pay a price in the developed world and, before long, in the developing world, as well. Because in the midst of a global environmental crisis, neither old world nor new, first or third, developed or developing, will tolerate rogue businesses sucking the very life out of the earth.

To put this in consumerist terms, if you're failing to deliver sufficient value to justify the toll you take on the environment, if you're squandering valuable communal resources to no great end, who on earth is going to buy what you have to sell? And how can you justify your company's existence?

It's in the myopic nature of humans to think that the way things are is the way they will be forever. But history tells us that that is never, ever the case. Change is constant. With that in mind, consider the fact that our mass consumer society is little more than a hundred years old. Our current way of life is nothing but "a time-bound historical creation," as William Leach wrote in *Land of Desire: Merchants, Power, and the Rise of a New American Culture*.

Consumer culture began in another era, when global issues of growth, energy consumption, and the environment were viewed in a completely different light and the ideal of "democratic abundance" was a distant goal. In a world constrained by global warming and other borderless environmental threats, consumption itself will be the subject of new and vigorous scrutiny. It has already been put under the microscope by best-selling authors Michael Pollan, Eric Schlosser, and Bill McKibben. A new generation is poised to enter the discussion, weighing the ethical and environmental consequences of our way of life.

As we grapple with these complex issues, brands will come under increasing pressure to deliver authentic, sustainable value. Environmental impact will increasingly become a basis for evaluating the goods and services we buy. And that scrutiny will begin with the final consumer product and work its way back down the supply chain—all the way to the raw materials that feed the manufacturing source. Companies will have to be able to justify their actions at each step of that process. And they will have to provide a measure of their environmental impact from start to finish.

> Environmental impact will increasingly become a basis for evaluating the goods and services we buy.

Tesco, the largest grocery chain in the United Kingdom, offers a glimpse of the very near future. The company has vowed to cut its own energy use in half by 2010. But that's just the start. In addition, Tesco has begun an expensive and labor-intensive effort to measure the carbon footprint of each of the seventy thousand products the chain stocks. It has also pledged to cut back on products that are shipped by air—the most GHG-intensive form of transportation.

For years, supermarkets like Tesco had an incentive to stock as many products as they could profitably sell. In the new era, that logic is beginning to erode—not only because products shipped by air will have to pass a new threshold to merit inclusion but because each and every product in the store will be measured by a new standard.

That standard is simply this: Is the product valuable

enough to justify its carbon footprint? What about new products? Is a new product, which must be introduced to consumers and must compete with established products, worth the shipping and shelf space it will require? Does it justify the creation of yet more carbon? Conversely, will old consumer standbys be displaced by new competitors bragging about their smaller carbon footprints?

These are new kinds of questions, and they will play a new role in shaping a new kind of economy. Many products—and companies—may find they do not have the right answers. Perhaps their production processes are too dirty, or their product is ultimately too inessential, to pass the carbon test. After all, Wal-Mart and Costco, two stores synonymous with "plenty," already restrict many category offerings to just two brands. Is it so hard to imagine supermarkets across the country following suit?

In the fall of 2005, Wal-Mart unveiled its own environmental plan. The world's largest retailer, said CEO Lee Scott, wants to be a "good steward for the environment," ultimately using only renewable energy sources and producing zero waste. The company teaches vendors how to go green and insists they follow Wal-Mart standards in order to be included in the inventory mix. (We know—we sell our products to them.) Of course, naysayers contend that Wal-Mart's initiative is a ploy to save money. Hey, wake up—going green does save money, and what's wrong with that?

To survive what may well be a brutal era of creative destruction—one that appears to be right around the corner—smart companies are already positioning themselves on the green side. We are doing everything we can to be one of them. Since I joined the board of Conservation International twelve years ago, I've been working to educate myself about environmental issues. Getting to know Sylvia Earle, the world's greatest oceanographer, whom I lovingly call "Her Deepness," has enlightened me to the sad plight of our oceans and the depletion of fisheries. Jared Diamond, another friend, has influenced me, as well. His landmark book *Collapse* is a jarring reminder of how previous civilizations were agents of their own demise. These are voices of our age—speaking out for all of us to hear and heed.

When we launched FIJI Green, we didn't really know what we were getting into. There was no one in the industry we could use as a model. (Coke? Pepsi? Pleeeease!) There was no Carbon Trust to provide advice or facilitate the process. There was no road map showing how to proceed. There weren't even any reliable data to indicate how expensive the transition would be.

We have the luxury of being a private company. We don't answer to the nearsighted pack on Wolf Street. So we decided to take the green plunge and deal with the consequences—come what may. Want to know how naïve we were? Setting aside our conservation projects, including preservation of the Sovi Basin in Fiji, it turns out that FIJI Green's impact on our bottom line will be millions of dollars. Fortunately, the initiative will be *adding* millions to the bottom line, not *subtracting* them. As it turns out, we should have gone green long ago.

One of the most significant costs we have at FIJI is PET, the plastic resin that is an essential element of every bottle. PET is also a significant source of carbon. So by reducing the amount of PET in our bottles, we're going to reduce carbon and save money.

Similarly, our energy costs in Fiji are about twice as high as energy costs in California. By replacing our old energy infrastructure with wind turbines, we're going to save a lot of money on power over the long run—while simultaneously reducing carbon. I mentioned before that shipping by boat produces dramatically less carbon than shipping by truck. We're now serving not only the West Coast but the eastern seaboard, via the Panama Canal, by boat. By reducing our reliance on trucking, again, we're also reducing costs.

Lately, however, some environmentalists have taken issue with bottled water, citing two concerns. The first is that, unlike tap water, bottled water is, well, *bottled.* That means you create packaging to contain it and you dispose of that packaging after it's been consumed. Second is that, unlike tap water, bottled water must be transported from the source to the marketplace, thereby consuming energy and dispensing carbon into the atmosphere. I confess to being mystified by this argument. Here's why:

- People need to hydrate.
- In a mobile, fast-paced society, they frequently need to hydrate on the go, rather than in their kitchens.
- Even for those at home, tap water is suspect in many, many communities and a known hazard in others.

- Even when tap water is safe, it simply doesn't taste good to many people. They don't want to drink it.

In reality, bottled water does not even compete with the tap; it merely replaces less healthy beverages that are worse for the environment. According to Beverage Marketing Corporation, annual bottled water volume grew by 1.3 billion gallons over the past two years in the United States. Where did this volume come from? People aren't any thirstier, so the answer lies in the decline of other packaged beverages.

Carbonated soft drinks have lost 600 million gallons of consumption during the same period, and the full-calorie versions of these products have fared particularly badly. Sugary fruit beverages have lost an additional 200 million gallons. Meantime, there has been no material change in the consumption of tap water. In effect, the 1.3 billion additional gallons of water that consumers drank eliminated nearly one trillion calories from the American diet. But not only calories were eliminated.

The high-fructose beverage that water supplanted was likely soda, itself a packaged good that is transported to the marketplace. And harvesting, shipping, and transforming corn into syrup is an energy-intensive process.

What, then, would we achieve by removing bottled water from the marketplace, other than to encourage greater carbon and waste production accompanied by a rise in obesity, diabetes, and other health problems? Already, two liters of carbonated soft drink are sold for every liter of water. Is it really in society's interest to increase that ratio?

Bottled water accounts for two hundredths of 1 percent of U.S. oil consumption, and plastic water bottles make up one third of 1 percent of municipal waste streams. Even so, we're determined to do all we can to reduce FIJI's environmental impact.

· In addition to the previously mentioned measures, we're reducing the amount of overall packaging by 20 percent, and more of what remains will come from recycled materials. We already use rectangular bottles, which take up less space than round bottles and enable us to ship more product per cubic foot. We're also stepping up our efforts to encourage expanded curbside recycling and consumer incentive programs, such as container deposit laws that include water bottles.

Only eleven states have container deposit laws, and just four of those include water bottles. Yet most of the industry is opposed to recycling, since a container deposit raises the retail price of water bottles. We hope they'll see the light. Our laws, which preceded the emergence of the bottled-water industry, are antiquated. They need to be updated to account for the urgent environmental crisis we face.

The national recycling rate for plastic bottles is an abysmal 31 percent. Yet we know from Fiji's carbon footprint analysis that recycling a water bottle reduces its carbon footprint by at least one third. A ton of recycled plastic saves about 685 gallons of oil.

We're a small company. We represent only about 1 percent of the entire bottled water industry. Bottled water is here to stay; the industry is not going to disappear. On the contrary, it's going to continue growing as consumers become more aware of the health problems associated with soda and other artificially sweetened beverages. As consumers increasingly seek healthy alternatives, water will become a beverage of choice.

The transition to green isn't 100 percent perfect. We have to maintain higher inventories because our water, traveling by ship and, increasingly, by train, takes longer to reach its destination than it did when it traveled by truck. But that's a very small price to pay to be both carbon-negative and, in the long run, more profitable.

Our large customers have been very supportive, in part because they are getting pressure from *their* customers to show they are responding to the environmental challenge. Restaurant and hotel patrons are aggressively seeking green alternatives to the status quo. And, believe me, we all need them. Today, if you are served a liter of FIJI Water in a restaurant, that product represents carbon emissions of *negative* 114 grams as a result of our FIJI Green initiative. But what about that eight-ounce, grain-fed steak on your plate? That's a different story. By the time it's served up medium rare, your steak has left a trail of 8,300 grams of carbon in its wake. You would have to drink twenty-seven half-liter bottles of water to achieve the same environmental impact.

FIJI Water has begun offering advice to customers who want to reduce their own carbon footprint. In March 2008, we became the first privately held company to join the Carbon Disclosure Project, a voluntary organization dedicated to reducing carbon in business and encouraging carbon transparency. But we could sure use more support from other businesses and from the government. The best way, for example, to reduce carbon emissions in the bottled beverage industry is to use plastic instead of glass bottles and then to recycle them.

Until Google surpassed us with its own solar field last year, we were the proud owners of the largest solar field in California. Covering seven acres, the field provides 30 percent of the power to process our pistachio crop. We are currently building a new juicing plant for POM Wonderful that will burn discarded pistachio shells as part of our alternative power mix. We have transitioned POM Tea from glass containers to plastic. Our in-house consulting group has a division that focuses on sustainability. Its mission is to evaluate the carbon footprint of all our businesses, illustrate how sustainability can benefit our brands, strengthen our relationships with customers and consumers, cut costs, and realize our commitment to being a responsible company.

In addition, in California's Central Valley, we have built a totally green preschool for the children of our employees. Our corporate headquarters building is going green floor by floor. We're trying to do better at home, too. Almost every car in our family is a hybrid. Stewart and I are constantly reducing our energy use at home by changing appliances (the average refrigerator accounts for 15 percent of home energy consumption), redoing our windows with double panes, using energy-efficient lightbulbs, and so on.

Now that the head-in-the-sand era of Bush and Cheney is over, government will be able to do more to spur innovation and initiate changes to begin reining in greenhouse gases. But the private sector can't afford to wait. With the federal government no longer an obstacle, change is coming quickly. We're all going green—like it or not.

And if you don't believe in global warming? Well, you don't have to. Global warming is not the only factor influencing the green imperative. A number of geologists believe we have hit a point of "peak oil," meaning that our ability to extract the black gold that fueled industry and growth in the twentieth century is about to decline. Established oil fields are producing less, and new fields are increasingly rare. Production from oil sands and other alternative, difficult-to-extract sources is inefficient and expensive. Biofuels, depending upon the source, are costly and energy-intensive themselves (and can contribute to global warming instead of mitigating it).

Meanwhile, global demand for energy has soared in recent years. Oil consumption in high-growth economies, including China and India, has risen at roughly six times the rate of growth in developed economies. China already consumes more grain, coal, and steel than the United States and is putting huge numbers of new cars on its congested roads. Tata, India's largest industrial conglomerate, recently introduced a $2,500 automobile that promises to increase that nation's already enormous appetite for oil. As a consequence, even without global warming, we seem to be hurtling toward a serious global energy crisis that will change the shape of economies in the future.

Like the remorseless logic of global warming, the logic of energy shortage steers us back to consumption. Tens of thousands of new products are introduced each year. Given the energy required to produce them and the waste entailed in packaging and shipping, how many of these products will consumers decide they really need? How many are truly valuable and necessary in an economy defined by scarce energy supplies and environmental crisis?

Even if you don't believe that we are in the early stages of environmental crisis, it makes sound strategic sense to behave as if we are. So go ahead. Fake it.

"In many respects, the scientific debate is irrelevant," wrote Andrew J. Hoffman of the University of Michigan, author of a chapter entitled "The Coming Market Shift: Business Strategy and Climate Change" in *Cut Carbon, Grow Profits: Business Strategies for Managing Climate Change and Sustainability*. "The debate is thus strategic (not scientific) and companies taking voluntary climate action are not practicing philanthropy or pure social responsibility (although many couch their activities in the language of 'doing the right thing'). In fact, many companies are agnostic about the science of climate change. They engage the climate change issue as a way to protect their strategic investments and to search for business opportunities in a changing market landscape."

In other words, even if you don't believe, as I do, that we are in the early stages of environmental crisis, it makes sound strategic sense to behave as if we are. Go ahead, fake it.

Keep in mind that the definition of value has already begun to expand. In the future, it will no longer be restricted to the product or service you provide. It will include the toll taken on energy supplies and the global environment in the process. In this new era, climate science will exert enormous influence over companies, markets and even international trade. Bestselling author and *New York Times* columnist Thomas Friedman has said that green is the new red, white, and blue. But for business, green is the new black.

CHAPTER 10

Nurturing Brand Faith in an Age of Cynicism

There is a long list of American leaders in politics, business, sports, and the arts who have contributed more than their share to the erosion of public trust. Bill Clinton lied. George W. Bush lied. Ken Lay lied. Bernie Ebbers lied. Dennis Kozlowski lied. Many people assume that Barry Bonds and Roger Clemens lied. And it seems as if the audience of readers for anguished personal memoirs is supplied by an ever-expanding army of authors, some of whom, like James Frey, are willing to fabricate a few of the million little pieces of narrative that constitute a "nonfiction" book.

We've always been a nation of tall tales and confidence men—Paul Bunyan and P. T. Barnum, Johnny Appleseed and Donald Trump. Everyone loves a good yarn. When canned tuna was introduced to the marketplace, it battled for share with the reigning king of canned fish, salmon.

Tuna wrested the crown away by proclaiming that it was "guaranteed not to turn pink in the can." That story, by the way, is every bit as fishy as its subject. Yet it's been told countless times with endless variations and grace notes simply because we marketers enjoy telling it so much.

Each generation seems convinced that the world it has inherited is speeding to Hell in the latest handbasket, whether the vehicle is a chariot or a Hummer. Yet even with that in mind, the perception this time seems especially acute. In a 2007 Roper survey, 51 percent of Americans said they believed business ethics had gotten worse in the past five years. That's a pretty remarkable vote of no confidence in the business world, and the time frame—a mere five years!—is certainly impressive. Enron lives on.

In *Deep Economy*, Bill McKibben cites a lengthier and more ominous trend. The National Opinion Research Council has shown a steady decrease in happiness among Americans since the 1950s. The decline was accompanied by a doubling of median income in the same period, which may be the best proof yet that money can't buy you love or happiness.

Disillusionment with a half century of American politics and government surely plays a part. But business has provided ample kindling for cynicism. Grotesquely overpaid CEOs, unethical behavior, and lousy, even dangerous, products bear much of the blame. So does marketing.

Nearly a third of American adults are obese, according to the Centers for Disease Control and Prevention. Yet Pepsi and Coca-Cola spend billions of dollars a year marketing junk food and endless varieties of high-fructose corn syrup to people who are literally dying from the pleasure.

The lists of ingredients in "100% Natural" 7 UP, "healthy and delicious" Egg Beaters, "wholesome" granola bars, and vitamin "fortified" chocolate milk are sufficient to fell a mature water buffalo.

Brands that were once synonymous with American culture and optimism have undermined their own value and cast a pall over consumer products generally. The road to ill health is paved with Doritos. In the film *Super Size Me,* the filmmaker ends up in the hospital as a result of a steady diet of what passes for food at McDonald's. Ford and GM, once icons of glamour and quality around the world, have become symbols of self-doubt and, in their refusal to take responsibility for the automobile's impact on the planet, of self-delusion and environmental destruction.

Perhaps no industry exemplifies the damage done by marketing and manipulation more than pharmaceuticals. Americans are living longer lives today, and managing chronic diseases better, in very large part due to the genius of drug company scientists and technologists in creating new products to treat everything from high blood pressure to cancer. Yet despite having extended and improved the lives of tens of millions of people, the industry is reviled for its predatory marketing practices and held in contempt for its obstruction of any sincere effort to resolve the problem of 47 million uninsured Americans. It's not easy to elicit disgust from someone whose life you have just saved.

Between corrupting the medical profession, stalling the introduction of generic drugs, and spending millions on dubious, direct-to-consumer advertising, drug companies have somehow managed to pull it off.

My point? Marketing overstepped its natural boundaries. Drug companies have transformed patients into brand-conscious consumers, looking for the equivalent of a Gucci logo at their local pharmacy. Disney and MTV have transformed childhood into a marketplace of branded experiences. And brands have worked their way into the emotionally charged space in our lives that was once reserved for family, friends, and community. You think you've been welcomed into the warm embrace of the Pepsi Generation, but instead all you get is more calories than your body can burn. By encouraging consumers to build emotional relationships with brands, marketers have set us—and themselves—up for a fall. Too often, brands promise more than they can ever hope to deliver.

"Branding works its magic only up to the point of sale," McKibben wrote, "and then actual human need returns, unfulfilled; the advertiser is always pleased to offer a new round of promise and failure, but after a century it's probably time to pursue some other strategy."

There are only two explanations for a breakdown in the relationship between a brand and a consumer: Either the consumer has run out of money, or she has run out of faith. Betrayal is an unpleasant experience—whether the betrayer is a spouse, a friend, or a familiar brand. Yet the way the world is changing raises the stakes for brands that don't deliver real value. There will always be snake oil salesmen—and some portion of them will get away with their game for a while. But on an increasingly transparent globe, where information is available everywhere, that becomes significantly harder to do.

> Betrayal is an unpleasant experience—whether the betrayer is a spouse, a friend, or a familiar brand.

A disgruntled former employee armed with unflattering data and a blog can do millions of dollars in damage with a few words. As everyone knows, once information appears on the Internet, it's a permanent record. If you're not honoring your word, sooner or later the world will find you out.

Consumer power will continue to grow as a result of this new technology. The consumer protection movement, which started long before Ralph Nader, has ebbed and flowed with business cycles and cultural tides. It is due for resurgence. Under the threat of global warming and the reality of growing inequality, consumers have every reason to be interested in more than a bargain basement price. Prior to World War II, *Consumer Reports* rated products not only on the quality of their performance but also on the quality of their manufacturers' labor relations. After decades of declining labor power, pension rip-offs, and the erosion of middle- and working-class wages and job security, a similarly holistic approach to product evaluation is in store.

With the Internet clearing the way to greater transparency, the public will be privy to a broad range of quality assessments of a brand. Whether a brand delivers on its value promise will be chief among them. But in addition, many consumers will also want to know the measure of a brand's carbon footprint and how a company deals with its workers and local communities. Similarly, in order for companies to take advantage of the community brain power models of Wikinomics and so-called naked transparency, in which outside collaborators contribute to business projects managed on the Web like an open book, they will need to be models of ethics and social responsibility.

Brands that set high standards for themselves are doing well these days. Patagonia's promise of clothes manufactured in an ethical and environmentally sound manner, including the use of recycled materials, seems right in sync with the times. Target appears similarly intent on pairing value and values for less affluent consumers. Entrepreneurs are merging business and philanthrophy into new, hybrid models. For every pair of TOMS Shoes you purchase, the company donates a pair to a needy child in South America or Africa.

It's not always easy to do the right thing in business. Believe me, I know. One episode from my own experience that gives me a queasy feeling in my stomach to this day occurred at the Frankin Mint many years ago. We had been doing a great business in collector plates—so good, in fact, that we launched a program of "forced conversion," similar to that used by book clubs, record clubs, and the like.

By ordering one plate in a twelve-plate series, a collector automatically received the next eleven. This plan was flawed from the start. First, there was no way for our artist to create the art for twelve plates in such a limited time. The plates were fine art fired into porcelain—not cookie-cutter representations. Second, who wants to order one plate and a week later find, unsolicited, a box of eleven others on the doorstep? It was a terrible idea. I should have stopped it before it ever started.

In the end, we got our just desserts. Collectors were understandably annoyed, and the business suffered as a result. In fact, I can pinpoint that lapse in judgment as the moment when our lucrative collector plate business started going down the tubes.

Transparency is a lot easier to talk about than it is to realize. It can be awkward for all the obvious reasons—and even some not so obvious ones. I have always believed that if you get your accolades on Earth, by the time you get to Heaven the folks up there may not be thrilled to see you. Stewart and I have generally preferred anonymity when making charitable donations. That seems like a luxury we can no longer afford.

In an era in which attacks can come seemingly from nowhere, speed throughout the Internet, and hobble your business in days, you need to be able to draw on a reservoir of goodwill. To draw on it, however, you will first have to establish it through very public conduct.

We plan to be more forthcoming about our own activities. In addition to our gifts to large institutions, such as the Los Angeles County Art Museum and UCLA's medical center, we do a lot with our employees, including encouraging their own philanthropy. In our Roll Giving program, every employee receives $1,000 per year to give to the charity of his or her choice (provided it's not political or religious). Additionally, we match employees' personal charitable donations up to $5,000 per year.

In the California Central Valley, any employee's child who maintains a 2.8 grade point average receives a college scholarship. Once enrolled in college, we provide counseling to the students, many of whom are the first in their families to pursue higher education. We want to help them succeed. In addition, we have helped put arts back into the public schools through our association with P.S. Arts, created an after-school reading program, built a preschool, and created a program with Bard College to train seventy-five teachers a year who will work in schools in the Valley. We recently provided the funds for a 50,000-square-foot wing for the Children's Hospital in Madera, California. We focus much of our philanthropy on the Central Valley because we are the largest employer there. We also know that many who live in the Valley are ignored by government.

Perhaps it's ironic that a technological revolution is ushering in the values of a forgotten, preindustrial era. By reducing the amount of communicating we do face-to-face, the Internet has encouraged vicious gossip, baseless attacks, and unhinged polemics from every corner. But by making the world smaller, it is also reinforcing a certain level of small-town business mores. Who runs an honest shop and who is a cheat? Who looks out for the less fortunate and who is a Scrooge? In a small town, everyone knows the answers. So it will be in the Internet Age. Brands that fail to establish good faith will confront a public that is well informed, skeptical, and unforgiving.

> By making the world smaller, the Internet is also reinforcing a certain level of small-town business mores.

Ethical and socially responsible behavior will enable you to function and communicate in this environment. But it won't necessarily ensure that you will profit in it. In 2006, 182,000 new consumer packaged goods products were introduced in stores around the world, a new record. How long a tail will a stressed planet support? Value is the ultimate bedrock. Value builds faith, and faith builds the kind of solid, long-term equity that can withstand competition and overcome challenges.

When all is said and done, there is only one sure route to survival in any market, and one hedge against irrelevance and obsolescence: cultivate the rubies in the orchard. Locate the intrinsic value of your brand, work to understand it and nurture it—even when that brand is you yourself. Communicate that value honestly and creatively. If you do, you will build the kind of faith in your brand that can overcome tough competition, hard times, cheap shots, and even a roller coaster of a new century.

ACKNOWLEDGMENTS

Unless you are painting the *Mona Lisa*, there is no creative process you complete alone. Even then, someone has to stretch your canvas and clean your brushes—and there is always the crucial matter of inspiration.

I have been blessed with help from many people, starting with my parents. My father taught me not to be afraid of anyone or anything. I also inherited his creative genes and artistic talent. My mother has a legendary sense of humor, and is no slouch in the creative department, either. She never met a house she couldn't redecorate. I have been inspired throughout my life by her sense of style and design.

When Stewart and I married thirty-five years ago, we joined our families—and from the outset it just worked. My sons, Jason and Jonathan, were thrilled to have siblings so close in age, and Jeff, Ilene, and Bill immediately warmed to me and my boys. We have been a closely knit mélange ever since. Our children have gracefully accepted the mother who works, and our lives together have been more than I ever dreamed possible. I love my children with all my heart. I couldn't be more proud of the amazing adults they have become, and their wonderful mates—Blue, Daniel, Chris, and Doug—are great additions to our family circle.

My grandchildren are a constant inspiration. I hope that today, at seventeen, with her creativity spilling over into every activity of her life, Danielle no longer bemoans the fact that I am "not like normal grandmas, baking cookies and sitting on the porch knitting" till she comes home from school. Scarlett, on the other hand, told me the other day, "I don't want to be like you . . . I want to be you!" Now, that is a compliment. Lucy and Oliver are a constant source of joy and amazement.

I want to thank my team at Roll for making so many successes possible: Bryan Honkawa, my muse and head designer; David Layton, whose work on the book jacket and color insert was inspired; Liz Leow and Mike Perdigao, whose brilliant efforts in advertising, Web development, and photography were so essential. So many talented individuals in our in-house agency—aptly called FIRE STATION—have helped. There is no team on or off Madison Avenue that does it better.

Tom Mooney was the life force behind our green transformation at FIJI. Without his steadfast commitment, it would have taken many more months or years to complete our goal. Matt Tupper has been my partner at POM since 2003. His sense of honor and faith in the brand have enabled us to move light-years ahead. I thank Brian Fisher, Peter Sauerborn, and Lilie Rahimzadeh for their immeasurable help in creating the Internet primer. David Pinion is my proofreader par excellence. Craig Cooper is more than in-house counsel; he is *consigliere* to the Roll family of companies. Shawn Weidmann, Teleflora's president, and John Cochran, president of FIJI Water, offered support and tolerated their staffs' time-consuming contributions to this effort.

Without Rob Six, I wonder how I could have done all the work that comes after a book is done. He is a brilliant public-relations guru, a dear friend, and a tireless supporter. Julie Fields and Fiona Posell helped before and after the writing was done as well. Anita Ferry, my personal assistant, has been tireless in her work behind the scenes. She is simply the best.

Our family doctor, Leslie Dornfeld, who passed away a few years ago, was really the catalyst in discovering the health properties of the pomegranate. He and his lovely wife, Maria Grazie, are remembered and missed every day of my life. Dr. Harley Liker, together with Mark Dreher, shares my enthusiasm for the pomegranate's virtues and has directed the astounding scientific research on pomegranates and human health.

So many of my dear friends have believed in this project and shown their love and support. Thanks to Wendy Goldberg, Shelli Azoff, Lyn Lear, Jane Nathanson, Irena

Medavoy, Arianna Huffington, Lori Milken (a great, if undiscovered, writer), Marlene Malek, and Jan Greenberg (who reads all I write and offers sound advice based on her great writing talent). These are my dearest buddies. I never had time for girlfriends until my children were safely out of the house. I missed a lot by not seeking them out sooner, but what a great bonanza it is to have their love in my life.

I am also inspired by some men in my life: Leonard Goldberg, who read my first drafts and was clear and fair in his advice; Mike Milken, who proves that one person can really make a difference in this world; Norman Lear, whose extraordinary grace defies age; and Walter Isaacson, who has inspired me through his actions and shown me the need for every individual to care as deeply about the common good as they care about their own family.

People ask, "How long did it take you to write this book?" I answer, "All my life." The actual collaboration with Frank Wilkinson was an amazing, seamless process because Frank is such a pro, an exceptional writer—and so staggeringly smart. It also helped that I had written sixty pages before we met and had about six boxes overflowing with research ready when we began. Ivan Roth worked with me on those first drafts, and his humor and talent have been a huge delight.

Jennifer Walsh and Mel Berger, my agents at William Morris, whom I met through my dear friend Jim Wiatt, represented me beautifully and gave me great counsel about packaging the book. They also set up meetings with publishers. From the moment I met Roger Scholl, my editor at Doubleday, I knew he was the one. Roger has been there for me every step of the way, and I don't care who knows it—I worship him. There is a great team at Random House that also contributed to the success of this book.

The reason *Rubies in the Orchard* is dedicated to Stewart Resnick is because, above all others, he is my greatest friend, most honest critic, and the love of my life. Together we have created a wonderful family and a marriage and love affair worthy of great opera. In my career, he has been the rock of stability. I could never have done it without him. I certainly never wanted to.

ILLUSTRATION CREDITS

INDEX

HENRY   JAMES

1843=187(

HENRY JAMES

The Untried Years

L E O N   E D E L

J. B. LIPPINCOTT COMPANY
PHILADELPHIA   NEW YORK

Copyright, 1953, by
Leon Edel
Manufactured in the United States
of America
by H. Wolff, New York
Designed by Marshall Lee

Library of Congress
Catalog Card Number 53–5421

Second Printing

To live over people's lives is nothing unless we live over their perceptions, live over the growth, the change, the varying intensity of the same—since it was *by* these things they themselves lived.

Henry James

Contents

Contents

Illustrations

HENRY JAMES AT GENEVA *facing p. 161*

From a hitherto unpublished photograph now in the Houghton Library at Harvard taken during the winter of 1859–60

WILLIAM JAMES AT 25 *facing p. 192*

From a photograph in the Houghton Library

FROM HENRY JAMES'S SKETCH BOOK, 1869
facing p. 192

"The novelist had, he said, the painter's eye, adding that few writers possessed it." *John La Farge, quoted by his biographer, Royal Cortissoz*

HENRY JAMES AT NEWPORT, AGED 20
facing p. 193

A photograph taken at the time of the writing of "A Tragedy of Error" and "The Story of a Year." "I remember (it now comes back to me) when (and where) I was so taken: at the age of 20, though I look younger, and at a time when I had had an accident (an injury to my back), and was rather sick and sorry. I look rather as if I wanted propping up." *Henry James to Mrs. Frank Matthews, 18 November 1902*

MINNY TEMPLE AT 16 *facing p. 193*

From a photograph sent to William James by Minny Temple's sister. Her hair had been cropped during an illness. William in his characteristically humorous vein described the cutting of the hair as an act of madness. ". . . let's speak of Minny and her fearful catastrophe . . . I have often had flashes of horrid doubts about that girl . . . Was she all alone when she did it? Could no one wrest the shears from her vandal hand? I declare I fear to return home. . . . I shall weep as soon as I have finished this letter." *William James to Katherine Temple, September 1861*

INTRODUCTION

THIS BOOK IS THE STORY OF THE CHILDHOOD AND YOUTH OF HENRY James—a portrait of the artist as a young man. In a sequel I hope to tell of the fashioning of his great career during his "middle years" in Paris and London; and finally I hope to trace the evolution of the legendary "Master"—for so his peers came to call him— the architect of the modern novel. His was a large life and it requires a large canvas.

Henry James stands astride two centuries and reaches backward to a third; with him the American novel, in a single leap, attained a precocious maturity it has never surpassed. And it is now recognized that with Henry James the novel in English achieved its greatest perfection. By some queer irony, a writer from the New World—in an era when Americans were preoccupied with ever-widening frontiers and material things arrived upon the scene of the Old World to set the house of fiction in order. To this Henry James dedicated the whole of his life. He became, in his time—and

reaching over into ours—the first great theorist and scholar in the art which he himself practiced with such distinction.

So large an artist becomes visible only by degrees after his death. Those closest to him in our century knew only the old man, and perpetuated the man they knew; in the process they embalmed for posterity the heavy-lidded talkative Master of Rye and Chelsea, but overlooked the sharp-visioned, crisp and witty, bearded James of the 1880's, and totally lost sight of the shy but purposeful, and prodigiously creative, young American who arrived in Paris at thirty-two and consorted with Turgenev and the heirs of Balzac. The figure of Henry James remembered today is a curious and encrusted pastiche of anecdote and rumor, as Simon Nowell-Smith showed in his painstaking and urbane compilation, *The Legend of the Master*. Few have gone in search of the small boy James tenderly evoked in his autobiographies, or the sensitive troubled youth of the Civil War years enshrined in *Notes of a Son and Brother*.

The two volumes of his letters, published in 1920, four years after the novelist's death, have served the general purposes of a biography. Several volumes have appeared since 1935* containing much valuable documentation without, however, appreciably altering the portrait of the Henry James of the letters. These revealed Henry James's great epistolary style, his sustained verbal mastery, and the generous way in which he gave of the surplus of his genius to his friends. Nevertheless they suffered from a lack of concrete biographical data: they offered the Henry James of the drawing-room and the week-end visits rather than the James who wrote assiduously and sought in the market place of letters, to sell his precious

. . . .

* Ralph Barton Perry, *The Thought and Character of William James* (1935), which contains many early letters of Henry James; F. O. Matthiessen, ed., *The James Family* (1947), an anthology of James family writings which includes portions of the novelist's correspondence; F. O. Matthiessen and Kenneth B. Murdock, eds., *The Notebooks of Henry James* (1947); Edel, Leon, ed., *The Complete Plays of Henry James* (1949) and the correspondence with T. S. Perry in Virginia Harlow's biography of the latter (1950). F. W. Dupee's concise *Henry James* in the "American Men of Letters Series" (1951) draws on these new materials.

wares. The "working" Henry James was utterly lost from sight, and it was not until the publication of his notebooks, a quarter of a century after the letters, that at least the intimate side of his creation was in part unveiled. The task of Percy Lubbock, the editor of the letters, was not facilitated by the fact that many persons held back letters as being too "personal" or too "intimate"—unaware that Henry James's tone had been personal and intimate with every correspondent, lavish in feeling yet cautious in self-revelation. Also, many of James's correspondents were still alive and certain reticences had to be observed. The inordinate length of most letters made necessary considerable trimming; and also—inevitably in so constant a letter-writer—endless repetitions had to be dropped in the reader's interest, if not in that of the scholar. Most of the family letters were carefully pruned before they reached Lubbock, for the older members of the James family read the correspondence understandably in the light of privacy rather than of posterity. The result was an admirable compilation for the needs of its time, yet one which seems to us now lacking in balance, since its first 434 pages cover fifty-seven years of the novelist's life and the remaining 502 pages cover the last sixteen years. This must explain in part the perpetuation of the orotund James of the legend and the neglect of the rounded artist.

Critics have tended to dismiss Henry James, the man, as a figure that sat and wrote for half a century—a kind of disembodied Mind, a writing machine riveted to a desk creating characters without flesh and stories without passion. This view, for instance, was shared by Bernard Shaw, who once remarked that Henry James dealt with life in which "passion is subordinate to intellect and to fastidious artistic taste." We would venture to suggest that Shaw was describing the author of *Candida*, or of *Pygmalion*, rather than the man who gave us so sustained a work of passion as "The Beast in the Jungle" or a tale of compassion for the trials of an adolescent in "The Pupil," or even the author who could produce as crystal a note, as pure in feeling, as "Daisy Miller." The legend of Henry James as

intellect untouched by feeling or passion belongs distinctly to those who have sparingly read the works or stumbled upon such parts of it—particularly in the late period—as are supremely analytical. "Where there's anything to feel I try to be there," remarks Gabriel Nash, the bright and talkative young man in *The Tragic Muse*. He spoke for Henry James. "I am that queer monster, the artist, an obstinate finality, an inexhaustible sensibility," James wrote triumphantly just two years before his death, in reply to a sour dose of pessimism from Henry Adams. In writing this biography it is my intention to present both a picture of "that queer monster, the artist" and of the "inexhaustible sensibility" that was Henry James.

The time has come for biography to apply to Henry James those correctives which are possible only with the lapse of the years and the emergence of materials at first hidden from view, the departure from the scene of actors intimately concerned in the life under study, and the clearing of the air by the warm light of a balanced and searching criticism. To the explanation of the Jamesian anomalies and ambiguities—the legend, the distortion, the caricature of his personality—the biographer can now address himself with the aid of an overwhelming mass of evidence. And this is the task at which I have been working—with some interruptions—for the better part of a quarter of a century.

It is above all necessary to dispel the belief that there was, so to speak, no "life" behind the Art of Henry James, that his was a purely cerebrating genius. Was it true for Henry James, as some have insisted, that like his protagonist in "The Beast in the Jungle" he was "the man of his time, *the* man, to whom nothing on earth was to have happened"? Did nothing happen to Henry James except the writing of an extremely long shelf of books? And could a man produce so much having, as it is claimed, lived so little? Percy Lubbock argued, when he was editing the letters, that James's life was "no mere succession of facts such as could be compiled and recorded by another hand." The passage is significant and must be quoted:

When Henry James wrote the reminiscences of his youth he
shewed conclusively, what indeed could be doubtful to none who
knew him, that it would be impossible for anyone else to write his
life. His life was no mere succession of facts, such as could be compiled and recorded by another hand; it was a densely knit cluster
of emotions and memories, each one steeped in lights and colours
thrown out by the rest, the whole making up a picture that no one
but himself could dream of undertaking to paint. Strictly speaking
this may be true of every human being; but in most lives experience
is taken as it comes and left to rest in the memory where it happens to fall. Henry James never took anything as it came; the
thing that happened to him was merely the point of departure for
a deliberate, and as time went on a more and more masterly,
creative energy. . . . Looked at from without his life was unevent-
ful enough, the even career of a man of letters, singularly fortunate
in all his circumstances. Within, it was a cycle of vivid and in-
cessant adventure, known only to himself except in so far as he
himself put it into words. So much of it as he left unexpressed is
lost, therefore, like a novel that he might have written, but of
which there can now be no question, since its only possible writer
is gone.

This is a resounding challenge to the art of biography. Mr. Lubbock was, in fact, arguing that in certain cases—and in the supreme
case of Henry James—biography must abdicate in favor of autobiography. The present writer sees no reason for such an abdication.
It is obvious that a biographer cannot write what Henry James
would have written out of his own mind. But he can attempt to understand and describe what went on in this complex mind and in
this man of great feeling, to chart a course through the "densely
knit cluster of emotions and memories" and those day-dreams that
became the stuff of Henry James's fiction.

Henry James achieved that rare thing—an international as well as
a national identity. He was able to remain a great American
novelist—and to be a great European artist as well. Such creative
personalities are few indeed and especially in the history of the

novel. In the era when it was fashionable to dismiss Henry James as a failure because he had remained abroad most of his adult life and so (it was claimed) detached himself from his American roots, Vernon L. Parrington wrote: "It is not well for the artist to turn cosmopolitan, for the flavor of the fruit comes from the soil and sunshine of its native fields." It may perhaps not be well for certain artists to turn cosmopolitan; and indeed Henry James once recommended that one of his younger contemporaries be "tethered in native pastures even if it reduces her to a backyard in New York." But there was no need to tether Henry James. He belonged in the cosmopolitan pasture: his whole boyhood and youth had been a preparation for it; and when he began to record the history of the American abroad—the chronicles of the Daisy Millers and Francie Dossons, the Roderick Hudsons and Christopher Newmans—he was reaching into his own authentic experience. That his peers and his critics then and now, shut within their own domestic frames and suffering from a kind of national myopia, could not see how Henry James had placed himself on a superior plane of observation, a-wing over two worlds, the Old and the New, was perhaps inevitable. And it has taken many decades and a breakdown of old insularities, a bridging of space in the modern world, to give James the relevancy and relationship to a reading public lacking in his own day. Henry James, in his prophetic vision, foresaw that the great story of the Western World for years to come, would be the New World's re-discovery of the Old, and the Old's discovery of the New. The two worlds are still trying to accommodate themselves to each other's idiosyncrasies. He felt, too, that in this great balancing of values, moral and material, the Americans could face the old trans-Atlantic order unafraid and indeed rise on occasions superior to the complexities and corruptions of the Europeans. At the same time he was anything but blind to the shortcomings in culture and perception of his fellow-country men. "I think to be an American is an excellent preparation for culture," he wrote when he was twenty-four. (One must note the use of the word "preparation.") "We have exquisite qualities as a race and it seems to me that we are

ahead of the European races in the fact that more than either of
them we can deal freely with forms of civilization not our own, can
pick and choose and assimilate. . . ." There spoke the formed cosmopolitan. Ultimately he was to write: "I have not the least hesita-
tion in saying that I aspire to write in such a way that it would be
impossible to an outsider to say whether I am at a given moment
an American writing about England or an Englishman writing
about America (dealing as I do with both countries,) and so far
from being ashamed of such an ambiguity I should be exceedingly
proud of it, for it would be highly civilized."

It is in this light that we must try to see Henry James—in the
light of high civilization, a figure of large and noble dimensions, a
man indubitably of his time and place yet with his face turned to
the future, struggling with his craft and with the problems of the
market place, an often deeply anxious writer, yet one with an abiding sense of his destiny that invariably enabled him to triumph
over certain of his deeply-rooted inner problems. How distorted our
picture of him is, may be judged from a single significant example
which I will give, although it belongs to James's later years and is
not elaborated in the present volume. It has universally been believed that Henry James was a man who practiced letters from ne-
cessities other than those of earning a living. This has no foundation in fact. Henry James made his way by his pen, as a professional
writer, until he was past fifty. The modest income he inherited upon
the death of his father (when he was forty) was turned over entirely to his sister Alice; during his father's lifetime he took little
money from him that was not paid back by literary labor. If I have
thus anticipated my story, it is to demonstrate what palpable errors
have been disseminated and to what degree our perspectives must
be revised. To untangle his life, to bring order out of the web of his
many friendships, to throw light on the much-discussed "ambiguities," to see Henry James in that late nineteenth century world
laying "siege" to Rome, to Paris and finally to London, to catch the
life that throbbed behind the work, this is our task.

In this long quest I have had to explore large masses of material and to disregard Boswell's injunction to let the subject speak for himself at every turn rather than "melt down" the materials. The contemporary biographer is forced, by the mere dead weight of paper, by the mountains of letters and journals and newspapers, to melt his materials or be smothered by them. In the case of Henry James the biographical terrain, moreover, is beset with calculated pitfalls created by a novelist who was devoted to the private life and mindful of posterity; he had a kind of rage of privacy and dealt in mystification to confound those who would treat of his life. As a major step in this duel with the future, he burned most of his papers, shrouded in vagueness the history of much of his work and carefully erased the first person "I" in some of his essays. But what he could not burn were his own letters, and few of his friends heeded his injunction to commit them to flame. The present biographer has seen not only the transcripts of the hundreds which passed through Mr. Lubbock's hands (save for two or three boxfuls destroyed by the Germans who occupied Lubbock's Italian villa during the war) but thousands more besides, thanks to the extraordinary collection of James family papers presented to the Houghton Library at Harvard University by the late Henry James of New York, the novelist's nephew and literary executor. This collection has been greatly enriched by many of the novelist's correspondents. I have also seen much material in other collections here and abroad and have had as well the friendly help of William and Alice James, in whose home in Cambridge are kept alive the memories of a distinguished father, who was a philosopher, as well as the distinguished uncle, who was a novelist. Mrs. Henry James of New York gave me access to books and materials used by her husband during his lifetime in carrying out his task as literary executor, and Mrs. Mary James Vaux of Bryn Mawr, daughter of Robertson James, made available to me voluminous family papers dealing with the younger brothers.

I am indebted as well to a number of persons whose contributions to this work are duly recorded in the notes on my sources. I

wish in particular to thank here certain friends with whom this
work has been a shared experience and who in one way and another—by discussion, criticism, the reading of certain chapters, and
the free exchange of information—have contributed richly to it: I
refer, first and foremost, to Edna Kenton and to Allan Wade,
Jamesians on both sides of the Atlantic, who have for many years
richly illuminated the novelist's life and work; Donald Brien,
most critical and searching of collectors, and Rupert Hart-Davis, my
publisher in England, who has gone far beyond a publisher's line
of duty to aid a researching author. I am grateful to George Stevens,
of J. B. Lippincott Company, for unfailing editorial counsel and
for the generous view he has taken of the scope of this work. My
debt to my wife, Roberta R. Edel, is great indeed: she trod an independent path through the work of Henry James and brought fresh
points of view and a lively and critical questioning of meanings
that provided new insights and helped to revise or confirm old judgments. The expression of my gratitude to many others must await
the writing of the later sections of this biography.

LEON EDEL

Interrogation of the Past

THE SPECTRAL EYE

THE JAMES FAMILY WAS FOUNDED IN AMERICA BY AN IRISH IMMI-grant who arrived in the United States immediately after the Revolution. He was a Protestant from County Cavan and bore the name William James. His father had been a William also, and among the thirteen children the immigrant fathered in the New World there was still another William and also a Henry who in turn became the father of still another William and of a Henry, a philosopher and a novelist. The names had become dynastic symbols, as if the family were a royal line and there was a throne to be filled.

Henry James the novelist and grandson of the enterprising William who had fared across the seas, was to plead often against the confusing proliferation of Williams and Henrys; and doubtless his passion for finding the right names for his fictional characters stemmed from a sense that wrong names had been bestowed within his family experience. It was difficult to be an individual if one's name were a family tag pinned to the cradles of helpless babes.

19

Family legend has it that the founder of the line, who was eighteen when he set foot in the New World in 1789, brought with him a "very small sum of money," a Latin grammar and a desire to visit the fresh battlefields of the Revolutionary War—a desire he appears to have promptly gratified. He found employment as a clerk in a New York store and two years later was able to open his own establishment. In 1793 he settled in Albany, then a thriving town of five thousand set in frontier country. In the three decades that followed he lived—in fact helped to create—the traditional American success story. He purchased land in upper New York State and in Manhattan; he ventured into activities as diverse as banking and the manufacture of salt in Syracuse. He became an influential power on the upper Hudson (it was perhaps no accident that his novelist grandson bestowed the name of Hudson on his first important hero) and in due course the name of James was given to a street in Albany, another in Syracuse and to Jamesville, New York. He was one of the staunchest pillars of the Presbyterian Church and prominent in civic affairs; he was chosen to deliver the official oration at the completion of the Erie Canal and he was a trustee of Union College, Schenectady. He died rich and honored on September 19, 1832 and the Albany *Argus* said: "Turn where we may, and there are the results of his informing mind—his energy —and his vast wealth."

His wealth was vast even in terms of the later period of "tycoons" and multi-millionaires. William of Albany left an estate valued at $3,000,000 to be divided among his eleven surviving children and his widow, Catharine Barber, who out-lived him by twenty-seven years. And he left them a legacy of rigid Presbyterianism against which the elder Henry James rebelled all his life. This son was punished in the will with an annuity that yielded about $1,200 a year. The will also invested the trustees with wide powers to supervise the lives of the heirs "with a view to discourage prodigality and vice and furnish an incentive to economy and usefulness. . . ."

The children of William of Albany rose against this attempt of their father to police their lives from beyond the grave. They went

to court, Henry among them, and the will was broken. In the division of property, the elder Henry James received a large parcel of real estate in Syracuse that yielded him about $10,000 a year. He accordingly found himself, as he remarked, "leisured for life."

I

The elder Henry James was the fourth son of William of Albany's third marriage, the first wife having died in childbirth and the second two years after her marriage. He was a sensitive boy, strong of limb and keen of mind, with an abundance of healthy animal spirits. The father, preoccupied with his ever-growing business empire, found little time for his numerous progeny, save to exercise (and catechize) them in the rugged Presbyterian manner. The elder Henry, in later years, recorded his memories of Sundays in the Albany household in which the children were taught "not to play, not to dance nor to sing, not to read story-books, not to con over our school-lessons for Monday even; not to whistle, not to ride the pony, nor to take a walk in the country, nor a swim in the river; nor, in short, to do anything which nature specially craved."

"Nothing is so hard," the old man added ruefully looking back at his childish self of those long Albany Sundays, "nothing is so hard for a child as *not-to-do.*"

Yet the child is ever resourceful and Henry James, an observant, out-giving little boy, in that large family, found compensations and solutions. One was to arrive at church early on Sundays in order to occupy the corner of the large family pew right next to the window. He could by this calculated stroke combine entertainment with a brave appearance of piety. The window-blind had a reachable cord and tassels to be set a-swinging; in the street (barred to traffic after the manner of the time for the duration of the Holy Service) he could watch the picturesque parade of irreligious strollers in their Sunday finery enjoying a Sabbath idleness in which he could participate only vicariously. And always, just about the time that the sermon began, there was an added touch

of color and drama remembered by the senior Henry into his old age. Opposite the church stood the dwelling of a Justice of the Peace and every Sunday the housemaid would appear and shake out the crumb-cloth over the side of the steps. She did this unhurriedly and nonchalantly, studying the passers-by—and studied in turn by the small boy at the church window. "I was . . . unfeignedly obliged to the shapely maid for giving my senses so much innocent occupation when their need was sorest," the elder Henry wrote decades later. "Her pleasant image has always remained a figure of my memory . . . the fresh, breezy, natural life she used to impart to those otherwise lifeless, stagnant, most unnatural Sunday mornings."

The Devil could stalk the streets of Albany and sow temptations even more serious than a glimpse of a shapely maid through a church window. When Henry James Senior was ten—he later confessed this to one of his sons—he used to stop every morning on his way to school at a shoemaker's shop near his father's house for a nip of raw gin or brandy, and the ritual was usually renewed in the afternoon. This was not, he said, an occasional thing but habitual. If, on the one hand, it was a way of being a manly little fellow among drinking and card-playing schoolmates, it was also a way of defying God the Father who had created dull Sundays and that other father who, in the important Albany household, was virtually a god.

The son pictured William of Albany as a stern and uncompromising parent. What is more, Henry felt himself a helpless victim of parental disregard. "I cannot recollect that he ever questioned me about my out-of-door occupations, or about my companions, or showed any extreme solicitude about my standing in school." Nor does his mother seem to have filled the gap. She was "a law only to our affections," "a good wife and mother, nothing else—save, to be sure, a kindly friend and neighbor."

These were the senior Henry's feelings about his father and mother recalled in old age. The available evidence tends to show that within the stern Calvinistic frame that enclosed their house

at State and Green Streets, and later North Pearl Street, the parents distributed all the usual elements of love, affection, devotion, parental solicitude and parental anger, accompanied by the usual moments of gaiety and joy as well as the storms, rivalries and tempests of passion that are to be found in a numerous family in which big and little egos clash. Henry, sensitive and reflective, clearly felt himself pushed aside; and we can judge how unhappy the boy must have been by the candid words his older self set down in his autobiographical fragment: "I was never so happy at home as away from it."

If happiness lay away from home it was because home early became for the young boy a place where competition with his brothers and sisters was intense and where the two fathers—the prosperous and busy corporeal William of Albany and the invisible Almighty—kept him under their gaze and *not-to-do* echoed through its rooms. Years later in speaking of some of his contemporaries, the elder Henry James invoked spy and detective images to characterize them. Emerson had "no sympathy with nature" but was "a sort of police-spy upon it. . . . He is an uncommonly sharp detective, but a detective he is and nothing more." Similarly, Hawthorne "had the look all the time, to one who didn't know him, of a rogue who suddenly finds himself in a company of detectives." There spoke a man who all his life felt himself spied upon. The dark silent night, for the small Albany boy, "usually led in the spectral eye of God, and set me to wondering and pondering evermore how I should effectually baffle its gaze."

To baffle the detective gaze of a suspicious Calvinistic Deity, to find a benign and friendly God, this was to be the troubled quest of Henry James Senior. And it was to leave its indelible marks upon his gifted sons.

II

Away from home lay wood and field where the boy felt free. Venturing into the world of nature he could at least provisionally shake off the vocal prohibitions of the household in North Pearl

Street. "The dawn always found me on my feet and I can still vividly recall," he wrote when he was old, "the divine rapture which filled my blood as I pursued under the magical light of morning the sports of the river, the wood, or the field." For the son of William of Albany the days "bowled themselves out one after another, like waves upon the shore, and as a general thing deafened me by their clamor. . . . The common ore of existence perpetually converted itself into the gold of life in the glowing fire of my animal spirits. I lived in every fibre of my body. . . ."

There came a day when the dawn did not find him on his feet and when it seemed indeed that Divine punishment had finally been visited upon him for all his sins.

He was thirteen and attending Albany Academy. On summer afternoons the boys would meet one of their teachers in the park in front of the Academy to combine learning with sport. One of their favorite pastimes was balloon flying. The power was supplied by air heated by a flaming ball of tow that was saturated with spirits of turpentine. When one of the balloons ignited, the ball would drop and the mass of fire would be rapidly kicked about until extinguished.

On one such afternoon some of the turpentine was splashed over the pantaloons of Henry. The balloon rose and caught fire; the ball dropped and the boys swooped down upon it. A sharp kick sent the flaming mass through the window of a nearby stable. Quick to realize the danger, Henry rushed into the barn, climbed to the hayloft. In stamping out the ball of fire his turpentine-soaked trousers were ignited.

The burns he suffered were severe. In one leg "a morbid process in the bone" set in which "ever and anon called for some sharp surgery." It was sharp indeed in the era before anaesthesia when liberal doses of whiskey may have dulled but did not eliminate the terror of the knife. The robust boy survived the primitive surgery of the 1820's; but when he left his bed long months after the accident he had lost his leg. It had been amputated above the

knee. For two years on his back he had been face to face with the spectral eye, the God of punishment. He would no longer be able to pursue the sports of the river, the wood or the field. He was wedded, henceforth, to the pavement or wherever an artificial limb, first of wood and later of cork, could take him; largely he had to rely on the easy conveyance of horse and carriage. For him forever after the smoother walks of the cities rather than the free latitudes of the country.

A curious and important thing happened, however, during this time. He discovered that both his father and mother were not as unmindful of his existence as he had believed. He remembered, all his days, his mother, candle in hand, sleep-walking at night, coming to his bedside during his illness, covering his shoulders, adjusting his pillow, "just as carefully as if she were awake." He recalled his father's agony, standing by his son while the surgeons did their work; his sympathies were "so excessive that my mother had the greatest possible difficulty in imposing due prudence upon his expression of it." He could say thus that "my father was weakly, nay painfully, sensitive to his children's claims upon his sympathy; and I myself, when I became a father in my turn, felt that I could freely sacrifice property and life to save my children from unhappiness." In recording this he reveals to us that where sensibility was concerned, his mother possessed greater self-control than the father.

He would have remembered William of Albany as an "indifferent parent" if the accident had not revealed "his tenderness to me . . . so assiduous and indeed extreme as to give me an exalted sense of his affection." However, the original struggle with his father was never resolved. The years of his illness only mitigated it; they offered compensations—at best poor ones—for a more serious handicap. But *not-to-do* now was a law because he simply couldn't do. To the frustrations imposed in childhood by Father was added now the frustration imposed by an act of God that seemed highly arbitrary. It had deprived him of his freedom to roam with his fellow-men. If he felt himself belatedly appreci-

ated, in his pitiable condition, surrounded by doctors and attending anxious parents (and later tutors) he also felt increasingly that there existed between man and the God of his father "a profound natural enmity." The thoughtful boy had time, during those long months, to day-dream and to read, and to develop a feverish mental life which, from now on, had to be a substitute for physical activity. And with this he mastered a rhetorical, vigorous, aggressive eloquence, that was to be transmitted to his four sons and to his daughter—picturesque phrases, conceits, elaborate flights of the imagination, a mordant wit as if some fragment of the knife that had pierced his bone had remained in his mind: all this became part and parcel of this dismembered young man who one day found himself at the end of his adolescence, erect again, facing the world on a solitary foot.

I I I

The elder Henry James entered Union College, Schenectady, in 1828, in conformity with William of Albany's wishes and asserted his recovered manhood by becoming a spirited young blade, if one can use that term for a young man-about-town of Schenectady of that era. Liberated from his bed of sickness—and from home—Henry indulged himself freely in un-Presbyterian luxuries —cigars, smart clothes, books of an undevout character, oysters. William of Albany had always kept the loose change for the household expenses in a drawer of his dressing table and when Henry, at seven or eight, had incurred expenses by constant frequentation of a confectioner's shop down the street (and later the informal "bar") he relieved himself of his debt by two or three times borrowing freely ". . . without any thought of making restitution." This surrender to Satan remained with him as a deeply disturbing memory. When he ran up debts, however, at Schenectady, there was no convenient drawer into which he could plunge his hand for some silver. Instead, he quite simply gave his creditors drafts on his opulent parent.

A letter from William of Albany to a friend has survived in

which the explosive paternal anger emerges in short breathless sentences . . . Henry had "so debased himself as to leave his parents' house in the character of a swindler etc.etc.—details presented today—are the order which I enclose as a specimen of his progress in arts of low vileness—and unblushing falsehood . . . a fellow from Schenectady was after him today for 50 to 60 drs—(in a note I understand) for segars and oysters. . . ." All this, William of Albany concluded, would certainly "lodge him in a prison." The elder Henry's novelist son, alluding to this episode as a "misunderstanding, if not . . . a sharp rupture," recalled that there had been a tradition that his father "had been for a period quite definitely 'wild.'" The father didn't, however, end up in prison. He ran away to Boston instead.

It was not an easy pilgrimage for a one-legged man in the days when there was no railroad from Albany to the city of his flight. But he made his way to New England and it is interesting to note, in the light of the later legend that the Jameses were New Englanders, that this was the father's only departure from the Hudson Valley in his youth and he was not to return to Boston, save for brief trips, until much later, when his children, also natives of the Hudson Valley, were advancing toward manhood.

In Boston he found a position as a proof reader, lodged himself comfortably, and enjoyed the society of the city's first families, where he was cordially received. The Boston excursion is important only as it underlines the break between father and son; and although he later established a truce with Albany and went back to Union College (he graduated from it in 1830) Henry neither completely placated his parent nor made peace with his own troubled spirit. He attempted the study of law, in accord with his father's wishes; he participated for a spell in the editing of an Albany publication; but he was restless and ill at ease.

The death of his father only exacerbated the deep emotional problems fixed in the sturdy battered frame of the young man who now confronted the world on his own with a comfortably filled purse, yet did not know where to turn. Seeking to understand his

misgivings over religion and to comprehend his relationship with God, the elder Henry gravitated to Princeton Theological Seminary —almost as if to do penance to the ghost of his father. This was in 1835, three years after William of Albany's death. The gesture of submission to the Deity of William was not for long. How could so intense a rebel accept religion, conformity, blind belief? And yet, he confessed, the conviction of God's supernatural being "was burnt into me as with a red-hot iron." He has left a vivid picture of his disturbed state of mind—the conflict within him between belief in a hostile God and in the laws of Nature which he deemed asserted themselves to save him from the revengeful Deity . . .

The thought of God as a power foreign to my nature, and with interests therefore hostile to my own, would have wilted my manhood in its cradle, would have made a thoughtful, anxious, and weary little slave of me before I had entered upon my teens, if it had not been for Nature's indomitable uprightness. . . . I doubt whether any lad had ever just so thorough and pervading a belief in God's existence as an outside and contrarious force to humanity. . . . I am sure no childish sinews were ever more strained than mine were in wrestling with the subtle terror of his name. This insane terror pervaded my consciousness more or less . . . made me loath at night to lose myself in sleep, lest his dread hand should clip my thread of life without time for a parting sob of penitence, and grovel at morning dawn with an abject slavish gratitude that the sweet sights and sounds of Nature and of man were still around me. . . .

He felt that he had escaped being "thoughtful, anxious" and the weary slave of terror during the juvenile years. Yet during those years he seems to have found some escape from anxiety only when away from home. Now he carried his anxieties with him and a perpetual sense of guilt He could find no peace. He abandoned his theological studies, he settled in New York, he married and became a father, but he remained troubled, as one who never had

found quite what he was looking for—nor known quite what he sought. He derived some solace in the friendship of Ralph Waldo Emerson, whom he met shortly after his marriage, and in the marks of respect men began to pay him for his fervor of speech, his intensity, his incisive wit and his devotion to the Scriptures.

In 1843, when his second son—the subject of this biography—was only six months old, he took his family abroad to England. There, in one horrible hour, came the dark breakdown foreshadowed in all the years of his inner conflict. After that came the revelation.

VASTATION

IT CAME (IN THE IMAGE USED BY HIS SON YEARS LATER IN ANOTHER but related context) like some beast in the jungle that had long crouched within him for the spring. He had spent the winter in and out of London, meeting Carlyle and the writers and free-thinkers who frequented the sharp-tongued Scotsman's home in Chelsea. He had worked for long hours and days at his desk, seeking an answer in the pages of Genesis to the struggle between physical well-being and Calvinistic spiritual well-being. He had settled his family in a cottage near the Great Park of Windsor. His health was good, he was in cheerful spirits and he was interested in his work. It seemed to him that at last he could make some contribution to an understanding of the word of God.

I

One day, toward the end of May 1844, the elder Henry James ate a
good meal and remained at the table after his wife and boys had
left it. The afternoon was chilly and there was a fire in the grate.
He gazed contentedly into the embers "feeling only the exhilara-
tion incident to a good digestion." Relaxed, his mind skirting a
variety of thoughts, he suddenly experienced a day-nightmare. It
seemed to him that there was an invisible shape squatting in the
room "raying out from his fetid personality influences fatal to
life." A deathly presence, thus, unseen had stalked from his mind
into the house. Or was this again the sense of being spied upon,
this time the spectral eye of the Devil?

He recognized that "to all appearance it was a perfect insane
and abject terror, without ostensible cause"—but it was terror nevertheless and not to be talked or reasoned away. "The thing had
not lasted ten seconds before I felt myself a wreck; that is, reduced
from a state of firm, vigorous, joyful manhood to one of almost
helpless infancy." He kept his seat in that haunted room—or rather
that room haunted with the terror of his mind—wanting to run
like a child to the foot of the stairs and shout as if calling for his
mother, or to the roadside to "appeal to the public to protect me."
He did neither at first. He remained motionless "beat upon . . .
by an ever-growing tempest of doubt, anxiety, and despair" until
he was able to struggle to his feet and confide the "sudden
burden of inmost, implacable unrest" to his wife.

He consulted eminent physicians who told him he had over-
worked his brain and urged upon him open air, cheerful company
and a water-cure. The elder Henry obeyed; however, his curious
and active mind brooded upon his illness. He went to an English
watering-place where the waters did not help but where he was
struck by the pastoral beauty of the countryside; and we find him,
in recalling this, and after dwelling on the morbidity, insularity
and prejudice of the English, wishing himself a sheep, grazing
on a "placid hillside" and "drinking in eternal dew and freshness
from Nature's lavish bosom." Later in the account he muses also

on the "heavenly sweetness in the soul of the patient over-driven cab horse, or misused cadger's donkey." Thus this intellectual now sought identity with the animals, the lowly creatures, subdued and passive—and beaten—servants of man. He discovered that he no longer wanted to study the Scriptures. He retained the notes he had taken for the rest of his life but never again looked at them. He became convinced that he had never really wanted to discover Scriptural truth, "but only to ventilate my own ability in discovering it." He experienced a sense of "my downright intellectual poverty and dishonesty" and wondered that he could have even pretended to an ability to ferret out the word of God. "Truth must *reveal itself* if it would be known. . . ." He mentions also that his depression and despair were such that to go for a walk or to sleep in strange surroundings called forth an effort such as might be required to plan a military campaign or write an epic.

The amputation had been a physical breakdown experienced when the stout boyish frame could triumph over the shock. The second experience, twenty years after the first, was a collapse of his mental well-being. Evil, to put it in theological terms, in that shape that squatted invisible, had come to reveal to the elder Henry James that he must not question the word of God but await the Truth of Divine Revelation. On psychological ground, we might say that he was suffering from nervous exhaustion after years of inner conflict. The inner terror of defying Fathers and escaping spectral eyes was finally too much for him. He chose the one escape possible: a relapse to the innocence and passivity of childhood. "I had nevertheless on the whole been in the habit of ascribing to the Creator . . . an outside discernment of the most jealous scrutiny, and had accordingly put the greatest possible alertness into his service and worship, until my will, as you have seen— thoroughly fagged out as it were with the formal, heartless, endless task of conciliating a stony-hearted Deity—actually collapsed."

The time had come in the life of the elder Henry James to make his peace with the Gods household and universal so that he should have to conciliate neither; for if the task were endless, life itself

would lose its meaning and he would live forever on the edge of
the abyss. That way lay madness. He did not reason it thus; but
within him the will to live, the will to manhood, eventually triumphed over the disintegrating forces of the divided self. The revelation came in unexpected form through the medium of a mother-
like figure whose name has been preserved for us only as that of
Mrs. Chichester.

II

She lived in the vicinity of the watering-place and was considered
by the elder Henry as "a lady of rare qualities of heart and mind,
and of singular personal loveliness as well." One day she asked
him what had brought him to seek a water-cure. Her sympathetic
inquiry provoked a ready response; he poured out to her the story
of his visitation in all its horror. She listened attentively and then
she spoke to him to this effect:

"It is, then, very much as I had ventured to suspect from two
or three previous things you have said: you are undergoing what
Swedenborg calls a *vastation*; and though, naturally, you yourself
are despondent or even despairing about the issue, I cannot help
taking an altogether hopeful view of your prospects."

These words were balm for Henry James. He inquired about
Swedenborg, he was not familiar with his writings. Mrs. Chichester
explained that the *vastation* was, in Swedenborgian thought, one
of the stages in the regenerative process of man—awakening, pur-
gation, illumination—and that a new birth for man was the secret
of Divine Creation and Providence. She admitted she was but an
amateur in these matters, but he had heard enough. He journeyed
post-haste to London and purchased two of Emmanuel Swedenborg's works—*Divine Love and Wisdom* and *Divine Providence*.
The doctors had warned him not to exercise his brain; he began
therefore by merely nibbling at the books. This he found a torture;
his interest grew "frantic"; finally he threw caution to the winds
and plunged in.

He read with a palpitating interest. He said later that his heart

divined, even before his intelligence seized, the truth he found in Swedenborg. His strict Swedenborgian readers later agreed; they said that Henry James projected into Swedenborgian thought many of his own beliefs and ideas. However that may be, the Swedish seer provided the ailing man with a kind of mental healing that strengthened and saved and altered the whole course of his life. For what, in effect, had the motherly Mrs. Chichester told Henry but that what had happened to him had happened to other men, that he could be reborn and recover his manhood and undergo rejuvenation, that he must not be afraid of confronting God, his Father, for God intended him to be reborn. Henry formulated it himself, "I had no doubt that this being or self of mine . . . came originally as a gift from the hand of God; but I had just as little doubt that the moment the gift had left God's hand . . . it became as essentially independent of him in all spiritual or subjective regards as the soul of a child is of its earthly father. . . ." And independence of his earthly father was what he needed to effect his cure, even though his father had been dead for more than a decade. His novelist son was to recall later that his father never traveled without the red-bound Swedenborgian volumes in his luggage; he remembered them as a "majestic array" forming "the purplest rim of his library's horizon." With the discovery of Swedenborg the senior Henry "passed rapidly into that grateful infinitude of recognition and application which he was to inhabit for the rest of his days."

He discovered finally that there was for him a God residing in infinite wisdom and love. Since Man was made in God's image, Man too could dispense love and wisdom. Henry James began to lecture and give of himself in brilliant talk, in friendship and in at times an almost ecstatic devotion to his family. He no longer was in overt struggle with the Deity of Discipline and Absolute Obedience. He could now remake the God of his father—and by the same token his father too—into his own image. He could *be* his father. In this manner he found a God that corresponded with his own naturally expansive spirit. Thus finally did the elder

Henry James lay the parental ghost. Emmanuel Swedenborg contributed to his spiritual liberation, teaching him that "God's great
work was wrought not in the minds of individuals here and there,
as my theology taught me, but in the very stuff of human nature
itself, in the very commonest affections and appetites and passions
of universal man, a transforming, redeeming, regenerating work,
which shall lift all mankind into endless union with God. . . ."

III

In Swedenborg Henry James had found the New Heaven. Now in
Charles Fourier he found the "scientific insight" for the new life
on earth. Fourier furnished the "disclosures of the harmonies
which are possible to humanity, in every sphere whether of its passions or active administration, as stamped with God's own truth."
Fourier's "practical" social science could in a sense be read as
complementing the doctrine of Swedenborg. Man made in the
image of God had God-given instincts. To inhibit them, as civilization did, was to violate the will and the intention of God. "Every
appetite and passion of man's nature is good and beautiful, and
destined to be fully enjoyed," James wrote in consonance with
Fourier, whom he began to read and study while he was still recovering from the *vastation*.

Fourier's ideas had taken firm hold of America in those early
decades of the nineteenth century. "We are all a little wild here
with numberless projects of social reform," Emerson wrote to Carlyle in the autumn of 1840. "Not a reading man but has a draft
of a new Community in his waistcoat pocket." In 1846, two
years after Henry James's discovery of Swedenborg, the French
social thinker had an estimated two hundred thousand followers in
the United States. His proposals to establish communal societies,
social units (*phalanxes*) from which the competitive complexities
of civilization might be banished and a harmonious social order
achieved, constituted an enlargement of the very ideas which the
Transcendentalists at Concord were preaching—the fuller realiza-

tion of man. Brook Farm was for a time Fourierist and Fourier continued to be studied and discussed in America long after his greatest vogue had passed. We know that some twenty years after the elder Henry's first reading of Fourier his name was still respectfully invoked in the James family. Henry Junior's boyhood friend, Thomas Sergeant Perry, recalled that "it was near Lily Pond [in Newport] that we long discussed Fourier's plan for regenerating the world. Harry had heard his father describe the great reformer's proposal to establish universal happiness, and like a good son he tried to carry the good news further."

The future novelist was a very small boy when his father, turning from the self-centered analysis of his relations with God began to contemplate society around him. As with Swedenborg he adapted Fourier to his own needs, and these doctrines sufficed for a lifetime. The elder Henry's last book, published three years before his death, reflected this wedding of Society and God; it bore the title, *Society the Redeemed Form of Man and the Earnest of God's Omnipotence in Human Nature*. His son William later said that he had devoted his life to the elaboration of "one single bundle of truths," a fresh conception of God and of our connection with him. Evil for him were the constraints which civilization put upon the individual; they prevented him from fulfilling his God-given destiny since the individual owes all he has to his inheritance and to the society in which he is born. "Make society do its duty to the individual, and the individual will be sure to do his duties to society. . . ." With this the elder James had supreme confidence that God would not fail man in his hour of need. He believed that chastity and purity belonged to marriage rather than to celibacy in the sense that the passions and appetites of man, clothed with the "sunshine of God's recognition" are a "solace and refreshment to our spiritual faculties." He looked to the day when "the sexual relations will be regulated in every case by the private will of the parties; when the reciprocal affection of a man and a woman will furnish the sole and sufficient sanction of their material converse."

To a correspondent he wrote: "Let us permit divorce whenever the parties desire it, in order that the name of marriage may be utterly dissociated with the idea of bondage."

I V

His life after his return to America was no longer an exhausting battle with himself, although his mercurial temperament remained unchanged and there were bound to be bad hours to off-set the good. A growing family of four boys and a girl testified to his fertility and now his writings began to multiply also. He published them at his own expense. If they never reached a wide public, if they contained the evidence of a continual self-questioning and an unfinished search for complete inner harmony, if they reflected the welling-up of emotion that sometimes clouded Logic and Reason, they nevertheless came to constitute a body of religio-social thought essentially "Jamesian" with all the stamp of the father's individual eloquence and rhetoric. He could throw off quaint conceits: "If the Deity were an immense Duck capable only of emitting an eternal quack we of course should all have been born webfooted, each as infallible in his way as the Pope, nor ever have been at the expense and bother of swimming-schools." He found sharp images to frame his ideas; and ideas and words to express them came with ever-increasing ease. His style at its best is pithy, enthusiastic, good-humored; yet it is recondite. William Dean Howells observed that his interpretations of Swedenborg "which sentence by sentence were so brilliantly suggestive, had sometimes a collective opacity which the most resolute vision could not penetrate." Again Howells testifies that he lighted up his thought "with flashes of the keenest wit and bathed it in the glow of a lambent humor, so that it is truly wonderful to me how it should remain so unintelligible." It was Howells who observed that Mr. James had written *The Secret of Swedenborg*—but had kept the secret very well.

He lectured, he wrote letters to editors, he indulged in polemic, he even had a few disciples. He was universally respected and became a local celebrity, known among the elite of New York and

New England. He was a friend of Greeley, Ripley and Dana. Through Emerson he came to know the Transcendentalists—Margaret Fuller, William Ellery Channing, Bronson Alcott. Carlyle he had met in London; Thoreau called on him when Henry Junior was in his cradle; the great Thackeray came to see him during an American tour. He had a host of trans-Atlantic Swedenborgian friends, most notable of these being J. J. Garth Wilkinson, a London doctor and writer. He was considered a genial and eminently likeable man. Emerson said he had "heroic manners," found in him a "serenity like the sun," and considered his lectures to be "brilliant." Thoreau, after first calling on him, said he had never been "more kindly and faithfully catechized." He found him "patient and determined to have the good of you." Carlyle discovered "something sly and skittish in the man, but a brave heart intrinsically, with sound, earnest sense, with plenty of insight and even humour." And again Howells: "His written style had traits of . . . bold adventurousness, but it was his speech which was most captivating. As I write of him I see him before me: his white bearded face, with a kindly intensity which at first glance seemed fierce, the mouth humourously shaping the mustache, the eyes vague behind the glasses; his sensitive hand gripping the stick on which he rested his weight to ease it from the artificial limb he wore."

The elder Henry James, on his side, was filled with love for his fellow-men and was an unusually affectionate individual. He began always by liking; but often the great of his time, from their position of authority, seemed to him like gods, fathers, dictators, who could not always be reconciled with brotherly love: and hidden hostilities would escape from the tip of his tongue or his pen. Even the benign Emerson was not spared. Henry James could see him as "a soul full of doors and windows" and find that an "unmistakable breath of the morning encircles him, and the odor of primeval woods"; he could call him, also, a "man without a handle." Bronson Alcott, with whom he had sharp verbal tilts, was once informed that he was "an egg, half-hatched." He had seen Carlyle as "an artist, a wilful artist" yet finally he wrote

in disillusion that he was the child of Mother Eve's "most melancholy old age" who "used to bury his worn, dejected face in her penurious lap, in a way so determined as forever to shut out all sight of God's new and better creation." The Scotsman, he found on renewed acquaintance, was "the same old sausage, fizzing and sputtering in his own grease."

A man who could caricature with so free a hand apparently had a compelling need to trim his fellow-mortals to the measure of himself. "My intelligence is the necessary digestive apparatus for my life," he once said and indeed the regenerated Henry James fed hungrily upon all that came within his purview, criticized, argued and always proclaimed the greater glory of God. His contemporaries felt that he lived too much by his intelligence; and there remained something rather ineffectual about him—he seemed so an addict of talk without thought for action that the more active Fourierists felt indeed that here was a man for whom the dream of a utopia seemed to suffice. He appeared to conceive of society as a kind of happy anarchy. The personality moulded in the Albany household, with the strong effervescent spirit of Ireland transmitted to his mind and speech, conditioned by the accident, "leisured" by the enterprise of the immigrant father, was a passive intellectual. He could lecture on art, on property, on democracy, on theology, be touched by idea and opinion, but he remained fundamentally aloof from the core of action. Thus he never interested himself in the details of Fourier's planning, embracing only his ideas on the brotherhood of man and exalting the general principles that might bring it about. His opponents might indeed have applied to him the strictures he applied to Carlyle. One of them, having something of Henry's verbal gifts, did attack him as belonging to the "class of purely ideal reformers, men who will lounge at their ease upon damask sofas and dream of a harmonic and beautiful world to be created hereafter . . . a mere *jet d'eau* of aspiration, reaching a higher elevation at some point than any other man, but breaking into spray and impalpable mist, glittering in the sun, and descending to earth with no weight or mechanical force to effect

any great end." The elder Henry continued to lead an inner life, sallying forth among men but returning quickly to his hearth, to be at his greatest ease next to his wife, who mothered him as she mothered her offspring.

v

Henry James was married four years before the *vastation* to Mary Robertson Walsh, sister of a fellow-student at Princeton Seminary. The Walshes were a prosperous family, as stoutly Presbyterian as the Albany Jameses. They were descended from Hugh Walsh, an Irishman of English extraction who came from Killingsley, County Down, in 1764 and settled at Newburgh, New York, and from a Scotsman, Alexander Robertson, who arrived in the United States on the eve of the Revolution and attained civic prominence in Manhattan. The future mother of a cosmopolitan novelist and a great American philosopher was a woman of sterling domestic virtues, strongly Calvinist and of a down-to-earth literalness of mind. She and her younger sister Catherine Walsh would sit in the family parlor in Washington Square and listen to the strange and vivid eloquence of the young Albany scion, as he expounded his unorthodox religious views; and the flames of his words warmed the inscrutable Mary Walsh as they did her handsome sister. Both were charmed and spell-bound. In due course he proposed to the older sister and was accepted. Whatever drama—if indeed drama there was—in this wooing is lost to us; we know only that later Catherine Walsh became a member of the James household, lived and travelled with her sister's family and was in every way a second mother to the James children. Lively, spirited, with much wit, she was more out-giving than her older sister. She married, late in life, but perhaps she had waited too long, for shortly afterwards she and her husband parted and she resumed her perpetual role of the family aunt among her kinfolk.

In later years, in talk with Emerson, the elder James told him that on seeing Mary Walsh "the flesh said, It is for me, and the spirit said, It is for me." So successful was he in weaning Mary

Walsh from orthodoxy that she consented to a purely civil marriage. "To mark the rueful rupture," her son wrote, "it had invoked, one evening, with the aid of India muslin and a wondrous gold head-band, in the maternal . . . 'parlours' [No. 19 Washington Square] . . . the secular nuptial consecration of the then Mayor of New York—I think Mr. Varick." The evening was July 28, 1840. The mayor was not Mr. Varick but Isaac Leggett Varian. The bride was thirty, her husband twenty-nine.

They did not set up house immediately. There were spacious family houses in Albany and New York to accommodate the newly-married. They spent some time near Catharine Barber James. Then they moved briefly into No. 5 Washington Square and thereafter lived at the Astor House, the great new hotel of Manhattan of that day. Here the first son was born in January of 1842 and it was probably this which prompted the elder Henry to seek a more permanent home. In February he purchased No. 21 Washington Place for $18,000 from his younger brother, John James, a large house a block off the Square, near Greene Street. By March the family was installed. This was the month the elder Henry met Ralph Waldo Emerson for the first time and, it is said, brought him home to see the new-born babe, named William after the grandfather.

A year later, directing Thoreau how to find him in Washington Place, Henry James described the street as running from the Square to Broadway "flanked on one corner by the university and on the opposite by a church." In this home, within a stone's throw of these symbols of organized religion and systematized scholarship—from which he was always to remain aloof—was born in April 15, 1843 "another fine little boy" as the father proudly announced to Emerson. "Tell Mrs. James," Emerson replied, "that I heartily greet her on the new friend, though little now, that has come to her health."

KEYSTONE OF THE ARCH

MARY JAMES, THE WIFE AND MOTHER, MOVES WITH SO QUIET A STEP and for so brief a space through the pages of her son's copious memoirs that we glimpse only a phantasmal form and catch only a distant echo of her voice—as if it were drowned in the clamor of her children and the undisciplined eloquence of her husband. The senior Henry spoke of her "sleepless" sense of justice and Henry Junior described as "soundless" her "all-saving service and trust." Her daughter Alice spoke of her "selfless devotion." *Soundless, selfless, sleepless,* linked with such words as justice, service, trust and devotion convey an image of an august and omniscient personage walking with unheard step through a household where justice and mercy had to be dispensed even-handed and with generosity among contending factions. Implied also was a figure devoted and loyal, vigilant and unrelaxed. It was as if she simply "embodied the unconscious essence of wife-and-motherhood" her daughter said. "She was our life, she was the house," Henry Junior wrote in his notebook just after her death; he added, "she was the keystone of the arch."

I

The picture that has come down to us describing Mary James as "self-effacing" suggests a weakness or at least an impassivity that clearly did not exist. To have been the "keystone" of the James family arch required strength and firmness and an ability to control and weather high emotional tempests. This Mary James appears to have been able to do all her life. Holding "a firm rein," she wrote once in a letter to her son Wilkinson, "is especially my forte." It was. She was a strong woman, strengthened by the worship of her husband and the love of her four sons and daughter who accepted her not only as their devoted mother but as the exalted figure of their father's veneration. It was the era of Victoria

in England and the image projected from over the seas of a Supreme Queen reigning with a Consort was thoroughly familiar to the little Jameses.

Mary James seems to have governed with a certain grace and a quiet and unperturbed dignity. Her domain itself was, however, far from quiet. Two accounts of mealtime in the James household, when the boys were in their 'teens, give us a picture not only of a commingling of food and disputation, but of the happy turbulence that could prevail; Garth Wilkinson makes a remark and is challenged by his younger brother Robertson. Henry Junior emerges from his silence to defend Wilky. William joins in. Finally the father seeks to act as moderator. Ralph Waldo Emerson's son Edward, who describes this scene as he saw it at Newport, goes on to say that the voice of the moderator "presently would be drowned by the combatants and he soon came down vigorously into the arena, and when, in the excited argument the dinner knives might not be absent from eagerly gesticulating hands, dear Mrs. James, more conventional, but bright as well as motherly, would look at me, laughingly reassuring, saying, 'Don't be disturbed, Edward; they won't stab each other. This is usual when the boys come home.' "

"I remember . . ." writes another witness, E. L. Godkin, the founder and editor of the *Nation*, "it was not unusual for the sons to invoke humorous curses on their parent, one of which was, that 'his mashed potatoes might always have lumps in them!' "

Mary James was quite equal to this pleasant family rivalry which emerged in the presence of eye-witnesses, and even to the stormier tussles and bursts of open warfare at other moments. The mother has left us a vivid bit of testimony of the infantile struggle for power which takes us back into the James family nursery in Albany. In 1846 she wrote to Mrs. J. J. Garth Wilkinson, Wilky's English godmother:

Your little Wilkie has come out for himself since the birth of little Rob. He seemed thereupon to take the hint, and seeing that

he was about to be shoved off, concluded to let us see how well he could take care of himself. He began to walk when the baby was two weeks old, took at once into his own hand the redress of his grievances which he seems to think are manifold, and has become emphatically the *ruling* spirit in the nursery. Poor little soul! my pity I believe would be more strongly excited for him were he less able or ready to take his own part, but as his strength of arm or of will seldom fails him, he is too often left to fight his own battles.

Allowing for possible maternal embellishment, we are given the impression that Mary James followed a not always happy policy of *laisser-faire* in the nursery. Indeed the battles continued far beyond infancy.

For relaxation I go to the Jameses, the parents are away, and those unhappy children fight like cats and dogs. [wrote T. S. Perry when he was a student at Harvard and the James boys in their late 'teens] The other evening I went there, and stayed for about an hour and a half, during 3/3 of which time Willie [Harry?] was trying to obtain solitude in the library, with the rest of the family pounding at the door, and rushing in all the time. He so far forgot himself at one time as to try to put and lock me out of the house. It was a terrible sight, and I can assure you I pitied poor Harry, and asked him to come and stay with me.

How much of this was a happy lark and how much a real struggle we cannot now judge; but it suggests that the James residence was rarely a mansion of peace and quiet while the boys were growing up.

I I

A photograph of Mary James, taken two years before her death when she was seventy, shows a woman in the characteristic pose of resigned elderly maternity: the black taffeta trimmed with lace and the graying hair parted in the middle upon which has been mounted the carefully-composed lace cap; the hands are folded,

the lips pursed to a single, hard line. The nose is prominent, the eyes are keen, the forehead is high. If we make allowance for the fact that sitting for one's photograph then was a somewhat more intense matter than it is today, her countenance suggests a purposeful, strong-willed and determined woman. Her daughter Alice remembered her as the central source of comfort and security in the family: "Father's sudden return at the end of thirty-six hours —having left to be gone a fortnight—with Mother beside him holding his hand, and we five children pressing close round him 'as if he had just been saved from drowning' and he pouring out as he alone could the agonies of desolation through which he had come." And we glimpse her in middle life in a few casual words set down by William James in a letter: "Mother is recovering from one of her indispositions, which she bears like an angel, doing any amount of work at the same time, putting up cornices and raking out the garret-room like a little buffalo." Mary James herself left this brief self-sketch in a letter to William: "The poor old Mater wears well I am happy to say; strong in the back, strong in the nerves, and strong in the legs so far, and equal to her day." She was indeed equal; and the emphasis must be placed, perhaps, on the phrase "strong in the nerves."

During the early years of the marriage the family tore up its roots continually so that Henry Junior was later to speak of himself and his brothers and sister as having been "hotel children." In addition to moves between New York and Albany there were two trips to Europe, major undertakings for that time, with sojourns in England, France and Switzerland. The young children had to be cared for under conditions of travel far-removed from the modern trans-Atlantic liner and in an era when the stage coach and carriage were still important adjuncts to the primitive railroads. Mary James always had the domestic help she required and took an American nursemaid with her to Europe when the children were small. She also engaged indigenous assistance—French maids, governesses, tutors. In addition she was aided by her only sister, Catherine Walsh, the "Aunt Kate" of Henry James's letters and

memoirs. Her lot, thus, was eased considerably by her husband's comfortable means; but there were always responsibilities and worries, illnesses and accidents. The older sons suffered ill-health through their young manhood; the two younger boys went off to the Civil War and were physically broken by it and the daughter suffered a series of nervous breakdowns that left her a chronic invalid.

Despite these cares there were the compensations of a busy maternal life: she took justifiable pride in her growing children; she was surrounded by affection; she was devoted to her husband and wrote of him with deep feeling: "All that he has to say seems so good and glorious and easily understood to him, but it falls so dead upon the dull or skeptical ears who come to hear him . . ." She participated in his dream of a Heaven on earth:

. . . my dear Henry and I have lately been receiving a whole flood of light and joy and hope . . . by an insight into the glorious plans and prospects which Fourier opens for the world. Henry has been reading to me a most charming little book by Mad. Gatti de Gamond and translated by our old friend Mrs. Chichester. As fiction it is more beautiful than any romance I have ever read, but if true (and I feel that it must be so, or if not, as my hopeful loving Henry says, something much better must be) it will not only banish from the world, poverty with its long list of debasing evils, but it will remove every motive to cruelty, injustice and oppression to which the present disordered state of society has given birth and nourished in the selfish heart of man . . .

Her novelist son described her as always sitting on the steps of her husband's "temple" of Swedenborg, which stood in "the centre of our family," catching the "reverberations of the inward mystic choir." Apparently the reverberations sufficed. The father once said, with the extraordinary candor characteristic of him, that his wife had not been "intellectually speaking" a "liberal education" to him—but, he added, "she really did arouse my heart. . . ."

III

In her later years Mary James devoted every Sunday morning to the writing of letters to her scattered sons, dispensing brief, factual reports of the local happenings in Cambridge, interlarding counsel with concern about health and with affectionate platitudes and in general revealing those attributes we would associate with a "typical" American mother who has a firm hold on her family. She speaks in one of these of "my pen which runs so fluently and lovingly every *Sunday* . . . over a full sheet, sometimes more." The letters are indeed fluent, but literal, the spelling not always certain, the formulations homely, prosaic, the handwriting precise, sharp, thin. "God bless you my darling boys and help you to be manly and generous in your intercourse with one another and with all about you. . . ." "All are well—Father has gotten over his sleeplessness and Aunt Kate is flourishing. . . ." "Deal honestly with yourself and with us, and try and observe closely what effect perfect rest has upon you, and act accordingly. . . ." "Harry went to Newport for a few days, Mrs. Frank Shaw is there. Your Boston friends keep you *au courant* of what is going on there. There is no news here. Love from all."

Not all her letters had such a homely, gossipy air. She could smother Henry with maternal solicitude and denounce William, during his prolonged period of ill-health, as a too-articulate hypochondriac. "The trouble with him is that he *must express* every fluctuation of feeling and especially every unfavorable symptom," she wrote to Henry. "He keeps his good looks, but whenever he speaks of himself, says he is no better. This I cannot believe to be the true state of the case, but his temperament is a morbidly hopeless one, and with this he has to contend all the time, as well as with his physical disability." In a later letter she says: "If, dear Harry, you could only have imparted to him a few grains of your own blessed hopefulness, he would have been well long ago." Her characterization of her oldest son at a difficult point in his life has a quality that we cannot associate with a "self-effacing" mother any more than we can the possessiveness she showed toward her

second son. She tells him shortly after he has settled in London that what is lacking in his life is the affection she could give him were he at home ". . . your life must need this succulent, fattening element more than you know yourself. . . ." Since she cannot be with him in England, she offers him the familiar motherly counsel that he take a wife: "You know Father used to say to you, that if you would only fall in love it would be the making of you. . . ."

When William was twenty-six and travelling in Germany, the admonition came from Quincy Street: "Beware dear Willy of the fascinations of Fräulein Clara Schmidt, or any other such artful charmers. You know your extreme susceptibility, or rather I know it, so I say *beware*." And when Henry at thirty was travelling in Italy and Switzerland, he was still receiving counsel: "You will without doubt fall some day soon into the arms of Mrs. Lombard and Fanny, who I am told are to spend the summer in Montreux. They are both I imagine great invalids, so avoid committing yourself further than you can help with them." Or she might simply complain, in a manner likely to arouse distinct feelings of guilt or uneasiness in her favorite son: "Another mail dear Harry, and no letter. I am trying not to be anxious."

There was something strong-yet-yielding, firm-yet-soft about Mary James. Behind the façade of "selflessness" was a quiet method of holding the "firm rein" of which she boasted. She was, in Henry's words "our protecting spirit, our household genius" and yet there was an ambiguous quality about her protection. She could voice opposition to her children's ideas or plans, yet if in turn she was firmly resisted, she could yield with confusing promptness. She was inconsistent in her firmness; and this firmness itself was in contradiction with her husband's theory that children should be "free and uncommitted." A parental tug-and-pull upon the emotions of their offspring that was alike irrational and anxiety-provoking gives a deep significance to Henry James's remark in later years that in childhood "we wholesomely breathed inconsistency and ate and drank contradictions." When he was

younger he did not find this "wholesome." On the contrary it
showed a too-generous contempt for facts. His life was to be a long
search to understand this perversely ambiguous world of his childhood.

I V

In retrospect Henry James was conscious of "our sense of her
gathered life in us and of her having no other . . . " He also describes his mother as the "so widely open yet so softly enclosing
lap" of his father's "liberties and all our securities. . . ." Thus in
the junior Henry's picture the mother envelops the family, the father disappears in her "enclosing lap," the children are taken up
in her softness and she becomes all-encompassing. "She *was* he,
was each of us," he wrote after she had been dead thirty years.
"She was patience, she was wisdom, she was exquisite maternity," he had written at the time of her death. This is an exaltation
of the mother to a supremacy not uncommon in American house-
holds. Nevertheless it is striking that both Henry and William
James, who talked often of their father in later years, had little to
say of the mother. And when Henry came to write of his parents
in *Notes of a Son and Brother* he gave her only a few ambiguous
paragraphs. When his nephew, William's oldest son, inquired into
the reason for this, the answer was: "Oh! my dear Boy—that
memory is too sacred."

The memory undoubtedly was "sacred." Yet the remark could
also have been an evasion, for the brief passages concerning the
mother in the autobiographies reveal to us to some extent Henry
James's difficulty in seeing her as she really was. He tries with all
his artistic honesty: he asks questions, he wonders, he justifies, but
mainly he idealizes. We may speculate that he experienced difficulty simply because he was emotionally confused by his memories of his mother and rather than record the confusion he took
refuge in the "sacredness" of the tomb. The confusion, however,
does emerge in spite of himself, and nowhere more sharply than
when he begins to muse about her identity. "The only thing I might

well have questioned . . . was the possibility on the part of a self-lessness so consistently and unabatedly active, of its having any-thing ever left *acutely* to offer. . . ." He refers to this also as her "inaptness for the personal claim" and leaves us wondering how much Mary James did "offer." He tries to explain: "She lived in ourselves so exclusively with such a want of use for anything in her consciousness that was not about us and for us, that I think we almost contested her being separate enough to be proud of us—it was too like our being proud of ourselves." It is almost as if he were saying that without her family Mary James ceased to have a personality and ceased, also, to be an individual.

She makes her sole appearance in *Notes of a Son and Brother* as a "pipeline" or conveyor of "Father's ideas" to her son—ideas he held himself "little framed to share." It was the way in which she listened to her husband with her "complete availability" that gave them some meaning for Henry Junior. He pictures Mary James as a support "on which my father rested with the absolute whole of his weight." She listened with the "whole of her useful-ness" and also "the whole of her tenderness" and "with a smooth-ness of surrender that was like an array of all the perceptions."

Henry Junior saw his father as living only by his mother and what he observed as a small boy was borne out for him when fully grown. After his mother's death, the father was incapable of going on without her: "he passed away or went out, with entire simplicity, promptness and ease, for the definite reason that his support had failed." It showed the son "more intimately still what, in this world of cleft components, one human being can yet be for an-other, and how a form of vital aid may have operated for years with such perfection. . . ." However much the father was an in-dividual in his own right, robust and essentially active, what struck the small boy was his dependency on Mary James. He gives us a vivid glimpse of a little parental drama. The children were allowed to go to ballets and plays but not to the elder Henry's lec-tures. He remembered his mother putting him to bed and then leaving with the father. Henry Junior climbs down to the parlor

in the Fourteenth Street house and from the window watches the departure. (We are, so to speak, in the opening pages of *Du Côté de Chez Swann*.) There is a little act of pantomime at the carriage door. By the light of the street lamp the father produces from a coat-tail pocket his lecture notes and shakes them in the face of his companion. The mother is the central figure in the pantomime. It is she, earnest and confident, who makes sure that the father has forgotten nothing.

It was the father who, at Christmas, weakened and gave his children a snatched view of the packaged gifts with the adjuration not to tell the mother. It was to the father that little Alice wrote: "We have had two dear letters from you and find you are the same dear old good-for-nothing home-sick papa as ever." His homesickness was but one of the established family jokes. Henry Junior remembered that "we all used brutally to jeer at him; and I doubtless as hard as the rest." The son records a crucial instance. "The happiest household pleasantry invested our legend of our mother's fond habit of address, 'Your father's *ideas*, you know—!' which was always the signal for our embracing her with the last responsive finality (and, for the full pleasure of it, in his presence). Nothing indeed so much as his presence encouraged the license. . . ."

"We were delightedly derisive with her," Henry adds, "even about pride in our father." We pause over the pleasure the son derived from this good-humored defiance and mockery of the parent and especially at the supreme moment of embracing the mother "in his presence." That Henry Junior should have made a point of this, records it all the more as a triumph of possession and of alliance with strength against what seemed to him weakness. William James participated in such occasions as well. Once when the father was at work on one of his abstruse volumes William sketched the frontispiece for it: a picture of a man flogging a dead horse! The household pleasantries, however bright and funny, were not without an undertone of contempt.

Before the little boy's observant eyes there was this ever-present picture of ambiguity and reversal of relation: a father strong, ro-

bust, manly, yet weak and feminine, soft and yielding, indulging his children at every turn; and a mother, strong, firm, but irrational and contradictory. It is no suprise to us therefore to discover this formulated in the opening pages of Henry James's first major novel. Ralph Touchett, musing about his parents in *The Portrait of a Lady* thinks with fondness of his father who "ministered most to his sense of the sweetness of filial dependence. His father," the novelist adds, "as he had often said to himself, was the more motherly; his mother, on the other hand, was paternal, and even, according to the slang of the day, gubernatorial." In the guise of fiction it was much easier for Henry to describe the observations of his boyhood; and behind the elaborate formulations of *Notes of a Son and Brother*, this is, in effect, what he is trying to say to us many years later.

v

It was easy enough for the future novelist to accept the Queenship of his mother and her authority; it was less easy to understand the strange light in which this reversal of parental roles placed the father. The portrait that Henry James drew of his father in *Notes of a Son and Brother* some sixty years removed from childhood accurately reflects the ambiguity a child would experience in discovering the male parent in such a situation. Behind the warm show of tenderness and affection, reflecting his conscious feelings towards the senior Henry, we catch his uncertainty and emotional confusion. Every now and again the father peeps from behind his son's flowing sentences as a rather ineffectual old man; and Henry occasionally slips in an undesigned word of mild contempt. "Our dear parent . . ." we find him saying at one point, "could have told us very little, in all probability, under whatever pressure, what had become of anything." He "could answer . . . with the radiant when one challenged him with the obscure"; he also responded "with the general when one pulled at the particular." It was a matter of concern to the little Henry that he could not give his father a paternal identity that conformed with the

identity of other fathers. The senior Henry seemed unlike them in more respects than that of his missing limb. Henry Junior pressed him to say how he could describe him to his schoolfellows. "Say I'm a philosopher, say I'm a seeker for truth, say I'm a lover of my kind, say I'm an author of books if you like; or best of all, just say I'm a student." This was hardly helpful, Henry ruefully felt, when other boys could describe their fathers as merchants, doctors or lawyers. The father listed no occupation for himself in the New York directory until 1854-55 when he finally inserted "author" after his name.

We have no evidence as to Henry Junior's feelings concerning his father's amputated state.* He makes no allusion to it save as "a grave accident in early life" in A *Small Boy*. In *Notes of a Son and Brother* however he does specify that the accident "lamed him for life." In this volume he equates the lameness with his father's inability to be a large literary success. In fact he begins the portrait of the elder Henry with the observation that his writings brought him "no ghost of a reward." He then goes on to describe the good qualities in his prose but criticizes him for not having a characteristic "style." "I so suffered . . . under the impression of his style, which affected me as somehow too philosophic for life, and at the same time too living . . . for thought." It is " monotonous" and "verbally repetitive" and he records a "shade of irritation" at finding it "narrow," devoid of imagery and above all lacking in variety. His father was not explicit and his books did not sell. And he wonders whether there is any relationship between his father's crippled state and his apparent ineffectuality.

. . . .

* William James's interest in amputated persons is attested by a paper entitled "The Consciousness of Lost Limbs" (*Proceedings of the American Society for Psychical Research*, Vol. I, No. 3). In writing this paper William sent out a questionnaire and interviewed a number of amputated persons, collating the replies of 185 of these. There is an apparent allusion to the elder Henry James when William mentions that "The oldest case I have is that of a man who had had a thigh amputation performed at the age of thirteen years, and who, after he was seventy, affirmed his feeling of the lost foot to be still every whit as distinct as his feeling of the foot which remained."

Henry decides that there is. "The two acceptances melt together for me—that of the limits of his material action, his doing and enjoying, set so narrowly, and that of his scant allowance of 'public recognition' or of the support and encouragement that spring, and spring so naturally and rightly" from a message "richly and sincerely urged." Fortunately his father's daily bread did not depend on his writing although he wrote, Henry explains, as if it did. The novelist was recording this fact in the knowledge that in this respect he had far out-distanced the father. What the son overlooked was how successful, within its limits, his father's life had been despite his accident, what resources of fortitude and faith he had even if his books were obscure. In his middle years the son also was to struggle with the problem of "public recognition" but on grounds other than a physical infirmity.

VI

From the day-dreams recorded in his notebooks, from his tales, from his observations in the memoirs, we can fathom the effect on the young Henry of this view of the parental relationship which remained with him throughout his life. At some stage the thought came to him that men derive strength from the women they marry and that conversely women can deprive men of their strength and life. Mothers—women—apparently were expected to give themselves wholly, submerge themselves (he uses the word *availability* twice in describing Mary James) in their family. Men used women, were propped by them and sometimes could not go on living after the woman was dead. This meant that women could control the lives of men and this he believed was what happened to his father. A father demanded the mother's complete attention ("the whole of her usefulness . . . the whole of her tenderness"). Similarly women could command the abject worship of men.

This led to further considerations. What happens to anyone who gives himself to another? To love—was not that to renounce? Did not the mother give all of herself? What did she have left *acutely* to offer? Selfless, sleepless, soundless . . . ("There are few things

more soundless," Henry wrote in one of his novels "than a deep devotion.") Is the man therefore a threat to the woman in a love relationship? (It was clear enough to him that the woman could be a threat to the man.) Would the man collapse and become weak (like the senior Henry) if he ever allowed himself to love a woman? To be a man and to take a woman for wife—was that not something to be feared? might it not mean collapse into a stultifying dependency—and one in which love and death seemed to be coupled? In the James family annals there seemed to be answers: women were strong and survived their men, or if they did not, then somehow the men could not continue to live. In either case the man seemed doomed. The Grandmother James had lived on in triumphant old age reading the lady novelists with a tall candle set straight between her eyes and the page. Mary James was strong— the father revealed this by all his words and deeds—and when she died the Sacred Fount from which the father had derived life and strength was dried up. There was his mother's cousin Helen, whose husband, was a "spectral spouse," a "dim little gentleman." Once a seafaring man, he walked the length of his two parlors as if they were the deck of a ship; and Cousin Helen ruled her wards, Albert and Henry, with an iron hand. On all sides strong-minded firm-handed women swallowing up their men.

The considerations thus formulated undoubtedly were not reasoned in this form by Henry James: they emerge however as fictional themes: and in particular, what we might call the "Vampire Theme," elaborated in three of his works, early, middle and late, recording the observed reality of his father's subservience to his mother and the perhaps less consciously observed fashion in which she in turn took strength from him. In "De Grey: A Romance," a blood-and-thunder short story written when he was twenty-six, an old family curse destines brides of the De Greys to early death. When the curse is resisted it is reversed; De Grey himself must die. The prospect of marriage proves fatal in this case for the man. In "Longstaff's Marriage" written at thirty-five, Longstaff is dying of his love for Diana but recovers miraculously when she rejects

him; then it is she who fades and dies. The prospect of marriage can prove fatal to a man unless the woman is removed. And finally in the short novel of Henry James's fifty-seventh year, *The Sacred Fount*, the theme attains its full morbidity: an acute and hypersensitive observer spends a week-end in a country house studying what he believes to be a young man drained of his youth by an older wife who grows younger in the process, while another man is acquiring intelligence and wit from a brilliant female companion who grows dull and is drained of all intellect. From *Roderick Hudson* to *The Ambassadors* and in the *nouvelles* and tales the permutations and combinations of this situation are played out: at all times the observer is obsessed by the relationships between people as if the little Henry, observing his father and mother, had never quite apprehended what occurred between them. Mothers in James's novels are sometimes the negative and long-suffering Mrs. Hudsons or the unperceptive Mrs. Millers, or sometimes terrifying creatures who dominate the lives of their progeny. Both types mirror the two aspects of Mary James. Fear of women and worship of women: the love theme plays itself out in striking fashion throughout Henry James's work. And usually love, in these fictions, as one critic has put it, is "a deterrent to the full life." It is more: it is a threat to life itself.

In a list of names he set down in his notebooks when he was fifty, Henry James included that of "Ledward" and then, as was often his custom, he improvised several variants, apparently as they came into his mind: "Ledward—Bedward—Dedward—Deadward." This appeared to be a casual rhyming of led-bed-dead. It was, in effect, a highly-condensed statement springing from Henry's mind of the theme of "De Grey," "Longstaff," *The Sacred Fount* or that story of Merimée's he had liked so much in his youth, "*La Vénus d'Ille.*" To be led to the marriage bed was to be dead.

Henry James accordingly chose the path of safety. He remained celibate.

MERE JUNIOR

THE MALE CHILD BORN IN 1843 IN WASHINGTON PLACE WAS NAMED Henry after the father, even as his older brother had been named William after the grandfather. For the next forty years the novelist was destined to be known as Henry James Junior. All his works, up to and including *The Portrait of a Lady*, carried the junior label on their title pages. Throughout his life Henry volubly protested against the parental failure to let him have a distinctive name and (by the same token) an identity of his own. He pleaded always with vehemence against the conferring of juniorhood upon a "helpless babe." When William James's second son was about to be named William (the first having been promptly named Henry) the novelist sent a fervent plea from London to Cambridge adjuring his brother to cut short the family confusion. William, however, paid no heed. The new William James grew to manhood, married, had a son. And the novelist, by now an Olympian of three score and ten, promptly renewed his plea to the new generation, this time in two thousand vigorous words, against a practice to which he could never be reconciled. He had argued that the name given to a child can affect his whole life, and now he couldn't "but feel sorry that you are embarking upon that unfortunate *mere* junior. I have a right to speak of that appendage—I carried it about for forty years . . . disliking it all the while, and with my dislike never in the least understood or my state pitied. . . ." But it was to no avail. The "interminable career of the tiresome and graceless 'Juniors'" clearly could not be arrested in the James family.

As late as 1882, the year of the elder Henry's death, the father and son were being taken for one another since they both wrote and published and on occasions appeared in the same table of contents of the *Atlantic Monthly*. This resulted on one occasion in a critic incongruously congratulating Mr. Henry James on his

travel essay, "Roman Rides," written in his "usually charming graceful style" and on "another article in quite a different vein entitled 'Modern Diabolism,' which is interesting and very original." Mary James quite justifiably commented to her son, "You will each soon be groaning under this double weight of honor." There exists a letter of 1882 in which Henry Junior gives his father's address to an autograph seeker who had written to him in error. It was not, however, the confusion of names that really agitated the novelist. Some sons are proud to bear their father's given name and Henry was protesting through no lack of filial devotion. Deeply emotional reasons as well as practical ones are reflected in the acute feeling he conveyed in his various appeals. Foremost among these was his struggle in that family of competing egos to find his own identity. William's name recalled the long-dead Albany grandfather. Garth Wilkinson James, born after Henry in 1845, honored an English thinker, a Swedenborgian. Robertson, the youngest boy, born in Albany in 1846, was named after the maternal grandfather. Henry alone had a shared name within the family circle. The very word "junior" had a diminishing sound, at least to the novelist. His dislike of the "appendage" is clearly evident in the signature he evolved up to the time of his father's death. Use of the "Jr." often caused him to curtail the first name to an initial. At first the "Jr." was quite legible and in early days even written out in full. As the years passed it was finally reduced to an unreadable flourish over which floated a seemingly inexplicable dot—sole evidence that he intended the letter "j" to be there.

The dot and the flourish were dropped upon the death of Henry Senior and the novelist thereafter wrote his name in full, large letters. Yet when, at sixty, he revisited America he scrawled across the top of one of the scribblers that served him as notebook "H. James Jr. Journal, March 1905." Here indeed was a return to the past. Rediscovering "home" after his prolonged absence (he had been away ever since the year of his father's death) he retraced the familiar, the disliked signature, that of his younger self

—and reduced the Henry again, for the first time in decades, to an initial.

I

Readers of Henry James's novels and tales discover at every turn the writer's predilection for second sons. Sometimes he kills off older brothers or turns them into villains; sometimes his hero is an only son, usually with a widowed mother. He thus confers on them an ideal fatherless and brotherless state. In his memoirs he has told us how he envied his orphaned cousins: "parentally bereft cousins were somehow more thrilling than parentally provided ones." They constituted his first childish conception of the possibilities residing in their "enviable lot . . . to be so little fathered and mothered."

Thus Henry James's first major hero, in his first important novel, *Roderick Hudson,* is the second son of a Virginia slaveholder. His "ugly-faced" older brother has been killed in the Civil War. (In later editions of this novel, Henry indulgently altered the description to "plain-faced.") "I have to fill a double place," Roderick explains. "I have to be my brother as well as myself. . . . I was the curled darling. . . . I stayed indoors to be kissed by the ladies while he made mud-pies in the garden. . . . He was worth fifty of me!" Significantly Roderick, on arriving in Rome, executes first a statue of Adam and then one of Eve. Having thus created the father and mother of mankind he identifies himself promptly with their oldest son.

Abel doesn't interest him. However: "I have been thinking lately of making a Cain, but I should never dream of making him ugly. He should be a very handsome fellow, and he should lift up the murderous club with the beautiful movement of the fighters in the Greek friezes who are chopping at their enemies." Valentin de Bellegarde, in *The American,* embodies grace and romantic charm; need we add that he is a second son? and that his older brother, the Marquis, is a monument of fatuity and corruption? Owen Wingrave, in the ghostly tale, has an older brother who has been com-

mitted to an asylum, and his father was killed by a sabre thrust in India. Morgan Moreen of "The Pupil" is the sensitive and perceptive member of a mendacious family whose first-born, Ulick Moreen, is anemic and ineffectual, with a "buttonhole but feebly floral and a mustache with no pretensions to type." But it is in the late novel, *The Wings of the Dove,* that he gives us a concrete reflection of the feeling of fraternal inferiority he harbored in the depths of his consciousness. Kate Croy, lives in "a state of abasement as the second born, her life reduced to mere inexhaustible sisterhood."

For Henry, life in the James family, was a state of mere inexhaustible brotherhood, as if, he wrote in *A Small Boy,* William "had gained such an advantage of me in his sixteen months' experience of the world before mine began that I never for all the time of childhood and youth in the least caught up with him or overtook him." William was "always round the corner and out of sight, coming back into view but at his hours of extremest ease. We were never in the same schoolroom, in the same game, scarce even in step together or in the same phase at the same time; when our phases overlapped, that is, it was only for a moment— he was clean out before I had got well in." The image of an absent, elusive, distant William persisted to the end. The novelist "seems often to think that my father is here, *tho' not in the same room,*" William's oldest son wrote during Henry James's last illness.

Thus on the ninth page of the novelist's memoirs is established that difference between himself and his older brother which constitutes the refrain of the autobiographies—sometimes good-humored, sometimes a trifle mocking, but mostly filled with self-pity and utter "abasement." Henry was not alone in this curious feeling of "inexhaustible" brotherhood in that emotionally stimulated family. A fragment of reminiscence left by the youngest brother, Robertson, who was a highly gifted and poetic individual, similarly illuminates the fraternal and familial relationships. "I often like to contemplate myself as a baby and wonder if I was really as lit-

tle appreciated as I fully remember feeling at that time. . . .
At a very early age the problems of life began to press upon me
in such an unnatural way and I developed such an ability for
feeling hurt and wounded that I became quite convinced by the
time I was twelve years old that I was a foundling." These are
strong feelings to have been carried—as they were both by Henry
and Robertson—into old age; they reflect indeed the way in which
the rivalries of the nursery common to all children can linger and
emerge in later life.

The very titles of the memoirs, A *Small Boy and Others* and
Notes of a Son and Brother reflect Henry's need to put himself
into the forefront of the family picture. What he described as
"an attempt to place together some particulars of the early life of
William James" emerged as autobiography. Henry responded
to an overwhelming need to make himself instead of William the subject of the book. It is Henry who is the Small Boy;
and it is Henry, not William, who looks out at us from the Matthew Brady daguerreotype which serves as frontispiece—looks at
us with a gentle, quiet stare from bright boyish eyes, his hand rest-
ing on his father's shoulder. We may indeed rejoice that the novelist chose to give us autobiography rather than biography for that
circumstance resulted in a remarkable recreation of a childhood,
but we must note at the same time the curious nature of the circumstance. By the end of the volume the Small Boy has reached
his teens and the account of William remains to be written; the
broad background of their common childhood has been brilliantly
established but this, however, on Henry's, not William's terms.*

A second volume thus became imperative. Once again Henry
took the foreground for himself. *Notes of a Son and Brother* are,
of course, Henry's notes. He argued that the only honest picture
he could give of William and his father was in the light of his
own observation and relationship to them, and he freely altered

. . . .

* Usually accurate in dating events, the novelist errs in giving the date of
William's birth in this book—January 9 instead of January 11, 1842.

the texts of their letters, from which he quoted. He was yielding, however, to dictates deeper than these, which belong to the craft of authorship. The others were of a psychological order and they are revealed to the full in the contents of the two volumes: Henry's buried sense of his subordinate position alike to father and brother. The terms in which he talks of his father, a mixture of admiration and of mild indulgence and depreciation, and of his brother, a mixture of affection and praise always coupled with humility, tell a story that the author never intended us to know, nor indeed was fully aware of himself.

II

We are confronted with brotherly rivalry at the start of A *Small Boy* when Henry is brought crying and kicking to the Dutch House in Albany—that house which James described with care in the opening pages of *The Portrait of a Lady*. Isabel Archer's revolt against attending it is not explained in detail* by her creator; but in A *Small Boy* he makes it amply clear why little Henry James, aged five or six, rebelled. The rage that welled to the surface in the form of kicks and screams in front of the yellow-painted colonial structure was provoked by the discovery that William was there ahead of him, seated at his desk, serene and "in possession." Henry's vocal retreat left William "once for all already there, an embodied demonstration" that Henry was foredoomed to arrive invariably "belatedly and ruefully. . . ."

The infantile Henry revolted; the adolescent sought equality when he and William were in Geneva and attained it when he was able to attend the Academy where William had been enrolled ahead of him; then, during their young manhood, at Newport, he picked up pencil and paint brush, seeking to emulate his senior

· · · · · · · · · ·

* In early editions of the novel James merely stated that "having spent a single day" in the school Isabel "expressed great disgust with the place, and had been allowed to stay at home." In the New York Edition this was altered to "having spent a single day in it, she had protested against its laws and had been allowed to stay at home. . . ."

who was studying art in William Morris Hunt's studio (William drew "because he could, while I did so in the main only because he did.") Later still, when William went to Harvard, Henry in due course followed him there. His brother's pasture always seemed greenest until he actually reached it and then, feeling himself "outclassed" by William, he had to turn away.

The terms in which he described his descent upon Harvard at twenty, written half a century later, show how the old feelings, however submerged, persisted. William was studying medicine and Henry, who briefly attended the Law School, could have created an independent student career. Nevertheless he recalls his student days almost exclusively as a relationship with his brother in which he played the inferior role. He describes William's easy faculty for taking hold of an environment in a desire to demonstrate his admirably alert qualities of mind and his capacity for gregarious association with his fellows. What he conveys, however, even more, under the guise of a generous acceptance of his own inferiority, is his insecurity in the same environment.

"At Cambridge of course"—and the "of course" is intended to denote the inevitability of it—" I . . . was further to find my brother on the scene and already at a stage of possession of its contents that I was resigned in advance never to reach; so thoroughly I seemed to feel a sort of quickening savoury meal in any cold scrap of his own experience that he might pass on to my palate." He fed himself on "the crumbs" of William's feast and upon "the echoes of his life." This is a tribute to William but a curious self-portrait. If it lends emphasis on the one hand to the respect inspired in him by his brother's *savoir faire* it suggests a disagreeable humility. There were many ways in which the seventy-year-old Henry James could have sketched his relationship to William; and yet the picture evoked, even if we allow it to whimsicality or irony or euphemism, is that of a groveling beggar picking up cold scraps and crumbs from a brother's table and finding life in the echoes of his senior's undergraduate occupations. Here indeed was the complete abasement of younger brotherhood.

Henry does not stop here. He announces that he wished to live, if only "by the imagination, in William's adaptive skin." He thus characterizes himself as unadaptive, aloof, lacking in William's social qualities, and expresses clearly what he has always wanted to be—his brother. What else could he be if he were in his brother's skin?

III

William had been taken first to the theatre while little Henry was left at home by the lamplight in a "vivid vigil" to imagine the stage and the actors and to nurse "my view of paternal discrimination." William had presided authoritatively over boyish games. William pointedly put Henry in his place with "I play with boys who curse and swear!" when Henry proposed to accompany him. Henry, of course, didn't curse and swear. And the old man, remembering his older brother's insult, looked self-pityingly at his younger self and added: "All boys, I rather found, were difficult to play with. . . ." (An analogous reminiscence is to be found in the father's autobiography in which he testified that he "now and then violently repelled the overtures of a younger brother who aspired to associate himself with me in my sports and pastimes.")

This was not the only remembered instance in which William aggressively rejected his younger brother. The philosopher recalled later in life how Henry, combining authorship with his attempts at drawing, sketched a mother and child clinging to a rock in the midst of a stormy ocean. Beneath the drawing he bravely wrote: "The thunder roared and the lightning followed." We might pause here over Henry's choice of subject: the image of a child clinging to a mother in the fearsome surroundings of a tempest—a dramatization of fear and dependency. But it was not the subject which arrested the precise and scientifically-minded William when he came upon the young author-illustrator. That Henry should put thunder before lightning was a meteorological blunder inviting high derision. It is not in the nature of elder brothers to correct the mistakes of their juniors with indulgence. With all the weight

of his seniority, William pounced upon Henry's work and tormented his brother to such an extent that he promptly enacted a portion of his story. He ran for maternal protection. William was punished for his too enthusiastic display of his exact knowledge at Henry's expense. If the incident ended in triumph for the younger brother, it emphasized once again the elder's overlordship. It may well explain, in part, the reticence and secrecy with which Henry surrounded his literary efforts both early and late. There had been too many prying brothers, too much merciless criticism and childish lampooning. Garth Wilkinson, who was in turn Henry's junior (and described by him as my "extremely easy yokefellow and playfellow"*) reported to T. S. Perry in 1860 from Geneva: "Harry has become an author I believe, for he keeps his door locked all day long . . ." Apparently at sixteen and seventeen the feuding continued, for Wilky also reported that "Willy and Harry have been getting along very well indeed this last winter" which suggested other winters when there was less well getting along. William was to continue to the very end of his life to be a sharp and not always friendly critic of Henry's work.

I V

We are indebted to T. S. Perry for a significant glimpse of Henry at Newport. ". . . When we got to the house and the rest of us were chattering, Henry James sat on the window-seat reading Leslie's *Life of Constable* with a certain air of remoteness." There lay escape from the frustrations of his juniorhood: in books, in the imagination, in writing. He couldn't draw like William, but he could read books about art and artists. He couldn't act, or felt that he couldn't, but he could invent stories about himself doing some of the things his brother did. William could be impulsive, filling each moment with imagination translated into action. Henry, possessing an equal capacity for action, translated it into
. . . .

* Henry James wrote that he had during those years "one exposure, rather the northward, as it were, to the view of W. J., and the other, perhaps the more immediately sunned surface, to the genial glow of my junior."

imagination; he discovered that there was a virtue to immobility: if he could not participate in William's adventures he could actively employ his mental resources: he could observe, and his memory clung tenaciously to all that it absorbed. They might urge upon him greater activity; he sat back and looked, looked at everything with the calm yet hungry eyes of childhood and the aid of his fostered and stimulated imagination. It is no surprise that he attached so much importance to his eyes—that the heroes he most identified himself with were those he endowed with the finest perception and that he gave first place always to his "observer" in his fiction and to the "point of view" from which he narrated his tales.

The evidence of Henry James's life points to a curiously paradoxical element in his personality: he was an active and masculine individual who finding direct action impossible—and with this direct expression of his individuality—realized this activity and individuality through a prodigiously creative and highly productive art, while remaining to all appearances passive in the extreme. The small boy cultivated a quiet aloofness; nothing would happen to him if he withdrew and used his eyes and his mind in that turbulent family. Inside the little mind great worlds were created, great achievements, great aggressions planned. For frustration, engendering aloofness, engendered also rebellion, and rebellion in turn had to be smothered to maintain his façade of passivity. He confessed late in life that his favorite fairy tale in childhood had been "Hop-o'-my-Thumb." Little Hop-'o understandably caught Henry's young imagination; is he not the merest of mere juniors and yet the greatest of little adventurers? Youngest of seven boys, deserted with his brothers by his parents, and yet a monument of resourcefulness, he takes charge—becoming thus Senior instead of Junior—outwits the ogre, obtains possession of the Seven League Boots and ends up as the benefactor of his entire family, including his unhappy parents. "It is the vague memory of this sense of him," James wrote, "as some small precious object, like a lost gem or a rare and beautiful insect on which one might inadvertently tread, or might find under the sofa or behind the window-cushion,

that leads me to think of *Hop 'o my Thumb* as my earliest and sweetest and most repeated cupful at the fount of fiction." But it was not Hop-'o's *smallness* alone that counted; it was that, being tiny, he yet conquered worlds. And Henry James, reduced to inexhaustible younger brotherhood, making himself small and quiet among the other Jameses, turned into the depths of himself to fashion a fictional world based on the realities around him in which older brothers were vanquished, fathers made to disappear, mothers put into their place. But it was not as easy as all that. Such day-dream accomplishments—and aggressions—had their concomitant fears and anxieties and guilts, the criss-cross of emotion within the outwardly serene little boy. Yet in this fashion, by controlling his environment, suppressing his hostilities, electing the observer's role, rather than the actor's, he was able to act in his own highly personal way and conquer. He came to be his mother's favorite son. He was called "angel" in the family circle. At the time of his parents' death he had achieved international celebrity; he had surpassed his older brother who was to win renown some fifteen years after Henry's first novel was published. The elder Henry, shortly before his death, wrote to the son that bore his name: "I can't help feeling that you are the one that has cost us the least trouble, and given us always the most delight. Especially do I mind mother's perfect joy in you the last few months of her life, and your perfect sweetness to her."

The victory within the family was complete. But beyond the family lay the great outer world, hard and competitive, and it would have to be faced in a new struggle—it was really a renewal of the old. Henry James was to discover that one could cease writing the Junior after the name and still have to go on contending with the problems that had prevailed when it was there. And he was to discover that the mask of immobility, the maneuver to control the environment, did not always succeed. Sometimes the people and the surroundings defied control. Nevertheless, a personality had been moulded in this difficult familial process—and an artist as well.

Henry James tells his London publisher (Macmillan),
in a letter from Boston after his father's death, that he
has dropped the "Jr."

NOTES ON A NIGHTMARE

IN THE OPENING PAGES OF "A SMALL BOY AND OTHERS" HENRY JAMES
set forth explicitly his sense of being a perpetual younger brother
forever in pursuit of William who had the good fortune to arrive

in the world sixteen months ahead of him. This passage comes to mind as 350 pages later we reach the vivid account of a nightmare dreamed by him many years after childhood and never forgotten. The remembered dreams of our lives are comparatively few and seldom recorded; they are evanescent tales told by ourselves to ourselves, built of the tissues of timeless experience. There is no question here of seeking to interpret Henry James's nightmare. It is doubtful whether the most skilful explorers of the unconscious could do very much with it save indulge in gratuitous speculation. We do not know when, or in what circumstances, the nightmare was dreamed. Many years elapsed before it was recorded. It exists, however, as a literary record in a volume crowded with associations and memories and in this context can be studied as we might study any of the tales written by Henry James —as something which sprang from this particular mind and was recorded at a particular time within the frame of this mind's life and experience.

I

He called it a "dream-adventure"—using a descriptive phrase his friend Robert Louis Stevenson had employed in an essay on dreams long before. His recollection of the nightmare was provoked by a memory of visits with William to the Louvre. The train of association that leads him to relate the dream takes us with the two boys as they walk along the Parisian quays during their residence in the French capital in 1856-57 when William James was fourteen and Henry thirteen: their progress from book-stalls to print shops on the Left Bank, their leisurely stroll along the Rue de Seine as "little gaping pilgrims" in high black hats and gloves "the childish costume of the place and period." The distance of Paris traversed, the walk up the Rue de Tournon in its cobbled and grass-grown days past the old Café Foyot at the end of the street and the arrival at the Luxembourg Palace—this route of boyhood happens to be exactly the path trod by Lewis Lambert Strether, the hero of *The Ambassadors*, on his arrival in Paris.

It was a remembered walk and apparently repeated, one of the great walks of Henry's life. In the Luxembourg Palace, which harbored the newer works of art, he saw Couture's "Romains de la Décadence" and remembered that William Morris Hunt, the American painter, had been one of Couture's pupils—Hunt who at Newport later taught William James. Henry invokes also the landscapists Troyon, Rousseau, Daubigny and Lambinet (Lambinet through whom we enter the most remarkable chapter of *The Ambassadors*, Strether's Maupassantesque day along the Seine in the Paris *banlieue*). Henry James recalls that he once visited Couture's studio and wonders how "poetry had swooped down, breathed on him for an hour and fled." Then he turns to a more durable reputation: that of Eugène Delacroix. From the first, he tells us, William had discerned his greatness and had copied his works. ("Eugène Delacroix, our next young admiration, though much more intelligently my brother's than mine . . . an effect of my brother's sureness. . . .") Henry's recollections go back to *his* admiration of work of another order, Paul Delaroche's historical paintings—such as "Les Enfants d'Édouard," the "long-drawn odd face of the elder prince, sad and sore and sick," and his paintings of Lady Jane Grey and of Charles I.

Thus far the recollections are almost entirely of art and great reputations and of William's aspirations to be a painter. Henry's linking of art, artistic reputations and his brother's studies now flow into a recollection of the Louvre to which the boys retraced their steps from the Luxembourg.

Here the profusion of paintings first "simply overwhelmed and bewildered me. It was as if they had gathered there into a vast deafening chorus." Elsewhere he speaks of being at first "appalled" by their assault on his senses. With this comes the memory of the Galerie d'Apollon. At the mention of this great picture-hung gallery, Henry launches into a passage of eloquent rhetorical description not of paintings but of the collective impression of grandeur that transcended the works themselves and which, curiously, he translates into sound:

I shall never forget how—speaking, that is, for my own sense—they filled those vast halls with the influence rather of some complicated sound, diffused and reverberant, than of such visibilities as one could directly deal with. To distinguish among these, in the charged and coloured and confounding air, was difficult—it discouraged and defied; which was doubtless why my impression originally best entertained was that of those magnificent parts of the great gallery simply not inviting us to distinguish. They only arched over us in the wonder of their endless golden riot and relief, figured and flourished in perpetual revolution, breaking into great high-hung circles and symmetries of squandered picture, opening into deep outward embrasures that threw off the rest of monumental Paris somehow as a told story, a sort of wrought effect or bold ambiguity for a vista, and yet held it there, at every point, as a vast bright gage, even at moments a felt adventure, of experience.

Well might this great gallery have inspired such thoughts: its two hundred feet of length seemed endless to the American boy and its vaulted ceiling with its elaborate frescoes evoked bold themes out of mythology. The subjects themselves had a dream-inspiring quality. In the center of the vaulting was a great painting by Delacroix, "Apollo's Victory over the Python." Other subjects were "Night and Dreams," "Evening or Morpheus," "Dawn" painted by Charles Lebrun, architect and artist who rebuilt the Galerie d'Apollon for Louis XIV after it was swept by fire in 1661. Over the entrance was Guichard's "Awakening of the Earth," and over the south window Lebrun's "Awakening of the Waters or the Triumph of Neptune and Amphitrate." Tapestry portraits hung there in rich colors and in glass cases were Byzantine mosaics, Limoges enamels, ecclesiastical ornaments, reliquaries, statuettes, crown jewels, flashing gems—the reflected glory of ancient things

It was here that Henry James discovered for the first time the meaning of "Style." He crossed "that bridge over to Style constituted by the wondrous Galerie d'Apollon." And the bridge to Style, the glorious, ornate hall, led James into a "prodigious tube

or tunnel through which I inhaled little by little, that is again and again, a general sense of *glory*."

"The glory meant ever so many things at once, not only beauty and art and supreme design, but history and fame and power, the world, in fine, raised to the richest and noblest expression." And he adds, after this significant recollection—and reflection— that for the little boy the world meant also the "local present fact, to my small imagination, of the Second Empire." The Galerie d'Apollon, the Apollonian name, thus evokes for us another name synonymous with the Second Empire—Napoleon. Apollon and Napoléon—pronounced in French, as the small boy was able to do, it was almost as if one were saying the same word.

I I

The small boy was in the Paris of the Second Empire. The name of Napoleon was still heard everywhere even if the Napoleonic tradition had shrunk to the stature of Charles-Louis Napoleon. The banners still waved, the eagles still flew, the sound of trumpets still echoed through the streets. Henry glimpsed the pageantry of this era—with its suggestion of "the generations and dynasties and armies, the revolutions and restorations they had seen come and go"—as represented in those paintings at the Luxembourg which recalled princes assassinated and monarchs beheaded. The small boy had watched the infant Prince Imperial out for his airing on the Champs Élysées and in the Tuileries, and his progress through Paris to Saint-Cloud "in the splendid coach that gave a glimpse of appointed and costumed nursing breasts and laps, and beside which the *cent-gardes,* all light-blue and silver and intensely erect quick jolt, rattled with pistols raised and cocked." He remembered the public holiday of the Prince's baptism at Notre Dame, the fête of Saint-Napoléon, which he was later to rediscover in the pages of Zola's *Eugène Rougon,* wondering whether the French novelist had been there in the same crowds, a small future creator of fiction even as the young American. . . . "The sense of that interminable hot day, a day of hanging about and

waiting and shuffling in dust, in crowds, in fatigue, amid booths and pedlars and performers and false alarms and expectations and renewed reactions and rushes, all transfigured at the last, withal, by the biggest and brightest illumination up to that time offered even the Parisians, the blinding glare of the new Empire. . . ."

The elegance of the Second Empire, successor to earlier Imperial glories and harking back to the first Napoleon, stimulated the historic vision of the young boy already steeped in books and plays and acutely conscious of the recent past. In later years he was to read avidly in Napoleonic lore and to count among his acquaintances Bonapartists and Bonaparte Princesses. In his library, at his death, bound in red morocco—a binding he accorded exclusively to his most valued books—were nine volumes of Napoleonic reminiscences and anecdotes which he purchased and devoured during the 1890's. The "general sense of glory" persisted far beyond the years of his childhood. Balzac, who later became his supreme literary model, had placed as a sole ornament in his study in the Rue Cassini a plaster statuette of Napoleon and written under it: *"Ce qu'il n'a pas pu achever par l'épée, je l'accomplirai par la plume."* James also in later life thought of himself as conquering worlds with his pen; the exhortations to himself which he wrote into his notebooks were summonses to literary conquest and power "splendid and supreme creation . . . *à l'oeuvre, mon bon, à l'oeuvre . . . roide!"*

Napoleon represented, in a Europe in which he was but thirty-five years dead when the small boy was there, the power and the glory of a recent and heroic past. If in the Louvre—the Louvre of Napoleon, the gallery of Apollo—Henry James found his initiation to Style, then Style remained associated for him thereafter with the pomp of Imperial power. Were not many of the works of art in the great Palace the fruit of Imperial conquest and reconquest? When Henry years later recalled the old apartment in Paris where he wrote the first portion of *The American*, he remembered the "light of high, narrowish French windows in old rooms,

the light somehow, as one always feels, of 'style' itself." The rooms, we know, were in an old house close by the Place Vendôme with its Napoleonic column recording the great victories of the post-revolutionary era. Style itself, intensity of tone, the "high homely style" of an older day, as he put it in *The Ambassadors*, where his first call on Madame de Vionnet in the Rue de Bellechasse finds Lambert Strether "making out, as a background of the occupant, some glory, some prosperity of the first Empire, some Napoleonic glamour, some dim lustre of the great legend; elements clinging still to all the consular chairs and mythological brasses and sphinxes' heads and faded surfaces of satin striped with alternate silk." Henry James knew the Rue de Bellechasse well: here he had spent evenings in the home of Alphonse Daudet where the memory of the Impératrice was cherished long after the advent of the Third Republic.

The small boy found Napoleonic memories at every turn; not the least significant, during a residence at Boulogne, was that placed on the steep cliff, the monument to the Napoleonic vigil over the Channel with England lying just beyond his reach beyond the water. The monument struck Henry "as futile . . . as that enterprise itself had proved." He had stood and played on the historic ground. History was all around the small boy.

It is in the passage of his memoirs immediately preceding the account of his nightmare, when he muses on Style, that Henry James begins to wonder about "the sources at which an intense young fancy (when a young fancy *is* intense) capriciously, absurdly drinks?—so that the effect is, in twenty connections, that of a love-philtre or fear-philtre which fixes for the senses their supreme symbol of the fair or the strange." In the next sentence he recalls that the Galerie d'Apollon was the scene of the "most appalling yet most admirable nightmare of my life." *Love and fear. Fair and strange. Admirable and appalling.* We weigh these balanced alternatives and antitheses and note that to Apollon and Napoléon we must now add another word—*appalling*. Here is a consonance of syllable and association which emerges in this

closely-woven chapter of reminiscence: Apollon-Napoléon-Apalling the last word many times reiterated; and these can be translated into Art and Love, Power and Glory, Fear and Terror.

III

He is defending himself, in terror, against the attempt of someone to break into his room. He is pressing his shoulder against a door and someone is bearing down on the lock and bolt on the other side. Suddenly the tables are turned. Nightmare is routed. Terror is defied. It is Henry who forces the door open in a burst of aggression—and of triumph. Now he is no longer afraid. Now he is triumphant. . . . He experiences an extraordinary sense of elation. Then, in one of those curious transpositions of dreams, "the figure retreated in terror before my rush and dash . . . out of the room I had a moment before been desperately, and all the more abjectly, defending by the push of my shoulder." The figure had tried to appal Henry. But now it is appalled by him. The pursuer, the attacker, becomes the pursued.

. . . Routed, dismayed, the tables turned upon him by my so surpassing him for straight aggression and dire intention, my visitant was already but a diminished spot in the long perspective, the tremendous, glorious hall, as I say, over the far-gleaming floor of which, cleared for the occasion of its great line of priceless *vitrines* down the middle, he sped for *his* life, while a great storm of thunder and lightning played through the deep embrasures of high windows at the right. The lightning that revealed the retreat, revealed also the wondrous place and, by the same amazing play, my young imaginative life in it of long before, the sense of which, deep within me, had kept it whole, preserved it to this thrilling use; for what in the world were the deep embrasures and the so polished floor but those of the Galerie d'Apollon of my childhood? The "scene of something" I had vaguely then felt it? Well I might, since it was to be the scene of that immense hallucination.

For Henry the "lucidity, not to say the sublimity, of the crisis had consisted of the great thought that I, in my appalled state,

was probably still more appalling than the awful agent, creature
or presence, whatever he was, whom I had guessed, in the sud-
denest wild start from sleep, the sleep within my sleep, to be making for my place of rest." *Sublimity* was indeed the word for it:
to resist nightmare, to turn the tables and counter-attack, was con-
sonant with the sense of triumph and glory and conquest and
power. Attacked, Henry James had fought back. And he had won.

He dreamed it in a summer dawn years after his childhood
visits to the Louvre. He recaptured it on awakening. He set it
down when he was seventy. But seven years before this he had
used it as the germ for his tale, "The Jolly Corner." Recalling this
in his notebook in 1914, James wrote of the ghostly tale that "my
hero's adventure there takes the form so to speak of his turning
the tables, as I think I called it, on a 'ghost' or whatever, a visiting or haunting apparition otherwise qualified to appal *him*; and
thereby winning a sort of victory by the appearance, and the evidence, that this personage or presence was more overwhelmingly
affected by him than he by *it*."

This is a curiously inaccurate account by James of the story he
had written. The novelist here substitutes the nightmare for the
story. In the story the hero does not appal the ghost, but is appalled and overwhelmed by it. James was able to be more courageous in the dream wrought by his unconscious than in the more
consciously-wrought tale—which is probably why he remembered
the nightmare better than the story he derived from it.

IV

The nightmare appears to reflect—and we are here speculating—
the fears and terrors of a "mere junior" threatened by elders and
largely by his older brother. William would appear to figure in
the dream in a context of art, represented by the Galerie
d'Apollon with its Delacroix fresco. But this gallery also represents glory and power. Henry's unequal struggle for power is set
forth, as we have seen, in the early sentences of the same book in
which the nightmare is recorded: "We were never in the same

schoolroom, in the same game, scarce even in step together or in the same phase at the same time." William James we recall was always in the Other Room. The figure in the dream is out of the room in a moment and in Henry James's earlier account of William "when our phases overlapped . . . it was only for a moment —he was clean out before I had got well in." And as we read of the "visitant . . . a diminshed spot in the long perspective" of the gallery we also recall that Henry James had written 350 pages earlier, "I never for all the time of childhood and youth in the least caught up with him or overtook him. He was always round the corner and out of sight . . ." even as the figure in the nightmare. And it is significant that Henry during his last illness thought of William as always present "tho' not in the same room."

The thunder and lightning in the Galerie, as he pursues the vanquished figure, likewise tempt us to speculate on their relationship to William's derision over the thunder that roared and the lightning that followed. But these, we must emphatically remind ourselves, are *our* associations not the dreamer's and have relevance only because they arise largely in the same book as the nightmare. Rather do the passages which precede and follow the dream illuminate it for us and it is from these that we can obtain at least some clue to the significant equations of art and love which become also glory and power as well as fear and terror.

The opening passage, with its account of Henry James's taste for forgotten painters and William James's perception of the greatness of Delacroix is once again Henry's statement of William's assurance in a world in which he feels himself insecure. The painters listed by Henry as interesting him are those who had momentary reputations and fell from sight: men who achieved ephemeral glory. The note of glory is struck repeatedly: glory on the heroic, Napoleonic scale. The very paintings he mentions are of people in high places, the assassinated and beheaded, whose glory was ephemeral as well: the Princes in the Tower, Charles I, Lady Jane Grey. "Style," which he discovered in the Louvre and in the Luxembourg—the Senate of the Empire—as well as in the build-

ings of Paris, is associated with Imperial Glory, Empire, Royalty. The Louvre itself, Palace of Kings, had but lately been paced by the great Napoleon, remodelled by him and its collections expanded through his efforts. Had not Napoleon been a kind of supreme Apollo of his time, a giver of sunlight, a creator of states and colonies and at the same time an inspirer of music, poetry and art? It was an era of great art and great artists. When Henry James reached Paris in 1855 Balzac was but five years in his grave; Berlioz was alive and creating; George Sand was actively wielding her pen, Alfred de Musset was alive but dying, the name of the great Rachel was on everyone's lips and Victor Hugo very much an immortal among the mortals.The memory of Chateaubriand and of Madame de Staël was still fresh. Henry was, at twelve, in a Paris alive with the great voices of the nineteenth century and the echoes of the eighteenth—and keenly aware of them. And in the gallery of Apollo he found a synthesis or vast chorus of all the voices, past and present. The same word which expressed Apollonian and Napoleonic glory was, for him, however, also the word for sudden and overwhelming fright. Well might there be thunder and lightning in such a context for the thunders of Zeus killed the son of Apollo and he in turn killed the Cyclops who manufactured the thunderbolts. Aggression and counter aggression among the gods. The *love-philtre* and the *fear-philtre*, Apollon and appalling!

But why did he also experience fear? He tells us in a brief passage near the end of the chapter how fear was provoked in him by his first visit to the Louvre. The James family had arrived in Paris in July of 1855 and taken rooms at a hotel in the Rue de la Paix. They had engaged the services of an Italian courier, Jean Nadali, in London and here he was promptly charged to take the two oldest boys to the Louvre. "I hang again, appalled but uplifted, on brave Nadali's arm. . . ." (The word appalled continues to slip into the text.) The novelist goes on to describe the effect on his boyish self of the great world of art; he felt alarm, he experienced bliss:

"The bliss in fact I think scarcely disengaged itself at all, but only the sense of a freedom of contact and appreciation really too big for one, and leaving such a mark on the very place, the pictures, the frames themselves, the figures within them, the particular parts and features of each, the look of the rich light, the smell of the massively enclosed air, that I have never renewed the old exposure without renewing again the old emotion and taking up the small scared consciousness."

A freedom of contact . . . really too big for one . . . the small scared consciousness. Henry James was "scared" by being given a sudden view of power, glory, style "really too big" for his young consciousness. For all the twelve years of his life he had been accommodating himself to the world by sitting back, using his eyes, measuring and absorbing his environment, making it a part of himself. Now he was suddenly plunged into a great gallery in a great Napoleonic palace where pictures, art, grandeur, assailed him from all sides and in his young mind were translated into a thundering roar of sound. It is not surprising that the Galerie d'Apollon appalled him while at the same time Jean Nadali offered reassurance and guidance. Alarm and bliss. His conversion of art into sound, associated with thunder and lightning—heavenly wrath—might have ingredients of guilt, as Lionel Trilling has eloquently argued, growing out of his "imperious fantasy" exemplified in the counter-aggression of the nightmare. But it seems partially explicable in the boyhood terror of an environment he could not promptly assimilate. In due time he returned to the Louvre for other visits; by degree familiarity enabled him to enjoy the great works and his young sensibility felt itself almost "rub for endearment and consecration, as a cat invokes the friction of a protective piece of furniture" the "incomparable Seine-side front of the Palace."

However, there was another component of the fear and this belonged to Henry James's sense of the past. "If in my way I collected the new . . . I yet cherished the old." James's cherishing of the old was also a merging of the philtres of love and fear. The

past could inspire and it could also frighten. It seemed so completely dead and safe and secure—but was it? The great terror of the hero of the unfinished *Sense of the Past* is that having returned to an earlier time he may become a prisoner of it and not be able to move forward again to his own era. Likewise the hero of "The Jolly Corner" searching for himself in the past—himself as he might have been—is terrified by what he discovers.

v

There is a postscript to Henry James's great dream of the Galerie d'Apollon. When he was seventeen and the hours of his stay in the old world had shrunk to but a handful, he slipped from his bed on the fifth floor of the Hôtel des Trois Empereurs in the Rue de Rivoli one September morning and looked out upon Paris from the balcony. There was the wide, open Place du Palais Royal with a ceaseless swarming movement in it. On one side was a cab station with the drivers asleep on the top of their box-like fiacres, while their horses stamped and whisked their tails. He had seen soldiers parade there, with a mixture of waddle and swagger. Across the way loomed the new wing of the Louvre. Against the great palace wall were the statues of Napoleon's young generals—Hoche, Marceau, Desaix. At that moment "what it somehow came to was that here massed itself the shining second Empire, over which they stood straight aloft and on guard, like archangels of the sword, and that the whole thing was a high-pitched wonder and splendour, which we had already, in our small gaping way, got into a sort of relation with. . . . We were present at something it would be always after accounted a privilege to have been concerned with, and that we were perversely and inconsiderately dropping out of it. . . ."

Thus he sensed that he had been present at a moment of French history that was now mingled with personal history.

It meant, immensely, the glittering régime, and *that* in turn, prodigiously, something that would probably never be meant quite to

any such tune again: so much one positively and however absurdly said to one's self as one stood up on the high balcony to the great insolence of the Louvre and to all the history, all the glory again and all the imposed applause, not to say worship, and not to speak of the implied inferiority, on the part of everything else, that it represented.

The Louvre again is Napoleon and his generals and glory. The Louvre loomed for James as the supreme palace of the western world "the most peopled of all scenes not less than the most hushed of all temples." It was the Temple of Apollo and the Palace of Napoleon and the Palace of Art which in the end became mixed and interchangeable with the House of Life.

Scenes from a Boyhood
1843=1854

THE TWO SQUARES

I

HENRY JAMES ALWAYS STOUTLY MAINTAINED THAT HIS EARLIEST memory was of the Place Vendôme in Paris with its column celebrating the victories of Napoleon. He had been taken to England when he was six months old and France was visited during the following year. The James family returned to America in 1845 and then years elapsed before they ventured abroad again. This means that Henry's remarkable "recollection" of the Place Vendôme could have been only of his second year.

As he set it down, he remembered he was still "in long clothes" seated in a carriage on somebody's lap opposite his father and mother when he was "impressed with the view, framed by the clear window of the vehicle as we passed, of a great stately square surrounded with high-roofed houses and having in its centre a tall and glorious column." When he spoke of this later in childhood, his parents compared notes in surprise. Neither Albany nor New York had such a square, nor was there anything like it in

81

London where he had been taken at an even earlier age. "Conveyed along the Rue St. Honoré while I waggled my small feet, as I definitely remember doing, under my flowing robe, I had crossed the Rue de Castiglione and taken in, for all my time, the admirable aspect of the Place and the Colonne Vendôme."

Was this the loom of memory at work, weaving backward and forward among things seen early and late? Whether the brilliant infant had really absorbed and remembered so concretely we cannot know. What we do know is that his awakening consciousness was first exposed to Europe. It was there that he emerged from the cradle and began to assimilate, with his alert senses, the world around him. We know also that he had a precocious memory and a tenacious one.

Henry James reached the infantile age of recognition and perception during the period of the *vastation*, in a little cottage between the Great and Little Parks at Windsor, next to the residence of the Duchess of Kent, fronting the entrance to the Little Park which was within the range of vision of Queen Victoria herself from her great castle windows. "Willy and Harry," the senior Henry wrote to his mother in Albany, "from the nursery windows may hold delightful converse with the sheep and cattle brousing beneath." They also had the view of the long broad meadows of the Park "dotted with the noblest oaks of England." It is not surprising that when Henry returned to England at twenty-six he had a deep sense of the familiar or that beneath noble trees the opening pages of Isabel Archer's story invite us to join in the English ceremony of afternoon tea. The infant had been taken from the edge of cart-crowded Broadway in New York across an ocean and opened his eyes before the august beauty of the English countryside at the very spot where it was designed to regale the eyes of a Queen. Something of the English, the European, *ambiance*—the color and tone of the buildings, the grandeur of squares and boulevards—inevitably lingered.

The future novelist was doubtless too young to seize consciously on the images of Windsor Park but apparently not too young to

record in his mind's eye some months later the impression of the Place Vendôme in Paris. Whether the memory was of this time or a merging of later impressions with pictures seen in books, it is significant for us that Henry James should have fixed as his first recollection a great Parisian square, associated with the memory of the first Napoleon.

II

If the novelist's first glimpses of the world were European, his emerging consciousness caught hold, on native grounds, of another square in the city of his birth which was to give its name to one of his most celebrated works. In the early pages of *Washington Square* he allows himself a striking autobiographical digression or what he calls a "topographical parenthesis," almost as if he wanted to make certain that his own identity with that Square would be permanently enshrined in a work of art.

I know not whether it is owing to the tenderness of early associations, but this portion of New York appears to many persons the most delectable. It has a kind of established repose which is not of frequent occurrence in other quarters of the long, shrill city; it has a riper, richer, more honorable look than any of the upper ramifications of the great longitudinal thoroughfare—the look of having had something of a social history. It was here, as you might have been informed on good authority, that you had come into a world which appeared to offer a variety of sources of interest; it was here that your grandmother lived in venerable solitude, and dispensed a hospitality which commended itself alike to the infant imagination and the infant palate; it was here that you took your first walks abroad, following the nursery-maid with unequal step, and sniffing up the strange odour of the ailanthus-trees which at that time formed the principal umbrage of the Square, and diffused an aroma that you were not yet critical enough to dislike as it deserved; it was here, finally, that your first school, kept by a broad-bosomed, broad-based old lady with a ferule, who was always having tea in a blue cup, with a saucer that didn't match,

enlarged the circle both of your observations and your sensations. . . .

He telescopes events perforce. If he were not writing this reminiscence within a fictional frame he might have specified that his "first walks abroad" were indeed "abroad." He is alluding here of course to his first walks in Manhattan from his maternal grandmother's home to which the James family briefly went on their return to America when little Henry was two and a half. We note also in these few lines the role the novelist quite properly gives to the small nose and palate, infantile avenues to discovery. Concerning the school he has left us other recollections. It was not his first: the Dutch House in Albany had provided the official beginning of his education after his original rebellion. He had finally accepted the tutelage there of a Miss Bayou or Bayhoo—he remembered only the sound of the name. The school in the Square was a later and better remembered affair, presided over by a Mrs. Daly in one of the small red houses on the south side of Waverly Place. Stout, red-faced, apparently Irish, Mrs. Daly viewed her little pupils as "so many small slices cut from the loaf of life and on which she was to dab the butter of arithmetic and spelling; accompanied by way of jam with a light application of the practice of prize-giving." The ferule alluded to in the Jamesian parenthesis was bestowed by him on a different teacher in A Small Boy, a tall spare lady named Miss Rogers, whose face was framed in ringlets and who wore a light blue dress. She "beat time with a long black ferule to some species of droning chant or chorus in which we spent most of our hours."

These were but three of a series of ladies who administered "small vague spasms of school" to the future novelist. But before his schooling began there had been further displacements. The elder Henry had brought his wife and two boys back from Europe after the residence at Windsor where he had experienced his vastation. Mary James was then carrying her third child, who was born in New York on July 21, 1845 and named Garth Wilkin-

son. A few months later the father gravitated anew with his family toward his mother in Albany. He resided at No. 50 North Pearl Street, a few doors away from Catharine Barber James who lived at No. 43 and from his brother Augustus and his family, who lived at No. 47. Here the James family remained until 1847 and here Mrs. James gave birth to still another son, Robertson, on August 29, 1846.

A FLAVOR OF PEACHES

I

WHEN HENRY JUNIOR IN LATER YEARS SPOKE OF "INFANTILE ALBANY" he meant his third and fourth years spent near his grandmother in a veritable settlement of Jameses. Catharine Barber James ("the most democratic person by temperament I ever knew," the senior Henry said of her) lived in the large old-fashioned house which her grandson later minutely described in the opening pages of *The Portrait of a Lady*. She exercised, "within the limits of the family, a high hospitality. . . . There was a constant coming and going . . . grandmother's sons and daughters and their children appeared to be in the enjoyment of standing invitations to arrive and to remain, so that the house offered to a certain extent the appearance of a bustling provincial inn kept by a gentle lady who sighed a great deal and never presented a bill." Catharine James's grandfather had been a judge of the Court of Common Pleas and her father and two uncles had served in the Revolutionary Army. One uncle was detailed by George Washington to be an aide to

Steuben. John Barber, Catharine's father, returned from the battlefields to his native Montgomery, Orange County, New York, to
become an associate judge of the County Court, a member of the
State Legislature and a Church elder, a post he held for fifty
years. Late in life Henry James sought, after his long residence in
England, to discover some shred of English ancestry in his family among his Scotch-Irish antecedents. He represented Catharine
Barber James as providing "for us in our generation the only
English blood—that of both her own parents—flowing in our
veins." The novelist was seeking to mould fiction into fact. Catha-
rine Barber's grandfather came from Ireland and he married a
Jeannet Rhea or Rea of Montgomery who is nowhere listed as
English in the James family annals.

II

All of Henry James's memories of Albany had a flavor of peaches.
There were certain "capital peach trees" in the great expanse of
garden behind the grandmother's house and the small boy required no urging to do justice to them. For Isabel Archer in
the early pages of *The Portrait of a Lady* peaches and Albany are
synonymous and in Henry James's third story published when he
was twenty-three the heroine makes an entrance bearing "a plate
of early peaches." In *A Small Boy* he remembers mounds of Isabella grapes and sticky Seckel pears. But ah "the peaches
d'antan!"

. . . bushels of peaches in particular, peaches big and peaches
small, peaches white and peaches yellow, played a part in life from
which they have somehow been deposed; every garden, almost
every bush and the very boys' pockets grew them; they were "cut
up" and eaten with cream at every meal; domestically "brandied"
they figured, the root of the year, scarce less freely—if they were
rather a "party dish" it was because they made the daily whenever
they appeared, and when ice-cream was added, or they were added
to it, they formed the highest revel we knew. Above all the public

heaps of them, the high-piled receptacles at every turn, touched
the street as with a sort of southern plenty . . . We ate everything
in those days by the bushel and the barrel, as from stores that were
infinite. . . .

In matters of food the small boy was inevitably less discriminat-
ing than his later fictional characters. The small boy would not
have been satisfied with the *omelette aux tomates* and bottle of
straw-colored Chablis ordered by Lambert Strether and Madame
de Vionnet on the Paris quayside. He consumed large quantities of
ice cream at every turn; he swallowed hot cakes and sausages and
molasses on the hospitable porch of a neighbor later, when the family was back in New York; doughnuts were consumed on Broadway when young Henry wasn't using his pennies for the more
tempting fare offered at Barnum's Museum, and waffles "by the
hundreds" were eaten after school ("the oblong farinacious compound, faintly yet richly brown, stamped and smoking, not crisp
nor brittle, but softly absorbent of the syrup dabbed upon it").
There were "small amber-coloured mounds of chopped cocoanut
or whatever other substance, if a finer there be." Later, on the
Continent, there were to be the melting *babas* and criss-cross
apple tartlets with other delights of the French pastry shops. At
seventy Henry seemed to be smacking his lips over his hearty boyish appetite.

He remembered more than the peach trees in Albany although
these always came first to mind: the swing on the covered piazza
to the rear of the grandmother's house, the long garden sloping
down to the stable, the library of William of Albany, full of books
"with frontispieces" which the child climbed on a chair to take
down, guided in his selection chiefly by the pictures; the "office"
beyond the library with its musty smell and ancient pieces of furniture and the schoolhouse across the street from which came the
"hum of childish voices repeating the multiplication table." Albany constituted the first stage in the novelist's experience of his
native land; and the scene was crowded with the faces of the

James clan at its most numerous before separations and deaths—
already begun—cut its ranks and dimmed the fading splendor of
the merchant-founder's domain.

58 WEST FOURTEENTH STREET

IN 1847 THE JAMES FAMILY MOVED BACK TO NEW YORK. HERE MRS.
James gave birth on August 7, 1848 to her fifth and last child, a
daughter, named Alice. After a brief residence at 11 Fifth Avenue
in a house later razed to make way for the Brevoort, the elder
Henry settled his brood in the then fashionable "uptown" resi-
dential neighborhood near Union Square—first in a rented house
and then at No. 58 West Fourteenth Street near Sixth Avenue in
a building which he purchased. It was not a new mansion; the
plasterer and the paperhanger were summoned and little Henry
watched the yellow-grained paper with a pattern of dragons and
sphinxes being applied to the walls. The New York of *A Small
Boy and Others* in which the future novelist roamed between his
fifth and twelfth years, was largely constituted for him by the area
between Sixth and Fifth Avenues down to Washington Square and
up eastward to Union Square which, in that era, was enclosed by a
high railing, had a fountain and was presided over by a solitary
amateur-looking policeman, "a strange superannuated, dilapidated
functionary, carrying a little cane and wearing, with a very copious and very dirty shirt front, the costume of a man of the
world." This was the "old liquor-scented, heated-looking city, the

city of no pavements" with the "blistering summers" recorded on its face. On the corner of Eighth Street the boyish nostrils eagerly sniffed the warm smell of the bakery with its cookies, cream cakes and pies; on the corner of Fifteenth Street and Fifth Avenue he remembered a great mansion which seemed to him the finest in New York. As the boys grew older New York widened for them. There were excursions downtown to the theatres of Chambers Street, or Park Place and walks up and down Broadway and the farther reach of Forty-Second Street beyond which everything was clearly suburban. New York was a city of mixed buildings, vacant lots filled with weeds, theatrical billboards and wooden fences. The squares were fenced, there were poplars in the important thoroughfares and stray pigs and poultry wandered in the side streets. The grass plots in front of City Hall were known as "the park," Hoboken was a "genteel resort" and the rotunda of Castle Garden echoed with the music of precocious Adelina Patti while earlier all New York had talked of Jenny Lind.

It was the "small warm dusky homogeneous New York world of the mid-century." The house on Fourteenth Street was large and well-furnished. In the winter evenings the fires burned brightly in the hearth and the quiet little Henry spent intervals before bedtime looking at pictures and reading books. In the front parlor there was hung a large painting of a Florentine view by Thomas Cole; the rear parlor boasted still another Italian scene, a Tuscany landscape by Lefèvre, hung over the sofa; between the two rear windows stood the bust of a Bacchante with vine leaves in her hair and her breasts imperfectly covered. Certain visitors used to pause by the bust and pronounced the marble lady rather "cold" for a Bacchante.

Henry remembered Mr. Emerson seated on the sofa in the rear parlor between his parents, in the dusk before the lamps were lighted, "elegantly slim, benevolently aquiline." The great man showed an interest in the small boy, inviting him to draw nearer, off the hearth-rug, and the "sweetness of the voice and the finish of the speech" established for the future novelist the fact that the

human tone could evoke personality and arouse emotion. In the library one day he saw Mr. Thackeray who had come to America to lecture on the English humorists. Henry was dressed after the fashion of the time in a tight jacket adorned in front with a row of brass buttons and, hovering near the door of the sun-filled library, heard himself summoned by the enormously big English gentleman: "Come here, little boy, and show me your extraordinary jacket!" Thackeray peered through his spectacles alike at the garment and the boy. He then carefully explained to Henry that if he were to go to England he would be addressed as "Buttons."

It is possible from these fragmentary reminiscences to put together the house at 58 West Fourteenth Street—parlors front and back, a sunny library, a guest room (known as "Mr. Emerson's room" to the little Jameses) bedrooms for the four boys and for Alice, the maternal and paternal quarters, the attic in which theatricals were staged by the enterprising William and doubtless servants' quarters as well as a large old-fashioned kitchen. The childhood of Henry James was spacious alike in home and in city in the sense of providing him with a world rich and various, wrapped in outward security and, as he put it, "floating in such a clean light social order." Henry could "dawdle and gape" at his ease and observe to his heart's content. The old New York was to remain with him all his life and he was to image it in his work long after it had changed its face and wedged itself up the island into the era of the automobile and the skyscraper.

PICTURE AND SCENE

I

BETWEEN THE FRONT PARLOR WINDOWS IN THE FOURTEENTH STREET
home stood a piece of furniture which housed volumes of Gavarni's caricatures, a set of Béranger enriched by steel engravings
and the four tall folios of Joseph Nash's *Mansions of England in the Olden Time*. Here on winter afternoons, in the fading light and the glow of a red fire, the small boy lay on his stomach on the drawing-room hearth-rug studying the Nash pictures all
unaware that some day he would be an honored guest in England's mansions; in Gavarni he delighted in the pictures of the
sturdy French women who came to life on the page and resembled
the short-skirted Mlle. Delavigne, one of his teachers. (He was
later to characterize Gavarni as "the wittiest, the most literary and
most acutely profane of all mockers with the pencil.") And
here he read *Punch*. Between his seventh and twelfth years the
front parlor was associated with Henry's discovery of wider horizons than those embraced by Broadway and Union Square, Chambers Street and the big brown house at Eighteenth Street where
he sometimes admired the two or three little elegant cows, the nibbling fawns and other "browsing and pecking and parading creatures."

Every year Henry's parents talked of going again to Europe
and every year they just as surely changed their minds. Meanwhile all England seemed to unfold from the pages of *Punch* and
mainly London—the names of London streets and theatres, Ken-
sington Gardens and Drury Lane, the very sound of the name
Piccadilly seemed to be there, people riding in the Row, cabmen
and costermongers, little pages in buttons, bathing-machines at the
seaside, small boys in tall hats and Eton jackets, elaborately
dressed gentlemen hunting foxes, pretty girls in striped petticoats
with their hair dressed in the shape of mushrooms. Long before
he had seen it he was acquainted through Leech's drawings with

the aspect of Baker Street in December. He was to discover in due course that if *Punch* had represented London to him, London in turn was *Punch*. Everything looked familiar once he was able to pace the great city and everything seemed to have been drawn by Leech.

The transition from pictures in books to pictures in galleries was made early. New York at the mid-century favored large canvases and bright colors—as large "as the side of a house and of a bravery of colour and lustre of surface that I was never afterwards to see surpassed." The Duesseldorf School, as exemplified in the work of Leutze's celebrated painting of Washington crossing the Delaware, commanded the market and its paintings were almost constantly on exhibition on Broadway, in a "disaffected church where gothic excrescences and an ecclesiastical roof of a mild order helped the importance." The first exhibition of the Leutze painting was an occasion never forgotten, for the James family attended in force, taking the crosstown omnibus on Fourteenth Street at an hour of the evening when Henry was usually in bed. There it was, the painting, in a "wondrous flare of projected gaslight" with little Henry taking in "the sharpness of the ice blocks . . . the sickness of the sick soldier . . . the protrusion of minor objects . . . the strands of the rope and the nails of the boots . . . above all . . . the profiled national hero's purpose" which seemed to be that of "standing *up*, as much as possible, even indeed of doing it almost on one leg . . ." The Father of the Country was thus promptly identified with Henry's own father.

Less thrilling was another evening spent at Bryan's Gallery of Christian art viewing a collection of "worm-eaten diptychs and triptychs, of angular saints and seraphs, of black Madonnas and obscure Bambinos" all certified "primitives." He heard later that this collection fell under suspicion and he believed it consisted largely of frauds and fakes. "I have never since stood before a real Primitive," he wrote, "a primitive of the primitives, without having first to shake off the grey mantle of that night."

What is clear from these fragmentary early memories is the ex-

tent to which the Picture entered into the experience of the young Henry; he was to link it to the "scene" that he learned also as a boy to watch on the stage; and he was to seek a wedding of picture and scene long afterwards in his novels. In fact, at the end, he tended to see his own life as a series of images and scenes ". . . the only terms in which life has treated me to experience . . . I cherish the moment and evoke the image and repaint the scene . . ."

II

His father had taken him to visit an uncle on his estate at Rhinebeck, on the Hudson, "Linwood"—one of the most beautiful sites on the river. He remembered peaches, roses, grapes, the hum of insects, a wide view "great bright harmonies of air and space." One evening little Henry wandered to the eminence overlooking the Hudson accompanied by his cousin Marie, who was a year older than he was. Small, brown, with shining black eyes, she was an object of special interest because Henry had heard she was "spoiled." That made her particularly interesting since the James boys had never been spoiled. It gave her a romantic status to Henry who only half understood the meaning of the term. His uncle, Augustus James, at a given moment, remarked with some emphasis that it was Marie's bedtime. The words must have fallen with some weight; by implication it was probably Henry's bedtime too. Marie objected. There was an emphatic rejoinder from Uncle Augustus. Marie appealed to her mother, and Henry, then eleven, heard these sharp words which were emphatically registered: "Come now, my dear; don't make a scene—I *insist* on your not making a scene!"

That was all the witchcraft the occasion used but the note was none the less epoch-making. The expression, so vivid, so portentous, was one I had never heard—it had never been addressed to us at home; and who should say now what a world one mightn't at once read into it? It seemed freighted to sail so far; it told me

so much about life. Life at these intensities clearly became
"scenes"; but the great thing, the immense illumination, was that
we could make them or not as we chose.

Henry James considered that evening at Linwood a landmark
in the history of his imagination.

III

After pictures came books. Visits to the bookstore "fondest of my
father's resorts" were frequent and even before he could read
young Henry sniffed at the fresh paper and the printer's ink—he
called it the "English smell" because so many of the books were
imported from England. The small boy learned to read early and
in due course his father was describing him as a "devourer of libraries." He remembered that he had accompanied his father one
summer's day on one of his visits to the New York *Tribune* in
Nassau Street where the elder Henry usually called on his friend
Horace Greeley. Here Henry Junior was impressed by a conversation about the French theatre and of tales of a new great town
springing up in the west, a conglomeration of shanties and wooden
plank sidewalks called Chicago. Someone handed his father a volume by Solon Robinson, a staff member of the paper. It was
called *Hot Corn*. Little Henry promptly wanted to get his sensitive nose into this book but one of the men suggested that the
volume wasn't for little boys. A glance at the book, with its lurid
pictures of New York slum life ("The Story of Little Katy" who
sold hot corn on Manhattan's sidewalks, "The Rag Picker's
Daughter" and "Wild Maggie") explains why. Henry Junior at
seventy remembered the "soreness of the thought that it was I
rather who was wrong for the book." This, to say the least, was
"somehow humiliating." He never read *Hot Corn* although the
title remained with him long after the book was forgotten.

As a consolation he was given Maria S. Cummins's *The Lamplighter* then enjoying great vogue on both sides of the Atlantic
and it was suggested to him that this was a "grown-up" book. In

his memoirs Henry James implies that the small boy wasn't
fooled. He had his reserves as to whether such a book could be
"really and truly grown-up" although he confessed that the tale
of the little orphan adopted by the lamplighter with its pathos
and moralizing received an "absorbed perusal." Something else
happened, however, to give young Henry his real taste of what a
novel could be.

AN INITIATION

I

ONE DAY WHEN THE FAMILY HAD FLED THE NEW YORK HEAT AND
was staying at New Brighton, on Staten Island, the elder Henry
took the boat to New York accompanied by Henry Junior to do a
number of chores. These included the usual visit to the bookstore
where the father purchased a number of volumes including a novel
for the mother's reading. This book was handed to young Henry
to carry. They made their way back to the boat and the small boy
clambered into the little cabin or sitting room for the brief journey. Here he waded into the book. It was called *The Initials*
and was by a woman with the picturesque name of the Baroness
Tautphoeus. "It came over me with the very first page," he later
wrote, "assimilated in the fluttered little cabin . . ." that "*The
Initials was* grown-up."

It is easy to see, even today, what appeal the first page of this
novel by Jemima Montgomery, Baroness Tautphoeus, had for the
young Henry. It has an atmosphere not unlike the first page of

Daisy Miller: a young Englishman named Hamilton has alighted at a Munich inn and is taking a sophisticated view of his continental surroundings. In a few minutes an "international" situation develops, a mysterious note, merely initialled, is delivered, and in due course Mr. Hamilton has met the proud German beauty Hildegarde and her sister Crescenz and the book, with a freshness and lightness that has not faded from its pages after a century, carries us into masquerades and suppers, visits to little towns (even to Berchtesgaden long before it was to have its garish moment in history), inspection of cloisters and monasteries, hare hunts, the Hôtel d'Angleterre in Frankfort (how many Hôtels d' Angleterre Henry was to stay at in later years!). The Baroness was an Irishwoman who had married a Chamberlain to the King of Bavaria and she was one of a group of English writers of her time who skilfully illuminated foreign manners for Anglo-Saxon readers. She is entirely at home abroad and little Henry, aged eleven, seems to have felt himself at home also in her pages. What was a sentimental story of an orphan and a lamplighter compared to a tale, romantic and witty, set in the Bavarian Alps, containing a lurid suicide, a struggle of lovers against cruel fate, even a quasi-elopement in which, however, the hero observes all the niceties after registering the heroine at a Mainz hotel and being taken for her husband. "I will go at once across, and if there be any rooms to be had, not quite on the other end of the town, I shall not return until morning." The precision of the "not quite at the other end of the town" could only be an anticipation of the early Henry James Junior. The Baroness's novel was distinctly a forerunner of the tales which would be written by the small boy when he grew up.

II

Henry James indeed discovered that day on the New Brighton boat what real fiction could be, fiction sophisticated and written with a bright, facile charm, "the history of the long-legged Mr. Hamilton and his two Bavarian beauties, the elder of whom, Hil-

degarde, was to figure for our small generation as the very type of the haughty as distinguished from the forward heroine (since I think our categories really came to no more than those). I couldn't have got very far with Hildegarde in moments so scant but I memorably felt that romance was thick round me—everything, at such a crisis, seeming to make for it at once."

The "romance" that took the small boy from fiction to life was his discovery that "lurking" in the same public cabin-sitting room were two little girls whom he recognized as the "Boon Children" of the New York stage scheduled to perform that evening at the New Brighton Pavilion. Thus Henry, not quite the long-legged Mr. Hamilton, could fancy himself as being "in relation" with two beauties, not quite Bavarian. They had come down to the cabin supervised by a female in whom "the strain of the resolute triumphed over the note of the battered." They lurked "out of more public view as to hint that they weren't to be seen for nothing."

The Boon Children were weary and sleepy and young Henry "found the histrionic character and the dramatic profession for the first time revealed" to him. He was fascinated yet somehow afraid. The girls were rather frightening in their assurance, their lack of interest in anything and anybody; they expressed "melancholy grace and a sort of peevish refinement, yet seemed awfully detached and indifferent, indifferent perhaps even to being pinched and slapped, for art's sake, at home." Ever after, Henry James was to have a certain contempt for actors and actresses— exception made for such brilliant personages as Fanny Kemble or Elizabeth Robins in whose lives the stage had only a partial role. He considered actors "self-exhibitionistic" creatures whose view of the world was narrowed to the contemplation of their own form in a mirror. This, however, did not dull his admiration for their art at its best, of which he became both an acute observer and recorder.

On this occasion the boy Henry was sharply conscious of being ignored. The Boon Children seemed unaware of his presence.

He thought of himself quite as one of the "little louts" peeping through a hole in the canvas of a tent at two circus performers. Henry remained the observer. Looking at the Boon Children constituted adventure enough on that historic day—historic in the sense of providing a capital initiation. Henry discovered that experience existed alike in the pages of a book and in the life around him: that fiction at such moments became life and life fiction.

THE DICKENS IMPRINT

HIS MOTHER HAD TOLD HIM IT WAS BEDTIME. BUT THE SMALL BOY was as reluctant as all small boys are to obey when there is a visitor in the house. An Albany cousin had arrived and the elders were gathered in the library; the cousin was to read aloud the first instalment of Mr. Dickens's new novel, *David Copperfield*.

Henry feigned a withdrawal upstairs but retreated instead to cover in the library, "the friendly shade of some screen or drooping table-cloth." Behind this protection, doubled up and hugging the carpet, he listened.

He listened holding his breath as the story unfolded. Finally the "tense cord . . snapped under the strain of the Murdstones" and the elders assembled in the room became aware of a loud sobbing.

This time he was effectively banished to his bed. But the "ply then taken was ineffaceable." Dickens was woven into the fabric

of the young Henry's life. The familiar characters were emerging freshly then in magazine and volume and also were being thrown hastily upon the stage by play tinkers seeking to give bodily form to the Micawbers and Scrooges, Pickwicks and Copperfields, Oliver Twists and Paul Dombeys whose very names assured a full house. In his later writings Henry alluded to Dickens always in charmed retrospect yet he never devoted a critical article to him. He wrote of George Eliot and Anthony Trollope, he devoted articles to Robert Louis Stevenson and even a late essay to Thackeray but Dickens figured in reminiscence rather than criticism, and only once did he review one of his novels. When James was invited to contribute the Dickens volume to the "English Men of Letters" series for which he wrote the Hawthorne, he hesitated for a long time and finally declined. Dickens "laid his hand on us in a way to undermine as in no other case the power of detached appraisement . . . he entered so early into the blood and bone of our intelligence that it always remained better than the taste of overhauling him." So Dickens remained "hoarded in the dusty chamber of youth." Henry preferred it that way. To deal with Dickens as a novelist and craftsman would have been quite another matter; about Dickens's art and sense of life Henry James was to have distinct reservations and they are incorporated in the remarkable review he wrote, as a young man, of *Our Mutual Friend.*

In that same chamber of youth and sentiment were hoarded the memories of the dramatized Dickens, the actor Burton as "a monstrous Micawber, the coarse parody of a charming creation, with the entire baldness of a huge Easter egg and collar-points like the sails of Mediterranean feluccas." This memory and that of Lizzie Weston as Smike in *Nicholas Nickleby* "all tearful melodrama" was retained through the years as a striking portrait of "Nicholas's starved and tattered and fawning and whining protégé." Decidedly the "force of the Dickens imprint, however applied, in the soft clay of our generation" resisted "serenely the wash of the waves of time."

A SMALL BOY AT THE THEATRE

WHEN HE SAW THE DICKENS PLAYS HE WAS ALREADY AN INVETER-
ate theatregoer of nine or ten. Henry James's theatrical memories
are a striking part of A *Small Boy and Others* whose four hundred pages cover only the first fourteen years of his life. Yet
one-eighth of these is devoted to a detailed recounting of nights
at the play—pantomimes viewed in early childhood, the memory
of the old theatrical billboards with their lurid synopses of the
plays and the picturesque names of the stage folk, as well as the
excursions to the theatres of New York and later of London and
Paris. William was taken to the theatre first; Henry tells that
story twice, in two separate books: and since he names the play
to which he was not taken (Charlotte Cushman in *Henry* VIII)
we can estimate, from the date of her performance, that at seven
little Henry was not considered quite ready for the theatre. But
at eight the curtain rose on what was to be a lifetime of theatre-
going.

James believed that his first play was A *Comedy of Errors*. He
remembered the work was read to him during the day and he recalled the "sacred thrill" once inside the theatre before a green
curtain that refused to go up: "One's eyes bored into it in vain,
and yet one knew that it *would* rise at the named hour, the only
question being if one could exist till then."

Young Henry was taken to all the leading theatres of the time
—Burton's, the Broadway, the National, Wallack's Lyceum, Nib-
lo's Gardens and Barnum's, attached to the "Great American Museum." It was the era when many theatres, in the lingering Pu-
ritanism, still masqueraded as gardens, lecture rooms, lyceums,
baptized with innocent titles while openly plying their lively and
profane trade.

At Burton's, in Chambers Street, he saw such familiar farces
as *The Toodles* and *The Serious Family*; at the Broadway the

super-spectacle of *The Cataract of the Ganges* or *The Rajah's Daughter* (with a cataract of "real water") and the popular *Green Bushes*; at Wallack's the clever comedies of Dion Boucicault (then written Bourcicault), *London Assurance* and *Love in a Maze*. Always there is the vivid recollection of the actors: William Burton, as Aminadab Sleek, Mr. Toodles or Paul Pry, "his huge person, his huge fat face and his vast slightly pendulous cheek, surmounted by a sort of elephantine wink, to which I impute a remarkable baseness"; Madame Ponisi, the Oberon of *A Midsummer Night's Dream*, "representing all characters alike with a broad brown face framed in bands or crowns or other heavy headgear out of which cropped a row of very small tight black curls"; Madame Céline Celeste "straight out of London" in *Green Bushes* (J. B. Buckston's play which James wrongly attributes to Boucicault), "whose admired walk up the stage as Miami the huntress, a wonderful majestic and yet voluptuous stride enhanced by a short kilt, black velvet leggings and a gun haughtily borne on the shoulder is vividly before me . . ."; Miss Julia Bennett "fresh from triumphs at the Haymarket . . . in a very becoming white bonnet, either as a brilliant adventuress or as the innocent victim of licentious design, I forget which, though with a sense somehow that the white bonnet, when of true elegance, was the note at that period of the adventuress." We can multiply examples of these crowded recollections, sometimes accurate in all details, sometimes mistaken, as when he assures us he saw Fanny Wallack in *London Assurance* "as Lady Gay Spanker, flushed and vociferous, first in a riding-habit with a tail yards long and afterwards in yellow satin with scarce a tail at all." Fanny Wallack's last appearance in America was in June 1852 and *London Assurance* wasn't produced at Wallack's until 1854 with Rosa Bennett as Lady Gay.

Henry saw one important drama that was to remain a landmark in the American theatre for successive generations. In November 1853 Barnum mounted his production of *Uncle Tom's Cabin* at his Broadway Museum and here he saw the play for the first time

with Emily Mestayer, red-faced, "her swelling bust encased in a neat cotton gown" giving an intrepid and graceful performance of Eliza's flight across the ice. This was an abridged version with a happy ending. Later Henry saw the full version in six long acts at the National—eight tableaux and thirty scenes—an evening particularly remembered because it happened to be the occasion of his first theatre party. He was able to play the role of critic: he could compare the two versions. He was certain the second Eliza was less dramatic than Miss Mestayer: but the ice floes at the National seemed more genuine than Barnum's obvious carpentry. And Henry James, writing of this evening late in life, felt that the occasion was all the richer for him in that its humor and melodrama and pathos were collectively shared. He was absorbed as much by the junior audience as by the play. The little sophisticates had gone to *Uncle Tom's Cabin* with some detachment but found themselves swept along by the play's strong currents. It was initiation into social as well as aesthetic adventure.

. . . AND OTHERS

I

THE UNITED STATES AT THAT TIME CONSISTED FOR HENRY JAMES OF "the busy, the tipsy, and Daniel Webster." The "busy" were all around him—and there was no shortage of the "tipsy." He knew that people went to offices and stores (though his father never did) and that they made money—yet the process of making it was forever a mystery to him, money-conscious though he was

from his earliest days. He later came to give New York's Uptown and Downtown special meanings related to money. Downtown was the world of the money-makers that he didn't know and couldn't write about. Uptown represented leisure, largely feminine (since the males were Downtown making the money), and this world was useable in his books.

Early in life there came to him faint echoes of the Mexican War; he caught a glimpse of an uncle in uniform and later was introduced to Winfield Scott on Fifth Avenue. Then he remembered two uncles arriving at their Fifth Avenue apartment, just before they moved into Fourteenth Street, to announce excitedly to his father the triumph of the revolution of 1848 in France and the flight of Louis-Philippe. Henry was six when the country reverberated to the discovery of gold in California, but the Jameses had their eyes turned toward Europe as the covered wagons moved westward. These major events had reality for the boy only as stories told by persons around him, as news broadcast by word of mouth on the Avenue. Beyond the perpetual circle of relatives he began to pay attention to an ever-widening group of callers at his father's house. There were artists, Thomas Hicks, A. J. H. Duganne, C. P. Cranch, Felix O. C. Darley and they talked of others, names that had common currency then, Cropsey, Cole, Kensett, Ives, Powers, Mozier. There were writers, George Curtis, Parke Godwin, George Ripley, Charles Dana, Rufus Griswold and N. P. Willis with talk of Bryant, Washington Irving, Poe and the familiar Mr. Emerson. He remembered meeting Washington Irving on the steamboat to Fort Hamilton. Irving told his father that Margaret Fuller had been drowned with her husband and child off Fire Island in the foundering of a ship during the storm of two days before.

Thus gradually was constituted an atmosphere around the small boy and his brothers and sister in which figured people doing things, men with reputations, a world of books, talk of art. Closest to Henry Junior were the maternal and paternal relatives; he dubs them "a company of characters" and proceeds to sketch them

in his memoirs in a brilliant series of profiles. They are the "Others" outside his immediate family in the title of his autobiographical volume. Mainly there are cousins on all sides, even as we find them later in his novels in groups and clusters, people one could or could not be "in relation with" and who are also "other." "Everyone was a little someone else," he wrote in a late story. In A *Small Boy* he tells us that he was "constantly eager to exchange my lot for that of somebody else, on the assured certainty of gaining by the bargain." He is careful at the same time to explain that this was not "jealousy." In contemplating the qualities of his orphaned cousins in particular he reveals how low a value the small boy placed on himself; and when this is the case it does not permit any such acute passion as jealousy. His desire to be "somebody else" was the equivalent of a small boy's view, he explained, of sweets through a plate glass window. The glass will never melt. To be "other, almost anyhow, seemed as good as the probable taste of the bright compound wistfully watched in the confectioner's window; unattainable, impossible, of course. . . ." Therefore jealousy wasn't involved. Accepting the idea of the unattainable meant also removing himself from competition. "I never dreamed of competing—a business having in it at the best for my temper, if not for my total failure of temper, a displeasing ferocity. If competing was bad, snatching was therefore still worse, and jealousy was a sort of spiritual snatching."

Little Henry thus reduced himself to his favorite pastime of watching. He observed his relatives closely. William of Albany's family had been large; and there were maternal relatives as well. The human material close to the future novelist was abundant.

II

They pass before us in these sketches and portraits; they constitute a "chronicle of early deaths, arrested careers, broken promises, orphaned children." The father's relatives to whom he alludes in this fashion receive less notice than the mother's; and

the mother's are all "strong" females, holding their men under their thumbs, from Great-aunt Wyckoff, "an image of living antiquity . . . that I was never to see surpassed" to Cousin Helen, his mother's cousin, with her "fine old New York ignorance and rigour." The Great-aunt probably sat for Juliana Bordereau in *The Aspern Papers* "throned, hooded, and draped" as the small boy saw her. Cousin Helen with her suppressed husband could have been the inspiration for "Georgina's Reasons"—Henry James's sensational tale which he sold to a newspaper syndicate years later, in which Georgina suppresses her husband to the point of never acknowledging his existence. Cousin Helen's husband we noted was described as a "dim little gentleman" and a "spectral spouse." He is also a "shade of nullity," "a blank," "a zero" and a "natural platitude." But Henry makes it clear that it is Helen who has utterly reduced him to this status. He was "Mr." to his own wife. This seemed to Henry to sum up the situation.

Under Cousin Helen's authority fell Albert Wyckoff, her nephew, who seemed an independent spirit since he was among those neither fathered nor mothered; yet in the end Cousin Helen sufficed for both. He too lived in the Fourteenth Street "other house" to which little Henry frequently went (and where he read *Oliver Twist*). The "Spectral Spouse" paced it from street end to piazza at the back; he was partially bald, his hair standing up on both sides; he wore neckcloths that seemed to elongate his neck. He talked of the grand tour he would some day make. Finally after half a century he sailed for England. The shock was too much for him. There was a "snap of the tense cord . . . he just landed and died." Helen also had charge of Henry Wyckoff, her brother, and of his ample fortune. She gave him a dime a day on the theory that he was "not to be trusted" with money. When finally his guardian died, he failed quite to rise to his estate after almost half a century of this discipline. "He did feel rich, just as he felt generous; the misfortune was only in his weak sense for meanings." Henry James decided that not his heart but his imagination had been starved. Years later Henry Wyckoff became

the subject of the novelist's best-realized stage comedy, *The Reprobate.*

The small boy saw only the beginning of these stories of his relatives but he lived longer than most of them to be present also at their endings. There were other cousins and uncles who died almost before their lives began: Minny Temple, the second daughter of the senior Henry's second sister, Catherine James, a small Albany cousin known briefly to the small boy, but later destined, on re-acquaintance at Newport, to play a large role in his life; Gus Barker, the second son of Jeannette or Janet James, Catherine James's oldest sister, whose mother died giving birth to him. A guerrilla's bullet cut him down at twenty-one during the Civil War and we capture him, during his brief bright life, through Henry Junior's eyes, clad in the uniform of the military school he was attending and much admired by his cousin, "the most beautifully-made athletic little person, and in the highest degree appealing and engaging" and again without uniform, in fact without clothes, "perched on a pedestal and divested of every garment" being drawn by William James in Hunt's studio at Newport. Henry kept William's sketch; presently it was all that remained of the genial Gus.

There was Gus's brother, Bob Barker, with his promise as a sculptor; Johnny James, with a talent for music cut short by death; the four uncles, Augustus, John, Edward and Howard, the first presiding in grandeur over Linwood, the last three figuring as customers of Mrs. Cannon who sold ties, collars and the essence known in old New York as "Cullone" somewhere near Fourth Street; little girl cousins encountered in Paris; Vernon King with his European background and his sad end—a tale told twice in *A Small Boy:* the conflict between Vernon, the blond-bearded short-of-breath dandy of Paris and Newport and his mother, Charlotte, who had Southern sympathies, Vernon's promise not to return to battle after he was wounded in the Civil War, his violation of the promise, his untimely end at Richmond or Petersburg and

his burial at Newport under a stone that makes no allusion to his soldier's death.

The dimmest ghost of all perhaps was the memory of Aunt Ellen King James, "softly spectral" with ringlets who died at twenty-six—when Henry was six. This was in Albany and he remembered a call at her house in Elk Street, the memory being fixed mainly by the fact that she had married Smith Thompson Van Buren, the son of a President of the United States. The visitable past of the James family could lead Henry even to the White House.

The Nostalgic Cup
1855-1860

THEORY OF EDUCATION

IN THE HISTORY OF LITERATURE AND IN THE LIVES OF A MAJORITY of the nineteenth century novelists, Church and School figure as twin institutions coloring their childhood and casting shadows, for good or bad, across the adult years. The discipline of the spirit and of the mind was imposed by precept and sermon in those rigorous decades or firmly injected by the broad and generous application of strap and ferule. In how many novels do we sit with the struggling hero or heroine through interminable Sunday mornings—such as those commemorated by Henry James Senior —and long classroom hours over Latin and sums? The era of *The Way of All Flesh* and Wackford Squeers left Henry Junior relatively untouched. Although he was born, as we have seen, in a house hard by a church and a university he grew up unencumbered by religion and formal education. The elder Henry, remembering his joyless childhood, shrank from anything that would be "narrowing" for his children. A cheerful anarchy character-

ized the schooling of the little Jameses. As for the Church, Henry himself described his relations with it as "pewless."

I

"What church do you go to?" his schoolmates challenged. Little Henry was as bereft of an answer as he was when asked to name his father's profession. The question, put in turn to the senior James by the puzzled boy, again received a baffling reply: "It was colder than any criticism, I recall, to hear our father reply that we could plead nothing less than the whole privilege of Christendom, and that there was no communion, even that of the Catholics, even that of the Jews, even that of the Swedenborgians, from which we need find ourselves excluded. With the freedom we enjoyed our dilemma clearly amused him: it would have been impossible, he affirmed, to be theologically more *en règle*." To have all the churches and all the religions was really to have none. And this may explain why Henry James, during adult life, indulged in periods of intense churchgoing, as if to compensate for past omissions. At twenty he wrote from New York to T. S. Perry that he had filled two Sundays with the sermon of a Presbyterian preacher and visits to a revival meeting and to a "congregation of the new dispensation." The Presbyterian preacher was listened to with particular curiosity because he had officiated in a church attended years before by Henry's mother. "Darkly must her prospect of Heaven have been obscured!" mused her son. "The old man is now eighty, but he still finds strength with great reinforcements of tobacco-juice, to fulminate against back-sliders and evil doers. I may emphatically say he gave us hell. . . ."

From this divine Henry went on to hear the preaching of Mrs. Cora V. L. Hatch in an Astor Place basement. A committee, selected on the spot, decided upon her subject: "The Evidence of the Continued Existence of the Spirit After Death." Cora, after invoking Divine aid, began to speak in "a string of . . . arrant platitudes" and we promptly recognize the type of female oratory we will encounter thirty years later in *The Bostonians*. At

the "congregation of the new dispensation" he listened to "a grand oration (tremendous) from the female on the right and singing from her on the left." Henry was taking his father's account of their universal church membership literally. His taste in church services was to remain eclectic.

Churchgoing for Henry, whether in London or while paying country visits in later life, was essentially a participation in a social phenomenon rather than a religious experience. "James's churches of any denomination," one critic has remarked, "are a humane crystallization of the scene—moments, aspects, tones, with little sectarian dispute to disturb the atmosphere." On Sundays, in his stories, we walk across the English countryside, past the old tombstones into the old small church whose bell long before has musically been chiming through the hollow and here dramatic incidents sometimes occur: the ghost of Sir Edmund Orme suddenly stands in the pew or little Miles demands that he be sent back to school. If Henry James can be said to have had a personal religion, it was a mysticism compounded of meditation and communion with spirits and forces, vaguely discerned yet acutely felt, in a dim intuitional "beyond." On the one hand he accepted the supremacy of reason and on the other inclined toward Pascalian intuition. He worshipped in solitary visits to churches and cathedrals much after the manner of George Stransom in "The Altar of the Dead." Within the orbit of "consciousness," Henry James had constructed, by middle life, his series of shrines—the shrine of art, tradition, morality, his own religion of beauty and the "religion of consciousness"—a worship almost pagan, were it not so highly sophisticated, of the "powers and forces and divinities to whom I've ever been loyal . . ." that included the guiding spirit of his writing table, whom he familiarly addressed as *mon bon,* the unseen but strongly experienced strength within him that was his creative power. This, combined with the curious private prayers he wrote out in his notebooks—more invocation to the special Jamesian Muse than prayer—constituted the "religion" of the nov-

elist. He never seems to have prayed to a specific Deity in his writings and his admiration for Catholicism was exclusively for that portion of it which provided for "retreat," for meditation and communion with a Deity—but really a Deity of his own choosing (much like his father's) together with a delight in the color of Catholic ritual. "The Great Good Place" for him was a monastery of the mind.

For Catholicism as a functioning religion, and for some of its manifestations, as he saw them at Rome, he occasionally had a critical word, the word of a Protestant born if not bred. The absence of formal religion in his upbringing did stimulate a curiosity about religious experience; he wondered, for instance, at the absence of clergymen in the James household although he found them present in most English novels read as a boy; but he did have the case of his father and the revolt against Calvinism. During his boyhood he was exposed at the most to his father's discourses on Swedenborgianism, his diatribes against organized religion and an occasional Sunday reading of the Scriptures. He was exposed much more to religious *feeling* than to religion itself. This resulted in his reviewing in later years such works as Père Chocarne's *Inner Life of Father Lacordaire* or Count de Falloux's *Life and Letters of Madame Swetchine*—works in which the religious sentiment is paramount. And it was this which was reflected in his discussion of Alphonse Daudet's *L'Évangéliste* —with its portrait of a "theological vampire" who is a Calvinist —which gave the initial impulse to *The Bostonians*. Henry James complained that Daudet not only did not understand Protestantism, but he lacked any "natural understanding of the religious passion." That "province of the human mind" James added "cannot be *fait de chic*—experience, there, is the only explorer." James undoubtedly felt that through his father he had had this experience. Nevertheless the "religious passion" is absent from his novels. It was not absent from his life, where it was constantly being translated, in full measure, into his art.

11

"School" was present in Henry's life with much greater regularity than Church. First there were the "educative ladies"—the long line that began with Miss Bayou or Bayhoo. They included a Miss Sedgwick, a Mrs Wright (Lavinia D.), a Russian lady with an accent whose name was forgotten, a Mlle. Delavigne, who taught French, and a Mrs. Vredenburg, who maintained a summer school at New Brighton on Staten Island. Then, when he reached ten, he was sent to the Institution Vergnès in lower Broadway, "a sordidly *black* interior . . ." It occupied the first and second floors of a building past which stage coaches and horse cars rattled and heavy carts were painfully dragged and where he could hear the "promiscuous human shuffle of New York." M. Maurice Vergnès was an old and rather irritable individual, or seemed to be to the young Henry, and the school swarmed with small homesick Cubans and Mexicans. The entire staff of this institution was "constantly in a rage." "I remember infuriated ushers, of foreign speech and flushed complexion—the tearing across of hapless 'exercises' and *dictées* and the hurtle through the air of dodged volumes; only never, despite this, the extremity of smiting. There can have been at the Institution no blows instructionally dealt—nor even from our hours of ease do any such echoes come back to me. Little Cubans and Mexicans, I make out, were not to be vulgarly whacked—in deference, presumably, to some latent relic or imputed survival of Castilian pride. . . . In Vergnès air at any rate I seem myself to have sat unscathed and unterrified—not alarmed even by so much as a call to the blackboard; only protected by my insignificance. . . ."

In due course the elder James, always experimenting, removed William and Henry to the greater establishment of Mr. Richard Puling Jenks at 689 Broadway where they were pupils during 1853-54—that is during Henry's eleventh year. Mr. Jenks was a rotund, bald man with a *barbiche*, who nursed his ferule and whacked occasionally, although Henry had no recollection of ever

being the recipient of so much attention. Mr. Coe was the draw-ing master, tall, white-haired and affecting a great cloak. What impressed little Henry was that so tall an individual produced such miniature drawings "as if some mighty bird had laid di-minutive eggs." Mr. Coe, he added, laid his "all over the place" and Henry in his old age could remember the very smell of the tiny panels he painted. He taught the boys to draw crooked cot-tages, feathery trees, browsing beasts. The third member of the Jenks faculty was the writing master, Mr. Dolmidge, "a pure pen-holder of a man" who taught the boys how to make complicated flourishes. The school itself was recalled by Henry as a couple of "middling rooms, front and back, our close packing, our large un-accommodating stove, our grey and gritty oilcloth, and again our importunate Broadway. . . . Up out of Broadway we still scram-bled—I can smell the steep and cold and dusty wooden staircase; straight into Broadway we dropped—I feel again the generalized glare of liberation. . . . We must have knocked about in Broad-way, and in Broadway alone, like perfect little men of the world; we must have been let loose there to stretch our legs and fill our lungs, without prejudice either to our earlier and later freedoms of going and coming." The stove scorched without warming and Henry wondered how he could have been put into a school with such a "deficiency of landscape." For Henry there had been noth-ing comparable to the playing fields of Eton, only the dusty, noisy streets of old New York.

In the following year they changed schools yet again. This time, Henry recalled, they were moved to the establishment of "Forest and Quackenboss" at Fourteenth Street and Sixth Avenue. How-ever no such school is given in the New York directory of that year although two teachers included therein list their names as Quackenbos. George P. Quackenbos lived at 292 Henry Street and George C. at 124 Leroy; a William Forrest is listed as a teacher in the 1854-55 directory at 71 West Fourteenth Street which would be near Sixth Avenue at that time. At any rate Henry studied with a Mr. Forest or Forrest, a massive individual

in a black dress coat and white neckcloth and found him "the driest of all our founts of knowledge." William had Mr. Quacken-bos—the two teachers may have occupied the same premises—and was "lost on upper floors, in higher classes, in real pursuits." We gather that Henry day-dreamed much in this class over the prospect of Europe which loomed as an approaching reality.

III

Henry James Senior's theory of education was comparatively simple. He feared pedantry and rigidity; he had a horror of dogma and of moral judgments. He wanted to spare his children the sufferings of his own boyhood. His solution was to throw them into many schools and to let them find their own feet. He reasoned that there was Divine Truth in the world and this the children were bound to discover for themselves under Divine Guidance. "The literal," Henry Junior said, "played in our education as small a part as it perhaps ever played in any. . . . Method certainly never quite raged among us."

The father's desire to surround his boys with "an atmosphere of freedom" was itself surrounded by contradictions. When William at one point expressed a desire to go to Union College, his father burst out that colleges were hot-beds of corruption where it was impossible to learn anything. Later he agreed to William's attending Harvard. When Henry first expressed a desire to follow William, the father said it was "wholly unpracticable." Some months later, in a different mood, he informed Henry there was no obstacle to his going. "To have deprecated the 'college course' with such emphasis," his son reflected, "only so soon afterwards to forswear all emphasis and practically smile, in mild oblivion, on *any* Harvard connection I might find it in me to take up, was to bring it home, I well recall, that the case might originally have been much better managed." This was still another case of having to breathe inconsistency and drink contradiction.

The "theory"—if the elder James's ideas on education can be called anything so formal—produced in young Henry the feeling

that he had been given no standard by which to judge the facts of the life he saw around him. He felt himself forced, he reasoned much later, to pay attention to everything and by this process could seek to bring order and reason and common sense out of the world's chaos. The senior Henry gave him, he felt, no sense of values save to realize the value of *all* life and *all* experience. At one point the novelist likens his brother and himself to Romulus and Remus, disowned by the parent, thrown into the Tiber of life, left to flounder as best they could and called upon to build Rome—that is to have the right answers to the Divine Truth which the father affirmed was all around them. The novelist reasoned that this free-and-easy mode of education—or absence thereof—was the best thing that could have happened to him: it made him "convert"—everything had to be translated into his own terms and rendered in the light of his own inner resources which in the end helped him to bring order into his world. He had a terrible need for order, for design, for apprehending—and later communicating—the world around him in an elaborately organized fashion. It stemmed undoubtedly from the disordered fashion in which, as a boy, he was asked to cope with it. In a sense the circle came full round: William of Albany sought to impose discipline and order on the senior Henry; the elder James carefully refused to impose such order upon his novelist son, who in the end imposed it, as a consequence of inner needs, upon himself.

Reflecting in his old age on the years spent in the New York classrooms, Henry was struck by his separateness and isolation, even in the midst of the "elbowing and kicking presences" of his classmates. The gifted little boy was as withdrawn and shy in class as at home. He neither attracted attention nor was molested by his thoroughly down-to-earth schoolfellows. He gives the impression that he was perturbed by this, yet at the same time aware of the ground upon which he stood as a little observer of the human scene. "I lived and wriggled, floundered and failed, lost the clue of everything but a general lucid consciousness (lu-

cid, that is, for my tender years) which I clutched with a sense of its values." It was this lucid consciousness that enabled him to remember the appearance and the dress of his teachers, the very smell of the classrooms and the aspect of the bustling Manhattan in which he moved. He had the novelist's eye—for detail, for picture, for scene—and the sensual awareness from the first. There was "self-abandonment . . . to visions" in the obscure classrooms and in doing this he carried on "in the midst of the actual . . . an existence that somehow floated and saved me even while cutting me off from any degree of direct performance, in fact from any degree of direct participation, at all."

He "converted." The small boy's imagination could make "all pastors and masters, and especially all fellow-occupants of benches and desks, all elbowing and kicking presences within touch or view, so many monsters and horrors, so many wonders and splendors and mysteries, but never, so far as I can recollect, realities of relation, dispensers either of knowledge or of fate, playmates, intimates, mere coevals and coequals." What the small and exceptional boy could do was to endow them with the richness of his creative imagination, so that far from indulging in a flight from reality, he achieved something that did not exist at all for his fellow-pupils. "They were something better—better above all than the coequal and coeval; they were so thoroughly figures and characters, divinities or demons, and endowed in this light with a vividness that the mere reality of relation, a commoner directness of contact, would have made, I surmise, comparatively poor."

Henry's conclusion was that "no education avails for the intelligence that doesn't stir in it some subjective passion and that on the other hand almost anything that does so act is largely educative." There remains indeed the significant fact that not all little boys had a subjective passion that could be stirred.

THE THAMES AND THE SEINE

HENRY JAMES THE ELDER HAD BEEN SETTLED ONLY A FEW MONTHS in the house on Fourteenth Street when he began to speak of taking his family abroad. This time, however, he did not act precipitately. The project was discussed for six years before he acted and meanwhile the small boy and his brothers were able to push down roots in Manhattan that otherwise would never have sprouted. As early as August 1849, when Henry was six and they had been in New York less than a year, the father wrote to Emerson a since much-quoted letter about his boys and their education. The family had grown, the Fourteenth Street house required enlargement, a country place was needed for the hot summers. . . . "These things look expensive and temporary to us, besides being an additional care," the father wrote, "and so, looking upon our four stout boys, who have no play-room within doors, and import shocking bad manners from the street, with much pity, we gravely ponder whether it would not be better to go abroad for a few years with them, allowing them to absorb French and German and get a better sensuous education than they are likely to get here. To be sure, this is but a glimpse of our ground of proceeding—but perhaps you know some decisive word which shall dispense us from further consideration of the subject." This was indeed a large request and Emerson's reply was a model of tact. "I hear with some terror that you are going to Europe, I who never see you. . . . New York looked available and intelligent whilst I knew you were in it." Years later, Henry Junior, quoting from his father's letter in his memoirs, altered "get a better sensuous education than they are likely to get here" to read "get such a sensuous education as they can't get here." In this way he proclaimed the absence of proper facilities in America for "sensuous" schooling and at the same time sought to create

the impression that his father's decision to go abroad was not an arbitrary act but one of necessity.

In 1851, two years after writing Emerson, the debate was still going on in the elder Henry's mind. "We are still talking of Europe for the boys," he wrote to Dr. Wilkinson. And he added a remark that has a highly modern sound: "Think you there will be peace for two years more out of England?" To Edmund and Mary Tweedy, he wrote: "We may go to foreign parts . . . and educate the babies in strange lingoes." But they remained in New York from year to year with Europe always on the horizon. Finally the decision was taken and the preparations made. On the evening of June 26, 1855, the elder Henry wrote to S. G. Ward: "We are having a golden sunset to pace our last evening at home." The next day he stomped aboard the S.S. *Atlantic* of the Collins Line with his wife and five offspring and a French maid, Annette Godefroi, who came from Metz and had been engaged for the journey in New York. The great adventure, the "re-exposure" to Europe, "to air already breathed and to a harmony already disclosed," was begun. Henry Junior was then twelve.

The "nostalgic cup," he wrote years later, "had been applied to my lips even before I was conscious of it." He had been "hurried off to London and to Paris immediately after my birth and then and there, I was ever afterwards strangely to feel, that poison had entered my veins." The nostalgic cup was about to be offered to him again or, in another image which he also used, the golden nail was to be driven in once more, this time not into an infant kicking his feet in his flowing child's robe on someone's knee in the Place Vendôme, but to a keen-eyed little product of Manhattan, all his senses alert to the wonders of the world.

I

They disembarked in Liverpool on July 8, 1855 and forty-eight hours later Henry was sitting beside a coachman on a vehicle piled high with luggage and packed with his brothers and sister,

gaping at the spectacle of London. The remainder of the stay in
the capital of mid-Victorian England was the memory only of a
curtained four-poster bed in the Euston Hotel. Henry suddenly
developed malarial chills and fever, a hangover from the sojourn
on Staten Island the previous summer. He remained in bed "with
the thick and heavy suggestions of the London room about me
. . . and the window open to the English [July] . . . and the
far off hum of a thousand possibilities."

A few days later the James boys were on a balcony of the Hôtel
Westminster in the Rue de la Paix looking down upon the Paris
of the Second Empire. It was at this moment that Jean Nadali
took Henry and William to the Louvre for their memorable first
visit. The curious small boy remembered also that across the street
from the hotel he could see one of the dress-making establishments for which the French capital is famous—busy young women
sewing far into the night. The James family did not linger long
in Paris. They pushed ahead whenever Henry's fever and chills
subsided. They took the railway to Lyon and there put up for
two days at the Hôtel de l'Univers where Henry spent more
time in bed. The hours passed in this hostelry prepared him,
he felt, for the French *vie de province* he was to experience in
his later travels and in the pages of Balzac. There was no railway between Lyon and Geneva, their ultimate destination, and
the father engaged two travelling carriages to complete the journey. They set forth with young Henry stretched out on an improvised couch, formed by a plank across two seats and a small
mattress fortified by cushions, and with an elaborate retinue—a
costumed postilion, the black-mustached Nadali and the fresh-
colored, broad-faced *bonne Lorraine*, Mlle. Godefroi. For Henry
this was "the romance of travel." He was to yield to it in one
way or another, all his life.

And so while in the United States new generations of Americans were striking westward in covered wagons, the James family,
products of the eastern seaboard, had pushed still farther east,
across an ocean, to travel in this colorful fashion over the Franco-

Swiss highways into the Alps. If this parallel is here invoked it is not to contrast pioneering with the sophisticated travel of the Jameses, but rather to emphasize that the generation of critics which condemned Henry James for not writing about American life failed to reckon with the facts of his boyhood. Henry James could not write about prairie schooners but he could write about Americans spending the fruits of their native wealth in Europe and riding in travelling carriages through Switzerland. The capital event of this journey, during which the young Henry sat propped among his pillows like some young princeling, was "an hour that has never ceased to recur to me all my life as crucial, as supremely determinant." The carriages mounted and mounted and at one point there was a halt at the doorway of an inn in the cool sunshine. Henry munched cold chicken and surveyed the scene. The village street was unlike any that he had ever observed: it opened into a high place upon a fresh, a significant, in fact an epochal revelation: a castle and a ruin.

The only "castle" Henry had ever seen was the elaborate villa with its towers at the New Brighton summer resort; and he had never before viewed a ruin. Below the slope he spied a woman at work, attired in a black bodice, a white shirt, a red petticoat, a pair of sabots, the first peasant he had ever seen. Here was a "sublime synthesis" of Europe for the future novelist and it was as such that he remembered it: a castle (with a tower), a ruin, a peasant woman in sabots engaged in some sort of field labor. Memories came to little Henry of books, of his lonely readings in Fourteenth Street and now the imagined scenes out of the absorbed pages suddenly focused into reality.

"Europe mightn't have been flattered, it was true, at my finding her thus most signified and summarized in a sordid old woman scraping a mean living and an uninhabitable tower abandoned to the owls. . . . It made a bridge over to more things than I then knew." The young Henry James—or the old Henry James recalling the past—had fixed on the very symbols of "Europe" selected by Goethe in his *Poems of Wisdom* dedicated to America:

America, you fare much better
Than this old continent of ours
No basalt rocks your land enfetter
No ruined towers. . . .

The memory of that day was embodied by Henry James some
years later in one of his early stories, written when he was twenty-
six and on the verge of his first adult journey to Europe. In
"Gabrielle de Bergerac" there is the castle of Fossy, lifting
its "dark and crumbling towers with a decided air of feudal arrogance from the summit of a gentle eminence in the recess of a shallow gorge . . . offering the hospitality of its empty skull to a colony of swallows. . . ." The hero talks as if he had been reading
Goethe: "It's haunted with the ghost of the past. It smells of
tragedies, sorrows, cruelties." The heroine evokes Knights and ladies, a lover on bended knee, a moat sheeted with lilies, all the
trappings of feudal romance. The young man isn't interested.
Could he have counted on being a Knight in that old order? The
reality, he observes, is that he would have been a "brutal, senseless peasant, yoked down like an ox, with my forehead in the soil."

"I should have liked to live in those old days," sighs the heroine.

And her young lover answers: "Life is hard enough now."

High on the road into Switzerland that day Henry James seized
the romance and the ruin of Europe, the contradictions of old
and new, the symbols human and material of the old feudal order.
He had seen a peasant woman with her "forehead in the soil." A
vivid slice of life, a whole world of history, floated in through the
window of the travelling carriage. Past and present, the old order
and the new—the Old World and the New—this was to be the
heart of Henry James's half-century of creation.

II

In Geneva the James family established itself during August in an
old house, the Villa Campagne-Gerebsow, sublet by an invalid

Russian lady who assigned five or six rooms to her guests and kept a wing for herself. The grounds led down to the junction of the Arve and the Rhône. There was a view of Mont Blanc and the garden was whitened with orange blossoms. All this for $10 a week, the elder James triumphantly announced in a wordy letter to the New York *Tribune*. Henry remembered the Russian lady who could be seen regularly on her chaise longue under a mushroom hat and green veil in a corner of the garden. He watched her from afar while Wilky, more gregarious and fearless, made her acquaintance and reported to Henry on her identity and history. In most of his tales of Switzerland later shadowy Russian ladies figure in the background and are sometimes alluded to as Muscovite "tartaresses."

He was still spending feverish days in bed. William and Wilky were placed at a Swiss boarding school, the Pensionnat Roediger at Châtelaine where Henry was scheduled to join them upon his recovery. The elder Henry extolled the school in a second letter to the *Tribune* for having a playground as big as Washington Square and providing the young with gymnastic facilities; he also, praised the participation of the teachers in the boyish games, was deeply impressed by the absence of rowdyism, the cultivation of the arts, the staging of concerts, and in subsequent letters stressed also the fact that the students were given a large measure of freedom to amuse themselves on Sundays. The James parents attended one of the Sundays at the school. There was a grand dinner at five in the afternoon, followed by singing and dancing; the senior Henry was pleasantly struck by the way in which the Sunday was converted into a day of "pure festivity."

Henry Junior recalled the spaciousness of the Geneva villas, the cool houses, the green shutters, the placid pastoral scenes, the great trees, the afternoon shadows and the polyglot character of the school where a babble of English, French, German and Russian was constantly heard. The boys were to be sent to the Institution Haccius, a celebrated establishment dedicated to teaching languages to young Americans—but the father changed his mind when

he discovered that the American language "reigned there almost unchallenged." The stay in Switzerland, begun with parental enthusiasm, was soon curtailed. In fact, by the time the father's enthusiastic letters were appearing in the *Tribune* he was writing his mother that Swiss schools were "over-rated" and that he and his wife had decided "home tuition" would be best for the children. This was in late September, a bare two months after they had arrived in Geneva.

Early in October the elder Henry decided to spend the winter in London. "We had fared across the sea," Henry Junior wrote, "under the glamour of the Swiss school in the abstract, but the Swiss school in the concrete soon turned stale on our hands." This time without Nadali, but with a new Swiss governess to replace him, they clambered aboard the big postal coach between Geneva and Lyon, "vast, yellow and rumbling." It was wholly filled by the Jameses. To the last there was note of romance: an expatriate cousin, Charlotte King, emerged from a rural retreat and ran alongside the carriage pleading with the conductor that he slow up *"rien que pour saluer ces dames."* The coach didn't slow down much, but the enterprising Charlotte achieved her brief breathless visit with her ambulatory relatives and "dropped as elegantly out as she had gymnastically floated in."

Two days later they were in Paris. Then, late one evening, tired and hungry, they were in London, at the Gloucester Hotel close to Berkeley Square, where they ate cold roast beef, bread and cheese and washed it down with ale while an exuberant father extolled the English scene: "There's nothing like it after all." From here they moved into a small house at No. 3 Berkeley Square and then, after a month and before their first English Christmas, into a furnished house in St. John's Wood above Regent's Park at No. 10 Marlborough Place, where they had Dr. J. J. Garth Wilkinson and his family as neighbors. "You have a home-feeling in London. . . ." The elder Henry wrote to his mother. We get something of the flavor of that Christmas in the opening sentence of one of the father's letters to the *Tribune*, dated, "Christmas Day,

1855." "From the bobbery which the children have been making for several hours past upstairs," he wrote, "I conclude that St. Nicholas, the merry old elf, crossed the water to us last night, and that we are in for at least five stockings full of overflowing jollification."

In the interval the father had advertised in the *Times** for a tutor and selected from an overflow of candidates a fresh-complexioned clear-eyed Scot with a tendency to trip over his long legs, Robert Thomson (James wrongly spelled it Thompson in his memoirs). Thomson engaged rooms in Titchfield Terrace over a baker's shop to be near his charges and from morning until noon he taught them—exactly what Henry could not remember. He recalled only that Thomson once rewarded him by giving him a copy of Lamb's *Tales from Shakespeare*, that he pitched ball with the boys in the large garden of their house and on days when they did their work in his rooms, at recess time, a little girl, looking like a Dickens orphan, would come up from the shop with a big stale cake which the young Jameses heartily consumed.

Thomson did not confine education to books or ball-playing. He took the boys on long exploratory rambles—the length of Baker Street, which Henry had studied in *Punch*, the landmarks of the English novelists, and the past: the Tower, St. Paul's, the Abbey, not to speak of Madame Tussaud's. Years later, Henry discovered that the warmly-remembered Scottish tutor, after leaving his American pupils, had taught still another future novelist, and a later friend of Henry's, Robert Louis Stevenson.

Their French was not neglected. Mlle. Amélie Cusin, who had come from Geneva to London, carefully officiated over the family's use of the Gallic tongue. She was but one of a list of governesses

. . . .

* The advertisement appeared in the issue of November 14, 1855, Page 3, Column 3: "To teachers.—The advertiser wishes to ENGAGE a TUTOR, by the month, for three or four hours a day, who is competent to give his boys instruction in Latin, and the ordinary branches of an English education. None but well qualified persons need apply. Address H. J., 3, Berkeley-square, between 5 and 7 in the evening."

who appeared in the James family during their European travels, "a longish procession of more or less similar domesticated presences" whose ghostly names Henry retained and inscribed in his memoirs: Mlle. Cusin, Augustine Danse, Amélie Fortin, Marie Guyard, Marie and Félicie Bonningue, Clarisse Bader. Mlle. Danse was apparently the favorite, "her of the so flexible *taille* and the so salient smiling eyes . . . the most brilliant and most genial of irregular characters. . . ." She was abruptly dismissed, however, and someone hinted she had been an adventuress. That made adventuresses interesting for Henry. He, at any rate, had admired Mlle. Danse's "sophisticated views" and she had shown the James children much "solicitude." He likened her to a distinguished governess of fiction, Becky Sharp—he who in *The Turn of the Screw* was also to create an unusual governess.

They took endless walks. They haunted the Pantheon in Oxford Street studying the vast canvases of Haydon; they visited Marlborough House and looked at the works of Maclise, Mulready, Landseer, David Wilkie and Charles Leslie. Maclise's "Play-scene in Hamlet" with Ophelia looking as if she were cut in silhouette out of white paper and pasted on the canvas attracted Henry and he "gazed and gazed again" at Leslie's "Sancho Panza and the Duchess." They went to the Royal Academy and saw the fresh flowering of the Pre-Raphaelites—exemplified in Millais's "Vale of Rest," his "Autumn Leaves" and his "Blind Girl."

Playgoing in London was an elaborate and calculated ceremony, a ride through foggy tracts of the town from St. John's Wood to the West End. The British capital offered the excitement of the Christmas pantomime and also Charles Mathews, Frederick Robson, Alfred Wigan and Charles Kean. The "momentous" event of the London stay was Kean's production of *Henry VIII*. For weeks afterwards the James children sought to reproduce in water colors Queen Katharine's dream-vision of beckoning and consoling angels. "The spectacle had seemed to us prodigious—as it was doubtless at its time the last word of costly scenic science." Henry saw the stunted Robson, heard his hoarse voice, his grotesque de-

livery. Robson leered and snarled; he used to grind his teeth and roll his eyes but he created comedy and painful intensity for the young American. At the Olympic he saw Tom Taylor's *Still Waters Run Deep* with Wigan; Mathews he saw in *The Critic*. He remembered the nights at the Olympic in Wych Street approached through squalid slums, an "incredibly brutal and barbarous" avenue to the make-believe of the theatre.

For Henry the London people themselves offered a wider field for observation than the theatre. They had an "exuberance of type" and a wealth of costume—postmen in their red frock coats and black beaver hats, milkwomen in shawls and enormous boots, footmen hooked behind coaches, grooms with riders in the Park. The little boy took in London in minute detail and was to return to it as an adult to recover all the links established between it and his younger self. He remembered in particular one evening, a return from the Continent to London with his father, a long ride in a Victorian four-wheeler westward from the station at London Bridge. It was June: the light lingered softly and there were swarming crowds everywhere. Little Henry looked upon gas-lit patches of street that seemed like the London of Cruikshank (and, as he later recognized, of Hogarth). The Artful Dodger and Bill Sikes and Nancy were in the streets that night and Henry caught a glimpse from the cab window, as a framed picture, of a woman reeling backward from a blow to the face given her by a man. Violence—that side of life excluded from his novels—was not unfamiliar to him. There were "embodied and exemplified 'horrors' " in the streets—and "horrors" was added to Henry James's special lexicon of words surrounded by quotation marks, that is words having special meanings and associations for him. To narrow the meaning was to be specific: to start naming the horrors was to limit the imagination. To use the word "horrors" and leave it at that, was to suggest *all* the horrors a reader wanted to imagine.

III

From the London of the 1850's to the Second Empire was a small jump—yet it was a progress to another world. St. John's Wood was abandoned in the early summer of 1856 in favor of the French capital. The James boys said good-bye to Robert Thomson and in due course were entrusted to M. Lerambert, who was apparently as good a teacher although a more detached individual. They lived first in a house rented from an American who divided his time between Louisiana and France. Henry remembered glassy floors, a perilous staircase, redundant mirrors, clocks, ormolu vases, white and gold panels, brocaded walls, sofas and chairs in red damask. Lerambert was spare and pale, wore a tight black coat and spectacles and came from the Rue Jacob on the Left Bank where he lived with his mother and sister. He had written a volume of meditative verse which the great Sainte-Beuve had sympathetically noticed. He had neither Thomson's ease nor a capacity for playing ball, nor for taking the boys on touristic walks. Henry's memory was of long sleepy mornings in a pavilion on the Champs Élysées between the Rond Point and the Rue du Colisée spent beside windows opening on a clattery, plashy court, rendering La Fontaine into an English that was admired and commended by his parents.

In the afternoons there was the wonderful Mlle. Danse, with her smiling eyes, to take the boys for walks along the Champs Élysées. She devoted herself mainly to Henry and the younger brothers and wasn't interested in William whom she considered rather a "bear," because he insisted on precise and scientific answers to his questions. She was fondest of the youngest, *l'ingénieux petit Robertson.*" Henry was beyond the age when children delight in mere puppets; nevertheless he still relished Guignol and Gringalet on the Champs Élysées; more than this he relished the beauty of Paris introduced to him by the loquacious and ever-lively governess. She "vouchsafed us all information for the free enjoyment— on the terms proper to our tender years—of her beautiful city." It was not then as beautiful as it is today. Baron Haussmann had

not yet cut his prodigious boulevards through the city. It was the old Paris, the Paris of the Revolutions, with its multiplicity of little streets and small squares, its lively Parisiens and Parisiennes. Yet in the Paris of the Second Empire the eye could take in the Tuileries and the grandeur of the Arch while cafés and houses with gardens and terraces were to be discovered along the Seine in a kind of "dusty ruralism" that merged with the Bois. The Jardin d'Hiver "looped itself at night with little coloured oil-lamps, a mere twinkling grin upon the face of pleasure." Beyond the Arch was the beginning of suburb and the two lodges of the *octroi* stood guard on either side, suggestive of revolutions and restorations. The young Empress, "more than young, attestedly and agreeably *new* and fair and shining," was constantly to be seen riding in state. The father's contemporary report of their view of royalty was: "We saw the Empress yesterday promenading *en voiture,* and shortly after the Emperor [with] his American swagger. Certainly it is a high compliment to our country that he should thus adopt one of its most distinctive institutions. We see the infant hope of the Empire every bright day, of which we have had a great many lately. . . ." He added: "On the whole then we are too well off here, to think of returning just yet." Paris of that era had a "homely grace" and the Jameses set up their fireside for another winter abroad. By September 1856 they had left the plush house for an apartment at No. 19 Rue d'Angoulême-St. Honoré (now Rue de la Boëtie) with many windows from which Henry could survey the full flow of life of his *quartier:* the inevitable *boulangerie,* the *crêmerie,* the *épicerie,* the *écailère* or oyster-lady, the blue-frocked workers and stout or spare cabmen, all thoroughly *bavard* and critical, as their descendants are to this day; the *marchand de bois* with his neat faggots and logs stacked around him and so on, the whole series of local shops, sociable and domestic, that make up the individual streets of the French capital.

From this Paris Henry was still maintaining his links with New York. The earliest boyhood letter of Henry James preserved

is a missive still in its narrow envelope addressed in a bold hand to "Master E. Van Winkle, 14 st. N. York." The recipient, Edgar Van Winkle, son of a lawyer, lived two doors from the Jameses and "walked in a maze of culture"—at least so Henry remembered him. (He served later for many years as chief engineer of New York's Department of Parks.) "Dear Eddy," it runs, with a brevity the novelist was seldom to achieve in his later correspondence, "As I heard you were going to try to turn the club into a Theatre. And as I was asked w'ether I wanted to belong here is my answer. I would like very much to belong. Yours Truly H James."

In Paris the staunch little playgoers were reduced to the level of circuses—the perpetual Cirques d'Été and d'Hiver and the Théâtre du Cirque. The plays in the French capital were, as Henry put it, "out of relation to our time of life . . . our cultivated innocence." The plays of Manhattan, and even of London, had been directly addressed to such innocence. Out of this Paris he remembered only a couple of plays with Rose Chéri and Anaïs Fargueil; and of hearing the name of Rachel invoked with awe. There remained with him, however, the memory of a walk with some girl cousins who had more ready access to the French theatre than he did and who related how many times they had seen Madame Doche in *La Dame aux Camélias* and what floods of tears she made them weep. For Henry James the name of Dumas *fils* forever evoked the distant memory of little girls in the Palais-Royal giving a curious aesthetic role to the handkerchief in the theatre and the memory, too, of the strange beauty of the title, and the complete unawareness, shared by himself and his cousins, of the social position of the lady of the expensive flowers.

During the autumn of 1856 Henry and William began their long walks through Paris that led them to the Luxembourg and the Louvre. In due course M. Lerambert was dropped by the father in favor of a Fourierist school discovered in the Rue Balzac, the Institution Fezandié. M. Fezandié was bald, with a melancholy eye and a delicate beard. The school was frankly experimental; it was

part *pension,* part classroom. Elders of both sexes and of many nations were taught French side by side with the children. Henry saw "ancient American virgins," "long-haired and chinless compatriots," a host of young Englishmen finding the food at the *pension* "rotten" and speaking of everyone within view as "beggars and beasts"—expressions "absent from our domestic, our American air." Here Henry became familiar with the *pension* as institution, such as he was later to study in the pages of *Le Père Goriot.* In particular, he met those Americans abroad he himself was to portray and satirize in the bright pages of his early works.

Dictation was read to the mixed class by M. Bonnefans who seemed to Henry to go all the way back to the Revolution. He tended to be contemptuous of Americans and to ridicule their pronunciation of the all-important word *liberté.* They pronounced it *"libbeté"* and M. Bonnefans would, with a show of r's that sounded like a drum roll, demonstrate how it should be said. Bonnefans was a candid if whispering "subversive" opposed to the monarchy and as full of dark hints about police spies as some of James's characters later were to be in *The Princess Casamassima.* Bonnefans would recite with bravado from *Le Cid:*

> *Nous nous levons alors!*

and in the process would move from a crouch to a terrific leap. It was from instructors such as these, as well as from the constant reading of French novels, that Henry gained his extraordinary fluency in French. He had a thorough knowledge of the riches of the language and consciously cultivated gallicisms in his English, even as he liberally sowed his earlier prose and even the late with French words. He corresponded effortlessly in later life with his French contemporaries—despite his complaints that he found it difficult. The French letters that have been preserved are neither labored nor perfunctory. They read often like extraordinary accurate renderings into French of Henry James's characteristic prose style.

IV

The family moved into still another apartment in the spring of
1857, this time at No. 26 Rue Montaigne—a large and costly establishment which required many servants. Mary James estimated
her annual household expenses here at $2,200. That summer
they went to Boulogne-sur-mer, where they set up house at No. 20
Rue Neuve Chaussée. Boulogne had a large English colony: blue-
jacketed British schoolboys, little English ladies with mushroom
hats, English water colorists. Henry assiduously explored the town
of Colonel Newcome and its waterfront, with its fishermen and
boatmen, and acquired impressions that were to find their way
into his first anonymously published story a few years later. He
studied the fishing boats, tramped over the cobbles, visited the
Napoleonic monument. He seems to have been a regular customer
at the English lending library, kept by a Mr. Merridew, who supplied him with Victorian three-decker novels which he consumed
unendingly. "Henry is not so fond of study, properly so-called, as
of reading," his father wrote that autumn. "He is a devourer of
libraries, and an immense writer of novels and dramas. He has
considerable talent as a writer, but I am at a loss to know whether
he will ever accomplish much." The elder Henry's attitude both
toward William's early ambition to be a painter and Henry's
youthful writings tended to be constantly depreciatory. Art was
frivolous, vain, "narrowing" in a world where there prevailed the
fundamental truths of science and religion. But he was of fixed
mind also that "whatever befalls my dear boys in this world, they
and you and I are all alike, and after all, absolute creatures of God,
vivified every moment by Him, cared for every moment by Him,
guided every moment by an infallible wisdom and an irreproacha-
ble tenderness. . . ."

Since Henry was "an absolute creature of God" he was allowed
to continue his reading even as William was allowed to study art.
At the same time both were made aware of parental depreciation
of their choice of pursuit. This was not, psychologically speaking,
a happy situation. It created feelings of doubt and also of guilt.

We have no record of Henry's readings, but his constant allusions to novels and novelists, letter writers and biographers, in his early criticism, could be made only by one saturated with literature, and especially fiction, both in French and English, from boyhood.

There came a day in Boulogne—it was in September of 1857—when Henry developed symptoms of illness and remained in his bed through the afternoon with the sounds of the port floating in through half-open windows. As daylight waned he was conscious of mounting uneasiness, a sense of being increasingly unwell. He tumbled out of bed to summon help and then knew only the "strong sick whirl of everything." It is with this dramatic moment, "the gravest illness of my life," that the novelist concludes his account of the *Small Boy and Others*. "My Harry has been very ill with typhus fever," the elder James wrote to a friend, "but he is now better, and we hope the best results. He was for several days delirious, and he is now extremely weak and low. . . ." To Albany he wrote that "we trembled more than once for the issue." He called in an Irish homeopathic physician named Macoubrey who carefully ministered to Henry. For him the rest of the stay in Boulogne was a dreary blur. He was in bed the best part of two months.

By the end of October Henry was convalescent and the Jameses moved back to Paris. Now, for the first time, there was heard the whisper of financial difficulties. The elder Henry James had taken his family abroad during a period of booming American prosperity. The era of railroad expansion had begun; during the Jameses' first year abroad 3,400 new miles of rail were laid. Land speculation was at its height; business inflated itself in anticipation of new markets and much of the inflation rested on credits dispensed by unstable banks. In the summer of 1857 loans began to contract under the effects of an unfavorable trade balance, rail stocks began to fall, a great insurance and trust company went bankrupt and a characteristic American "crash" was under way.

Its effect on the senior Henry was marked. To a brother he wrote: "It is something new for us to feel anxious for the future.

. . . I wrote to Ma to ask you and Augustus and Howard to aid her to contribute as large a sum as you can, to be put to my credit at Samuel G. Ward's in Boston. We shall get home as soon as we can command the means. . . . Was ever anything clearer than that these commercial disasters inflict the widest *social* disease in the community? The lack of the sentiment of brotherhood—the prevalence of self-seeking—this is the disease of the common mind." This was on October 28 and within the week Mary and Henry James had made their plans. In Paris they were paying eight hundred francs a month for their elaborate apartment in the Rue Montaigne; they would retrace their steps to Boulogne, where they could find adequate quarters for as low as two hundred francs a month. Instead of a retinue of servants and tutors they would do with one or two and the children could attend the local schools. For forty dollars a month the education of all the children would be assured, including music and dancing. The father wrote to a friend on November 2, 1857: "We have been very nearly sent home by these dreadful commercial disasters on the other side. As it is I think we shall consult duty by retracing our steps to Boulogne, and passing the winter there. . . . It is a most agreeable place, with good schools and a capital market, and a population much more manly, or rather more womanly (for it is of those remarkable fisherwomen that I speak particularly) than that of Paris."

Later that winter, when they were installed again in Boulogne, at No. 29 Grande-Rue, in smaller and less elegant quarters than those of the preceding summer, the elder Henry wrote to the same correspondent: "The children wish you a merry Christmas. They have no idea as yet, poor souls, that Christmas can ever be otherwise than merry to every one.— We *have* lost some of our income by the crash at home , , I don't know where another year may find us." It is doubtful whether teen-age children, as observant and sensitive as the young Jameses, would have been as innocent and as unworldly as their father painted them in these remarks. The changed circumstances were not hidden from them;

the sudden frugality of their parents was apparent and they were aware of trans-Atlantic happenings. The parental anxieties of this time were remembered by Henry—remembered over the decades— and they emerged in the poignant tale of "The Pupil," describing an itinerant American family in Europe, under perpetual financial embarrassment. In the tale it is a second son who suffers from the spectacle of the mendacity of his parents and their happy-go-lucky habits. While these parents bear no resemblance to the novelist's, the plight of young Morgan recaptures the anguish of an adolescent for whom the world has no anchors, and who thus remains afloat among uneasy values and unrelieved anxieties. That he should develop an almost morbid dependency on his devoted tutor, who offers him the only loyalty and devotion he can find, is inevitable. The tale is a masterpiece of conveyed feeling, evolved from the depths of Henry's own adolescence in Europe.

For a while, still convalescent from his typhus, Henry was assigned a tutor at home, a M. Ansiot, whom he described later as "a form of bland porpoise, violently blowing in an age not his own." For all his dreariness, his greasy texts (extracts of classical writers), his "drowsy lapses and honest aridities" M. Ansiot left something with his young pupil: a "working" sense of *le vieux temps*, a glimpse of a past world which Henry felt later to have had a wealth of value for him.

At the Collège Imperial Henry found himself no longer a young aristocrat, privately tutored, but member of a class constituted of the sons of local shopkeepers, mechanics, artisans and fishermen. He remembered in particular the son of the local pastry-cook, a youth with a pug nose named Coquelin, whom he was later to admire on the stage of the Théâtre Français and to entertain in London—the inimitable creator of Cyrano de Bergerac.

A winter at Boulogne sufficed for the parents. If the children now had a schoolful of playmates, the adults tended to find restricted opportunities for a social life in the Channel port. And the elder Henry was again fretting about his children's education, his chronic excuse for displacement. "I have no doubt from all I

can gather," he wrote to his mother, "that our own schools are
. . . much superior to the European schools." After that it was inevitable that the Jameses should at long last turn their faces westward again. They remained at Boulogne to the end of the school
year. Robertson James recalled being present at the Commencement, and his memory was characteristic of his sense of isolation
in that family:

Boulogne-sur-mer and the Collège Municipale and its stone
vaulted ceiling where Wilky and I went and failed to take prizes.
But the day when the Mayor of the City distributed these I do
remember, and somehow I think that tho' it was not a prize we
both had souvenirs or a reward of some kind—for I recall a beautiful book with gold figures. But around the mayor who stood on a
platform with great civic splendor and officials in uniform, I see
yet the fortunate scholars ascend the steps of his throne, kneel at
his feet, and receive crowns or rosettes, or some symbol of merit
which *we* did not get. The luck had begun to break early!

They had been abroad three years and the young Henry was
now a sturdy youth of fifteen. Early in the summer of 1858—the
depression in America was running its short-lived course—the family set sail, their destination, for the first time, New England.

NEWPORT IDYLL

THEY WENT TO LIVE AT NEWPORT, RHODE ISLAND, THEN A QUIET
seaside perch to which the elder Henry James was drawn by the
presence of his old friends, Edmund and Mary Tweedy, foster-
parents of his nieces, the four orphaned Temple girls. "We are set-

tled very comfortably at Newport for the present . . ." the father wrote that summer. "Mary is very well, though still concerned about many things, such as inkspots in children's shirts and rents in their trousers, which deflect her from the strait path of conjugal rectitude and devotion. The boys however are as good as good can be, inside of their shirts and trousers, and utterly abandoned to the enjoyment of their recovered liberty, boating and fishing and riding to their hearts' content. They have not fairly recommenced their studies."

Little more than a year later, he was writing: "I have grown so discouraged about the education of my children here, and dread so those inevitable habits of extravagance and insubordination which appear to be characteristic of American youth, that I have come to the conclusion to retrace my steps to Europe, and keep them there a few years longer. My wife is completely of the same mind, and though we feel on many accounts that we are making personal sacrifices in this step, the advantages to the children are so clear that we cannot conscientiously hesitate. I am a good patriot but my patriotism is even livelier on the other side of the water."

Abroad the children went again with their indefatigable parents, to Switzerland and later to Germany, and then they once more returned to Newport. The novelist, in his old age, reviewing these itinerant chapters of his life, found them disturbing. The restless crossings of the Atlantic seemed to testify too eloquently to a lack of purpose in his father—and they made for confusion in the narrative. It was artistically more satisfying, in writing his reminiscences, to keep the family in Europe for a full five years and then return them, once and for all, to America. He explained his reasoning to his nephew, the oldest son of William James, one day (August 23, 1913) at Lamb House. The nephew made a record of the conversation:

"H. J. at lunch said 'There is one thing about your father's early life in respect to which you mustn't give my *Small Boy*

away. I've covered over the fact, so overcome am I by the sense
of our poor father's impulsive journeyings to and fro and of the
impression of aimless vacillation which the record might make
upon the reader—that we didn't go to Europe twice, but once. I've
described our going abroad the first time, and am saying that the
year '60 found us back at Newport.' "

The nephew noted that this struck him as "a ridiculous sub-
jectivity on the part of a biographer" (although he was not allowing for the fact that Henry in reality was writing not biography
but autobiography). He told his uncle accordingly that "I was
surprised by his feeling so and that it seemed to me that it made a
real difference to a boy in the '50's (or now) whether he was
brought up solidly for five or six years in Europe after the age of
13, or whether he was dipped for 15 months in the middle of
the period into his native American bath. Uncle H. rather pooh-
poohed this, saying 'Yes, if you want to be very *analytical*; but
nothing happened in that 15 months. The family went abroad in
'55, came to Newport for the summer of '58, took a house for the
summer and another for the winter, went to Europe again in late
summer or autumn '59 and returned to America in '60.' "
The nephew noted: "Uncle H. evidently has a very lively consciousness of his father's vacillations and impulses—as if the possibility of going home or going to Europe, going from one place to
another, were always in the air and often realized to the disturb-
ance of his, Uncle H.'s equanimity. He is also evidently self-
conscious about the fanciful and inconsequent explanations and
reasons which his father used to give to people, who expressed
surprise or made inquiries."
There is no doubt that the "equanimity" of the young boy was
disturbed and this malaise was still present in the old man. In a
letter written to T. S. Perry at the time of the publication of *Notes
of a Son and Brother*, the novelist confessed that he suppressed
the 1859 journey to Europe to avoid giving the impression that
his father was "*too* irresponsible and too saccadé in his generous

absence of plan and continuity." He added that he found himself, in his memoirs, enumerating "so many choppings and changes
and interruptions and volatilities (as on our parents' part, dear
people) in our young education that the aspect of it grew in a manner foolish on my hands." Consequently he simply "dropped,
for worry-saving, certain stitches." We can now recover them
thanks to the correspondence preserved by Perry out of that distant time and the extant letters of the senior Henry.

I

After their sojourn by the Thames and the Seine, after the galleries, palaces, schools, pensions and theatres of the Old World, the
James boys finally set foot in New England. A reasonably brief
ocean voyage had brought these sons of the Hudson Valley from
the Second Empire of Louis Napoleon to the America of President Buchanan. They arrived at a time when the slavery issue was
entering an acute phase. Lincoln was about to begin his debates in
the West with Douglas. The stage was being set, the historic forces
were at play, for a great and bloody civil war. But for the young
Jameses these things were reserved for the future. For the moment
their return to America—or to the rim of America—was a return
to happy native conditions, the rediscovery of certain cousins now
grown up like themselves and the making of new and important
friendships. Henry felt in later years that Newport was "the one
right residence in all our great country." The old town seemed
indeed, with its crooked streets and small buildings, its old wharves,
its associations with Bishop Berkeley, its historic cemeteries, to
be a bit of Europe or an European outpost on the soil of America.

Newport was more: it was a corner of the eighteenth century
that had lingered into the nineteenth. It possessed in the 1850's a
"quaint shabbiness." Thames Street recalled the lately deserted
London, the great houses faced the sea and behind them lay the
Avenue along which Henry James often strolled and where stood
in their grey nudity, in contrast to the elaborate modern dwell-

ings, the shingled boxes that had been the dwellings of another day. Newport had a landscape and a seascape; it had indeed some of the characteristics of the European watering places and for the little James pilgrims, freshly returned from far-away lands, it served as an ideal stepping stone to reconciliation with their homeland. In discussing Newport, Henry James used a term he often repeated in this context: *disconnected*. The James boys had been "disconnected" from America. Newport seemed the "one marked point of reattachment." It had an active social life; there was a colony of artists; old American families lived in the town; there were cultivated elderly gentlemen and a vast summer population of elegant wives with their children sent away from overheated New York or Boston mansions to enjoy sea breezes while the husbands wilted bravely in their offices. The old-fashioned streets echoed to the footfalls of attractively dressed young women. There was, above all, the constant vision of land and sea, more sea than land. There were walks to be taken along moss-clad rocks and over the sand-choked grass with the ocean as a constant companion. There were a "thousand delicate secret places dear to the disinterested rambler." In his late book, *The American Scene*, there is almost a rhapsodic note—certainly a lyrical one—as he comes upon Newport after a thirty-five-year absence and remembers "far-away little lonely, sandy coves, rock-set, lily-sheeted ponds, almost hidden, and shallow Arcadian summer-haunted valleys with the sea just over some stony shoulder: a whole world that called out to the long afternoons of youth." And the afternoons were long indeed.

I I

Henry James has left us a detailed record of the old aspect of Newport. He revisited the town in 1870, a decade after his first residence there, when he was already launched on his career, to write a travel paper for the *Nation*. He promptly acknowledged that "I suffer from knowing the natural elements of Newport too well to attempt to describe them. I have known them so long that

I hardly know what I think of them." Thirty-five years later, again revisiting the spot, he wrote "The Sense of Newport" and observed that he had known the place "too well and loved it too much for description or definition." It wasn't, however, until three years before his death, when Newport was half a century distant, that he sought to evaluate the role of the town in the young creative consciousness that began to find itself there in 1858 and 1860.

For Henry James the place was to have always a "shy sweetness" and one suspects that the words betrayed his own state of feeling as much as what he saw in the town. "Shy" probably refers more to his first encounters with young women, for the female population of Newport was large. The theme that runs through his two papers on Newport and is explicitly expounded in his memoirs, is the sense Henry James had in this resort of being an "outsider" in America and different from Americans. He could not be a part of an American society "where the great black ebony God of business was the only one recognized." He had known only the other gods: the gods of art, of culture, of educated talk, of the life of the spirit. He recognized that this was a spot devoted to the so-called leisure class, to people like his father "leisured for life." He is concerned over idleness in a national community that was energetically attending to material things in the months before the Civil War. He recalls that as a boy he "felt it tasteless and humiliating that the head of our little family was *not* in business." Everyone else in America seemed to be. For him Newport represented disconnection not only from Europe but in a sense from America itself, even though it was a point of attachment.

This was his feeling late in life as he surveyed these early years. At the time, disconnected though Henry James undoubtedly was by temperament and upbringing, and by his long deep draught from the nostalgic cup, he felt a deep attachment for Newport itself. His roots, pulled up when they were tender, from the banks of the Hudson, found new and fresh American earth at Newport; taken abroad once more by his ever-restless father, they accepted

the fertilization of Europe but resisted, for the time, the transplanting. His letters reflected a nostalgia for Newport and the Newporters, "surrounded with a halo, in my mind which grows brighter and brighter . . ." and again "Geneva has endless lovely walks, but I think Lily Pond, Cherry Grove, Purgatory, Paradise and Spouting Rock (how I delight to write the names) . . . how I wish I was going to migrate there!" In Europe, during these years of his adolescence and emergence into young manhood, he had been able to make only casual friends; how could he do more in the swift and ever-changing shifts from place to place and school to school? The James boys were thrown a great deal upon each other's company. The elder Henry was aware of this for he spoke in a letter to a friend of the fact that the boys had been "all along perfectly starved on their social side." Newport filled a serious gap in Henry's life; for museums and galleries, books and theatres and lonely European promenades he could substitute at last important human ties. Henry Junior was young enough, when he arrived in this sea-blown corner of his native land, and sufficiently adaptable, to live himself into Newport's life and to attach himself to his new-found friends. When the time came to go abroad once more he found it difficult to leave them.

III

Two friendships formed by Henry James at Newport embraced letters and art and exerted a deep and enduring influence. Thomas Sergeant Perry was perhaps the first and closest friend; two years younger than Henry, and also a second son, he lived even more than the future novelist in a world of books. John La Farge, the painter, was seven years older. He proved to be an extraordinary mentor, sensitive and devoted, especially during the later phase of Henry's Newport residence. Friendships formed in young manhood sometimes are beacon lights for the future and for Henry both Perry and La Farge nourished mind and spirit at a crucial time. La Farge could guide and offer illumination; Perry

was a companion with whom there could be a constant exchange of ideas and books. He had a formidable ancestry: his mother was a direct descendant of Benjamin Franklin; his father was a son of Commodore Oliver Hazard Perry who won the victory on Lake Erie in 1813, and a nephew of Commodore Matthew Calbraith Perry, who drew Japan to the West. Young Perry was precocious and passive, with a tendency to substitute books for action; and he was a faithful companion. Henry James's tribute to him, in *Notes of a Son and Brother,* describes him as a great lumberjack of the library, felling volumes and sets of volumes as if they were trees in a forest, absorbing whole literatures at a time. In the life of young Henry and Sargy Perry the Redwood Library loomed large and its name may have suggested the lumber-image. It was the pride of Newport with its fifty-foot long reading room, windows at each end, a dome, and more than one hundred paintings on its walls. This was not the Galerie d'Apollon, but it was a haven for the literary Henry who spent many hours there with Perry.

T. S. Perry met the James boys in June or July of 1858 shortly after they had settled in Newport. He used to box with William, he was a friend of the genial Wilky, who was his own age, but he was for the most part with Henry. His diary, carefully kept over years, discloses how often they were together, in and out of school where they were classmates. The latest educational institution to which Henry was committed was the Berkeley Institutue headed by the Reverend William C. Leverett, curate of Newport's Trinity Church, who was addicted as much to delivering orations on things "as such"—his favorite expression—as to coming to grips with the concrete materials of education. Perry remembered that Henry James was an "uninterested scholar." The school was located in the Masonic Building and contained a large study room and "recitation rooms." One day a week they declaimed pieces from Sargent's *Standard Speaker.* "H. J. in his books speaks without enthusiasm of his school studies," Perry recalled, "but he and I read

together at Mr. Leverett's school a fair amount of Latin literature. Like Shakespeare he had less Greek."

John La Farge too had lived abroad and so carried about him the aura of "Europe" as did the Jameses. He was of French descent, a Catholic of ample means and wide horizons. His father, like Henry's grandfather, had amassed a Hudson Valley fortune, in real estate, and he had been brought up in the same tight old New York world as the future novelist. Like Henry he had lived in Paris but with the difference that in the capital he had glimpsed the literary elite, encountered through a relative of his mother's, the critic Paul de Saint-Victor. He could thus speak of Saint-Beuve, Baudelaire, Flaubert and the Goncourts with a certain impressive familiarity.

La Farge shared with Henry the latest copies of the *Revue des Deux Mondes* as they arrived in their salmon-colored wrappers. The artist had sketches of European scenes, water colors of Breton peasants, costumes, interiors, bits of villages and landscapes. He took Henry on long rambles across the rocks. And he could talk; he filled the afternoons with a full measure of talk, and more than this, ideas. He acquired with young Henry "an authority . . . that it verily took the length of years to undermine."

Perry too remembered their walks. "A thousand scrappy recollections of the strolls still remain," Perry wrote after Henry James was dead and he was approaching his eightieth year, "fragments of talk, visions of the place." Near Lily Pond they talked one day of Fourier. Another time they were full of their reading of Ruskin and Henry devoted himself to the "conscientious copying of a leaf and very faithfully drew a little rock that jutted above the surface of Lily Pond. . . . We read the English magazines and reviews and the *Revue des Deux Mondes* with rapture."

The first part of the Newport idyll lasted from early 1858 until the autumn of 1859. Presently the Jameses were in New York again and (it was October 8, 1859) Henry was writing to his Newport friend, Sargy, "You see by the date that this is our hour for sailing. . . . I can scarcely sit still to write this and feel myself

thinking much more of what I leave behind than what I expect to find. . . . Good bye to you and every body and every thing! Yours very truly H. James Jr."

THE RHÔNE AND THE RHINE

ONCE AGAIN THEY TURNED THEIR FACES EASTWARD. THE STEAMSHIP *Vanderbilt* made the crossing in eleven days of unrelieved bad weather. They landed at Le Havre and spent a day there, "plenty of time to find out what a nice little place it is" (remaining just about as long as Caroline Spencer was to do in James's "Four Meetings"). They spent two days in Paris revisiting familiar places. Five days after landing they were in Geneva.

The James family had gone abroad in 1855 "with an eye to the then supposedly supreme benefits of Swiss schooling" and had ended up by the Thames and the Seine. Now, four years later, they had retraced their steps to the city of Calvin and of Rousseau, and, we might add, of Gibbon and Madame de Staël and even Voltaire. Henry and Mary James took rooms in the Hotel de l'Écu at the edge of the rushing Rhône. The two younger sons were placed in the Pensionnat Maquelin just outside Geneva: Alice remained with the parents. William enrolled at the Academy which later became the University of Geneva and Henry was dispatched to the Institution Rochette—a preparatory school for engineers and architects!

I

This was perhaps the most curious of all of Henry James's miscellaneous schools. As he gently put it many years later he had been "disposed of under a flattering misconception of my aptitudes." He found himself among students whose goals were far removed from literature; he was called upon to study mathematics and his brave attempt to make some sort of showing was "mere darkness, waste and anguish. . . . It was hard and bitter fruit all and turned to ashes in my mouth." What astounded Henry in later years as he looked back on this episode, was his failure to protest "with a frankness proportioned to my horror." And again, as before, he explains his ordeal as an under-estimation of self; he considered himself inferior to others in not being able to attack geometry and algebra and he was determined to overcome the inferiority. It was a hopeless battle. The attempt broke down utterly and Henry withdrew or was withdrawn "not even as a conspicuous" but "only as an obscure, a deeply-hushed failure."

The Institution Rochette was selected, and apparently with Henry's concurrence, because it was the best school in Geneva other than the Academy and the Gymnasium, neither of which he was qualified to enter. There is no evidence that the parents intended to make either an architect or an engineer of their second son. No such intention could be imputed to the father's theory of education. He might have been tutored at home, as in the past; this, however, would have provided no companionship and no opportunity for talking French. At the Rochette school he was cloistered with some twenty fellow-students and for the greater part of the day, five and a half days a week. It was understood from the outset that Henry was not to receive the full pre-science training; as he put it to Perry, "I am the only one who is not destined for either of the useful arts or sciences, although I am I hope for the art of being useful in some way." In his letters to Perry, Henry kept up a bold front, assuring him repeatedly he was getting on "very well." By Easter it was clear that he wasn't; mathematics was clearly a waste of time and without giving details Henry told

Perry that "the yoke, if the expression is not too tragic, has been considerably lightened." He had dropped all subjects at the Institution Rochette except German, French and Latin and he had arranged to sit in at a number of courses at the Academy instead. Thus his bitter-sweet year in Geneva ended with his attaining a certain level of equality with his older brother, after an inequality all the more emphasized by the disagreeable doses of a subject which induced only a feeling of utter helplessness.

The letters to Sargy Perry during these months give no suggestion of gloom; they are buoyant and filled with the healthy observations of an unusually wide-awake young man of seventeen. Nowhere do they suggest that "eternity of woe" James described in the opening pages of *Notes of a Son and Brother*. However, the contemporaneous account does not appear to be in contradiction with that written fifty years later. On the contrary, James's memory is prodigiously accurate in the details. It was not to be expected that young Henry would pour out his woe to Perry; for him he recorded the more joyful aspects of his European sojourn with a zealous adherence to fact rather than to feeling. The year was certainly not one of unmitigated gloom even if it was one of hard—and unsuccessful—study. As Henry puzzled it out toward the end of his life, his parents had "simply said to themselves, in serious concern, that I read too many novels, or at least read them too attentively—*that* was the vice." Moreover, they had "got me in a manner to agree with them." The experiment designed to form his mind through the approaches to science failed and Henry consoled himself as usual that it was not entirely a waste of time. There had been a harvest of impressions—and these we get to the full in the letters he wrote back to Newport.

II

Geneva itself, as he described it after a later visit, was "a strongly-featured little city, which, if you do not enjoy, you may at least grudgingly respect." It had no galleries, museums or interesting churches, but it did possess a natural beauty; there were "liquid

sapphire and emerald" in the surface of Lake Leman and the "divinely cool-hued gush of the Rhône beneath the two elder bridges" was "one of the loveliest things in Switzerland." It must have seemed to Calvin, James mused, "as one of the streams of the paradise he was making it so hard to enter." The town itself presented a sordid aspect that nevertheless fascinated Henry when he first explored it—explored it and described it to Perry with uncommon skill and concreteness that revealed a writer formed, a young master of the resources and rhythms of the English language: "Such dingy old streets and courts and alleys, black with age some of them are, steep and dirty, such quaint old houses, high and sombre are very picturesque." The sentence may be lacking in completeness, but it has conjured up a distinct picture. We can look with young Henry out of the window of the Institution Rochette, down into the street: "Perhaps you would like to know about my school. The building is wholly unlike that of the Berkeley Institute. It is a dilapidated old stone house in the most triste quarter of the town. Scarcely a soul passes by it all day, and I do not remember to have seen a wheeled vehicle of any kind near it since I've been there. Beside it is the prison and opposite the Cathedral of St. Peter, in which Calvin used to preach. It seems to me that none but the most harmless and meekest men are incarcerated in the former building. While at my lesson in a class room which looks out on the door, I have once in a while seen an offender brought up to his doom. He marches along with handcuffs on his wrists, followed by a gendarme in 'spick and span' uniform. The gendarme knocks on the door, which is opened by some internal spring, shoves in his charge, the door closes, the gendarme retraces his steps. What happens after the prisoner is inside I don't know, but as the only officer I have ever seen about the prison is a diminutive little porter with a most benign countenance, I am inclined to think that the most inoffensive subjects are sent to him to deal with. . . ." We wonder how Henry knew the door opened by some internal spring, we may smile at the "diminutive little" but there is no denying the care and system of the narrative; it

is further testimony incidentally to Henry's interest not in the Institution Rochette but in what was going on around it.

Henry didn't have much time for relaxation. He rose at six-thirty in the winter dark; he breakfasted alone in the Hotel de l'Écu. By eight, in the dawning light, he has reached the school. Four hours later he walks back for lunch. He is at his school bench again an hour later. At five he returns to the hotel. He dines; he studies till bedtime. And so it goes, from Monday to Saturday, with a half day off Thursday. During the Thursday afternoon he reads, he idles, he looks out of the hotel window, he explores the shops, he walks around the edge of the lake. He is very much alone. His brothers are scattered. He doesn't make friends with his schoolmates; he, an English youth and a young Russian, are the sole foreigners in their midst. (He remembered himself as a "lost lamb, almost audibly bleating" in the school.) He talks to his fellow-foreigners. The English youth "is the only one with whom I have been able to become the least bit friendly. . . . When I first went there no one spoke to me, I had to commence every conversation myself. I think that if a Frenchman had come to Mr. Leverett's he would have been more hospitably received. . . ."

On Sunday the family gathers at the Hotel de l'Écu: Wilky and Bob come in for the day from the Pensionnat Maquelin; Alice is there; William on occasions mingles with them unless, Henry recalls, he can find "livelier recreation." Toward the end of the winter there seems to be a little more social life. Henry is going to parties. "I go twice a week to a dancing school . . ." he tells Perry, "and seldom have I seen a more hideous collection of females than I do on those occasions. They all sit on benches ranged along one side of the room and the cavaliers stand up against the wall on the opposite side—for a fellow to sit down on one of their benches would be a most heinous crime. In the intervals of the dancing therefore we have occasion to contemplate them as they sit with their eyes modestly cast down upon the floor. I learned to dance because at the parties here that is the sole amusement"; and the young American with the ever-hearty appetite adds char-

acteristically and patriotically: "they do not even have supper but hand round little glasses of syrop and 'helpings' of ice-cream about twice as large as a peach pit!! Be thankful that you are born in our free and enlightened country."

He is now liberated from his rigorous educational schedule; he has time for newspapers and magazines. The new *Cornhill Magazine*, edited by Thackeray, has arrived and he reads it avidly ("Strokes of the great Victorian clock," the old Henry James wrote, remembering the first issue which particularly brought him Trollope "charged with something of the big Balzac authority"). He is now studying French literature and natural philosophy at the Academy (the self-same Academy which Winterbourne, in the revised versions of "Daisy Miller" attends ". . . Winterbourne had an old attachment for the little capital of Calvinism; he had even gone, on trial—trial of the grey old 'Academy' on the steep and stony hillside—to college there . . ."). Henry was there "on trial." He listens to H. F. Amiel, vaguely aware of him as a "mild grave oracle." With a bow to science he studies anatomy. "I went the other day in company with half a dozen other students to see a dissection at the Hospital," he told Perry. "It was a most unlovely sight. The subject was a strapping big gendarme who had died of inflammation of the lungs. The smell was pretty bad, but I am glad to say that I was not in any way affected by the thing." William is invited to join the Société de Zoffingue, the Swiss student organization for "brotherhood and beer." He takes his younger brother with him to the village of Moudon near Lausanne where they drink, smoke German pipes and sing. The local clergy participate: "they drank as hard, sung as loud and gave as many toasts and jolly speeches as the most uproarious student." The students swear allegiance with a great "swilling down of beer, of grasping of hands, of clashing of rapiers, and of glorious deep-mouthed German singing."

Despite the ups and downs of this winter Henry has been quietly scribbling. Wilky, writing to Perry, reports peeping into Henry's room and seeing "some poetical looking manuscripts lying

on the table, and himself looking in a most authorlike way."
William had been reading aloud satiric odes to his sister Alice
and other members of the family and Wilky observes "the only
difference there is between Willy and Harry's labours is that the
former always shows his productions while the modest little Henry
wouldn't let a soul or even a spirit see his." Commenting on this
after his friend's death, Perry wrote that Henry seldom entrusted
his early efforts "to the criticism of his family—they did not see
all he wrote. They were too keen critics, too sharp-witted, to be
allowed to handle every essay of this budding talent" and we
might add there was too strong a fund of rivalry and aggressive-
ness there; if the senior Henry lampooned his contemporaries, his
offspring lampooned one another. Perry adds their comments on
Henry's work "would have been too merciless; and hence, for
sheer self-preservation, he hid a good part of his work from
them. Not that they were cruel, far from it. Their frequent solitude in foreign parts, where they had no familiar companions, had
welded them together in a way that would have been impossible
in America, where each would have had separate distractions of
his own. Their loneliness forced them to grow together most har-
moniously, but their long exercise in literary criticism would have
made them possibly merciless judges of H. J.'s crude beginning's." Perry perhaps minimizes the fund of plain boyish high-
spiritedness that prevailed, the usual tendency among growing
youngsters for self-aggrandizement at each other's expense. He
questioned Henry about Wilky's disclosure of his literary efforts
and was told in reply: "A fearful vengeance awaits Wilkie's fool-
hardy imprudence in disclosing, as he did, my secret employment."
But he does not deny it. Perry having asked him what "style of
work" he is cultivating, he volunteers readily, "I may reply that
to no style am I a stranger, there is none which has not been
adorned by the magic of my touch." And as if to demonstrate to
Perry his facility he begins his next letter with an extravagant imitation of the eastern romances he has been reading: "The morning broke! High into the vast unclouded vault of Heving rode the

Awb of Day, chasing before it the fleeting clouds that enshroud the slumbers of men. . . ." And so on describing the awakening of " 'Enry James de Jeames" on his couch "covered with the skin of a leopard, which he had killed with his own hands in the burning wastes of Arabia." He stretches forth his arm on which the "cerulean veins swelled like ivy creepers round a giant oak, and grasping a time piece more glittering with brilliants than an eastern monarch's diadem he. . . . Nay—but a truce to this idiotic strain. This meaneth in plain English that your good friend Henry James Jr. Esquire was awakened by the sun . . ." and so on. Perhaps Henry had not been boasting; he was not a stranger to many styles and no stranger to good humor and geniality either. Of his studies that spring he told Perry not a word. But in *Notes of a Son and Brother* he remembered that he read Livy and Virgil with a M. Verchère, Schiller and Lessing with a ruddy, noisy little German professor, and that he was "almost happy" with M. Toeppfer with whom he read Racine and who described for him Rachel's playing of *Phèdre*, her entrance "borne down, in her languorous passion, by the weight of her royal robes—*Que ces vains ornemens, que ces voiles me pèsent!—*"

Now the Swiss spring was at hand and Henry practiced swimming in the deep-blue lake water and enjoyed the Alpine views; he wandered along the verdant hedges, stopped to peer at the iron gateways up long avenues of trees leading to châteaux: yet he thinks also of Newport. "I suppose you will soon see the commencement of the annual migration to Newport," he writes to Perry. "How I wish I was going to migrate there!" The family plans however called for a summer at Bonn and a stay next winter at Frankfort. Before going to Bonn, William and Henry went on a week's walking tour through the mountains. They crossed the Mer de Glâce, went to the Canton du Valais by way of the Tête-Noir and from Martigny, with the aid of a guide and a mule, they climbed the St. Bernard. The scene as they neared the celebrated hospice called forth this passage from the future novelist to Perry;

at seventeen he was distinctly beginning to master that "spirit of the place" which he was to invoke in his later travel writings. . . .

At about three hours distance from the hospice the scenery becomes most wild dreary and barren. Everything indicates a great elevation. The growth of everything but the enormous rocks is stunted—not a blade of grass or straggling mountain pine. The tinkling of the last cattle bell dies away, you see the last hardy Alpine sheep climbing over desolate heights which would seem to afford no nourishment and then you enter upon the snow which lies all the year round.

At the hospice they were received by one of the Fathers, given warm slippers, hot broth and mutton and slept on the hard mattresses "apparently stuffed with damp sand." In the morning they saw the "noble, majestic, tawny" dogs which Henry observed had the same "stately courtesy" as the Fathers themselves. Henry visited the morgue where the bodies of those found in the mountains were placed. "As they cannot be buried they are stood around the walls in their shrouds and a grim and ghastly sight it is. They fall into all sorts of hideous positions, with such fiendish grins on their faces! faugh!" The region was mournful indeed and Henry, with that sense for tone and color marked in his later writings, describes the scene: "The sky is of a liquid twinkling sort of blue, and the gigantic grey and white rocks rise up against it so sharply-cut and so barren, and the stillness that reigns around and the apparent nearness of every object from the greater tenuity of the atmosphere!"

On the following day they went to Loèche-les-Bains and walked over naked and rugged terrain down narrow steep zigzags ending their trip at Interlaken where they met, as scheduled, their father, mother, Alice and Wilky. Robertson had gone off with his teacher and classmates toward the Italian Alps with Venice as his ultimate destination after which he was to rejoin the family at Bonn. The Jameses travelled from Interlaken to Frankfort, sam-

pling the hot springs and visiting the gambling tables at Wiesbaden. Then they went by the Rhine to Bonn. It all seemed pretty tame to Henry after Switzerland.

III

They arrived at Bonn in July of 1860. Henry and Wilky were installed in the pension of a Dr. Humpert, Latin and Greek professor, situated at No. 190 Bonn-Gasse near the birth house of Beethoven. William was housed with a Herr Stromberg, whose wife made fine pancakes and wrote tragedies. It was the elder James's wish that his sons should acquire a working knowledge of German during the coming weeks. He and his wife took rooms for themselves and Alice in a large brick mansion built like a feudal castle, looking across the broad expanse of river at the Seven Mountains—in reality a series of green hills. Henry found himself in characteristic Germanic surroundings. The Herr Doctor's family was composed of his wife, her sister, and his son, Theodore. There were also five young German pensioners aged six to fourteen. The sister, Fräulein Stamm, reminded Henry, when he recalled her in later years, of Hepzibah Pyncheon in *The House of the Seven Gables*, always wiping hock-glasses and holding them up to the light and bearing long-necked bottles and platters of food through the "greasy rooms" of the house. "This is an opportunity for me to see something of German life, in what would be called, I suppose, the middle classes," Henry wrote to Perry. "I naturally compare it with the corresponding life at home, and think it truly inferior. The women stop at home all day, doing the house-work, drudging, and leading the most homely and I should say joyless lives. I fancy they never look at a book, and all their conversation is about their pots and pans." He found their ignorance of the United States extraordinary. Fräulein Stamm wanted to know whether there was a King in America; their knowledge of his homeland was based, Henry discovered, largely on a reading of expurgated adaptations of Fenimore Cooper. Life he found was a round of German "conversation" centering on the stereotyped

amenities *Haben Sie gut geschlafen?* and *Wie geht?* Henry made
excursions, to nearby Godesberg and to the Drachenfels across the
Rhine which they climbed in a party with Henry's mother resorting to a donkey for conveyance. There were picnics and walks, in
the early morning, on the Venusberg when the dew was still wet,
and the pursuit in German orchards of pears, cherries and plums.
He walked in old Germanic woods and enjoyed the long vistas of
the river. He didn't learn much German, devoting most of the summer to a laborious translation of *Maria Stuart* after being taken
by his father one night in Bonn to see Adelaide Ristori in the
play ("the vulture counterfeiting Jenny Wren" was the elder's ver-
dict).

Although Henry enjoyed his Bonn experience on the whole he
was never to feel, as did William, a kinship with the German people and the German mind. When he revisited Germany in 1872
he satisfied himself once and for all that "I can never hope to
become an unworthiest adoptive grandchild of the fatherland.
It is well to listen to the voice of the spirit, to cease hair-splitting
and treat one's self to a good square antipathy. . . ." He satirizes
the Germans in a number of his tales and particularly in the
caricatured Dr. Rudolf Staub in "A Bundle of Letters" and his
sketch of the German diplomat in "Pandora." In only one tale did
he create a sympathetic German—who collaborates, on artistic
ground, with a Frenchman.

IV

They had been at Bonn only a few days when the elder Henry
James took an important decision which his second son promptly
and exuberantly communicated to Perry. "I think I must fire
off my biggest gun first. One-two-three! Bung gerdee bang
bang. . . . . !!! What a noise! Our passages are taken in the Adriatic, for the 11th of September!!!!!!! We are going immediately
to Newport, which is the place in America we all most care to
live in." William James, after many misgivings and much inner debate, had confided to his father that he didn't want to be a sci-

entist, as his parent had hoped. He felt his vocation to be that of a painter and he wanted to study with William Morris Hunt, the American artist, whom he had met earlier and who now had a studio in Newport. Hunt had agreed to accept William as a pupil. The elder Henry re-expressed his misgivings about artists and writers. William argued with him: "I am sure that far from feeling myself degraded by my intercourse with art, I continually receive from it spiritual impressions the intensest and purest I know. So it seems to me is my mind formed, and *I can see* no reason for avoiding the giving myself up to art *on this score.*" That summer at Bonn William was striking a blow not only for himself; he was, in effect, leading a family revolt against further wanderings and an education that, while of the freest and easiest sort imaginable, reflected too much the parental vacillations. Henry expressed this to Perry: "I think that if we are to live in America it is about time we boys should take up our abode there; the more I see of this estrangement of American youngsters from the land of their birth, the less I believe in it. It should also be the land of their breeding." He was to hold this view all his life. His own later expatriation, he felt, was the direct and logical outcome of his early "estrangement" from America. The international scene had been the "land" of his particular breeding. He therefore later took up his abode in it.

The father, writing to a friend on July 18, 1860, the same day that Henry expressed these views to Perry, threw still further light on the decision to return. He says that he is glad to go back and to allow William to study with Hunt; he adds, "The welfare of the other youngsters will, however, be as much consulted by this manoeuvre, I am persuaded, as Willy's. They are none of them cut out for intellectual labors, and they are getting to an age, Harry and Wilky especially, when the heart craves a little wider expansion than is furnished it by the domestic affections. They want friends among their own sex, and sweethearts in the other; and my hope for their own salvation, temporal and spiritual, is that they may 'go it strong' in both lines when they get home. Early

marriages are thought very bad as a prudential step here in Europe, but an immense deal of imprudence may yet be transacted in America with the happiest social and individual consequences." We smile as we read that "none" of the boys were cut out for intellectual labors; but the elder Henry was right in perceiving—at long last—that his children were starved for companionship.

The decision taken, the father promptly left Bonn ("where he can neither understand nor make himself understood," William wrote to Perry) and was joined in Paris by his wife and Alice, Robertson and Aunt Kate. They installed themselves in the Hôtel des Trois Empereurs to await the September sailing, while the three other sons completed their summer at Bonn. If the senior Henry deprecated Henry's addiction to novels, he nevertheless sent him copies of *Once a Week* which had begun to appear a few months earlier and in the pages of which his son first discovered Meredith and Charles Reade. William, reporting to his parents on life in Bonn, described Henry as working "pretty stoutly" at his studies and resisting all week the temptation to read the periodical. "Harry says he 'wakes up every day from his lethargy to wish he was in Paris' instead of availing himself of the little time he has here . . . [he] has not touched the *Once a Week* until today. . . ." In another letter the oldest son announces "We are going to put Harry through a slashing big walk daily" and he tells how Henry indulges in wrestling matches with Wilky "when study has made them dull and sleepy." Henry himself was quite articulate about his German impressions. In August he wrote to his mother— it is the earliest letter to her extant—in a vein of filial amiability, describing certain excursions, the conversations in the pension, the epistolary activities of his brothers who "are so free in their communications that I begin to suspect they simply despatch you blank sheets of paper, for what they can find to say about Bonn to fill so many pages is to me inconceivable . . . ." His hostess and Fräulein Stamm "seem to think it is the exception in going to America not to be drowned and assurances to the contrary are received with uplifted eyes and hands and raised eyes and in-

credulous 'Ohs!' and 'Achs,' and pious ejaculations. I wish we could take Madame Humbart [Humpert] to America with us as cook. She is by far the best one I ever saw. I wish you could come on and take a few lessons from her; I shall bring you a lot of receipts by which I shall expect you to profit next winter. I shall look for a *marked improvement* in the cookery department." The light touch, the graceful letter-writer, was already formed; and as for the German cooking, the time was to come when a more fastidious Henry would have the opposite of praise for the Germanic cuisine.

The weeks passed quickly enough and punctually on September 11 the three boys made the twelve-hour train journey from Cologne to Paris in a first class carriage which they shared with a French lady's maid, valet and coachman, "who chattered by the hour for our wonderstruck ears." They gave Henry a glimpse in their talk, on the one hand, of "servile impudence" and, on the other, of the life of the French upper classes. There were long stops at stations with trains going in the opposite direction carrying the French society of the time in its annual descent upon Homburg and Baden-Baden. He was to discover this society of the dying days of the Second Empire in the works of About and Daudet. During the day Madame la Marquise came to inspect her servants:

It was true that Madame la Marquise, who was young and good-natured and pretty without beauty, and unmistakably 'great,' exhaling from afar, as I encouraged myself to imagine, the scented air of the Tuileries, came on occasion and looked in on us and smiled, and even pouted, through her elegant patience; so that she had at least, I recollect, caused to swim before me somehow such a view of happy privilege at the highest pitch as made me sigh the more sharply, even if the less professedly, for our turning our backs on the complex order, the European, fresh to me still, in which contrasts flared and flourished and through which discrimination could unexhaustedly riot. . . .

"Europe" had begun for Henry with a glimpse of a peasant, a castle, a ruin; it ended with this glimpse of "happy privilege at the highest pitch," and the bemused view of the Louvre described in an earlier chapter. They sailed on the *Adriatic* on the eleventh, were in New York on the twenty-third and within a few days Henry was pacing the sands of Newport again with Sargy Perry. The European adventure was at an end. The Nostalgic Cup had been filled to the brim. Henry did not know it then, but this adventure had been the prelude to a life-long adventure in Europe.

PALETTE AND PEN

FOR THEIR SECOND AND LONGEST PHASE IN NEWPORT, THE ELDER Henry James settled his family in a rented house at No. 13 Kay Street near the Edmund Tweedys and the sons promptly resumed the idyllic life from which they had been torn fifteen months before. They lived here for the next two years, until the spring of 1862, and then in a large stone house at the corner of Spring Street and Lee Avenue which is still standing. Brief allusions in the youthful diary of Thomas Sergeant Perry gave us glimpses of their activities. Thus on January 2, 1861: "Went with Harry James to the 40 Steps. . . . Went after dinner with Jno [La Farge] and Willie J. to the Point." January 3: "Down town then with Harry J. Met Willie and with him to Belmont's. . . ." January 4: "In the morning down street with W. J. . . . dined at the

Jameses." Saturday, January 5: ". . . down street again with H. J."
And so the life went, a constant series of excursions "down street"
and to the scenic points in Newport, with abundant sociabilities.
Perry later wrote that "all the land and shore beyond the Avenue
was a wild pasture where the Jameses and I were the sole in-
habitants." On Sunday, January 6: "H. J. came to church with me in
the morning" and then Perry boxes with Willie till 1 P.M. On
Monday he and Henry go to the Redwood Library. The next day:
"walked after school to the Big Pond nearly with H. J." On January 13 a significant entry: ". . . to the Jameses. Introduced to
and to walk with their cousins, the Miss Temples." Mary and Edmund Tweedy, having lost their three children, had taken into
their home the four orphaned Temple girls, children of Catherine
Margaret James, the elder Henry's favorite sister and of Colonel
Robert Emmet Temple, a West Point graduate and a lawyer. Mrs.
Tweedy was a daughter of Colonel Temple by a first marriage and
thus not directly related to the Jameses. She was, however, referred
to always as "Aunt Mary" by Henry.

William had lost no time in starting to work under Hunt. Henry
"under the irresistible contagion" followed him to the studio. Apparently for the moment there was no thought of further schooling
for the younger son. He found the world of art, even though he
participated in it largely as a dabbler and observer, to be a
"rounded satisfying world." The experience gained here, together
with the renewed friendship with John La Farge and closer
acquaintance with Hunt, was to be carried over into his fiction.
Artists, studios, the whole special world of painting and sculpture,
figured in novel and story early and late, and Henry was to leave
behind a goodly body of art criticism and appreciation. He was to
be at home in the art world of London and Paris. From painting he borrowed a large terminology which he applied to his own
art. It was no accident that Henry James wrote a novel that was
a "portrait" of a lady, or entitled his travel sketches "portraits" of
places, or some of his critical essays *Partial Portraits*. He was on
the easiest of terms with the wielders of the palette and the

THE GRANDMOTHER
Catharine Barber James about 1855

THE AUNT
Catherine Walsh (Aunt Kate)

THE MOTHER
Mrs. Henry James Senior in middle life

HENRY JAMES SENIOR AND HENRY JUNIOR
From a daguerreotype by Matthew Brady 1854

HENRY JAMES AT GENEV
From a photograph

brush; he too, for a little while, laid down the pen to wield these in the strictest amateur sense.

I

The studio on Church Street in Newport was filled with plaster casts, canvases and the presence of the Quixote-like figure of the American master. William Morris Hunt had been a pupil of Couture whose "Romains de la Décadence" Henry had seen in Paris; he had studied later with Millet in Barbizon. In Newport he was the embodiment of the artist, the flowing beard, the velvet jacket, the scarlet sash. There were two spacious rooms on the ground floor of his studio where Henry was allowed to wander as he pleased, and the large studio proper upstairs where William, not yet twenty, worked together with twenty-five-year-old La Farge and Theodora Sedgwick, youngest sister of Mrs. Charles Eliot Norton. Henry remembered sitting alone in one of the grey cold lower rooms, trying to draw by himself, and day-dreaming that his copy of a plaster cast of the uplifted face of Michelangelo's "Captive," which he had seen in the Louvre and now tried to reproduce, might attract the attention of the Master. He remembered with gratitude an occasional friendly word, a gesture of kindness from Hunt himself. He felt that he had entered the temple of art here "by the back door" so to speak and was enjoying some fugitive golden hours ". . . in the studio I was at the threshold of a world."

One day he crossed the threshold. Wandering into the large studio upstairs he discovered his handsome young cousin, Gus Barker, standing on a pedestal, a gay, neat model "divested of every garment." It was Henry James's first glimpse of " 'life' on a pedestal and in a pose." The spectacle settled matters for him then and there. "I well recall the crash, at the sight, of all my inward emulation—so forced was I to recognise on the spot that I might niggle for months over plaster casts and not come within miles of any such point of attack." They were working in pencil and charcoal and Henry watched closely. His brother's ease at re-

producing the figure astonished him. There was no point, he decided, in seeking to emulate this.

On that day Henry James pocketed his drawing pencil. He rarely used it again.

I I

He had never really wanted to be an artist and he had now had a moment of awareness—his pursuit of art was in reality his pursuit of William. It is difficult to say now whether the decision to return to his own pasture was deliberate and conscious, or as vivid as he makes it out to be in his memoirs. What we can deduce is that he had found someone who took him seriously as a potential writer. The family had made light of his addiction to novels; he had been teased and baited; his parents had tried to turn him from his world of dreams and books. He had, on his side, always gone in pursuit of William and of William's pursuits. And now, in the benign surroundings of Newport, he found in John La Farge a much-needed ally, friend, guide. La Farge was not only willing to talk to him about books and about writing; he listened attentively to him; he bestowed, in effect, paternal sympathy, for he was older, and brotherly companionship as well. Henry remembered that at Newport in 1860 the future painter "opened up to us, though perhaps to me in particular, who could absorb all that was given me. . . ."

The painter was an attractive figure, riding on a chestnut mare across the shining Newport sands against a background of far sunsets, or emerging in cool white from top to toe, or wearing his artist's velvet jacket. Henry posed for him willingly and La Farge talked generously as he painted. There survives a portrait in oils which Henry James considered the best perhaps of La Farge's early exhibition of "a rare color sense." The portrait sets the young Henry in sharp profile against an opaline background, in dark attire, austere, almost priestly, as if he were a young seminarist. The head is bent and pensive, the lips firm, the forehead straight

and high; the painting suggests a sensitive youth set in colors that recall a stained glass window. La Farge was indeed to become a master of this medium. He was to invent opaline glass; he developed a deep interest in architecture and in aesthetics; he lectured and wrote on art and left behind him vivid accounts of travel in the Far East and the South Seas. His interest in stained glass and cathedrals was to set his friend Henry Adams upon the exploration of Mont St. Michel and Chartres. Thus John La Farge, who lived so large and full a creative life himself, fed the lives of two other creative personalities—the young Henry James and, in later life, Henry Adams. Adams considered La Farge "among the best talkers of his time."

For Henry James he opened "more windows than he closed." The windows he closed were those of the practice of art. He let Henry daub but encouraged him and pushed him to write. He taught him that the "arts were after all essentially one." He gave Henry the sense of a young man who feels secure, who knows what he wants to do "a settled sovereign self." And as Henry talked with him, he felt surer of himself, he too could become sovereign. It is doubtful whether La Farge knew just how helpful he was to his young protégé. It was the painter who introduced Henry James to the world of Honoré de Balzac. Balzac was then but ten years dead, and Henry read him with such attention that years later, on re-opening *Eugénie Grandet* "breathlessly seized and earnestly absorbed" under La Farge's instruction, he was "to see my initiator's youthful face, so irregular but so refined, look out at me between the lines as through blurred prison bars." The influence seems, in fact, to have been immediate, for T. S. Perry testifies to his writing at this time stories "mainly of the romantic kind" in which the heroines were sophisticated and seemed "to have read all Balzac in the cradle and to be positively dripping with lurid crimes." Perry added that he began these extravagant pictures "in adoration of the great master whom he always so warmly admired."

La Farge also introduced Henry to the short stories of Prosper Mérimée; the future novelist found himself "fluttering deliciously —quite as if with a sacred terror—at the touch of *La Vénus d'Ille*." It "struck my immaturity as a masterpiece of art and offered to the young curiosity concerned that sharpest of all challenges for youth, the challenge as to the special source of the effect." We suspect that this challenge was peculiar in the America of those years to Henry James, and his later critical writing discloses just how closely he studied the technique of the writers he read. In *Notes of a Son and Brother* he remembered that La Farge prodded him into translating Mérimée's tale of the ghostly Venus and sending it to a New York periodical "which was to do me the honour neither of acknowledging nor printing. . . ." In a reminiscence recorded in 1898 he spoke of having translated Mérimée's *Tamango* and *Matteo Falcone* and offering them to an illustrated weekly. He could recall "the rejected ms. cast at his feet again by the post, unroll, ironically, its anxious neatness. . . . Certain it is that from that moment he was sure Mérimée was distinguished." Years later Henry was to consider Mérimée's stories "perfect models of the narrative art . . ." and possessing a firmness of contour suggestive of hammered metal.

Thus La Farge was the original inspirer, the first to prod Henry to a constructive writing effort and to insist that once his manuscript was completed, he try to do something with it. Perry also testified that Henry went on to translate Alfred de Musset's *Lorenzaccio* and introduced into it scenes of his own. It was obvious that Henry needed no urging to write; what he did need was appreciation and now he had found it. He gives us an instance which reveals the extent to which La Farge filled a great want in his life. Browning's works had lain among his parents' books but Henry had never ventured to read the poet. La Farge had only to invoke Browning and Henry fell upon the volumes immediately. And the old Henry, gathering these old memories, throws in curious praise of La Farge at the expense of his parents.

"*They*," he noted, and he italicized the word, "had not divined in us as yet an aptitude for that author." *

III

Henry James was in America in 1910 when John La Farge died at seventy-five; and he was in Boston when a large commemorative exhibition of La Farge's work was held. The novelist, then sixty-seven, and removed from Newport by five decades, walked among the paintings and looked upon landscapes that suddenly "laid bare the very footsteps of time." As he stood there his mind wandered back to one incident which he recounted in his *Notes* with such evident pleasure that it reveals, more than anything else, the depth of the Newport—and the La Farge—attachment. "There recurs to me," Henry wrote, "one of the smallest of adventures, as tiny a thing as could incur the name and which was of the early stage of our acquaintance, when he [La Farge] proposed to me that we should drive out to the Glen, some six miles off, to breakfast and should afterwards paint—*we* paint!—in the bosky open air. It looks at this distance a mythic time, that of felt inducements to travel so far at such an hour and in a backless buggy on the supposition of rustic fare. But different ages have different measures, and I quite remember how ours, that morning, at the neat hostel in the umbrageous valley, overflowed with coffee and griddle-cakes that were not as other earthly refreshment, and how a spell of romance rested for several hours on our invocation of the genius of the scene: of such material, with the help of the attuned spirit, may great events consent to be composed."

. . . .

* This reproach does not appear to have been entirely justified. There was nothing to prevent Henry James from reading Browning and indeed once the father discovered that his son liked the poet he gave him at least one of his works. In the Lamb House library there was a copy of *Dramatis Personae* inscribed, "H. James Jr. from his aff. Father. Aug. 20. 1864." Earlier that year Henry also was given a copy of *Sordello* by his friend Perry. The copy is inscribed, "Henry James from T. S. P. Newport Mar. 2 '64."

La Farge arranged his easel and canvas, palette and stool while Henry "at a respectful distance" arranged his. He mused, in recalling the incident, as to why it had been remembered and why it had "really mattered." It did indeed matter, he told himself because there was "in the vagueness of rustling murmuring green and plashing water and woodland voices and images" the hovering possibility that "one's small daub . . . might incur appreciation by the eye of friendship."

"This indeed was the true source of the spell," wrote Henry, "that it was in the eye of friendship, friendship full of character and colour, and full of amusement of its own, that I lived on any such occasion, and that I had come forth in the morning cool and had found our breakfast at the inn a thing of ineffable savour, and that I now sat and flurriedly and fearfully aspired. . . ."

To the old man, standing there amid the work of his faraway friend, the posthumous exhibition was filled with more scenes than were depicted on those walls. His debt to La Farge must not be measured in terms of "influence." He lived in the "eye of friendship"—and it was a painter's eye. If Newport had been the real right place, La Farge had appeared in Henry's life at the real right time. The writer was haunted by John La Farge, and his image is preserved among those talkative, brilliantly vivid painters who pass across his fictional pages.

To the end the lessons of Newport remained with Henry James; he was to slip back again and again into doubt and anxiety but the example of that "sovereign" self, the memory of the breakfast near the Glen, the walks with La Farge and Perry, and a thousand other memories were to feed him, even as the writings of Balzac and Mérimée and Musset—and Browning. One has but to read the pages of *The American Scene* consecrated to Newport to understand what Henry James meant when he spoke of the "time of settled possession" and the "*pure* Newport time." None of the days that were to come would have such a crystalline purity.

The Vast Visitation
1861=1865

AN OBSCURE HURT

THE SOUTHERN GUNS OPENED UP ON FORT SUMTER ON APRIL 12, 1861,
and on April 15—Henry James's eighteenth birthday—Lincoln is-
sued his first call for volunteers. Presently T. S. Perry was noting
in his Newport diary: "April 27: We made bandages all evening."
"April 28: After breakfast we all rolled bullets."

Bandages and bullets! Abruptly the evidence of struggle confronted the young Henry James and his generation as the four
epic years of passion, of "blood and tears" (the words were written
in juxtaposition by the novelist long before their modern use) began. There was "hurrying troops" and a "transfigured scene" and
"the interest of life and of death" that involved the whole question of national as of personal existence.

From the perspective of the twentieth century and two world
wars the American Civil War seems in the long retrospect a rather
local, if bloody, conflict in which battlefields bore familiar names
and relatives could bring home the wounded and the dead after

the carnage. But in the spring of 1861 the moment, filled with excitement and terror, was unbelievable, and for young sensitive men such as Henry and William James it was almost unbearable. The paradise of paternal optimism and cheerfulness in which the Jameses lived, the free-ranging through countries, schools, books, galleries, was now at an end. On the brink of manhood they found themselves on the brink of an abyss, almost within earshot of the guns and confronted with the problem of whether they should go out and face them. Yet with the tension and the abrupt dawn of general insecurity and grief, there was also the drama of war, the bugle's blare, the waving of banners, the marching of men. The James boys run to the Armory to see the militia off. They are at the wharf to see the troops go by. And they see the ships returning, filled with wounded.

Stirring deeds, patriotism and also fear—and bafflement: a merging of the personal predicament and the national problem; there were all these elements in the complex of emotion that young Henry felt in the dawn of the struggle for the Union. As war broke out in 1914, when he was an old man, he suddenly recalled the older time "the sudden new tang in the atmosphere, the flagrant difference, as one noted, in the look of everything, especially in that of people's faces, the expressions, the hushes, the clustered groups, the detached wanderers and slow-paced public meditators." The stretch of more than half a century had still left a sharpness: for Henry "war" was to mean all his life the Civil War.

As usually happens in wars there is the first great burst of drama and then come the long periods of tense waiting as armies wheel into position and the civilians steel themselves for the ordeal. After Fort Sumter came the moment when North and South took a deep breath; then followed the Northern march on Richmond and in July the first battle of Bull Run. By then the North knew that the struggle would be difficult and perhaps long.

The youths in Newport took their usual walks that summer; they watched the soldiers; they read the newspapers. On July 4 the elder Henry delivered the Independence Day oration at the

invitation of his fellow-citizens. He entitled it "The Social Significance of Our Institutions" and displayed his rich rhetoric and
eloquence; it was a vivid statement, surcharged with the emotions
of the moment. From his criticism of the arrogance and the ignorance of the American wealthy and the British class structure it
was but a step to the denunciation of the iniquities of slavery.

Our very Constitution binds us, that is to say, the very breath of
our political nostrils binds us, to disown all distinctions among
men, to disregard persons, to disallow privilege the most established and sacred, to legislate only for the common good, no longer
for those accidents of birth or wealth or culture which spiritually
individualize man from his kind, but only for those great common
features of social want and dependence which naturally unite him
with his kind, and inexorably demand the organization of such
unity. It is this immense constitutional life and inspiration we are
under which not only separate us from Europe, but also perfectly
explain by antagonism that rabid hostility which the South has
always shown towards the admission of the North to a fair share of
government patronage, and which now provokes her to the dirty
and diabolic struggle she is making to give human slavery the
sanction of God's appointment. . . .

In mid-July Henry and Sargy Perry went on a walking tour in
New Hampshire, climbing Mount Lafayette and Mount Washington and returning a week later to Newport, tired, cheerful, penniless. Perry noted: "At and with Harry James to the Lily Pond. Lay
on the grass and talked." The idyllic life could, for the moment,
still go on. It was during this month (and not a year later as he
suggests in *Notes of a Son and Brother*) that Henry, again with
Perry, went one afternoon "to a vast gathering of invalid and convalescent troops, under canvas and in roughly improvised shanties"
on the Rhode Island shore, at Portsmouth Grove. This was his
"first and all but sole vision of the American soldier in his multitude, and above all—for that was markedly the colour of the whole
thing—in his depression, his wasted melancholy almost." He

talked with the men, strolled with them, sat by the improvised couches "of their languid rest." He drew from "each his troubled tale, listened to his plaint on his special hard case" and emptied his pockets for them of whatever cash he had. In his memories he identified the image of himself on this occasion with Walt Whitman "even if I hadn't come armed like him with oranges and peppermints." He felt himself under the spell of the same forces that later moved "the good Walt" to his "commemorative accents." He sailed back to Newport that evening with Perry "through the summer twilight . . . the hour seemed, by some wondrous secret, to know itself marked and charged and unforgettable."

In September William entered the Lawrence Scientific School at Harvard, abandoning his study of art almost as abruptly as he had begun it a year earlier. It is impossible to judge what role the Civil War played in this decision; certainly it was difficult for him to remain painting in the studio under the pressures and tensions of the time. Wilky and Robertson had been put to school at Concord the previous autumn, at Frank B. Sanborn's pioneering co-educational Academy. Here the younger Jameses, then sixteen and fifteen, found themselves classmates of Emerson's son, Edward, and Hawthorne's son, Julian. Henry was left alone at Newport with his parents, his sister and Aunt Kate. He proposed to his father at this time that he also should go to Harvard. The senior James brushed the suggestion aside and Henry stayed on, marking time while around him young men were springing to the colors. In due course the two younger brothers enlisted and before the war had run half its course two of Henry's cousins, young Gus Barker and William Temple had died in battle.

Henry James has left us no concrete record of his thoughts and feelings in those early weeks of the war. We know only from later evidence that for him, as for many others, the call to arms provoked an acute conflict. Temperamentally unsuited for soldiering, unable to endure violence, he had long ago substituted acute and close observation of life for active participation in it. He had from the first cultivated passive resistance to competition with his

brothers, and now he ran the risk of being called upon to take the field in direct assault upon his brother Americans. In Henry James the universal conflict—the reluctance of the citizen-soldier in a democracy to shoulder arms against his fellow-man—merged with the conflict that arose within his constituted personality. If peacetime competition had for him a "displeasing ferocity," what could he say of war?

The young man of letters experienced a certain amount of social pressure to which many of the youths of the time were subjected. This was reflected in verses such as Dr. Holmes indited to "The Sweet Little Man, dedicated to the Stay-at-Home Rangers," or his hortatory

> Listen young heroes! your country is calling!
> Time strikes the hour for the brave and the true!
> Now, while the foremost are fighting and falling,
> Fill up the ranks that have opened for you.

Nor was the senior Henry particularly helpful at this juncture. While public sentiment pulled in one direction he pulled in the other. "Affectionate old papas like me are scudding all over the country to apprehend their patriotic offspring and restore them to the harmless embraces of their mamas," he wrote very early in the struggle. "I have had a firm grasp upon the coat tails of my Willy and Harry, who both vituperate me beyond measure because I won't let them go. The coats are a very staunch material, or the tails must have been off two days ago, the scamps pull so hard."* It is difficult to tell from this letter whether the elder Henry is dramatizing matters somewhat for the benefit of his correspondent or merely reflecting the indecision of himself and his sons. He goes on to write, "The way I excuse my paternal interference to them is, to tell them, first, that no existing government, nor indeed

. . . .

* From a fragment of a letter to an unknown correspondent in possession of his granddaughter, Mary James Vaux.

any now possible government, is worth an honest human life and a clean one like theirs; especially if that government is likewise in danger of bringing back slavery again under our banner: than which consummation I would rather see chaos itself come again. Secondly, I tell them that no young American should put himself in the way of death, until he has realized something of the good of life: until he has found some charming conjugal Elizabeth or other to whisper his devotion to, and assume the task if need be, of keeping his memory green." (This last sentence could almost be a note for a portion of Henry Junior's Civil War tale, "The Story of a Year," which begins with the engagement of the young hero, on the eve of his departure for the war, to a girl named Elizabeth.)

Almost two years after the war began there seems to have still been indecision among the older sons. "I may say," the father wrote to his friend Dr. Wilkinson, "that my two elder boys Willy and Harry who have just come home from college, are thinking of going down to labour among the contrabands or now, thank God, the *freed* blacks. They have applied for places, but have as yet not heard of the success of their application. . . ."

Nothing came of this project. The elder Henry's two letters suggest a parent understandably concerned about his boys at this crucial time; but it is difficult to say whether he reflects his own state of mind or that of Henry and William. The letters do suggest that both sons, at various times, entertained plans to participate in the nation's struggle, and this only heightens our sense of the sharp inner dramas they were experiencing. Henry and William were not alone. The indecision of the older sons was in part a reflection of the indecision of the entire North. Compulsory service was not instituted by the Lincoln administration until more than a year after the first appeal for volunteers. The reluctance of the citizenry to respond, after the first rush to the colors, was exemplified in the bitter opposition to the draft which was finally instituted in March 1863; and even then Henry James had the option of finding a substitute or simply paying $300 which would

exempt him from service. It was no wonder that the cry arose of "a rich man's war and a poor man's fight" and the draft riots of July 1863, when New York counted one thousand killed or injured, bore testimony to the inequalities of sacrifice demanded and the confusion of the time. Long before this, however, an incident had occurred in Henry James's life that was to color the war years and the decades that lay beyond.

I

Henry James tells us in *Notes of a Son and Brother* that at the "same dark hour" as the Civil War he suffered a "horrid even if an obscure hurt." "Scarce at all to be stated . . ." he says, "the queer fusion or confusion established in my consciousness during the soft spring of '61 by the firing on Fort Sumter, Mr. Lincoln's first call for volunteers and a physical mishap . . . the effects of which were to draw themselves out incalculably and intolerably."

He called it a "passage of personal history, the most entirely personal" which he nevertheless associated with the "great public convulsion." The mishap occurred during "twenty odious minutes" and kept company "with the question of what might still happen, to everyone about me, to the country at large: it so made of these disparities a single vast visitation. One had the sense . . ." he adds, "of a huge comprehensive ache, and there were hours at which one could scarce have told whether it came most from one's own poor organism, still so young and so meant for better things, but which had suffered particular wrong, or from the enclosing social body, a body rent with a thousand wounds and that thus treated me to the honour of a sort of tragic fellowship."

The twenty minutes sufficed, James said, to establish a relationship with the world that was "at once extraordinarily intimate and quite awkwardly irrelevant." And he goes on: "I must have felt in some befooled way in presence of a crisis—the smoke of Charleston Bay still so acrid in the air—at which the likely young should be up and doing or, as familiarly put, lend a hand much wanted; the willing youths, all round, were mostly starting to their feet, and

to have trumped up a lameness at such a juncture could be made to pass in no light for graceful."

With this prelude he tells how "jammed into an acute angle between two high fences," in an awkward position, he and others managed to make "a rusty, a quasi-extemporised old engine" work sufficiently well to help put out what James characterized as a "shabby conflagration" in Newport.

What was interesting to him was that "from the first" he did not doubt in the least the duration of the injury. He does not describe it, nor give any further details. In the ensuing passage he says that he tried to "strike some sort of bargain" with his ailing condition, and spent much time in bed or on a couch on the theory that rest would help. Also he did not mention it to his family. Since, however, he did not mend, he finally confided his trouble to his father and received prompt and sympathetic attention although he felt that publicizing his hurt diminished the value of the comfort he was receiving. Early "that summer" he goes on to say (apparently the summer immediately following Sumter) he accompanied his father to Boston "for consultation of a great surgeon, the head of his profession there" who was also a friend of the elder Henry James.

"This interview," Henry continues, "settled my sad business" so that he was never afterward to pass the doctor's house without feeling the "ironic smug symbolism of its action on my fate." What happened was that the eminent surgeon made "quite unassistingly light of the bewilderment exposed to him." He gave no warnings, he treated Henry to a "comparative pooh-pooh." And Henry felt, ruefully, that he had to reckon on the one hand with his pain and on the other "with the strange fact of there being nothing to speak of the matter with me." He accordingly decided to act as if there weren't—but he continued to suffer for many months. Speaking of the choice of a course of action, he says, "I think of the second half of that summer of '62 as my attempt at selection of the best [alternative]." He decided once again that he would propose Harvard. This time his father consented.

11

This is all Henry tells us of the "obscure hurt" and it is a queer tale—queer since he has mingled so many elements in it and at the same time thoroughly confused us about the time sequence. If the accident occurred at the "same dark hour" as the outbreak of the Civil War, that is in the "soft spring of '61" then the visit to the doctor "that summer" must have taken place during the summer of 1861. But "that summer" becomes, at the end of the account, the summer of 1862. The details, as given by Henry, are meagre; and they bristle with strange ambiguities: in his characteristically euphemistic manner he makes it sound at every turn as a matter grave and ominous while at the same time minimizing its gravity.

The hurt is "horrid" but it is also "obscure." It is a "catastrophe," but it is in the very same phrase only a "difficulty." It is a passage of history "most entirely personal" yet apparently not too personal to be broadcast to the world in his memoirs, even though when it happened he kept it a secret and regretted the necessity of making it known. It is also "extraordinarily intimate" and at the same time "awkwardly irrelevant." This is perplexing enough. James compounds the mystery by giving no hint of the kind of hurt he suffered, although at various times during his life he complained of an early back injury, which he usually dated as of 1862. That he should have chosen to omit all specific reference to his back in his memoirs is significant; in some way he seems to have felt that by vagueness and circumlocution he might becloud the whole question of his non-participation in the Civil War. To the error of omission—"error" because of the consequences of his reticence—must be added the effect of his elaborate euphemisms: the use of the words *intimate, odious, horrid, catastrophe, obscure* and the phrase *most entirely personal*. These had an effect not unlike that of the unspecified "horrors" of *The Turn of the Screw*. His readers were ready to imagine the worst.

What, after all, is the most *odious, horrid, intimate* thing that can happen to a man? However much different men might have

different answers, in the case of Henry James critics tended to see a relationship between the accident and his celibacy, his apparent avoidance of involvements with women and the absence of overt sexuality in his work. Thus there emerged a "theory"—promptly converted into a rumor—that the novelist suffered a hurt, during those "twenty odious" minutes, which amounted to castration. In the April-June 1934 *Hound & Horn* issue, devoted entirely to Henry James, Glenway Wescott reported it almost as a fact: "Henry James, expatriation and castration. . . . Henry James it is rumored, could not have had a child. But if he was as badly hurt in the pre-Civil-War accident as that—since he triumphed powerfully over other authors of his epoch—perhaps the injury was a help to him." Stephen Spender quotes this passage in *The Destructive Element* and suggests that "Castration, or the fear of castration, is supposed to preoccupy the mind with ideas of suicide and death." He goes on to show how this is true of many of James's characters. Mr. Spender, however, does have a second thought and adds in a footnote: "The rumour of castration seems exaggerated and improbable, but it seems likely that James sustained a serious injury." F. O. Matthiessen in *The James Family*, speculates that "since Henry James never married, he may have been sexually impotent . . ." R. P. Blackmur, in his essay in the *Literary History of the United States* equates James with the emasculated Abelard "who, after his injury raised the first chapel to the Holy Ghost"; so James, he adds, "made a sacred rage of his art as the only spirit he could fully serve." And Lionel Trilling suggests that "only a man as devoted to the truth of the emotions as Henry James was, would have informed the world, despite his characteristic reticence, of an accident so intimate as his." The obscure hurt remained obscure to these critics; and to some of them highly ominous.

III

It is clear that Henry James's blurring of the date of the hurt (the "same dark hour" as the outbreak of the Civil War) served to

minimize his failure during the first six months to spring to the colors with other young men. To take his timing literally would fix the hurt as occurring in April or perhaps May of 1861. Had it occurred that spring, however, it is doubtful whether he would have climbed mountains in New Hampshire with T. S. Perry during July. Fortunately it is no longer necessary to speculate, since Perry comes to our assistance with specific dates. In a letter to James's nephew and executor, written shortly after publication of *Notes of a Son and Brother,* and alluding directly to the "obscure hurt" passage, Perry wrote that "the fire at West Stables was in the night of Oct. 28, '61." Hence the fateful incident occurred a full six months after Fort Sumter and three months after the first battle of Bull Run. The contemporary records of the fire are detailed. They include the newspaper accounts and the official report written by one of the firemen, now in the archives of the Newport Historical Society.

A high wind blew through the town on the night of October 28 and some time between ten-thirty and eleven a small blaze was discovered in the large stable of Charles B. Tennant at the corner of Beach and State Streets. In a few minutes the entire stable was in flames amid the screaming of horses and the scramble of an alerted town that rushed to give aid and to see the spectacle. The wind carried the fire to the adjoining stable of John West and the flames threatened the newly-built residence of Barney M. McGowan. By the time the fire-fighters had brought Engine No. 5 down to the Tennant stable there was little hope of saving it. Four horses perished and a number of vehicles were destroyed as well as substantial quantities of hay and grain.

The No. 5 engine had stopped en route at the Redwood Reservoir only to discover that the hose was not long enough to reach the scene of the fire. The engine accordingly was brought farther down and the requisitioning of wells in the neighborhood began. Two wells were pumped dry in rapid succession. In the meantime the fire had begun to spread in West's stable; a dozen horses and an equal number of carriages were removed to safety while a

stream from other cisterns was directed on the McGowan house which also caught fire. A small carpenter's shop belonging to Captain Josiah Tew was gutted and the firefighters tore down the dwelling of Perry Brown, directly in the path of the flames. This helped to arrest the fire and to confine it, so that about 1 A.M. the official report records that "there being no sign of any fire by this time we were ordered by the chief to return home which order was most willingly obeyed." At the height of the fire, reported the Newport *Mercury*, "clouds of sparks and smoke curled high up in the heavens and we have no doubt it was a great sight to the hundreds who congregated in the vicinity as idle spectators." The Newport *Daily News* said that "engine companies were on the ground and rendered all assistance in their power and succeeded in saving Mr. West's dwelling house and a building next to it, used as a carriage house." The entire loss was estimated by the press at $7,000. In terms of the time, the fire was much more than the "shabby conflagration" pictured by Henry James.

The high wind and the shortage of water would explain Henry's role among the volunteers that night. Apparently all available pumping engines were pressed into service and the novelist spoke of having helped induce "a saving stream to flow," probably that which kept the flames from the West residence. The accounts understandably make no mention of volunteers, since volunteer firemen were taken for granted in those days. There were no reports of any persons suffering injuries. Whatever hurt Henry received was suffered in silence; perhaps it went unnoticed and did not manifest itself until later.

Three days after the fire, on October 31, 1861, Perry's diary testifies to the fact that Henry James was well enough to travel. "Thursday, Oct. 31 [1861] At recitation in morning. Harry has gone to Boston." Perry by this entry identified (for James's nephew) the visit to William that Henry mentions in *Notes of a Son and Brother*. A letter from William to the family after Henry returned to Newport speaks of the "radiance of H's visit." Had Henry suffered anything approaching serious injury he would nei-

ther have been in condition for journeying nor visiting; nor does it seem likely that William would have found the visit "radiant." Henry remained for a long week-end. On November 5 Perry's diary says: "At school. Harry's before 12" and on the next day Henry walked with his friend to Easton's Point.

The next few months are those to which Henry alluded when he spoke of his seeking "to strike some sort of bargain" with his injury and his date of the summer of 1862—apparently early summer—for the visit to the eminent surgeon fits. However limited medical knowledge may have been in that era, it is quite clear that there would have been no "pooh-pooh" had the surgeon discovered a groin injury or a hernia. Hernia operations had been performed earlier in the century and any acute hurt would have been easily apparent to an experienced medical man. The "obscure hurt" was obscure indeed.

IV

Some years after the Newport fire Henry published a short story about a Civil War veteran who survives the conflict without physical injury but is stricken by illness at the end. The nature of the disorder is not disclosed; it is, however, "deeply-seated and virulent." The attending physician tells the hero, whose name is Colonel Mason, "You have opposed no resistance; you haven't cared to get well." Mason tries and is aided by an affectionate aunt who takes him to her home and gives him the care and attention of a mother. Staying with her is a beautiful niece, Caroline Hoffman, with whom Mason falls in love; he worships her, however, from afar; he gives her no intimation of his feelings. When he discovers that Miss Hoffman has been wooed successfully by his own doctor he has a relapse. "It's the most extraordinary case I ever heard of," says the doctor as his patient dies. "The man was steadily getting well." And again: "I shall never be satisfied that he mightn't have recovered. It was a most extraordinary case." The story, entitled "A Most Extraordinary Case," appeared in the *Atlantic Monthly* of April 1868 when Henry was twenty-five.

The extraordinary case was as mystifying to the doctor as the obscure hurt was to Henry James. The doctor was, however, unaware of the subjective elements which caused Mason to give up the fight; and Henry James was unaware of the subjective elements which conditioned and at the same time obscured his hurt. He gives us a very positive clue in his final account when he asserts "what was interesting from the first was my not doubting in the least its [the obscure hurt's] duration." This is a curious and significant admission. James admits to foreknowledge or to a feeling that his injury would have lasting effects. We can, of course, explain this in part by saying that James was an extraordinarily intuitive person. Still, to know in advance that the hurt would have a "duration" is not intuition; it is an attempt at prophecy; it suggests in effect a wish that the hurt might endure, or at least betrays an extraordinarily pessimistic frame of mind about it. It was a pre-judgment which the doctor in Boston did not in any way endorse. To understand the real ground for James's certainty that he had a serious hurt that would prolong itself, we must reach back into the events of his father's life before he was born.

Fire had a special meaning in the life of the James family. A fire in a stable had an even more special meaning. The senior Henry's cork leg had been the symbol through all of Henry Junior's life of what could happen to someone who becomes involved in putting out a stable fire. It was an enduring injury. We can therefore speculate, and the evidence warrants it, that this is the explanation for Henry James's sense, from the moment that he had hurt himself in circumstances analogous to those of his father, that his hurt too would have a long duration. And this is what happened. Henry was still experiencing his back-ache late in life.

The theory that there was an unconscious identification with the father at the moment of the accident is reinforced by a similar identification which occurs in the account set down in old age. Describing his hurt as keeping "unnatural" company with "the question of what might still happen to everyone about me, to the

country at large," Henry James said, as we have noted, that these "marked disparities" became "a single vast visitation." His use of these words evokes for us that other word which seems almost a portmanteau version of *vast* and *visitation*. . . . Henry James at the last could claim that he also had had his *vastation*.

v

Two letters of William James's supply independent evidence as to the nature of Henry's ailment and fix it in his back. In a letter of 1867 William speaks of having "that delightful disease in my back, which has so long made Harry so interesting. It is evidently a family peculiarity. . . ." In the same vein, when Robertson James complained of a back-ache in 1869, William, by then a medical student, wrote "even if we suppose that this recent matter of your back is a false alarm, yet in virtue of the sole fact of your fraternity with Harry and me, you must have a latent tendency to it in you. . . ."

Edmund Gosse remembered that early in the 1880's he called on James in London and found him stretched on his sofa. James apologized for not rising to greet him: "his appearance gave me a little shock," Gosse testified, "for I had not thought of him as an invalid." James "hurriedly and rather evasively declared that he was not that, but that a muscular weakness of his spine obliged him, as he said, 'to assume the horizontal posture' during some hours of every day, in order to bear the almost unbroken routine of evening engagements. I think," Gosse added, "this weakness gradually passed away, but certainly for many years it handicapped his activity." Seeing James in 1886 Gosse noted, "He had not wholly recovered from that weakness of the muscles of his back which had so long troubled him, and I suppose this was the cause of a curious stiffness in his progress, which proceeded rather slowly."

In 1899 when Henry was fifty-six he wrote to console his friend Howard Sturgis, then ailing ". . . if you have a Back, for

heaven's sake take care of it. When I was about your age—in 1862!—I did bad damage (by a strain subsequently—through crazy juvenility—neglected) to mine; the consequence of which is that, in spite of retarded attention, and years, really of recumbency, later, I've been saddled with it for life, and that even now, my dear Howard, I verily write *with* it. I even wrote *The Awkward Age* with it; therefore look sharp!" Three years later in a letter to Mrs. Frank Matthews, a daughter of Dr. Wilkinson, he mentions a photograph of himself taken at Newport: "I remember (it now all comes back to me) when (and where) I was so taken: at the age of 20, though I look younger, and at a time when I had had an accident (an injury to my back), and was rather sick and sorry. I look rather as if I wanted propping up. . . ."

In the privacy of his notebooks, James wrote a passage of reminiscence on the occasion of his return to America in 1905 in which he recalled a stay at Swampscott in 1866 where "I was miserably stricken by my poor broken, all but unbearable, and unsurvivable *back* of those (and still under fatigue, even of these) years." And again in another notebook entry he recalled his "suffering tortures from my damnable state of health. It was a time of suffering so keen that that fact might [claim?] to give its dark colour to the whole period. . . . Ill-health, physical suffering, in one's younger years, is a grievous trial; but I am not sure that we do not bear it most easily then. . . . Some of my doses of pain were very heavy; very weary were some of my months and years. . . ."

He alluded to his back-ache in an article published just seven months before his death. Recalling how J. T. Fields, the Boston editor and publisher, allowed him in the 1860's to read certain celebrated works in page proof, he remembered turning the ink-besmirched pages of *Essays in Criticism.* ". . . I can still recover the rapture with which, then suffering under the effects of a bad accident, I lay all day on a sofa in Ashburton Place and was somehow transported, as in a shining silvery dream, to London, to Oxford, to the French Academy, to Languedoc, to Brittany, to ancient Greece. . . ."

VI

In sum, the evidence points clearly to a back injury—a slipped disc, a sacroiliac or muscular strain—obscure but clearly painful. Perhaps the letter to Sturgis best describes it, "a strain subsequently . . . neglected." That the hurt was exacerbated by the tensions of the Civil War seems quite clear. Mentally prepared for some state of injury by his father's permanent hurt, and for a sense therefore of continuing physical inadequacy, Henry James found himself a prey to anxieties over the fact that he might be called a malingerer ("to have trumped up a lameness at such a juncture could be made to pass in no light for graceful") and had a feeling that he was deficient in the masculinity being displayed by others of his generation on the battlefield. This is reflected in all his early stories and contributed to the quite extraordinarily literal assumption by the critics that Henry James "castrated" himself in the accident. Of such substance are legends sometimes compounded. Yet even if we did not have the evidence of Henry James's activities immediately after the fire, his physically active later life and his monumental production would in itself undermine the legend. An invalid could hardly have accomplished what Henry James did between the ages of twenty-one and seventy-three. He rode horseback, fenced, lifted weights (to fight off over-weight), took long daily walks and was an inveterate traveller, indulging in an expenditure of prodigious physical energy, over and above his fecundity in creation, which in itself is deservedly legendary; he spent hours daily at his desk; he combined literary labor with a crowded and intricate social life. There was nothing of the eunuch about him either in appearance or action. Henry James himself, we suspect, would not have used the word *eunuch* so freely, as he did on occasions, to describe bad and unproductive writers, had he been physically one himself.

THE YOUNGER BROTHERS

IN CONCORD, WHERE THE MAJOR ACCENTS OF ABOLITION HAD SOUNDED, Garth Wilkinson and Robertson James now heard the more violent accents of the war. In 1862 Wilky, then seventeen, turned his back on the Sanborn school and sought a place in the Northern Army. A few months later Bob followed him.

The war thus emphasized a widening gulf between the four brothers that had hitherto been simply the result of their difference in age. Wilky and Bob were still busy with their schooling when William and Henry had gained comparative liberty in Geneva. There the younger boys had been set apart in the Pensionnat Maquelin, returning to the family at the Hotel de l'Écu only on Sundays. A similar isolation from family had occurred upon their return to America, in their prompt installation in Concord. Bob, in particular, had for some time "strained much at every tether," Henry observed. He had considered himself a foundling in the family; he talked of running off to sea. The war offered him a ready alternative. If their enlistment on the one hand was a reflection of a youthful desire for action, freedom, adventure, and a response to strong anti-slavery sentiment to which they had been exposed both at home and at Concord, it was also a leap to manhood and the sudden achievement of a superior position in the family hierarchy. By one swift bound they surpassed their older brothers, and the focus of family interest was turned upon them where it had previously treated them as juveniles and attached importance to William's artistic and later scientific career and Henry's bookishness. The younger brothers stepped into the bright and lurid light of war for their brief hour—and it turned out to be their only hour. Life after the Civil War was for them a long and painful anti-climax, while for William and Henry it marked a progression to careers and fame. The splitting apart within the family was permanent. The younger boys went their separate ways first of heroism

and then of frustration and suffering. Their story is a separate chapter in the annals of the James family, rich in idealism and courage, but also beclouded by pathos and decline.

During the Civil War the older brothers were the "stay-at-homes" and the younger boys took possession of the scene. Their vivid and excited letters from the field gave Henry a continuing picture of the life of the soldier and the life of action. Here were young Jamesian voices reporting what they had seen and done: and Henry listened with deep emotion. He remembered visiting Wilky when he was in the 44th Massachusetts at camp at Readville and marvelled that "this soft companion of my childhood should have such romantic chances and should have mastered, by the mere aid of his native gaiety and sociability, such mysteries, such engines, such arts. To become first a happy soldier and then an easy officer was in particular for G. W. J. an exercise in sociability." He remembered Readville as "an interplay of bright breezy air and high shanty-covered levels with blue horizons, and laughing, welcoming, sunburnt young men." Presently Wilky joined the dramatically-constituted 54th Massachusetts, the first regiment of colored troops, headed by Colonel Robert Gould Shaw. Henry was ill the day they marched out of Boston—May 28, 1863—"to great reverberations of music, of fluttering banners, launched benedictions and every public sound." That the moment seemed to him deeply important is testified to by the fact that he twice describes it in his memoirs, even though he was not present.

I

On July 1, 1863, as the battle of Gettysburg raged, Henry paced restlessly in a Newport garden, with some New York cousins "neither daring quite to move nor quite to rest, quite to go in nor quite to stay out. . . . This *was*, as it were, the War—the War palpably in Pennsylvania. . . ." Before the month was out war was experienced in the James household in Newport. There had been a courageous assault by the Negro regiment on Fort Wagner in Charleston Bay with the guns of Sumter playing on them. The

54th withdrew after two-thirds of its officers and nearly half its men had been shot down or bayonetted within the fortress or before its walls. Shaw had died, leading his men, a bullet in his heart; and Wilky James, his adjutant, had received a wound in his side and a canister ball in his ankle.

It fell to William James many years later (in 1897) to pronounce a eulogy of Colonel Shaw and his men at the unveiling of the Shaw monument by Saint-Gaudens in Boston. William, drawing on Wilky's memories, described the forced marches in the rain, the hunger of the men as they lay "in the evening twilight against the cold sands of Morris Island with sea-fog drifting over them, their eyes fixed on the huge hulk of the fortress looming darkly three-quarters of a mile ahead against the sky, and their hearts beating in expectation of the word that was to bring them to their feet and launch them on their desperate charge. . . ." He told of the fierce attack and finally described how the next day the rebels, having repulsed the assault, dug a ditch and threw into it the bodies of Shaw and his colored soldiers. "In death, as in life, then, the 54th bore witness," said William James, "to the brotherhood of man."

Wilky James probably would have been among the dead had not a rescuing hand intervened. Reported missing in the struggle at Charleston was Wilky's closest friend in the Army, Cabot Russell, whose father promptly went in search of his son. He did not find him, but he discovered Wilky among the wounded and brought him north by boat to New York and thence to Newport where, one August day in 1863, he appeared at the James residence with the wounded youth on a stretcher. They carried Wilky in, placing the stretcher just inside the door of the house. There he lay for days. The doctor ordered that he should not be moved. Henry remembered the moment of arrival in his old age as clearly as "some object presented in high relief against the evening sky of the west" —with himself sitting beside the stretcher and Cabot Russell's father "erect and dry-eyed at the guarded feast of *our* relief." In Henry James's second story, the bringing home of the young hero

from battle is described, much as it undoubtedly occurred at Newport, and the heroine wonders as Henry might have, whether the young soldier were not dead, "Death is not thinner, paler, stiller." A sketch of Wilky made by William at this moment shows him almost as one dead—open-mouthed, leaden-eyed, his cheeks sunken and his face covered with the stubble of his beard. "Poor Wilky cries aloud for his friends gone and missing, and I could hardly have supposed he might be educated so suddenly up to serious manhood altogether as he appears to have been," the senior Henry wrote to a friend at the same moment.

Wilky's recovery was slow but he pulled through and with a fine show of strength returned to the field in 1864, rejoining his own regiment. In spite of his freshly-healed wounds he was able to ride and march and he participated in the entry into Charleston. He was present when the American flag was hoisted over Sumter.

In the meantime Robertson had been made a lieutenant in the 55th Massachusetts. While Wilky was recovering, he was at Morris Island building earthworks and mounting guns in the southern heat with rebel shells playing on the troops so that they made for their breastworks "like so many land-crabs in distress." He suffered so serious a sunstroke during Seymour's raid on Florida that he was recommended for discharge. Instead, as soon as he had recovered, he took a staff post in the cavalry and later returned to his regiment before Charleston. He participated in a heavy fight, made an heroic charge ("I rammed my spurs into my own beast, who, maddened with pain, carried me on through the line, throwing men down, and over the rebel works some distance ahead of our troops"). This earned him a captaincy. The 55th later was the first body of Northern troops to enter Charleston.

11

Rereading the war letters when he was writing *Notes of a Son and Brother*, Henry re-experienced "the places, the hours, the stilled or stirred conditions" in which he had originally absorbed them fresh from the front. These conditions, he said, "settled for me into the

single sense of what I missed, compared to what the authors of
our bulletins gained, in wondrous opportunity of vision, that is
appreciation of the thing seen." Henry longed to live by his eyes
"in the midst of such far-spreading chances, in greater measure
than I then had help to. . . ." and his role was reduced to "seeing,
sharing, envying, applauding, pitying, all from too far-off."

The Civil War letters of his brothers form a logical bridge to
Henry's later reading of war memoirs and Napoleonic lore. The
passionate interest with which he absorbed the three volumes of
Marbot in the 1890's represented a continuation of the earlier experience; in other words, he continued over the years to read
other war letters cast in the form of memoirs, and the passages he
marked in Marbot are not unlike those he excerpted from Wilky's
letters—scenes of violence, storming of positions, the rugged life
and observations of men committed to action. When Field Marshal
Viscount Wolseley sent him his two-volumed *Story of a Soldier's
Life* in 1903 Henry wrote him: "To a poor worm of peace and
quiet like me—yet with some intelligence—the interest of communicating so with the military temper and type is irresistible—of get-
ing so close (comparatively!) to the qualities that make the brilliant man of action. Those are the qualities, unlike one's own, that
are romantic, that you have lived all your days by and with them
and for them, I feel as if I had never questioned you nor sounded
you enough. . . . I would give all I have (including Lamb House)
for an hour of your retrospective consciousness, one of your more
crowded memories—that for instance of your watch, before your
quarters, during the big fight in Ashantee—when the fellow was
eyeing you to see if you wouldn't get out of it. . . ." This was
doubtless true: Henry would have given much to have been able to
pass to vivid conquering action in his waking hours as he had
done in his nightmare of the Louvre: the measure of his offer was the measure of his passion.

III

When the war was over, Wilky and Bob, flushed with victory and imbued with the cause for which they had fought, embarked on a courageous if misguided venture: they set out to be plantation owners in Florida with paid Negro labor, as if the South no longer considered them "enemy" once the last shot was fired. They struggled valiantly, risked their lives, lost large sums of money advanced to them by their father, and finally gave up. The rest of Wilky's brief life was a series of efforts to find a place for himself in a disjointed America; sociable, as always, improvident, he drifted finally westward, worked as a railway clerk and died at forty after a period of prolonged ill-health. Robertson lived into our century, a brilliant, erratic individual, gifted, witty, deeply unhappy. Henry called him "our one gentleman of leisure." He too worked for a railroad for a while; he tried to paint, he wrote verses, he travelled and he experienced a series of religious conflicts much like his father—for a while he found solace in Catholicism, then he rebelled against the Church's authority and turned to the family religion, Swedenborgianism. The senior Henry's letters to him during these years are filled with brilliant exposition of his beliefs and with paternal counsel and solace. There were periods of heavy drinking and guilt, which Robertson expressed once in a pathetic poem that reveals nevertheless his strength of feeling and insight into his own sense of desolation:

> With Wine I slept, and sleeping did not hear . . .
>
> The night we live in, is the all of Fate,
> Oblivion's sleep will come, or soon or late;
> Drink deep! nor for some distant Heaven wait;
> And these, my friends, stayed on, until the Wine
> Was out—and then, they left me desolate.
>
> Nor did I wake for many an empty year
> Nor did I wish to wake, for very fear. . . .

The poem is an amalgam of the self-pity and sorrow that harked back to his boyhood. He died in the same year as William, in

1910, and Henry, mourning him, spoke of the "vivacity of his intelligence, the variety of his gifts" and his "easiest aptitude for admirable talk, charged with natural life, perception, humor and color, that I have perhaps ever known."

A PARTICULAR DIVERGENCE

THE DOCTOR'S POOH-POOH HAD OFFERED HENRY JAMES NEITHER A cure nor the awkward solace of invalidism. To remain at home at such a moment, with nothing more to show than a back-ache, however painful, while the great hurricane of the fratricidal war swept over the nation, could indeed "in no light pass for graceful." Henry James felt acutely that he had to "make some show of life . . . when everyone was on the move." He was, he told himself, "no less exaltedly than wistfully engaged in the common fact of endurance" like the soldiers themselves. Moreover, he found himself, at this moment, isolated in his own family. The younger brothers were gone; William was in Cambridge; and now his boon companion Sargy Perry was about to enter Harvard. This was clearly no time to remain at home. In September 1862 Henry James accordingly journeyed from Newport to Cambridge and registered at the Harvard Law School. In looking back at his young collegiate self, he felt that his act was similar to that of a young man joining a mustered army. "The Cambridge campus was tented field enough for a conscript starting so compromised; and I can scarcely say moreover how easily it let me down that when it came to the point

one had still fine fierce young men, in great numbers, for company, there being at the worst so many such who hadn't flown to arms."

Thus at nineteen the young cosmopolite, who had lived in New York, in London, in Paris, found himself at last on the New England scene. Newport, "with its opera-glass turned for ever across the sea" was not New England, was at best a stepping-stone to America. But now he was in the Back Bay itself and its academic suburb of Cambridge, in that city which the consummate Brahmin, Dr. Oliver Wendell Holmes, with a Bostonian complacency and civic pride that Henry was later to satirize, had characterized as "the thinking center of the continent." New England had been only a domestic geographical designation to Henry James, something discovered as a boy in Fourteenth Street through his reading of the Rollo books, or in the benign aspect of Mr. Emerson. It had, however, acquired a certain reality in the persons of three playmates who lived down street during those Manhattan years, Johnny, Charley and Freddy Ward. They exhaled, for the young Manhattanite, an atmosphere of apples and cheese, nuts, pies, jackknives, "domestic Bible-reading and attendance at 'evening-lecture' " as well as fear of parental discipline "and the cultivated art of defying it." The Wards were tough little New Englanders who talked of "squrruls," had warts on their hands, wore homespun and revealed "a brave rusticity." The words *rustic, rural, provincial* figure always in Henry James's picture of New England. He found Boston a "rural center even to a point at which I had never known anything as rural" and this was strange because the city was at the same time "stoutly and vividly urban . . . a town of history."

One felt there the "breath of the fields and woods and waters . . . at their domesticated and familiarized stage" which Emerson had brought into the Fourteenth Street parlor. New York might be described as "vulgar" and "homely" but the Puritan capital, with its plodding horse-cars and the afterglow in its sky of the great snowfalls, reflected "the higher complacency" and at the same time was New England "unabsorbed and unreconciled"—and also "the most educated of our societies without ceasing to be that of a vil-

lage." In his later sketch of Emerson and in his book on Hawthorne, as well as in his tribute to those Brahmins who became his mentors and friends, Henry James never forgot that while Nature, in New England, could inspire notes both lyrical and rhapsodic, its life constituted an "achromatic picture" of "a plain, God-fearing society . . . not fertile in variations." His book on Hawthorne is in reality a long discourse on the shortcomings of New England as a subject for the novelist; he speaks of its coldness, thinness, blankness, he contemplates the "lonely frigidity" of its social recreation, he calls it a "thinly-composed society." Between the rectitude and morality of meeting house and pulpit and the open fields and spreading elms there was that same disparity which the elder Henry had discovered between his Calvinistic home and the out-of-doors of his boyhood. (The father, in fact, had once described John Calvin as "a sort of model Bostonian.")

This was, however, Henry James's view of New England during his maturity and long after his saturation with the Back Bay life and Cambridge. The process began with Harvard and was to continue for the next six years. It flowered ultimately into *The Bostonians* and *The Europeans* and largely as satire and irony penned by the grandson of an Albany merchant, an immigrant, who could never reconcile himself to the gentility of the Brahmins and the frugality of Concord or the manner in which New England considered culture to be an arduous duty rather than a joy of life and of civilization. Wordsworth's "plain living and high thinking" summed up New England for one who came to it with visions in his mind of the London of Dickens and the Paris of the Second Empire. Henry James expressed the aberrations and deformities and frustrations, the starch that congealed the blood of some New Englanders, with an often ill-concealed, if urbanely-cloaked, animus. Yet within this environment he considered hostile to major creative art, lay the associations of his "untried years" so that Cambridge and Boston were regarded by him as repositories of old personal memories that had marked the launching of a career, *his* career. In the end his pictures of the old scenes are suffused with a

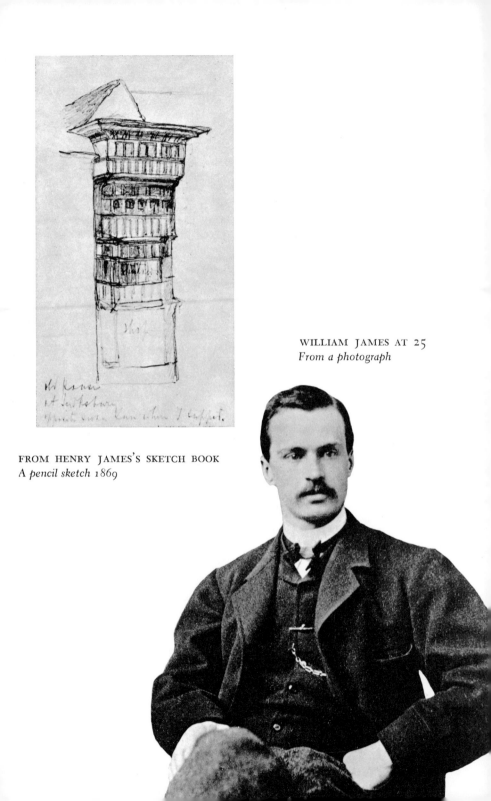

WILLIAM JAMES AT 25
From a photograph

FROM HENRY JAMES'S SKETCH BOOK
A pencil sketch 1869

HENRY JAMES AT NEWPORT
AGED 20
From a photograph

MINNY TEMPLE AT 16
From a photograph. Her hair h
been cropped during an illness.

kind of redeeming affection and tenderness. New England became a part of Henry James even if the strain was injected the wrong way.

I

Henry James had actually entertained the idea of a university education in Bonn, two years earlier, when he excitedly awaited his return to America. "I wish," he had written to Perry, "although I've no doubt it is a very silly wish, that I were going to college." He now had his wish. In his old age, however, it seemed "odd" to him that he should have wanted to go, and odder still that he should have elected the study of law. Law, nevertheless, appears to have been for him the only acceptable alternative in 1862. Harvard was then a college of some one thousand students and thirty teachers. Its curriculum had not yet acquired its modern amplitude. Nothing approaching "liberal arts" existed then except the rhetoric and oratory taught by Francis J. Child or the French and Spanish taught by James Russell Lowell. Henry was neither rhetorical nor oratorical; he had no need to study French and no desire to study Spanish. The Divinity School, the core of the institution, could offer little to a young man neither philosophical nor religious. He certainly had no desire to join William at the Lawrence Scientific School. Once he had excluded the clergyman, the scientist, the doctor, what remained but the lawyer? The law was the one field which seemed eminently "practical." It represented "life" and the "world." In reality it was the avenue of least resistance, for the moment, for a shy, observant young man who asked only to be just "literary." Harvard appeared to him "detached from any such interest" but that mattered little. For literature he could go to the library at Gore Hall, or when at home he had only to open the door of the big square closet in the Newport house where the pink copies of the *Revue des Deux Mondes* were piled "with the air, row upon row, of a choir of breathing angels." This had been his best school. In reality he wanted no other.

Henry James lodged with William for a few days after his ar-

rival in Cambridge until he found himself rooms in Winthrop Square, in an old house with "everything in it slanting and gaping and creaking." His sitting room commanded a view of distant hills and in an alcove there was a large desk where "even so shy a dreamer as I . . . might perhaps hope to woo the muse." In his short story "The Ghostly Rental," written some years later, the young Harvard graduate establishes himself "in a great square low-browed room with deep window benches," hangs prints on the walls and arranges his books "with great refinement of classification" in alcoves beside a high chimney shelf. We can imagine the young Henry doing this and taking "long and sustaining sniffs" at the "scented flower of independence." William was close at hand, to be sought out at will; T. S. Perry was as always a familiar companion. But now he had all Boston and Cambridge to explore, and the privacy of his room to which he could return to watch the flushed sunsets and the cloud scenery of which he makes so much in his early stories. New England now was all around him, and he had to "rinse my mouth of the European aftertaste *in order* to do justice to whatever of the native bitter-sweet might offer itself. . . ."

Harvard's setting at this time was entirely rural. In a matter of minutes he could find himself walking past shabby little meadows and scrubby little orchards, encountering crooked little crossroads and studying solitary dwellings on long grassy slopes under tall New England elms "with their shingled hoods well pulled down on their ears." Divinity Hall, where William had rooms in 1863, was remembered through a haze of Indian summers, with the vista of the nearby Norton woods massed in autumnal scarlet and orange "when to penetrate and mount a stair and knock at a door and, enjoying response, then sink into a window-bench and inhale at once the vague golden November and the thick suggestion of the room . . . was to taste as I had never done before the poetry of the prime initiation and of associated growth." "Europe" for the present retreated, leaving a more rustic and homespun scene to the contemplation of the earnest young man with penetrating eyes, high forehead and carefully-parted and already-receding

hair, who had become a cosmopolite without ever having been a provincial.

II

Henry joined William at meals three times a day at Miss Upham's board in her house at the corner of Kirkland and Oxford Streets. The young law student lost no time in translating the establishment into Balzac's Maison Vauquer, but agreed promptly that the Maison Upham, under the elms, had nothing of the sordid or sinister as in its French counterpart and that "in the matter of talk as talk we shone incomparably brighter." In fact it was "a veritable haunt of conversation." There was, of course, a major subject, the continuing war. The "torch flared sufficiently about Miss Upham's board" Henry remembered, but the spinster shoved it quickly away from her end of the table with heavy sighs as if hoping to extinguish the flame. From Henry's memoirs we can reconstitute the table at the boarding house: Henry sat beside William, who was brightly communicative, full of life and always ready to help "the lame dog of converse over stile after stile." There was little need to do this, for opposite sat Harvard's Chaucerian and collector of ballads, Professor Francis J. Child, round-faced, cherubic, fair-haired, wearing gold-rimmed spectacles and filled with discourse about the conduct of the war, his talk a "darting flame" when it came to the North's trans-Atlantic enemies, and gravely elegiac in keeping green the memory of the young men who had gone from his classes to war and death. Also at the table was John Bancroft, son of the historian, whom Henry had met at Newport and who was to become a valued friend; a young fellow student of Henry's, Beach Vanderpool Jr. and two friends of William's, Joe May, son of a New York Abolitionist, and a young theological student named Salter, with dark mustache and pointed beard, who looked like an old Spanish portrait and who was New England at its "sparest and dryest," and at the same time at its wittiest.

If Henry went conscientiously to the lectures in Dane Hall in the

mornings—and he marvelled at the extent to which he faithfully attended—it was because, he later felt, he could exercise his observer's role to his heart's content. The question of how people looked and "of how their look counted for a thousand relations" had existed for him from early days. Here he had a classroom filled with Americans to study at first hand. For the first time he found himself among his young contemporaries in his native land and he used his eyes constantly as he sat in the rear of the auditorium surveying his classmates, in the dusky half-smothered light coming from low windows, as if they were actors on the other side of the footlights. He felt that "when one should cease to live in large measure by one's eyes. . . one would have taken the longest step toward not living at all." He sought to fix "the weight, the interest, the function" of his fellow-Americans. He wanted to get to know the "types." The law students at Harvard came from a prosperous section of American society; this was apparent. They appeared to be standardized and homogenized New Englanders from Springfield or Worcester, Providence or Portland. Yet now and again they flowered into the "special type" of which Henry James was to make much in subsequent years. Their very names as we read them today, are redolent of New England—Wentworth, Lathrop, Pickering, Young, Kirkland, Sargent—and readers will find them used in the American novels and tales of Henry James. Curiously enough, however, with the exception of Salter, who was William's friend, and not a law student, Henry does not single out any New England classmates for the vivid sketches of his young contemporaries which are woven into his memoirs. The three fellow-students whom he recalls and describes are like himself "outsiders"—Beach Vanderpool Jr. "incorruptibly and exquisitely dumb . . . admirable, ineffaceable, because so essentially all *decipherable*," who came from New Jersey; an unnamed New Yorker, a "finished fop" (identified by T. S. Perry as Sam D. Craig) a comedy figure, a caricature with a tight umbrella under his arm, a toy-terrier at his heels, and a monocle in his eye when it was not being used in his hand as "a defensive crystal wall."

James admired his way of standing up to his classmates as an individual, never intimidated by their mockery and always consistent in maintaining the personality he had created. More important than either of these was a classmate designated as G. A. J. who reached "westward, westward even of New York and southward at least as far as Virginia" whom we identify as George Abbott James (not however a descendant of William of Albany) marked by Henry from the first "for a friend and taken for a kinsman"—sole member of the Harvard law class whose friendship the novelist cherished in later life. G. A. J. could kindle "bonfires of thought" and through him Henry could reach out, later, to create a Westerner such as Christopher Newman or a Southerner such as Basil Ransom.

The novelist hangs before us also three vignettes of his law professors: Dr. Theophilius Parsons, who sat beneath a "huge hot portrait of Daniel Webster" discoursing in "rich quavering accents," a provincial with accretions of unction, serenity, quality and homage to old superstitions; "Governor" Emory Washburn, from the depths of whose rusticity there emerged candor "as to his own pleasant fallibility," and Judge Joel Parker, with a tight mouth above an absent chin, representing "dryness and hardness, prose unrelieved," perhaps, observed Henry, because he was most master of his subject.

Only once during the year does Henry James seem to have stepped out of his observer's rôle in the Law School and this became a "black little memory." The Marshall Club of which Henry became a member, staged a moot court and Henry agreed, or was assigned, to represent the "defendant" in an arbitration suit. He found himself in a "perfect glare of publicity" which frightened him into virtual silence. The opposing counsel won the case with ease and Henry retired in deep discomfiture over his failure to think quickly on his feet. James's nephew many years later, seeking to discover more about this incident, learned that a classmate, George Gray, was the "judge" who found against the defendant, and that the case apparently was such that a real lawyer in a real

court could have stood no chance of winning. We suspect, however, that Henry couldn't have won even the easiest case. He had not studied his law books with any assiduity and, aside from this brave display of himself before his class, his connection with Dane Hall—a building long since gone from the Harvard scene—remained "as consistently superficial as could be possible" to one who was so "restlessly perceptive." Perceiving, James noted, had a distinct value: it "kicked up no glare." He invariably preferred to see rather than to be seen.

III

He went on long lonely rambles in Cambridge and Boston; he sat in Gore Hall reading Sainte-Beuve whom he discovered during that year, counting this as a "sacred date"—sacred, he felt, in the development of any historic or aesthetic consciousness; he wandered occasionally into other classrooms and on certain dark winter afternoons listened to James Russell Lowell discoursing by lamplight on English literature and Old French. The lectures were an "unforgettable initiation" and the lamplight illuminated the bearded face and expressive hands of the stocky Yankee Henry James was later to count as an intimate friend.

Henry was in Boston at the height of the Abolition fever. The burning question of slavery had touched him from his earliest days. He remembered how in Fourteenth Street the Norcom family arrived from Kentucky with three sons, Eugene, Reginald and Albert and set up a sausage-making contraption on their porch—pronounced by them "poo'ch"—proceeding to dispense Southern hospitality to the little Northern Jameses—hot cakes, sausages and molasses in prodigious quantities. They had brought with them precious pieces of property—two slaves, Davy and his mother, Aunt Sylvia (pronounced An'silvy). Davy became one of Henry's playmates, mingling in James family sports and talk until the day when both he and An'silvy quite suddenly disappeared. They had waked up to the fact that in the North they need not remain in bondage and one night made off "beyond recall or recovery." Little Henry,

fresh from his reading of *Uncle Tom's Cabin,* noted how the Norcoms were "shocked at such ingratitude." They could neither bring out the bloodhounds nor were there any blocks of ice for An'silvy to cross. Henry retained a sense, however, of having experienced at first hand a little of the crucial history of his time.

A milestone in this same history was his trip on New Year's day 1863 into Boston, through milling crowds, to the Music Hall, where an excited multitude celebrated Lincoln's Emancipation Proclamation with an uncommon Bostonian show of fever and emotion. On the crowded platform was the old family friend, Mr. Emerson, tall and spare, reading his "Boston Hymn" in ringing tones, the long-familiar voice. "He who does his own work frees a slave," Emerson had once written, and now he rendered the thought into verse, reading with stirring effect:

> Pay ransom to the owner
> And fill the bag to the brim.
> Who is the owner? The slave is owner
> And ever was. *Pay him!*

The North had at last articulated a long-demanded "war aim" that, while it did not transcend the struggle for the Union, touched the deep and human note.

Other moments during his year at Harvard were bound to be less historic. However, in the private history of Henry James there was an evening when he travelled into Boston to the Howard Athenaeum to see Maggie Mitchell in *Fanchon the Cricket,* translated from a German play which in turn was derived from a novel by George Sand. He had found that in the Boston audience there lingered the "half-buried Puritan curse . . . that intimation more than anything else perhaps of the underhand snicker," the "implication of the provincial in the theatric air, and of the rustic in the provincial." Miss Mitchell had played the one part up and down the United States—she "twanged that one string and none other, every night of her theatric life"—and yet there was nothing stale

about the charm she exercised upon the young law student. Henry returned entranced to his room in Winthrop Square and wrote Miss Mitchell a letter from which she should "gather the full force of my impression." Maggie reciprocated. She sent him an autographed "acting edition" of the play and Henry fancied himself quite the young Pendennis smitten by Miss Fotheringay.

The impression stimulated him to much more than a "fan" letter. He sat down at his desk in the alcove with his view of the distant hills "to enrol myself in the bright band of the fondly hoping and fearfully doubting who count the days after the despatch of manuscripts." His first piece of independent writing deemed fit to submit for publication thus dealt with a play and an actress. He adds coyly that "nothing would induce me now to name the periodical on whose protracted silence I had thus begun to hang. . . ." We do not know whether this spontaneous piece of drama criticism was ever published. Le Roy Phillips's bibliography of Henry James's writings lists nothing earlier than 1864 and in that year only criticism. But in December 1864 Wilky was writing from the front "Tell Harry that I am waiting anxiously for his 'next.' I can find a large sale for any blood and thunder tale among the darks." Some time between his departure from Harvard in 1863 and the appearance of his first unsigned criticism in the *North American Review* in the autumn of 1864 the young writer found his literary feet and took the path from which he would never stray.

Was this the turning point in Henry James's life? A friend—perhaps Howells—suggested to him after the turn of the century that it might have been (just about the time that Mark Twain was asked and was seeking to answer the same question). Henry James turned the matter over in his mind, as a few unpublished pages preserved among his papers testify. He had brought away from the Law School "certain rolls of manuscript that were quite shamelessly not so many bundles of notes on the perusal of so many calfskin volumes." These were notes of another sort, "small sickly seed, no doubt, but to be sown and to sprout up into such flowers as they

might, in a much less trimmed and ordered garden than that of the law." His friend had argued that "I must then, in the cold shade of queer little old Dane Hall have stood at the parting of my ways, recognized the false steps, even though few enough, already taken, and consciously committed myself to my particular divergence."

Henry James goes on in the fragment to say that he welcomed the suggestion and thought about it, wondering whether "my youth *had* in fact enjoyed that amount of drama." He couldn't be sure. The fragment breaks off at this point leaving us without the final answer. However, James's recollections of his Harvard year contain no mention of a conscious choice between law and letters, the world and the study. He drifted into the law school and he nowhere mentions how or when he drifted away from it. But he leaves no doubt that he was as ill-fitted for the law as he had been for his "scientific" studies at the Institution Rochette. Dane Hall may not have marked a "turning point" so much as the turning of a corner. There were to be no more "false steps."

ASHBURTON PLACE

THE CIVIL WAR, AS WITH ALL WARS, WAS A PERIOD OF TERMINATIONS and beginnings. The Emancipation Proclamation had marked the triumph—and the end—of the Abolitionist cause. Boston had never lacked causes or their advocates, but this cause had been at once

the noblest and the most deeply felt. It had engaged common sympathies. Men had laid down their lives to defend it; with it nineteenth century New England touched its highest note of compassion and humanity. In intellectual Boston the war marked the end of an era of "radicalism" and a return to the old conservative virtues. Not that New England "radicalism" had ever been very radical; it reflected, however, in the mid-century, a certain enlightenment, a kind of Athenian glory—the dazzle of marble in the sun at high noon—and now the long afternoon had begun. The elder Henry James, arriving on this scene from Newport, was impressed, as an outsider might be, by the geniality, intelligence and high-mindedness of the Bostonian elite; he did not, however, allow their shining virtues to blind him to their easy complacency and self-assurance. The Brahmins struck him, at moments, as "simmering in their own fat and putting a nice brown on one another."

His son was to say many brilliant if unkind things about the Bostonians and to enshrine them and their city in a long, cold, and distinctly unpopular novel; but at twenty-one he found life in the Back Bay palpitating with interest. For him too the period was one of terminations and beginnings. The black despair engendered by war and ill-health now gave way to a feeling of high hope and elation. The senior Henry and his wife had moved to No. 13 Ashburton Place in Boston from a Newport that had become too lonely for them, and William and Henry thus were returned to the family hearth. The house, of red brick and set on a granite basement, was as substantial as Boston itself. Henry had a large green-shuttered room on the third floor overlooking the Place and here he was able to establish his working relationship with "the small inkpot in which I seemed at last definitely destined to dip. . . ." The very words Ashburton Place in later years were tinted with memories of coming-of-age, "the days, the hours, the seasons, the winter skies and darkened rooms of summer , , the old walks, the old efforts, the old exaltations and depressions. . . ." "Ah the things and the people, the hours and scenes and circumstances, the *inénarrables* occasions . . . the sense . . . of particu-

lar little thrills and throbs and day-dreams . . . of unforgettable
gropings and findings and sufferings and strivings and play of sensibility and of inward passion . . . ." In Ashburton Place Henry
James heard the news of Grant's victories and the surrender at
Appomattox. Here—on his twenty-second birthday—the shrill cry
reached him of an outraged and grieving America standing at the
bier of the assassinated President. Here, too, one morning, word
came that Hawthorne had died; half-dressed, on the edge of his
bed, in the dim light that filtered through the green shutters, he
found himself yielding "to the pang that made me positively and
loyally cry." And here, in these same surroundings, he one day
counted the first earnings of his pen, a dozen greasy dollar bills.

It was the springtime of his life and his memories were of
Boston springs, a dropping down from Beacon Hill for "those
premonitary gusts of April that one felt most perhaps where Park
Street Church stood dominant, where the mouth of the Common
itself uttered promises, more signs and portents than one could
count. . . ." The two years at Ashburton Place were festive, a kind
of prolonged celebration, as if he were moving "through an apartment hung with garlands and lights." He came of age here
in more ways than one: he became a writer.

I

When the young literary aspirant arrived on the Boston scene in
1864—as distinct from the collegiate scene in Cambridge of the
previous year—the *Atlantic Monthly* was seventeen years old and
the *North American Review* almost fifty. The *Atlantic* was under
the editorship of James T. Fields, a friendly, hospitable and benevo-
lent individual deeply attached to his mission of publisher in a city
that prided itself on its love of good books and the communion,
through the printed page, with great minds. He and his wife, as
Henry James recalled many years later, were "addicted to the cultivation of talk and wit and to the ingenious multiplication of such
ties as could link the upper half of the title-page with the lower."
Fields was a collector of literary relics, autographs, rare editions

and his house by the Charles was a veritable "waterside museum." The Fieldses maintained a salon ("so far as salons were in the old Puritan city dreamed of") in which were received the elite of the literary and artistic world from both sides of the water. They were host to Dickens and to Thackeray, to every distinguished visitor who came to Boston, and to all the Brahmins; and it was not long before the young Henry found himself welcomed as a writer of promise, having Sunday supper opposite the celebrated Mrs. Stowe who had a "nonchalance of real renown" to the eyes of a youth seeking renown and not at all nonchalant about it. It was Fields who, in due course, published Henry James's first important fiction in the *Atlantic* while complaining of his "strain of pessimism." "What we want," said Mr. Fields with perfect truth, "is short *cheerful* stories." Henry was ready to admit years later that he had been "precociously dismal" and that he was striking a note alien to a society that was fundamentally optimistic and which had its eyes upon transcendant things. The future novelist was taking the writing of fiction more seriously than any writer in that society—a society which tended to take poetry, the sermon and the essay, rather than the novel, as the hall-mark of literary achievement. James Russell Lowell characterized the limits of the writer in New England when he asserted: "Let no man write a line that he would not have his daughter read," and Henry James was to complain bitterly that American magazines sought to reduce him to the intellectual level of adolescent maidens. "Why should a man by choice go down to live in his cellar," Lowell argued, "instead of mounting to those fair upper chambers which look toward the sunrise. . . ."

The Brahmins indeed lived in fair upper chambers in ancestral homes. Henry James, even though he too was rarely to venture into the cellar, insisted that life had its sunsets as well as its sunrises; in his modest way, he began to introduce into the bookish air of the Puritan city, a sense of reality distinct from the romances of the time, and a theory of the novel. It was extremely modest at first. The young outsider could only, at this stage, stand

in the shadow of the celebrities of Boston and Cambridge—none of them novelists—who by the end of the Civil War were reaching comfortable middle age and were become New England oracles as well as men of letters. Oliver Wendell Holmes, the "autocrat" and wit, was fifty-five when the Jameses appeared in Boston. Longfellow was fifty-seven and Lowell forty-five. Fields, their publisher, was forty-seven. Longfellow and Lowell were buried too far between book covers to want to look at any life beyond the pleasing perspective they had from their study windows in their ancestral homes where at night the cry of the cricket and grasshopper from lawn and garden was the sole sound of the outer world to reach them. Lowell, it is true, stirred uneasily later, on becoming a diplomat, and acknowledged that books were "good dry forage" and that after all "men are the only fresh pasture." This said, he kept nevertheless to his old course. The New England elite fell roughly into two classes: the men who, like Emerson and Thoreau, had built a philosophy in communion with the out-of-doors, and the urban Brahmins, sons and grandsons of clergymen, whose creativity was fed by the creativity of the past. They were, most of them, but one generation removed from the pulpit. They still tended to preach. Hawthorne alone among the writers had expressed, for Henry James, the passive, haunted, imaginative side of the transplanted Puritan. Lowell was the antithesis of this: he represented New England prosperity and good health linked to a facile and erratic literary talent. A haze of cigar smoke surrounded him and he was always digging into books for recondite information. He had for James a "boyish simplicity" and later, when the novelist came to know him intimately during his ambassadorial life abroad, he saw him as an "erect fighting figure on the side of optimism and beauty."

Longfellow, who in Henry James's eyes had found "the large, quiet, pleasant, easy solution" in life and literature, had absorbed heavy doses of German culture and derived inspiration from a variety of European models. He looked to the past, an unreconstructed romantic, whose work James found "remarkably even, nei-

ther rising above nor falling below a level ruled as straight as a line from a copybook." The youngest of the Brahmins in 1864—he was thirty-seven—was Charles Eliot Norton, son of a celebrated Biblical scholar, a friend of Ruskin, an art scholar, a lover of Italy. In his home, Shady Hill, which like Lowell's Elmwood was a Cambridge landmark, Norton had collected his trophies and spoils of Europe and in his long library he worked on his translation of Dante and carried out his "civilizing" mission, an apostle of Old World culture in the New World. The word "civilization" was often on his lips and Henry James remarked, in a late tribute to him, that the "representative of culture" had in those days "a great and arduous mission requiring plentiful courage as well as plentiful knowledge, endless good humour as well as assured taste." Norton brought to art the religious fervor of his forebears, he could "lose himself in the labyrinth of delight while keeping tight hold of the clue of duty."

In 1864 Norton and Lowell undertook to rescue the middle-aged *North American Review* from the staleness into which long-established periodicals often decline. And on July 30 of that year Henry James addressed to the editors from Ashburton Place a two-sentence letter, one of the least distinguished but most significant of his early epistolary efforts. "Gentlemen," he wrote, "I take the liberty of enclosing a brief review of [Nassau W.] Senior's *Essays on Fiction* published in London a few months ago. Hoping that you may deem it worthy of a place among your Literary Notices, I remain yours respectfully Henry James Jr." This done, he left to spend the summer at Northampton, Massachusetts.

I I

The choice of Northampton seems to have been dictated in part by its being in that era a comfortable health resort. Henry spoke of the town as "my small square patch of the American scene" when he put it into the opening pages of *Roderick Hudson*. It was, he wrote, the "only small American *ville de province* of which one had happened to lay up, long before, a pleased vision" and he

thought of the way in which Balzac, in his *scènes de la vie de province* had "done" Saumur, Limoges and Guérande. He didn't pretend to "do" it—there wasn't much to do with it and he felt, indeed, that he had failed in his emulation of the French master. The town has since grown to considerably larger proportions but when Henry James visited it in 1864—he prolonged his stay there from early August to December—it was a small New England settlement, with broad country streets and old white houses framed by box hedges and set off by high elms. Situated near an elbow of the Connecticut River and not far from Mount Holyoke, it provided Henry with a place of relaxation and rest, a spot where he could take a "water cure" and be near woods and rocks, red cedars, pines, "beauty sufficient for an artist not to starve upon it" as he said in his preface to *Roderick*. In that novel he introduces briefly those classical Balzacian figures, the town lawyer and the local clergyman; there is a picnic near the river such as James might have taken part in with his summer acquaintances and a sense of calm and dreamy peace which Rowland Mallet, the reflective observer, relishes—and from which Roderick, the artist, wants to escape. The choice of Northampton in James's first important novel was deliberate and autobiographical, as nearly all his choices of scene were. In this town Henry James, the American artist, was driving his pen in more professional fashion than ever before; it was therefore a fitting town in which to launch his fictional artist, and to impart to him those thoughts about the role of the creator in American society which Henry pondered as he walked through the American night and contemplated the moonlight among the lofty branches of the elms.

Nine days after dispatching his manuscript to the *North American Review* he had his answer. It was accepted—accepted with a show of enthusiasm that was flattering and with a prompt demand for more of his work. He replied that he would enjoy writing other literary notices if the books came "within my narrow compass" and he added, "I am frequently in the way of reading French works." Among the reviews he wrote at Northampton was one of

Harriet Elizabeth Prescott's *Azarian* and Mrs. A. M. C. Seemuller's *Emily Chester*. Before he returned to Boston his notice of Senior's essays was published in the October issue of the *Review*. He arrived at Ashburton Place at the end of November to find a request from Norton for a review of T. Adolphus Trollope's *Lindisfarn Chase* and did this for the January issue which contained three of Henry's reviews, all of them unsigned.

"I do *not* desire to notice novels exclusively," Henry wrote to Norton on December 1, "although I confess that that kind of criticism *comes most natural*. Other books which are not books of erudition, I shall always be glad to do my best for. Nothing would please me better, however, than to notice the novels of the next quarter in a lump, as you propose; so you may send me whatever appears in that line."

It was during this month that Henry James went out to snow-covered Cambridge in response to an invitation from Norton and spent a memorable half hour with him in his library at Shady Hill which he always considered as "a positive consecration to letters." The winter sunshine touched the serene bookshelves and pictures of the Dante scholar "with I know not what golden light of promise, what assurance of things to come: there was to be nothing exactly like it later on—the conditions of perfect rightness for a certain fresh felicity, certain decisive pressures of the spring, *can* occur, it would seem, but once."

The friendship formed that day was to endure for decades and to embrace Norton's immediate family and his sisters as well. It is doubtful whether it ever became intimate. Charles Eliot Norton did not inspire in Henry great warmth of feeling but a deep respect was there and the common ground of their love for the cultural riches of the Old World. Henry's letters to him are among his best: long, thoughtful, they contain a large body of comment on political events abroad absent from his other correspondence, as well as discussion of art, morality, Christianity and, criticism in apparent response to questions raised by Norton. And always, the American art scholar remained for Henry the man who had

opened one of the first doors to the world of letters. The *North American Review* paid Henry James $2.50 a page and his first review netted him twelve dollars. He had a sense of being launched, the first member of the family of the elder Henry James to have gone out into the world and taken a step toward earning his way. In a very general sense Henry James Junior had returned to the American path of William James of Albany.

I I I

Henry James's first book review which had received such prompt acceptance dealt with the art of fiction. It marked in every way an extraordinary debut as a critic for one destined to become a master of the art—almost as if, on the threshold of his career, he must consciously commit to print a theory of the novel he was to elaborate and practice during the next half century. What Henry's readers did not know was that the anonymous writer was not talking of fiction in a vacuum; that he had published at least one tale and was writing others soon to see print.

The essay is distinctly young and yet singularly mature. Its youth is testified to by its dogmatism, its attempt to demolish in cutting phrases, its forced mannerisms and above all by the desire of the writer to conceal his years. "Certain young persons . . ." he says at one point as if he were a somewhat older one, and ". . . youthful critics will be much more impartial at middle age" as if he knew all about middle age. It is doubtful however whether the casual reader of 1864 would have noticed this; he would have been impressed rather by the remarkable range of the writer's reading and his possession of a fund of original ideas on the art of the novel, whose form, then, was rarely discussed. The maturity that emerges from some of the stiff sentences derives from the evidence they furnish of Henry's intensive reading of fiction. He speaks as one who, for years, has been dissecting novels and examining how they were written, who feels that the time has come to set down if not an "Anatomy of Fiction," at least some suggestive thoughts on the subject. His very first paragraph strikes the note for his en-

tire career: "We opened this work with the hope of finding a general survey of the nature and principles of the subject of which it professes to treat. Its title had led us to anticipate some attempt to codify the vague and desultory canons, which cannot, indeed, be said to govern, but which in some measure define, this department of literature. We had long regretted the absence of any critical treatise upon fiction. But our regret was destined to be embittered by disappointment."

There spoke the man who was to write two decades later an historic paper on "The Art of Fiction" and who was to codify, in his late prefaces, at least those "laws" of the novel which had governed his own work. In this first essay he confined himself to making a few simple points which today may seem banal but which in their time were striking affirmations of the power and resources of the fictional form: fiction is a reflection of life, "even the most photographically disposed novels address pre-eminently the imagination," the public must be approached from its own level and not be preached at, fiction must become "self-forgetful," and not seek to instruct or to edify. It must, like *Waverley*, "prove nothing but facts." Men and women must be represented as they are, as motivated living creatures, not puppets. "Fiction?" queries the young man in discussing Sir Walter Scott's novels: "These are triumphs of fact. In the richness of his invention and memory, in the infinitude of his knowledge, in his improvidence for the future, in the skill with which he answers, or rather parries, sudden questions, in his low-voiced pathos and his resounding merriment, he is identical with the ideal fireside chronicler. And thoroughly to enjoy him, we must again become as credulous as children at twilight."

In demanding this evocation of reality even in such flights of the historic imagination as Scott's, Henry James ticks off the founders of the novel and rejects them: Richardson, Fielding, Smollett are "emphatically preachers and moralists"; *Tom Jones* "is like a vast episode in a sermon preached by a grandly humorous divine; and however we may be entertained by the way, we must not forget that our ultimate duty is to be instructed"; Richardson is "nei-

ther a romancer nor a story-teller; he is simply Richardson." Most
important of all, for the light they throw on the young aspirant,
are his asides which show him at grips with the form: "For our
own part, we should like nothing better than to write stories for
weary lawyers and schoolmasters. Idle people are satisfied with the
great romance of doing nothing. But busy people come fresh to
their idleness. The imaginative faculty, which has been gasping
for breath all day under the great pressure of reason, bursts forth
when its possessor is once ensconced under the evening lamp, and
draws a long breath in the fields of fiction." And so he defines the
function of the novelist as an artist who must meet distinct needs
of certain readers and at the same time know clearly how to go
about doing it. From the first he shows sensitivity over the
selection of names. "It is often enough to damn a well-intentioned
story, that the heroine should be called Kate rather than Katherine;
the hero Anthony rather than Ernest." Doesn't a novelist grow
weary grinding out "false persons and events"? He puts the question on behalf of the craftsman and answers it as if he has been
grinding them out for years: ". . . the best novelist is the busiest
man. It is, as you say, because I 'grind out' my men and women
that I endure them. It is because I create them by the sweat of my
brow that I venture to look them in the face. My *work* is my
salvation. If this great army of puppets came forth at my simple
bidding, then indeed I should die of their senseless clamor. But
as the matter stands, they are my very good friends. The pains
of labor regulate and consecrate my progeny. If it were as easy
to write novels as to read them, then, too, my stomach might rebel
against the phantom peopled atmosphere which I have given myself to breathe."

My work is my salvation wrote the young Henry James and when
he was fifty he put into his author's mouth in "The Middle
Years" an echo of those early words that was at the same time a
cri de coeur of his maturity. "We work in the dark—we do what
we can—we give what we have. Our doubt is our passion, and our
passion is our task. The rest is the madness of art." He couldn't

phrase it as compactly or as beautifully at twenty-one and only in middle life could he allow himself to doubt and wonder how much his work was really a fumbling in the dark. At twenty-one, however, Henry was approaching fiction more consciously and with greater deliberation than any novelist before him; the need to put the house of fiction in order and the need for precept, canon, codification, is there and clearly in evidence. Later it was to be expressed in a series of tales about misunderstood writers, all of them groping for an ideal world, a great good place in which art could flourish, freed alike from the pressures and disorders of society and the cares that beset the artist mind. For the novitiate in Ashburton Place, however, such complexities were unknown. *He* decidedly was not working in the dark.

Nearly all the early unsigned notices written between 1864 and 1866 in this journal and the *Nation* were collected in book form in 1921 under the title *Notes and Reviews*; assembled they show the young reviewer devoting himself almost exclusively to the novel. He lectures such writers as Miss Prescott and Miss Alcott on the need to create living characters, give them "a body, a local habitation, a name," but more than this reminds them: "The reader who is set face to face with a gorgeous doll will assuredly fail to inspire it with sympathetic life. To do so, he must have become excited and interested. What is there in a doll to excite and interest?" He advises the novelists to read Mérimée, to learn from the pages of Balzac how to set a scene and launch a drama and to study the realism of George Eliot. His concern is always with the reader who must be introduced to an atmosphere "in which it was credible that human beings might exist, and to human beings with whom he might feel tempted to claim kinship." The novelist must not describe, he must *convey*; characters once launched must *act* in certain ways consistent with their personality; the artist must not finger his puppets as a child besmudges a doll, he must endow them with their individuality and with life. Balzac is invoked as an example of the "scientific" novelist concerned with "the facts of things." James also lectures the novelists on their use of words. He

chides Miss Prescott for such phrases as "vermeil ardency" or such alliteration as "studded with starry sprinkle and sputter of splendor." The novelist must use his prose concretely: "You construct your description from a chosen object; can you, conversely, from your description, construct that object?"

It is amply clear from these reviews that whatever doubts and hesitancies Henry James had about his personal abilities he had none whatever about how fiction should be constituted and created. In a society addicted to happy-ending tales, he was a confirmed realist; in an age when the novel was generally regarded as an inferior form of art he had a profound faith in it as "history" and as "fact"—the words flow freely from his pen. We glimpse his sense of self-assurance where his craft is concerned in a journal entry some time between January and April 1865 made by Louisa May Alcott who in that year published her first novel *Moods*, which Henry James in due course tartly reviewed. Miss Alcott came to Boston and dined in Ashburton Place. "Henry Jr . . . was very friendly. Being a literary youth he gave me advice, as if he had been eighty, and I a girl." She adds, as if in extenuation of his presumption "My curly crop made me look young, though thirty-one." The truth was that the young man just turning twenty-two offered her important counsel, if we are to judge by his review of *Moods*. He observes there is no reason "why Miss Alcott should not write a very good novel, provided she will be satisfied to describe only that which she has seen." Elsewhere he remarks that the writing of a novel requires neither travel nor adventure nor sightseeing, "it is simply necessary to be an artist." This view he later elucidated by demonstrating that the artist worthy of his salt deduces from known facts and from experience.

At every turn he discloses the extent of his reading. Reviewing Miss Braddon's *Lady Audley's Secret* he invokes the names of Wilkie Collins, Mrs. Radcliffe, Walpole, George Eliot, George Sand, Hawthorne, Jane Austen, mentions the *Oresteia, Macbeth, Blackwood's Magazine* (of which he was an inveterate reader) and *Denis Duval*. He reviews *Felix Holt* and forgives George Eliot her

"clumsily artificial" plots because she delineates character, possesses human sympathy, poetic quality, microscopic observation, morality, discreet humor and exquisite rhetoric. As he nears his twenty-third birthday he reviews Dickens's *Our Mutual Friend* with a sense that the master has written himself out; the young Henry has seldom read "a book so intensely *written*, so little seen, known, or felt,"and concludes that Dickens knows men rather than *man* and that "it is one of the chief conditions of his genius not to see below the surface of things." As such he is the "greatest of superficial novelists." Dickens, the young critic finds, reconciles readers to the commonplace and to the odd, but he lacks an over-all philosophy, a capacity for generalizing the given case and so raising it to the level of the greatest art. The Dickens review is perhaps the most acute of all of Henry's early writings; he is freeing himself of an early idol and at the same time giving free play to his critical faculties. He is not intimidated by greatness and what is important for him is the elaboration and continued search for a viable theory of fiction.

This theory was derived not only from his close reading of novels. It bespoke a long saturation with French literature, largely through the medium of the *Revue des Deux Mondes*. A young man who had been carefully reading Sainte-Beuve and Taine, Schérer and Montégut, was equipped with serious critical tools; and a young man who had read—and reread and studied—the major French novelists as well as the minor, from Balzac to George Sand and Flaubert, as well as Edmond About, Octave Feuillet, Victor Cherbuliez, inevitably had standards of form, of style, of grace, of subtlety that did not exist in the as yet brief history of the American novel. The imprint of France was strong upon Henry James's early writings, both in the critical pieces and the fiction. At every turn French craftsmanship and French example are invoked in the reviews. The young Henry James had more theory in his head and a wider embrace of European models than any novelist then writing in the United States—and he had not yet written a novel himself.

IV

He had not written a novel but he was assiduously writing fiction. It has always been assumed that Henry James made his debut as a critic and then as a writer of short stories. The reverse was the case and the tale always regarded as his first—"The Story of a Year" —was in reality the first to which he signed his name. It had a significant anonymous predecessor. A full year before publication of "The Story of a Year" Henry wrote to Perry (in March 1864) that the printer's devil had been knocking at his door. "You know," he wrote, "a literary man can't call his time his own." This suggests the publication of something more than a book review and a few sentences later he proposes that he use Perry's mail address for correspondence with the *Atlantic* editors about a story. "I cannot again stand the pressure of avowed authorship (for the present) and their answer could not come here unobserved. Do not speak to Willie of this." The old victim of the thunder and lightning episode still felt himself vulnerable. But this letter reveals something more: that there had been "avowed authorship."

A chance remark in a letter, written by a Newport friend of the Jameses, now enables us to identify what was doubtless Henry James's first published, but unsigned, tale and thus advance by a year the formal beginning of his literary career. Mrs. George De Kay, mother of the future poet and critic Charles De Kay, wrote to her son, then at Yale, on February 29, 1864: "Miss Elly Temple has just come in looking very fresh and pretty—Henry James has published a story in the February Continental called a Tragedy of Errors. Read it. Smith Van Buren forbade Ellie to read it! which brought a smile of quiet contempt to Harry's lips but anger and indignation to those of Miss Minnie Temple."

Smith Van Buren was exercising an uncle's prerogative over one of his orphaned nieces. And Henry James's look of "quiet contempt" marked perhaps the first—and certainly not the last—time in his long literary career in which he stood accused of writing stories unfit for young people to read. The February 1864 issue of

the *Continental Monthly,* a journal devoted to literature and
national policy, contains a twelve-page tale, unsigned, entitled
"A Tragedy of Error." It is undoubtedly from the early pen of
Henry James Junior. French phrases, flowering on every page (and
those to which Henry was addicted), might aid identification
if we did not have Mrs. De Kay's positive statement about the
story's authorship. And the story fits more accurately than any of
the other early tales, the description of his friend Perry, that at
Newport he wrote stories in which the heroes were villains and
the heroines seemed to have "read all Balzac in the cradle and to
be positively dripping with lurid crimes."

The tale begins in the best manner of a French romance: "A
low English phaeton was drawn up before the door of the post office of a French seaport town. In it was seated a lady, with her
veil down and her parasol held closely over her face. My story
begins with a gentleman coming out of the office and handing her
a letter." Thus the drama—apparently at Le Havre—is launched.
The lady gives the gentleman her parasol to hold, lifts her veil to
show "a very pretty face" and "such persons as were looking on at
the moment saw the lady turn very pale. . . ." We note the "such
persons as were looking. . . ." Already Henry James is seeking to
cut the umbilical cord binding him to his story.

Hortense Bernier's paleness was caused by the contents of the letter. Her husband is returning. She must act, for she has taken a
lover in his absence. She has "half a mind to drown myself," she
tells Louis de Meyrau, but ends by making a pact with a brutal
boatman to drown her husband instead. The details are arranged
with care. The boatman will meet the arriving vessel beyond the
breakwater the next morning and offer to row her husband ashore.
It will be simple to do away with him en route.

'You want me to finish him in the boat?'
No answer.
'Is he an old man?'
Hortense shook her head faintly.

'My age?'

She nodded.

'*Sapristi!* it isn't so easy.'

'He can't swim,' said Hortense, without looking up; 'he—he is lame.'

'*Nom de dieu!*' The boatman dropped his hands.

The denouement is swift. Hortense has not counted on her lover deciding on his own course of action. He goes aboard the ship in the early dawn to greet the husband only to discover that Bernier has already had himself rowed ashore. He finds a waiting boat, however, and seats himself in it. He asks the boatman to take him to the Bernier house. "You're just the gentleman I want," says the boatman.

Meanwhile Hortense Bernier is pacing nervously in her garden. The last paragraph administers the shock. She utters a cry, "for she saw a figure emerge from below the terrace and come limping toward her with outstretched arms."

v

Thus in the earliest of Henry James's stories a limping husband is married to a woman capable of strong and determined action—even to the point of seeking to destroy him. The tale's plot is somewhat creaky and we are asked to assume that the lover, who is not lame, also cannot swim. But the narrative is lively, the talk vivid and little touches at every turn show how precociously Henry has studied his craft. There are calculated scenes, each with its own dramatic content: the Bernier maid, looking at Hortense through a keyhole, observes her swallowing brandy by the glassful and scanning the harbor with her opera-glass; the distracted woman's walk along the wharves; the boatman seizing a jug of milk from a boy and drinking it down, thereby revealing himself to Hortense as the predatory sort of person she seeks; the cautious conversation in which she becomes aware that he can be bought to commit a crime. The characterization of boatman, lover, and of the heroine herself,

is extremely adroit for a writer so young; Louis de Meyrau's hard-headed egotism is revealed in his first remarks; we know he will be of no help to Hortense. As for the distracted wife, she is the first of a long line of "bad heroines," capable of murder, yet exciting our sympathy. If Kate Croy and Rose Armiger are not yet on the horizon, their advent is forecast by Hortense Bernier.

A close analysis of the novelist's early tales has shown how they contain ideas and techniques basic to the later Jamesian work. There is such a foreshadowing in this tale. It is to be found in the series of interpolations, one of which has already been noted: "Such persons as were looking. . . ." Again and again it is not Henry James who sees what goes on but always someone else: "al-though to a third person it would have appeared . . ." "a wayfarer might have taken him for a ravisher escaping with a victim. . . ." On the way to the boat Hortense walked "as if desirous to attract as little observation as possible . . . yet if for any reason a passerby had happened to notice her . . ." The third person, the observer, the wayfarer, the onlooker, the passerby—a cloud of witnesses—is wafted across the pages and their testimony is presented to the reader. The tradition James invokes is closer to Defoe than to his nineteenth century contemporaries; at one point Henry James dis-closes to us that he wants us to consider that he is writing not fic-tion but the truth: "Though I have judged best, hitherto, often from an exaggerated fear of trenching on the ground of fiction, to tell you what this poor lady did and said, rather than what she thought, I may disclose what passed in her mind now. . . ." As if to add to the authenticity of his account the twenty-year-old author inserts a gloss to the sentence: "It was perhaps fortunate for Hortense's purpose . . . that she was a pretty woman." A footnote elaborates: "I am told that there was no resisting her smile; and that she had at her command, in moments of grief, a certain look of despair which filled even the roughest hearts with sympathy and won over the kindest to the cruel cause."

There was a conscious method in the narrative. The young man who talked of the art of fiction had the glimmerings of a design.

But many years were to elapse before he would develop it and explain it to his readers.

VI

Henry James had sailed confidently into Charles Eliot Norton's study as a critic. The publication of "The Story of a Year" seems to have been attended by greater difficulties. In a letter from Newport to T. S. Perry of March 25, 1864 he reveals to him that he has been rewriting "that modern novel I spoke of to you. . . . It is almost finished and will go in a day or two." He adds, "On the whole, it is a failure, I think, tho' nobody will know this, perhaps, but myself. . . . It is a simple story, simply told. As yet it hath no name: and I am hopeless of one. Why use that vile word novelette. It reminds me of chemisette. Why not say *historiette* outright? Or why not call it a bob-tale?"

He tells Perry that he is sending this tale to the *Atlantic* and is asking the journal "to send their letter of reject, or accept, to you." In October, while staying at Northampton he received word from Perry that an answer had come, for he replied to him, "The news . . . was very welcome altho' as you say, 'not unmingled with misfortune.' But I suppose I ought to be thankful for so much and not grumble that it is so little. One of these days we shall have certain persons *on their knees*, imploring for contributions." In the letter there is a sketch of a man representing the *Atlantic Monthly* kneeling before a haughty bearded individual. The letter suggests that there has been a qualified acceptance, ("I ought to be thankful, for so much. . . .") either a request for a certain amount of rewriting or perhaps the announcement of how little he would be paid for the tale. The drawing illuminates only the general situation; but it does suggest one other bit of biographical information—it would appear that by his twenty-first year Henry James had begun to grow the beard which he was to wear, after the fashion of the time, for the next thirty-five years, a thick neatly-trimmed growth, which he quite suddenly shed at the turn of the century. The acquisition of the beard coincided with the decision of Henry's hero

in "The Story of a Year" to "crop my head and cultivate my chin."

While no title is given in the letter, the words "novelette," "historiette," "modern novel" could all be applied to the first acknowledged tale which today we would call a long short story. It is, if we make allowance for its stilted moments and quaint formal expression, a story of considerable originality when considered in the context of its time and weighed as the performance of a young man: at every turn it is a calculated and scrupulously planned performance. The attention to detail revealed in the later notebooks of Henry James existed in this tale as in its predecessor: the way in which the character is suggested by action and speech, the manner in which relationships between people is dramatically established, the search at all times for precision in the narrative. Henry doesn't tell us what year this is the story of, but General McClellan's picture figures on the heroine's table beside that of the hero; the hero is wounded on the Rappahannock River in Virginia, where young Gus Barker was shot down by a guerrilla in 1863, and this, it would seem, was the year James was writing about; the heroine reads Jane Porter's *Scottish Chiefs*, a story of strife between Scotland and England—an older North and South, albeit a struggle between sovereign powers, across the sea. The principal characters bear Scottish names: Elizabeth Crowe meets a Robert Bruce (and his sister Jane) and refers to him as her "Scottish chief." There is the maternal name of Robertson in the tale and also the Scottish name of Mackenzie. When we recall that Henry's mother provided the sole Scottish strain in the otherwise Irish family we are tempted to remark that Henry has consciously linked his tale to his mother.

The three figures in the foreground were to reappear in many forms in James's later fiction—the determined mother, her ward or protégé or relative, and the young son in love, unsure of himself, fearing to assert himself, and if he does, paying for it by personal disintegration. Mrs. Ford is a somewhat fiercer Mrs Garland, John Ford an ineffectual and inartistic Roderick and Elizabeth a shallow Mary Garland. The situation recurs with quite other types in *The Portrait of a Lady*—Mrs. Touchett, Isabel and Ralph. In this first

tale the hero's mother, seated sewing, bites the end of her thread as if "executing a human vengeance" when her son discloses to her his engagement to Elizabeth. The hero gives up the fight even before he goes off to war; he is certain he will die: "My memory be hanged . . . what rights has a dead man?" and he is as furtive as Henry himself. He wants his engagement to be a secret ("My dread of the horrible publicity which clings to all this business"), but he doesn't keep it from his mother; she thereby has an advantage over the heroine, who believes her betrothal to be unknown. John Ford is brought back to his mother's door as Wilky James was returned, wounded in battle. Like the hero of the later "A Most Extraordinary Case" he has no desire to live. And so he gives up the fight and Lizzie, sitting at his bedside, is unaware that he sees her not as flesh but as stone. "He lay perfectly motionless, but for his eyes. They wandered over her with a kind of peaceful glee, like sunbeams playing on a statue. Poor Ford lay, indeed, not unlike an old wounded Greek, who at dusk has crawled into a temple to die, steeping the last dull interval in idle admiration of sculptured Artemis."

In this fashion Lizzie is converted into Artemis or Diana, goddess of the chase, the masculine-active yet all-mothering woman. In most of Henry James's early stories loved women are compared to statues. Only later does he become aware, if not of their flesh, at least of their heart and mind.

VII

"The Story of a Year" appeared in the March 1865 issue of the *Atlantic Monthly.* The senior Henry wrote to Wilky that it was "considered good" and that he was sending him a copy "so you can see his name in print." Henry was launched, and just how successfully he could measure when there appeared at Ashburton Place a handsome, vigorous man, an Irishman, named Edwin Lawrence Godkin. He had arrived in New York in 1856 after serving in the Crimean War and by 1865, at thirty-four, had thoroughly assimilated and identified himself with America and its future. A liberal

in the school of Bentham and Mill, he had zealously studied the progress of the Civil War and was convinced that the time was ripe for the launching of a weekly publication which would reflect the changing times and particularly the pressing problem of the freed slaves. He enlisted the sympathies of Norton and other Bostonians and succeeded in raising enough capital for his immediate needs. In July 1865 the *Nation* began its long and illustrious career. Godkin was to make the journal a guiding force in a confused country; he called for integrity in high office, he sustained the principles of nineteenth century liberalism and democracy and gave direction in the field of the arts to a level of criticism America badly needed. William James many years later described Godkin as "the towering influence in all thought concerning public affairs" and said that "indirectly his influence has certainly been more pervasive than that of any other writer."

The purpose of Godkin's call at Ashburton Place was to enlist the services of the two Henry Jameses on behalf of the new publication. Vol. 1. No. 1 contained unsigned reviews by both father and son—Henry Junior's review of a novel by Henry Kingsley and Henry Senior's review of Carlyle's *Frederick the Great*. From then on the junior Henry was a consistent writer for the *Nation*, first of reviews, later of travel sketches. For a brief period he was all but a staff member in New York; still later he was the *Nation's* informal correspondent-at-large in England, contributing political notes as well as brief items on British cultural life. In later years his contributions to the journal tapered off, especially after Godkin relinquished the editorship; yet his connection with it can be said to cover almost half a century. In 1915, when the *Nation* celebrated its fiftieth birthday, Henry James contributed a reminiscence of the founding, "Recollections of the 'Fairies' that attended its birth." He remembered that when he was asked by Godkin to contribute he had been "very young and very willing, but only as literary and as critical as I knew how to be—by which I mean, of course, as I had been able to learn of myself. . . . That winter at Ashburton Place, the winter following the early summer-birth of

the confident sheet, fairly reeks for me, as I carry myself back to it, with the romantic bustle of getting my reviews of books off." He got them off always too late to be able to read proof and his constant complaint was that there were typographical errors— these, it might be added, resulting almost exclusively from mis- reading by the printers of James's rapid handwriting.

"I was never 'cut' that I can remember," James wrote, "never cor- rected nor disapproved, postponed, nor omitted, but just sweetly and profusely and plausibly misprinted. . . ." Actually there were some delays in publication at times and occasional omissions, but on the whole James's relations over the years with the *Nation* were harmonious and fruitful. The friendship with Godkin was de- scribed by him as "one of the longest and happiest of my life." A majority of the writings for this periodical were unsigned and it is only through the resourcefulness of James's bibliographer, Le Roy Phillips, that they were identified and listed. This he was able to do in part by an examination of the *Nation's* account books kept by Wendell Phillips Garrison in which the payments made to James were faithfully recorded and the items named. They show that the *Nation* was never an important source of income to the writer: nevertheless it paid him, in an era when the dollar could purchase a great deal, especially in Europe, enough to provide mar- ginal funds, easy pocket money, in the 1860's and 1870's. During 1875 he wrote for the journal every week; he received anywhere from $3 to $10 for brief paragraphs, $12 to $25 for book reviews and $25 to $40 for travel articles and lengthier items. The range of subjects is wide and the contributions warrant study, for, in hav- ing access to the *Nation*, especially during his early years abroad, James became, in effect, a significant commentator for his country- men on the latest books and pictures, occasional theatrical develop- ments and trends in literature abroad, as well as a purveyor of tid- bits of political intelligence.

In those early months of the *Nation* in 1865 Henry James re- viewed two novels by Trollope, Dickens's *Our Mutual Friend*, dis- cussed Miss Braddon, the mystery novel and the ghostly tale, and

wrote the since much-quoted review of Walt Whitman's *Drum Taps* which later critics have singled out as indicative of James's immature critical sense, forgetting that had they been trying their critical wings in 1865 they too probably would have slated Walt— and with less urbanity than the young James. "It has been a melancholy task to read this book," wrote the bright young man of *Drum Taps* "and it is a still more melancholy one to write about it." He then proceeds to write about it without a touch of melancholy and with considerable zest. In later years James himself was to develop a deep affection for the personality of Whitman and his friends have testified that there were passages of the poet he knew by heart and on occasions liked to declaim.* This, however, was after he had read much more widely in poetry, of which he was never as wholly competent or perceptive a critic as he was of prose. No records have been found of any of his own poetic attempts during his youth, although there are allusions to some in the letters of his brothers. His early objections to Whitman were largely to the absence of ideas in his poetry: he found only "flashy imitations of ideas." Henry decidedly had been reading Matthew Arnold. Art, he informs Walt, "requires, above all things, a suppression of oneself, a subordination of oneself to an idea. This will never do for you, whose plan is to adapt the scheme of the universe to your own limitations." It was inevitable that the self-asserting Walt, raising his voice to glorify himself and his native land, should provoke a sharp criticism from the reticent Henry who particularly at this time was still seeking a self-identity

. . . .

* In the Lamb House library, Henry James's copy of *Leaves of Grass* was the Philadelphia edition (David McKay, 1900). On the end papers at the back he noted page numbers 48 and 62. On 48 he marked in the "Song of Myself": "This is the grass that grows wherever the land is, and the water is; This is the common air that bathes the globe ," Also the passage, "With music strong . . . I blow through my embouchures my loudest and gayest for them," On pages 62-63 he marked section 32 from "I think I could turn and live with animals . . . They bring me tokens of myself—they evince them plainly in their possession." On the flyleaf of the copy he signed, "Henry James. Lamb House Rye."

and had not yet arrived at an understanding of his relationship to America.

Henry James reflected in his remarks not only his own youthful literary decorum and his terrible need to be a conformist, so that he could find universal acceptance, but his sense, exaggerated by illness and war, of his personal inadequacies. Behind the elation of 1865, the launching of his literary self in three important journals and the liberation from the long-seated anxieties, remained the original fears of his childhood. His early acceptance as a writer was a distinct piece of good fortune as well as a recognition of his undoubted talents. Had he found himself in a society less receptive to the novice, or in a time when old periodicals were not being overhauled and new ones created, he might have had to face a much greater measure of discouragement than was his lot; and while this would not have submerged his creativity or affected his keen sense of his destiny, it would have delayed, we suspect, the launching of his career. He was ill-equipped to stand editorial rebuff; he was temperamentally unsuited for the more strenuous competition of the literary marketplace. He made his literary debut in a fashion that was devoid of frustration and distinguished in every way. He was to gain self-assurance as he continued to be published and read; but below the surface remained the fear of failure and of being considered a failure.

HEROINE OF THE SCENE

IN 1884, WHILE WRITING A LETTER TO THE EDITOR OF THE "ATLANTIC Monthly," Henry James made a series of slips of the pen. He was promising to write a serial for the following year and instead of 1885 he wrote 1865 at three different points in his letter. To have jumped backward in time by almost two decades—and not once but thrice—signifies to us the extent to which in his inner mind that year had an emotional importance for him. And this is corroborated for us by the exclamation recorded in his notebook late in life, "Ah, the 'epoch-making' weeks of the spring of 1865!" The spring was indeed epoch-making: in the national life the end of the Civil War and the discharge upon the face of the North of the great veteran army; in Henry James's private life, the year of his official debut as a writer of fiction and the year in which William James departed with a scientific expedition to the Amazon. It is Henry himself who adds William's sailing to the significant events of this significant year. He explains that William's departure left him, during that spring, "the more exposed, and thereby the more responsive, to contact with impressions that had to learn to suffice for me in their uncorrected . . . state."

To be "uncorrected" yet able to respond the more fully and freely to impressions: it is this sense of suddenly-discovered freedom which made 1865 seem to Henry ever after an *annus mirabilis* and which probably accounted, more than anything else, for the thrice-repeated slip of the pen. At one stroke he was freed of the deep and frustrating anxieties engendered by the war; and at the same time he found himself elevated, at least temporarily, into the position of the elder brother, freed of the lingering sense of being subordinate and supervised. The new-found freedom bursts through the lines of memory, "I literally came and went, I had never practised such coming and going. . . ." To be at large suddenly in the New England world, a young man of talent beginning to attract at-

tention, to have asserted himself as a creative writer and found favor in the process, to have shed the shackles of the war, all this represented a kind of personal triumph, or series of triumphs.

"I had never practised such coming and going. . . ." He paid repeated visits to Newport, spending happy days with John La Farge, who had married the sister of his friend, Perry. He spent golden hours in Lawton's Valley, a short ride from Newport, with the "Boston Muse"—Julia Ward Howe, who had written the "Battle Hymn of the Republic"—and he visited, also at Newport, the Edmund Tweedys "*their* house almost a second summer home to us." At the Tweedys lived the four cousins, the Temple sisters, and in particular, Mary Temple the younger, who for some time past had begun to assume an extremely important place in Henry's life. He also went "in particular, during summer weeks . . . to the White Mountains of New Hampshire, with some repetition." He does not tell us whom he visited in the White Mountains "with some repetition" at this point in *Notes of a Son and Brother*, but many pages later we discover that North Conway had almost, when recalled, "the force for me of a wizard's wand . . . the sense in particular of the August of '65 shuts me in to its blest unawareness not less than to all that was then exquisite in its current certainties and felicities." The White Mountains were visited "in particular . . . with some repetition" during that summer for the same reason that Henry gravitated to the Tweedy house in Newport. Minny Temple spent the summer of 1865 in the White Mountains.

I

In 1865 Minny Temple was twenty, the most radiant of his rediscovered Albany and New York cousins, "a young and shining apparition," slim, graceful, with a "wonderful ethereal brightness of presence." She was lithe and active, possessed of restlessness of body and mind and a "splendid shifting sensibility." She was always interested in those around her; she liked to draw out people in talk; she always had questions and sought for answers; she had a

fund of wit and a striking face—large eyes, a slightly upturned nose, full lips, largeish but not unattractive teeth. She talked with a charming toss of the head and walked with the "long, light and yet almost sliding steps" which Henry James imparted to several of his heroines. For him Newport was "vocal with her accents, alive with her movements." She remained for him always a dancing figure, possessing more humanity "than any charming girl who ever circled . . . round a ballroom." In the end she became for him above all "a disengaged and dancing flame of thought."

She might have her flirtatious moments, but for a girl addicted to the ballroom she had a serious mind. In one letter to a friend she observed, "Let us never give up one element of the problem for the sake of coming to a comfortable solution. . . ." The observation is characteristic of her quality of mind. And thus it was that she attracted to her young men who could not be satisfied by a pretty face alone. With Minny they could have the pretty face and wit and intelligence as well. It was no accident that she was courted, or at least admired, at this period, by a future philosopher, a future novelist, a future Supreme Court Justice and a future professor of law. All four were to attain national and international distinction. In those Civil War years they were simply "promising" youths drawn to Minny Temple's presence, making her, as Henry put it, "the heroine of our common scene." She was a heroine, he explained, not in the romantic sense of the word nor in the sense of seeking to dominate the scene. "She had beyond any equally young creature I have known a sense for verity of character and play of life in others, for their acting out of their force or their weakness, whatever either might be, at no matter what cost to herself; and it was this instinct that made her care so for life in general, just as it was her being thereby so engaged in that tangle that made her, as I have expressed it, ever the heroine of the scene. Life claimed her and used her and beset her—made her range in her groping, her naturally immature and unlighted way from end to end of the scale. . . . She was absolutely afraid of nothing she

might come to by living with enough sincerity and enough wonder. . . ."

He is here describing not only Minny but also the heroines
Minny was to become in his fiction: Isabel Archer, Milly Theale,
and the central figure of a group of stories, as well as the woman
to whom he consecrated the most moving of his chapters of memory in *Notes of a Son and Brother.* "Most of those who knew and
loved, I was going to say adored, her . . ." Henry wrote in his
memoirs. Henry *adored* Minny and between adoration and love
there can be a wide difference. The word explains why in the
retrospect of half a century he spoke of her alternately as angel
and human. He remembered her on the one hand as graceful and
quick "all straightness and charming tossed head," and on the
other as having "noble flights and such discouraged drops." To
have flights one must have wings. It is not strange that in these
circumstances he embodied his ultimate memory of Minny in *The
Wings of the Dove.*

11

Among the young men back from the wars was the junior Oliver
Wendell Holmes, a young law student William had met at
Harvard, who became an intimate of Henry as well. The friendship with Henry was between a sharp-witted young man, all action
and passion, touched with the fire of the conflict and thrice
wounded by it, and a sedentary literary youth, psychically wounded
by the same conflict, all hidden passion without action. Holmes
was now sitting in Dane Hall under Henry's old professors. The
future Supreme Court Justice was two years Henry's senior and
a good deal more at ease socially, in particular with young women.
"Harry never lets up on his high aims," Wendell later wrote to
William James, admitting that *he* often did. He added, "There are
not infrequent times when a bottle of wine, a good dinner, a girl
of some trivial sort can fill the hour for me." Wendell was
singularly pleasing to young ladies and his father pictured him

reciting his war exploits as "my white Othello with a semi-circle of young Desdemonas about him listening to the oft-told tale." Wendell was willing to put up with dull young girls if they redeemed themselves by having a pretty face; quite naturally he preferred pretty girls who weren't dull.

Henry James had scheduled his visit to the White Mountains for the end of July 1865 and he invited Wendell to join him. He had set Minny Temple room-hunting for them but with the summer influx she could find only a single room "the only one in the place, high or low—far or near. This," Henry exuberantly informed Wendell, "the wretch who owned it refused to furnish with two beds; but she took it and when we get up there we can pull his own out from under him. At any rate we are sure of a shelter, and I will tell Minny T. to keep her 'eye-peeled' for another room or another bed." The room was $2.50 a week and meals were to be obtained nearby for $5 or $6 a week.

Holmes meanwhile had been busy with his social life and with the Harvard Commemoration at which James Russell Lowell read his Ode to the Harvard dead . . . *Was dying all they had the skill to do?*

> In these brave ranks I can only see the gaps,
> Thinking of dear ones whom the dumb turf wraps,
> Dark to the triumph which they died to gain. . . .

Henry James was to read the Ode many times in subsequent years and to find its lines charged with the overtones of the old days; each time it seemed to him "more full and strong . . . more august and pathetic." That summer, however, only the echoes of the occasion reached him at Newport and he wrote to Wendell, "What adventures you must be having. What with the Commem. Gen. Meade and all the rest of it!" And he adds with a friendly jibe at Wendell's cheerful loquacity, "Pray don't tell the story to death before I see you. . . ."

On August 1, 1865 Henry travelled with Holmes, up the coach

road into the White Mountains, to North Conway. Holmes brought with him another young man fresh from the wars, a bearded fellow-student, and already a friend of Minny's, John Chipman Gray, who was destined to become one of Harvard's most distinguished jurists and for many years a member of its Law Faculty.

The scene Henry paints in *Notes of a Son and Brother*, without divulging the identity of Holmes or Gray, is touched with the warm brush of memory: ". . . the fraternising, endlessly conversing group of us . . . under the rustling pines." They talked of "a hundred human and personal things." It was "high talk" in the "splendid American summer drawn out to its last generosity" and he felt the talkers constituted "a little world of easy and happy interchange, of unrestricted and yet all so instructively sane and secure association and conversation, with all its liberties and delicacies, all its mirth and earnestness. . . ." They read the then fresh pages of Matthew Arnold, they talked of Browning and of George Eliot. In 1905, when Henry returned to this scene after an absence of forty years—returned by motor car over the old coach road—he surveyed the valley of the Saco and painted it as "the near . . . the far, country of youth," physically there yet recoverable only in memory. Much was changed in the man-made scene, but "the high rock-walls of the ledges, the striking sign of the spot, were there; grey and perpendicular, with their lodged patches of shrub-like forest growth, and the immense floor, below them, where the Saco spreads and turns and the elms of the great general meadow stand about like candelabra (with their arms reversed) interspaced on a green table." The woods were a "sacred grove" a place "prepared for high uses, even if for none rarer than high talk." The old Henry, on this revisited scene, found "latent poetry—old echoes, ever so faint." Forty years before, in similar woods and on similar meadows, he had walked with the Temple cousins and here, not far from Mount Washington's paternal face, had taken place a little drama, divided neither into scenes nor acts, and wholly without climax, that nevertheless

touched off in Henry's mind stories to be relived early and late
at his writing desk.

The drama resided largely in Henry's mind. For what happened at
North Conway during that August of '65 was merely that two young
Civil War veterans, apparently still in uniform, and Henry, gal-
lantly attended the Temple girls, devoting themselves particularly
to Minny. Henry, however, felt himself in a very special relationship to the veterans. The end of the Civil War, he noted in his
memoirs, had transported from the battlefields a "quantity of
military life" and "images of military experience" into the very
drawing rooms of New England. The bronzed, muscular young
men had come back full of stories and were "swamping much of
the scene as with the flow of a monster tide." Henry would not
have used such words had he not felt himself swamped by them;
and while he presented himself as "the dreaming painter of things"
seeking to absorb some portion of this common fund of history,
he felt himself once more on a footing of inequality among his
fellows. The "very smell" of having served in the war, he wrote,
seemed to his "supersensitive nostril . . . an emanation the most
masculine." The bronzed young men, fresh from the struggle,
constituted a challenge to Henry, who had not been a soldier; he
seems to have felt *his* masculinity questioned or at least diminished
by their presence. Every uniform, every sword-belt and buckle,
suggested a life of action that could never be a part of his life.
He had put this very clearly in his first story: "I have no intention
of following Lieutenant Ford to the seat of war. The exploits of
his campaign are recorded in the public journals of the day, where
the curious may still peruse them. My own taste has always been
for unwritten history, and my present business is with the reverse
of the picture."

The reverse of the picture was, for instance, Minny in earnest or
witty talk with Lieutenant-Colonel Oliver Wendell Homes, Jr., and
Judge Advocate John Chipman Gray, Jr., while Henry, the "mere

junior," the civilian stay-at-home, looked on from the outer rim of talk. He could claim the prerogative of a kinsman which he felt was also a handicap; he was almost, in that group, a host; he felt, as he put it later, he had a claim to special privilege because he had helped bring such a fine company together ". . . if we were just the most delightful loose band conceivable, and immersed in a regular revel of all the harmonies, it was largely by grace of the three quite exceptional young men who, thanks in part to the final sublime coach-drive of other days, had travelled up from Boston with their preparations to admire inevitably quickened." He added: "I was quite willing to offer myself as exceptional through being able to promote such exceptions and see them justified to waiting apprehension. There was a dangling fringe, there were graceful accessories and hovering shades, but, essentially, we of the true connection made up the drama. . . . If drama we could indeed feel this as being, I hasten to add, we owed it most of all to our just having such a heroine that everything else inevitably came. Mary Temple was beautifully and indescribably *that*. . . ."

The heroine was there but the would-be hero was eclipsed; "the interesting pair" Wendell and John had a "quantity of common fine experience that glittered as so much acquired and enjoyed luxury—all of a sort that I had no acquisition whatever to match." He could only rejoice that his friends had so much to show to Minny, such "brilliant advantage," even if he had "none of my own" to offer. The consolation of the observer remained, as always; with it, however, was the awareness—and it appears to have been acute—that his relationship to Minny in the circumstances was somewhat less than masculine. The "emanation the most masculine" came from the veterans of the Civil War; and Henry testified later in a letter to William that with his bad back and tendency to invalidism, he had lived in the hope of regaining "my natural lead" so that the friendship with Minny might have become "more active and masculine."

This was a recognition, a penetrating insight, into the shortcomings of the relationship. It is doubtful, however, whether Henry

would have acted otherwise, even had there been no other young men present to admire, to love, to adore Minny. A young man naturally shy and tending to hover in the background of any social situation, Henry in reality wanted only to worship Minny from a quiet and discreet—and we might add safe—distance. Henry was as uncompetitive in affairs of the heart as in matters of literary import; he left it to others to seek the attention of Minny by direct approach, relying upon his radiated emotion to assert his own claim to attention. To sit back and observe his cousin, to worship her from afar, to give her signs of devotion at the real right moment, this seems to have been the love stratagem of Henry—as it was of a number of his early young fictional heroes—those who do not go to the opposite extreme of tearing their passion frantically to tatters. He was too reticent and withdrawn to be an ardent wooer, too intellectual to accept romance on its own engaging terms; and he lived in an era when, particularly in the world in which he moved, there was much greater reticence among the sexes than prevails today. Henry James was in love, but it was love of an inner sort, the tormenting heart's rue, or that love which Voltaire framed in a conventional conceit when he sought to write a poem in English: *True love is best by silence known.* We might say that Henry loved Minny as much as he was capable of loving any woman, as much as Winterbourne, uncertain and doubting in his frosty bewilderment, loved Daisy, or the invalid Ralph loved Isabel: a questioning love, unvoiced and unavowed, and not fully fathomed.

True love is best by silence known. And such silence can have in it a component of fear. Love unafraid is not usually inarticulate; love afraid finds subterfuge in worship, adoration, a kind of desperate passive hope of acceptance that can reflect at the same time fear of rebuff. Henry James feared women and worshipped them and hesitated to express his feelings lest he be turned away. For him women could be as chaste and beautiful—and unattainable—as Diana; or else they were another kind of huntress, harsh and preda-

tory, literally dedicated to the chase—the chase of the husband—
and thus to be fled.

Minny was not only Diana, the bright-burning flame, chaste and
beautiful. If the first object of a young man's affection usually has
in her some of the attributes of the most familiar figure in his life,
namely his mother, this was certainly true of Minny. Her very
name, Mary, was his mother's; she was a kinswoman and she had a
capacity, similar to Mary James, for being all charm and simplicity
while holding back her feelings; she could "relate" winningly to
those around her with the familiar toss of the head and at the
same time draw down a flame-like curtain of inscrutability. "Heroine of the scene" she was for him and the very word "heroine"
suggests the extent to which he exalted her. But it is true that other
young men were also under her spell. Gray later said Holmes loved
her; Holmes said it was William James; and others said it was Gray,
for whom she does seem to have shown considerable partiality.
Some time later Henry wrote to William: "Every one was supposed,
I believe, to be more or less in love with her" and, while in this
letter he denied that he was, he added, "I enjoyed *pleasing* her
almost as much as if I had been. I cared more to please her
perhaps than she ever cared to be pleased." This is at once denial
and avowal: for to want to please there must indeed be a fund
of affection and the abundant evidence of the memoirs, and of
the role Henry James assigned to Minny alike in his life and in
his work, testifies to her role as an object of his affection. The
evidence is transparently written into a short story penned shortly
after the episode in the White Mountains. It is so transparent,
in fact, that he clearly was thinking of it when, in an eloquent
passage devoted to his early short stories ("these secrets of the
imaginative life"), he alludes to sending "the most presuming
of my fictional bids" to William Dean Howells. The first story
he sent to Howells was a tale of two Civil War officers and a
civilian. In the same passage he admits that his tales of that time
"referred to actual concretions of existence as well as to the

supposititious; the joy of life, indeed, drawbacks and all, was just in the constant quick flit of association, to and fro, and through a hundred open doors, between the two great chambers (if it be not absurd, or even base, to separate them), of direct and indirect experience." The tale of "Poor Richard" sprang from direct experience.

IV

This story, which Henry James wrote during the next year, was his longest effort to date and his fifth acknowledged tale. It appeared in the *Atlantic Monthly* in three instalments, June to August 1867, a substantial effort for a young man aged twenty-three. It is one of the three tales he wrote in which the Civil War figures as background. Its biographical interest resides in the central situation—that of a wealthy young heroine loved by three men, a Captain, a Major and the third, Richard Clare (whose name was changed to Richard Maule in a later revision of the tale), a stay-at-home. While neither of the military men appears to resemble Holmes or Gray, the hero is endowed with the feelings of Henry James. He suffers from a deep sense of inadequacy and though he pleads his love to Gertrude Whittaker in rather defensive and somewhat rough accents, he is conscious of his "insignificance" in the presence of the military suitors.

The two officers were already slightly known to each other, and Richard was accordingly presented to each of them. . . . His companions displayed toward their hostess that half-avowed effort to shine and to outshine natural to clever men who find themselves concurring to the entertainment of a young and agreeable woman. Richard sat by, wondering, in splenetic amazement, whether he was an ignorant boor, or whether they were only a brace of inflated snobs. . . . He writhed and chafed under the polish of tone and the variety of allusion by which the two officers consigned him to insignificance; but he was soon lost in wonder at the mettlesome grace and vivacity with which Gertrude sustained her share of the conversation. . . . As he gulped down the sickening fact of his

comparative, nay, his absolute ignorance of the great world represented by his rivals, he felt like anticipating its consequences by a desperate sally into the very field of their conversation. To some such movement Gertrude was continually inviting him by her glances, her smiles, her questions, and her appealing silence. But poor Richard knew that, if he should attempt to talk, he would choke; and this assurance he imparted to his friend in a look piteously eloquent. He was conscious of a sensation of rage under which his heart was fast turning into a fiery furnace, destined to consume all his good resolutions.

We cannot say now whether Henry, in the White Mountains, had similarly seethed with the rage which he imparted to his hero; however helplessness and frustration seem to have been there and the eloquence as well as minuteness with which Henry describes poor Richard's feelings have all the vividness of personal experience. The little episode in the White Mountains had become a dramatic situation which was to be carried over in due course to a major work as well. In *The Portrait of a Lady*, the heroine, Isabel Archer, avowedly modelled on Minny, also has three lovers, the invalid Ralph Touchett, Lord Warburton and Caspar Goodwood, and like her predecessor she marries none of them. Touchett, the invalid, has much in common with the ineffectual Civil War heroes; he assumes from the outset that he can never marry; he is the helpless and foredoomed lover. Richard belongs to a somewhat different category of Jamesian hero. He expresses his love, but later loses interest in the heroine because she shows an interest in another man—steps down from her exalted pedestal. In some respects he is a predecessor of Roderick Hudson and of Eugene Pickering. Gertrude, in "Poor Richard," has little in common either with Minny or Isabel. She is that impossible type of woman James often created—neither interesting nor even good-looking, difficult to see as anything but wealthy and motherly. However she is a moral force and loses this strength in the eyes of Richard when she accepts the mendacious Major.

Mid-way through the story Richard goes down with typhoid, an

illness Henry James was well qualified to describe. The Captain, who has loved Gertrude in silence—in Henry's fashion—has gone off to the wars and been killed; and when Richard recovers his health he discovers that Gertrude, who has really loved the Captain all the time, is now ill. "I've got my strength again," Richard exclaims, "and meanwhile you've been failing. . . ." The Jamesian "vampire theme" is here enunciated for the first time. It was to form the subject of a full-length story a year later and was to recur in stories early and late and in a late novel. Henry had linked himself to Minny as he had seen his father linked to Mary James. If she was the "heroine of the scene" then he could not be the hero. One or the other had to give way in Henry James's equation. The time was to come when he would equate his improving health with Minny's fading radiance. For the bright and shining flame was flickering. The seeds of tuberculosis were present in that slim body and were to manifest themselves in the coming months.

A Cambridge Life

1865=1869

THE SILVER MIRROR

IN 1881 HENRY JAMES RETURNED TO AMERICA AFTER AN ABSENCE
of six years in Europe. The day after Christmas, in the
family home at 20 Quincy Street in Cambridge, in the old back
sitting room which William and he used to occupy, he inscribed
in his notebook certain revived memories. "The feeling of that
younger time comes back to me in which I sat here scribbling,
dreaming, planning, gazing out upon the world in which my fortune was to seek, and suffering tortures from my damnable state
of health. It was a time of suffering so keen that that fact might
. . . give its dark colour to the whole period." And yet he remembered not the pain so much as "the joy of youth" and "the freshness of impression and desire, the hope, the curiosity, the vivacity,
the sense of the richness and mystery of the world . . . there is
an enchantment in all that which it takes a heavy dose of pain
to quench and which in later hours, even if *success* have come
to us, touches us less nearly. Some of my doses of pain were very

239

heavy; very weary were some of my months and years. But all that is sacred; it is idle to write of it today. . . ."

He turned instead to write of "the vision of those untried years. Never did a poor fellow have more; never was an ingenuous youth more passionately and yet more patiently eager for what life might bring." Life had now brought him what he had dreamed, and "success, if I may say so, now stretches back a tender hand to its younger brother, desire." (The image of *success*, personified in an older brother, seemed inescapable.) "I wanted to do very much what I have done." What struck Henry James was "the definiteness, the unerringness of those longings."

Many years later he could write ". . . *my* poor little personal C[ambridge] of the far-off unspeakable past years, hangs there behind, like a pale pathetic ghost, hangs there behind, fixing me with tender, pleading eyes, eyes of such exquisite pathetic appeal and holding up the silver mirror, just faintly dim, that is like a sphere peopled with the old ghosts." At the end he glanced fondly and often into the silver mirror.

JACOB AND ESAU

IN THE OLD TESTAMENT STORY, JACOB AND ESAU WERE TWINS, BORN but a few minutes apart, Jacob emerging from the womb clutching the heel of his brother, as if determined to be as little behind him as possible. The older of the two became the active one, a cunning hunter, the favorite provider of venison for his father. The

younger, a dweller in tents, a stay-at-home son, was beloved of the mother. Then one day Esau, driven by hunger, sold his birthright for a mess of Jacob's pottage. Later their father, Isaac, old and tired and near-blind, called upon his oldest son to bring him venison and to receive the paternal blessing. But while Esau hunted for the game with which to serve his father, Jacob, at the urging of his mother, supplanted him, donned his clothes, placed the skin of kids on his arms to give an effect of Esau's hairiness and brought his father meat carefully prepared by the mother. When Esau returned and discovered that Jacob had usurped his place and received the blessing, he raised his voice and wept: "He hath supplanted me these two times. He took away my birthright; and, behold, now he hath taken away my blessing."

There was neither birthright nor need for blessing in the James family, but between the ancient drama of rivalry in the tents of Israel and the brothers' drama in Quincy Street there are strange parallels—although Quincy Street saw neither deliberate acts of usurpation nor overt fraternal struggles. The parallels are there because the ancient story touched upon eternal truths.

I

William James returned from Brazil in March 1866 and resumed his medical studies. Henry's back-ache revived with his brother's return. He spent an uncomfortable summer at Swampscott, on Massachusetts Bay, twenty miles north of Boston. He read a great deal and wrote very little. A fugitive memory of this time, which slipped into his notebook years later, is that of "lying on my bed at Swampscott . . . toward the summer's end, and reading, in ever so thrilled a state, George Eliot's *Felix Holt,* just out, and of which I was to write, and *did* write, a review in the *Nation.* . . . I was miserably stricken by my poor broken, all but unbearable, and unsurvivable *back.* . . . To read over the opening pages of *Felix Holt* makes even now the whole time softly and shyly live again. . . ."

William spent this summer as an interne in the Massachusetts

General Hospital and in the autumn the brothers were reunited under the family roof, which was moved from Ashburton Place to 20 Quincy Street, a large comfortable house, facing the Harvard Yard. This was to be the last home of the James family. "Home" for them had been houses, hotels, pensions in a chain of cities—Albany, New York, Geneva, Paris, London, Newport, Boston. Their longest residence in one house had been in Fourteenth Street in New York. Now, in late middle age, the parents brought their wanderings to an end. Their sons were grown; the younger boys were conducting their experiment on their southern plantation. William, Henry and Alice were at home, but the older sons were restless and it was only a question of time before they would leave. Alice, now a girl of nineteen, was nervous and high-strung and was soon to manifest those attacks of nervous prostration from which she suffered during the remainder of her life.

Now it was William James, the vigorous and active older brother, who fell into a series of illnesses—back-aches, like Henry's, insomnia, eye-trouble, digestive disorders—a general state of exhaustion, nervousness and depression. The symptoms that manifested themselves were to continue for several years and disappeared gradually as William found his way into a career, married and established his own home. In the spring of 1867 he interrupted his medical studies and left for Germany in search of health and to profit, if possible, by research in German laboratories and study of the language.

Henry, on his side, showed prompt signs of improvement after William's departure. "I have felt quite strong since you sailed," he wrote his brother in May 1867; and eleven days later, "I have been feeling essentially better since you left." That same week the mother wrote to William that "Harry does you the compliment of choosing the same cloth for a summer suit as you had last year." It was almost as if, in the absence of the elder brother, Henry could step into his clothes—don, like Jacob, the raiment of Esau—and be, in role and in dress, the first son.

With Henry's improving health came resumed literary activity. He was so productive during the months of William's absence that

he earned $800 by his pen. This was a comfortable sum in an era when a room cost a few dollars a month and a steak a few cents. William on his side, who inquired into Henry's earnings, seems to have been troubled over his own inability to contribute, however modestly, to the family's resources. In September of 1867, in Berlin, he tried his hand at a book review, sending it to Henry for revision and possible publication. "I feel that a living is not worth being gained at this price," he wrote and then, apparently sensing that this remark was inappropriate to one who *was* earning his living by his pen, he crossed out the "not" in the sentence and substituted "is hardly worth being gained." He added: "Style is not my forte, and to strike the mean between pomposity and vulgar familiarity is indeed difficult." (Henry could hardly have relished this view of the horizons of literary art—a middle course between vulgarity and pomposity.) "Still," William James went on, "an' the rich guerdon accrue, an' but ten beauteous dollars lie down on their green and glossy backs within the family treasury in consequence of my exertions, I shall feel glad that I have made them." William wrote a few book reviews and articles under his brother's aegis and editing, and was paid for them on publication. He did not pursue this type of writing for long and was to emerge as quite a different sort of writer—a writer of vivid and lucid scientific papers, of works in psychology and philosophy, in a vigorous, muscular style that abounded in image and example and created an effect of rich spontaneous talk. It was essentially his father's style with clarity and discipline added to it. But that was to be two decades later, long after the younger brother had become a dominant figure in American and English literature.

In the autumn of 1868, after eighteen months abroad, William James came back from Europe. Henry promptly ceased to publish. His back-ache revived and he could bring himself neither to read nor write. Apparently the observation Henry had made about his new-found freedom and his "uncorrected self" on William's departure for the Amazon, reflected a distinct pattern: when his older brother was away Henry could feel a sense of release; he

could expand and flourish. The moment William returned, the old inhibiting forces in their relationship, which could reduce Henry to inaction and even illness, re-asserted themselves. Quincy Street did not seem capable of comfortably housing two Geniuses at the same time.

Mary James, faced with two ailing sons, tended to exacerbate rather than ease the hidden tension in Quincy Street. She had for a long time openly showed her preference for Henry, the quiet one, and not a little hostility toward William, the active and effervescent. She might fuss over Henry's aches and pains to which the household was quite accustomed, but she considered William's sudden acquisition of analogous symptoms without indulgence and with a singular lack of sympathy. While showing maternal concern, she treated William as a self-centered hypochondriac. Her letters make quite free with his condition; he complains too much; he has a "morbid sympathy" with every form of physical trouble; he worries excessively; "he must express every fluctuation of feeling," exclaims Mary James. Henry had taken illness with a kind of fatalistic resignation that made him easy to live with; the pronouncedly active William could be neither fatalistic nor resigned. Illness represented a sudden curbing of his vibrant personality and he experienced his fluctuations of mood with a lack of reticence that was at the same time voluble protest.

II

There was no open rivalry or strife between the two brothers. Had there been a healthy outlet for their submerged feelings, had William, like Esau, raised his voice and wept that Henry was for the moment surpassing him in material achievment, or had Henry on his side, not harbored a sense of guilt, there might have been flare-ups and scenes, but fewer symptoms. On the surface there was love and affection and mutual respect as well as close intellectual sympathy between the brothers, and interest in each other's progress and symptoms. The affection, indeed, was far beyond that which usually exists between brothers as different temperamentally as were

Henry and William. What happened was that the old brotherly equation of childhood, below the surface of the conscious and adult relationship, underwent a significant change. In 1866 a very important, and to William disturbing, reversal of role had occurred within the James family. Henry, the mocked and derided junior of old, who had secretly dispatched his manuscripts and used Sargy Perry's address for his mail to escape William's teasing, suddenly emerged as the only one of the four brothers who had his goals clearly in view and was proceeding toward them in a straight line. William, on the other hand, always sure of himself in the past, now appeared to be without fixed purpose. "Much would I give," he exclaimed to Wendell Holmes at this time, "for a constructive passion of some kind." Henry had long ago discovered such a passion. William, returning from South America, where he had believed himself to be the focus of family interest, discovered that Henry was in the center of the scene, exciting admiration and approval as a promising young man of letters. Jacob had supplanted Esau. William's behavior provides a striking series of clues to inner and concealed feeling. Thus even before his Brazilian journey, and immediately after the appearance of Henry James's first writings in the *North American Review*, he had dispatched to Norton a curious little note, that, for all the air of innocent humor it assumed, obliquely illuminated his desire to emulate his younger brother. "My dear Mr. Norton," he began, "As my friends and relations seem to be successful in their attempts to draw a revenue from the *North American Review* I am emboldened to try what I can do myself." And he proposes that he review Huxley's lectures on comparative anatomy. It is significant that here, as in the later letter from Berlin, William is concerned not so much about literary achievement as by the fact that Henry could "draw a revenue" from the journal for his writings.

Even more suggestive is the attitude which William adopted from the first toward Henry's literary work. He constituted himself promptly a judge of his brother's writings and during subsequent decades he delivered his verdicts and opinions, often *ex cathedra*.

William's criticisms at times took the form of a display of his own literary virtuosity while seeking to demolish that of his brother; on still other occasions he praised unstintingly and eloquently; critical discernment there invariably is in what he says, but the form is often a distinct body blow to the creative artist. This was the carrying out, on an adult level, of the thunder and lightning episode of childhood. We find William, shortly after arriving in Europe, firing off a series of critical salvoes at Henry. He criticizes Henry's "want of heartiness"; he tells him his stories are "thin." They "give a certain impression of the author clinging to his gentlemanliness though all else be lost"; also there is "want of blood in your stories. . . . I think the same thing would strike you if you read them as the work of another." That there was something stiff and precious in the style of the early tales there is no doubt; nevertheless William was throwing ice water at Henry. During the weeks that followed, William seemed to sense that this was what he had done. "I have the impression," he writes to Henry, "I assumed a rather law-giving tone." He re-assures him. "I feel as if you were one of the two or three sole intellectual and moral companions I have." When he read "A Most Extraordinary Case" in the April 1868 *Atlantic* he found better things in it: ". . . your style grows easier, firmer, and more concise as you go on writing . . . the face of the whole story is bright and sparkling. . . ."

III

In 1867 Henry, in a letter to William, mentioned he had received "overtures" from the *Nation*. Since he was a regular contributor to the journal this suggests that he had been offered a closer connection with it, perhaps an editorial post. All we know is that the "overtures" were turned down. A year later Charles Eliot Norton asked him to become an editor of the *North American Review*. Flattering this was, to a writer in his middle twenties and the post must have held promise of regular earnings and a well-marked career. Yet he unhesitatingly declined. There seems to have been no self-questioning, no doubts. Henry was not shrugging his

shoulders at the idea of a "safe" career. He had made up his mind what his career would be and was not allowing himself to be deflected by tempting proposals. Under no circumstances was he prepared to become a mere functionary in a magazine, concerned with the writings of others. Just how confident a measure he had taken of himself we may judge from the manner in which he told Perry, "I write little, and only tales, which I think it likely I shall continue to manufacture in a hackish manner, for that which is bread. They *cannot* of necessity be good; but they *shall not* be very bad." Henry underlined the words *shall not*. He was aware of his inner resources; and he had that confidence in them which makes for greatness in art and an unswerving and single-minded pursuit of the goal. To have doubted himself would be to have doubted his art. His training, self-organized, had been directed to making his pen proficient, his eye observant, his mind alert and watchful. His self-realization had been almost sub-conscious. When moments of decision came he made the right choice, perhaps because he consulted only his inner self and never yielded to the false whispers of the immediate and the external. And because he had such deep underground resources of observation, training, knowledge and imagination and such faith in them, he moved implacably forward in spite of the delays occasioned by his mode of life and his uncertain health.

He showed indeed a strange inertia by remaining in the family home in Cambridge. If, in retrospect, he characterized these as his "untried years" he seems at this time to have made singularly little effort to "try" them. He was securely anchored in Quincy Street, looking enviously on while William and Wendell Holmes and Sargy Perry successively went abroad. "Can Cambridge answer Seville?" queries Henry when Perry writes him from Spain. "Can Massachusetts respond unto Granada?" Apparently it could at least voice envy. "Bed-bugs? Methinks that I would endure even them for a glimpse of those galleries and cathedrals of which you write."

Why did Henry James linger in Quincy Street long beyond the

time when most young men leave home to make their own way
in the world? His health had improved; he was self-supporting;
the leading periodicals were only too pleased to welcome his work;
his parents were sympathetic and did not violently oppose his decisions. Nevertheless it is significant that he was twenty-six before he
ventured abroad and thirty-two before he took the final step to cut
the ties binding him to the family scene.

In a sedentary young man it was perhaps understandable that he
should hesitate to alter the established course of his life. It required no effort to allow the days to glide by and to accept all
the home-comforts provided by his doting mother. Yet it is abundantly clear that for Henry this existence was, often, an unmitigated and lonely bore. The young man who looked eagerly across
the sea to the literary world of London and Paris spoke of life in
Quincy Street as being "about as lively as the inner sepulchre." To
his brother abroad he complained: "I haven't a creature to talk to.
. . . How in Boston, when the evening arrives, and I am tired of
reading, and know it would be better to do something else, can
I go to the theatre? I have tried it, *ad nauseam*. Likewise *calling*.
Upon whom?" These then were the horizons of Henry James from
1866 until 1869—his twenty-third to his twenty-sixth years: the
writing desk, the book, the occasional play, the rare and usually
disappointing social call, the journey by horse-car from Cambridge
to Boston a full and chilly evening's adventure among the city's
deep snows or irksome and exhausting in the summer's heat.

Nor was this tone of complaint destined for his brother exclusively. "I have a pleasant room, with a big soft bed and good
chairs," he wrote to Perry at the end of the summer of 1867
during which, he boasted, he had remained in Quincy Street without leaving it for a single night. But he added, invoking Tennyson, it was "stiller than chiselled marble." He was sure that, before
the end of another year, "I shall have had enough" of Cambridge. He found no friends among the new generation of students at Harvard; as for the amiable Brahmins—Lowell, Norton,

Longfellow—they were "not at all to my taste, for the bulk of my society."

Was he really a fledgling who took longer than most to try his wings? Or was he a Jacob quite satisfied to dwell in tents and brew his literary pottage rather than roam afield? The truth was that he seemed to fly quite well when he was alone in Quincy Street and particularly during his brother's absences. Why did Henry James remain for so long under the parental roof? He had freedom of movement and an ever-widening career. There is no doubt that one reason was that he was waiting his turn to go to Europe; his ample earnings were not yet sufficient to provide funds for travel, and his father, with the younger brothers to be aided, and with William to support abroad, does not seem to have been prepared at this time to keep two sons in Europe simultaneously. The question indeed would not present itself were it not for the tales Henry was writing during this time, and these, as before, offer us some insight into the inner problems that were seeking a solution. Three tales were set down during William James's absence in Europe and each resolves itself into a similar situation. The first deals with the rivalry of two sisters for the hand of an Englishman who has come out to make his fortune in the colonies. The younger sister wins him but her triumph is short-lived; she dies in childbirth and, knowing how envious her older sister is, obtains a promise from her husband that her trousseau, carefully locked away, will be kept for her daughter. The older sister now is able to supplant the younger's place. She marries the widower and becomes the stepmother of the child. One bitter pill remains: she cannot put her hands on her sister's fine clothes. Finally she obtains the key to the trunk and like Bluebeard's wife opens the forbidden lock. Her husband finds her, at sunset, dead, with ten ghostly finger marks on her throat, lying beside the satins, silks, muslin and velvet she will never wear. The tale is called "The Romance of Certain Old Clothes." It was written, singularly enough, not long after Henry ordered from his tailor the suit of

clothes made from the same cloth as William's suit of the previous summer.

A second tale was also ghostly and melodramatic. It was about young De Grey whose bride refused to accept the old family curse which doomed her and in the process reversed it, so that instead of dying she found herself bringing about the death of her husband-to-be: ". . . she blindly senselessly, remorselessly drained the life from his being. As she bloomed and prospered, he drooped and languished. While she was living for him, he was dying of her."

But it was the third tale which crystallized this recurring theme of reversal of role and usurpation. "A Light Man"—a tale for which Henry James expressed particular fondness in later years— was one of the few early stories he esteemed sufficiently to revise and republish. It represented the first instance in which he used a technical device later to be developed to perfection: the device of self-revelation by the principal character with the author never intervening to describe or elucidate; the reader must figure out all the implications of the narrative himself. Maximus Austin is a cheerful scoundrel but we discover this only because James lets us read a few entries from his journal in which he candidly displays his improvidence, his opportunism, his dishonesty. He relates how he returns to America from Europe penniless; how Theodore Lisle, a friend of schooldays who treats him as if he were a brother, invites him to stay at the home of Lisle's employer, a wealthy eccentric. This man, brilliantly sketched, is weak, idiosyncratic, effeminate; combining in his personality both masculine and feminine traits, he acts as a kind of father-mother to both young men; indeed he has known in the past the father of one and the mother of the other and in this way another chain of invisible brotherhood is established between the two. The employer has drawn his will in favor of Theodore; but Maximus plays on the old man's erratic affections and receives from him the promise that he will make him the heir instead of his friend. The old will is destroyed; however the would-be benefactor dies before he can

write a new one. Not only has Max deprived Theodore of what might be considered his birthright—he has failed to obtain it for himself.

In all three of these tales we have situations involving a reversal of role between two persons closely linked and the supplanting of one by another: the older sister becomes the wife of her dead sister's husband and dies herself when she would wear her sister's clothes. De Grey's bride becomes a vampire-like destroyer of the man destined to be her husband in order to save herself; Maximus seeks to usurp the place held by Theodore in the household of a wealthy man and to obtain the birthright destined for his friend. Usurpation is central to the three tales.

Had Henry usurped William's place? Their roles were certainly reversed. In a sense he was wearing William's clothes and he had stepped into William's shoes; in the family in which he had for so long felt himself in a subordinate role, he had now achieved supremacy. While William was away he could be the first-born, with his brother's prerogatives of seniority. It was the same situation as the triumphal dream of the Louvre; there too roles are reversed, the pursued becomes the pursuer. We may speculate, therefore that Henry clung to Quincy Street because there he could enjoy, over and above the general amenities of home, a sense of power un-challenged; all-unaware he achieved a feeling of well-being dur-ing the long absences of his brother because he was alone and tri-umphant, even if at moments, as the stories showed, feelings of guilt developed and caused him to dream that fierce punishment is meted out to usurpers. Significantly, in these stories he seems to identify himself not with the younger or weaker individual, as in other of his tales, but with the older and stronger, the *usurping* individual. And in each case the usurper pays with his life or with defeat.

William James, on his side, enjoying Europe, was experiencing feelings of guilt as well. "It seems a sin to be doing such things while Harry is moping at home," he wrote in his diary. And in a letter to his sister he remarked: "I somehow feel as if I were

cheating Harry of his birthright." Thus the two brothers played
out their Jacob and Esau drama. The curious thing was that both
cast themselves in the role of Jacob.

VENUS AND DIANA

I

THE YOUNG MAN IN QUINCY STREET HELD BACK FROM THE WORLD
and this meant that he held back from women as well. He seems
to have seen little of Minny Temple during the Cambridge years;
there was only one more summer in the White Mountains, that of
1868, and he spent it at Jefferson, New Hampshire, in a "great
rattling tavern." The Temples were not at Conway. He wrote to
Minny's older sister, Katherine, to congratulate her on her engagement and discreetly inquired how Minny "in that deep inscrutable soul of hers contemplates your promotion. It is a rare
chance for Minny's cogitations—heaven bless her! If she could
drop me a line I should be very glad to have her views." Apparently they were not even corresponding at the time.

Minny was off at Newport, or New York, or suburban Pelham,
where she now lived, in a gay whirl of balls and dances and concerts but already racked by cough and suffering occasional lung
hemorrhages that subdued her dancing body and committed her to
silence and rest. There is no evidence that Henry was aware of her
condition; the immediate members of her family, in those medi-
cally primitive days, seemed to be without serious concern for her.
She was away in the distance, removed from Henry, a remote

Diana, chaste and active. Any closer view, any bubbling up of feeling between them, might have created problems for Henry. No feeling could bubble however; Henry continued to hold aloof.

In Cambridge itself he saw a goodly number of women, saw them as creatures to be observed and chatted with at tea; and he formed a series of friendships with various spinsters, notably of the Norton entourage, that endured for many years: the elderly Miss Ashburners, Theodora Sedgwick, Grace and Jane Norton, Frances Morse. Of these, the friendship with Grace Norton appears to have been the most rewarding; something in her personality, and in her troubled spirit, evoked a response in Henry James and inspired him to write to her some of the most felicitous letters of his middle years: they are long, detailed, spontaneous, filled with a running account of his literary life, his readings, his evaluation of persons encountered in the social world. The one hundred and sixty letters which Grace Norton preserved (he kept none of hers) are intimate yet without a suggestion of any depth of intimacy. Miss Norton, a rather rigid New England spinster, seems to have assumed for Henry the role of a maternal confidante, one to whom it was safe to speak of his feelings and of the general current of his life without engaging his affections too deeply. She, on her side, seems to have poured out her troubles to Henry and received advice, comfort, solace from him. It was largely a pen friendship for they were, for years, separated by the Atlantic. As she grew old in Cambridge and Henry grew famous, his letters became one of the great facts of her life, and she used to read them to her friends "with omissions" (William James once informed his brother) that suggested there were more deeply personal portions than was really the case. William once described her to Henry: she was growing stoutish, was plainly dressed, "but her voice is still in the major key and her intelligence, sociability and goodwill as great as ever. . . . She still seems to retain her aversion and contempt for female society." She shared Henry's interest in French writers and during her busy Cambridge years edited Montaigne, gave readings to women's clubs and circulated French volumes among her friends

gluing together certain of the more "offensive pages." She was one of Henry's cherished links with his homeland all his life.

A younger friend, intermittently at Cambridge and Newport, was Elizabeth Boott, who was also a friend of Minny Temple. She was the daughter of a widower, Francis Boott, of the elder Henry James's generation, who had lived long years in Italy. "The easy-fitting Bootts," Henry James once described them in a letter home. Lizzie had grown up a well-tended Americano-European girl, rather homely, shy, reserved, proficient in languages and dabbling in art and music. Henry thought of her later as "the admirable, the infinitely civilized and sympathetic, the markedly *produced* Lizzie" and she was to sit for the protrait of Pansy in *The Portrait of a Lady* even as Frank Boott, an amateur composer, whose songs had a certain vogue, gave the novelist the figure, if not the cruel character, of Gilbert Osmond, Pansy's father. Henry spoke of the Bootts as "inverted romantics." They had had their Europe when they appeared on the Newport horizon, had it to the full, and could now taste of their homeland. Henry was to see much of Lizzie at home and abroad and to enjoy her modest company. This was one of the few friendships of his life with a woman of his own age, and it remained strictly a friendship. There is not a word in Henry's letters—which Lizzie carefully preserved—that suggests even the shadow of a closer intimacy.

If she was a link to the Newport and Boston days she was to become also a link to the Italy of his middle life. A cluster of new memories were to form around her and her father in their Florentine Villa Castellani high on Bellosguardo. Lizzie worked hard at her painting and Henry watched her hoping she would paint eventually a little "less helplessly." He wrote at one time that she "produces hundreds of studies which remain only studies." The Bootts tended to drift between two worlds, Europe and America, and tended to latch on to the Jameses whenever possible. Henry, over and over again, speaks of Lizzie's "languid passivity" and of her sweetness. He valued her friendship greatly and did all he could to help her in her fruitless attempts to sell some of her

paintings in London. Ultimately she married Frank Duveneck, the American painter of the Munich school, whose work Henry was among the first to recognize and praise when it was exhibited in Boston.

In general Henry felt at Cambridge that the women he saw were "provincial, common, inelegant." They did not appeal to his fancy, he wrote Perry, but he did admit that "perhaps I am grossly insensible." Henry James could take the measure of his countrymen with a clear sense of their attributes and shortcomings. He could even try to take the measure of his countrywomen. Here, however, he ran into certain difficulties. He could describe them; he could reproduce faithfully their conversation and their manners; he might even try to give a picture of their mind; his intelligence could grasp them—but what were they? Fine pieces of statuary, yes, he could say that and did, likening them in his early tales to Venuses and Dianas and Junos, frozen in stone. They were, when they aroused feeling, or were encountered in the flesh, creatures of mystery and consequently of danger. Unfathomable. Sometimes when they seemed to be Jezebels they turned out to be purer than the Boston snows; and sometimes a mask of purity covered women who, like Browning's "Last Duchess"

> . . . liked whate'er
> She looked on, and her looks went everywhere.

Later, when he had observed English girls, he might write that they were "wholly in the realm of the cut and dried" and that they could not match the—what should he call it?—"intellectual grace" or the "moral spontaneity" of American girls. *Intellectual grace . . . moral spontaneity*. These were indeed concepts of the mind and not of feeling. He might thus find the formula for them without the certainty of emotional apprehension. What was his most famous story of some years later but that of a young man who tries unsuccessfully to fathom the innocent surface of a young girl named Daisy?

II

When Henry James wasn't writing stories of usurpation, he wrote of the mystery of womankind, of young men trapped by fickle females, of sad heroes betrayed, of curious men circling at a distance from the female world, the irrepressible *ewig Weibliche* of literary allusion. In his first acknowledged story the despairing hero goes off to the Civil War convinced of his impending death and ready to renounce his beloved; in his dying moments he sees her as a goddess in a Greek temple. In his second story "A Landscape Painter" the heroine is the "very portrait of a lady"—and her name is Esther Blunt! Her behavior bears out her name. She marries the hero for his $100,000 a year. He had thought he had successfully concealed this important fact from her and was being loved for himself. "It was the act of a false woman," the landscape painter blurts out when he discovers the truth. "A false woman?" Esther queries and then smiles: "Come, *you* be a man!" This Henry must have felt was a little too blunt an ending; the heroine's name was changed on revision to Miriam Quarterman, and her final speech to: "It was the act of any woman—placed as I was placed." If this tale reflects insecurity about personal worth it also reflects complete uncertainty about the trustworthiness of women. And just how dangerous woman could be to man in flesh or even in stone we have seen from the vampire tale of "De Grey" or James's fascination for the French story *La Vénus d'Ille* in which the statue of Venus, upon whose outstretched finger the hero has carelessly placed his engagement ring during a heated game of tennis, comes crashing into the bridal chamber to claim her "fiancé" and crushes him to death. Lovers preyed upon one another, women preyed upon men, and the supreme love of Venus could be all-destroying.

The sad hero of "The Story of a Masterpiece" discovers in the portrait of his fiance, which he commissions, disturbing qualities he had not discerned in her living self. Was she like the Last Duchess? Did she possess a "certain vague moral dinginess?"

Lennox is troubled until the night before his marriage; and then he finds a solution.

"Come," he tells himself as he looks at the portrait, "Marian may be what God has made her; but *this* detestable creature I can neither love nor respect." Seizing a poniard he thrust it "with barbarous glee, straight into the lovely face of the image. He dragged it downward, and made a long fissure in the living canvas. Then, with half a dozen strokes, he wantonly hacked it across. The act afforded him an immense relief."

In another tale, "Osborne's Revenge," the lawyer hero determines to avenge his dead friend Robert Graham, who committed suicide because of a broken heart. He seeks the acquaintance of the young woman, Henrietta Congreve, assured by a mutual friend that she was the destructive siren. He feels a "savage need of hating her." To his surprise, he discovers she can be hated only with difficulty; she is a gentlewoman, of fine intelligence and feeling. He sees no sign of remorse in her, nor any awareness that she had contributed to his friend's death. She refuses to discuss Graham with him. "I shall begin to think she's a demon," he says. He also speaks of her as if she were a vampire: ". . . she drained honest men's hearts to the last drop and bloomed white upon the monstrous diet." Yet if she did, it was behind a mask of goodness. "Ideally she had been repulsive; actually she was a person whom, if he had not been committed to detest her, he would find it very pleasant to like." He is puzzled that "a woman could unite so much loveliness with so much treachery, so much light with so much darkness."

Then he learns that the image he has compounded of Henrietta Congreve is false; in reality she never jilted Graham and it was Graham who was over-attentive and volatile. She did not even know of his suicide and believed his death due to natural causes. Thus a woman who seemed a flirt and a vampire turns out to be noble and virtuous and innocent of all the designs attributed to her by the vengeful hero. The tale is that of a man seeking to understand a woman and discovering that he has been in error

from start to finish. The misreading of Graham's character leads Osborne to misread the character of Henrietta and he has also listened too attentively to the gossip of prejudiced observers. Henry James was aware, from the first, as this tale reveals, of the disparity between appearance and reality; and in its primitive fashion it is, therefore, a forerunner of *The Turn of the Screw*. It is also a story of a man's bewilderment in comprehending the opposite sex.

III

William James, in a letter from Dresden of July 24, 1867 counselled: "Let Harry read (if he wants to) an essay by Grimm on the Venus de Milo . . . and compare it with the St. Victor one. Both are imaginative rhapsodies, but how much solider the German! (if I remember right.) It is worth reading, Harry. . . ." We do not know whether Henry read the Grimm essay or how he would have described the Saint-Victor essay; we do know that the latter was published in a volume entitled *Hommes et Dieux* in 1867 and that the book remained from then until the end of Henry James's life in his library. In the year before his death he scrawled his name on the flyleaf and below it affixed the dates, "1867-1915," thereby commemorating the volume's long life on his shelves and perhaps some intimate associations or memories it had for him. Paul de Saint-Victor endows the Venus de Milo with many qualities that must have struck a warm response in Henry James:

. . . the ambiguous visage of the Sphinx is less mysterious than this young head so naïve in appearance. . . . This is the Celestial Venus, the Venus Victorious, always sought, never possessed, as absolute as the life whose central fire resides in her breast. . . . She is the flame which creates and which preserves, the instigator of great things and heroic projects. . . . There is not an atom of flesh in her august marble . . . she sprang from a virile mind nourished by the Idea and not by the presence of the woman. She belongs to the time when statues expressed the superhuman character and the eternal thought. . . . From what avenue of the cen-

turies dost come to us, O young Sovereign. . . . To praise thee, we must have the three-stringed lyre which Orpheus sounded with religious gravity in the valleys of the new-born world! Soon your original character will be corrupted and degraded. . . . The poets will prostitute your Idea in their licentious fictions; they will roll your profane limbs through all the world's beds. The sculptors will make of you a Bacchante and a courtesan. . . . What does it matter? you emerge intact from these sacrilegious metamorphoses. . . . Who has not experienced on entering the Louvre and the hall where the Goddess reigns, that sacred terror—*deisadaimonia* —of which the Greeks spoke? Her attitude is proud, almost threatening. . . . There are no bones in this superb body, nor tears in its blind eyes, nor entrails in this torso. . . . Allow the charm to have its effect . . . rest at the foot of the august marble, as if under the shadow of an ancient oak. Soon a profound peace will course through your soul. The statue will envelop you in its solemn lineaments and you will feel as if you have been enlaced in its absent arms. It will elevate you quietly to the contemplation of pure beauty. . . .

William was right in speaking of Paul de Saint-Victor's subjective reverie as rhapsodic; yet its substance corresponds to Henry James's dream of fair women as beings beyond flesh, immortal Venuses, chaste Dianas, translated into imperishable stone where they may be contemplated by the Eye and the Mind and deified. A woman of flesh and blood could be a source of grave anxiety and bewilderment. In stone—or in death—she could be contemplated as beauty pure. One could even allow oneself to be enlaced by her absent arms. . . .

Venus, Diana—and Jezebel! There were many kinds of women in this world and a man had to be on his guard lest his inner feelings make him attribute things to them that in reality were not there; for women added to their worldly appearance embellishments, trickeries—and treacheries—that were at the same time elegance and luxury and civilizing attributes. When Henry James, in

October 1868, reviewed a trifling book entitled *Modern Women* in the *Nation* he disliked the aggressive tone of the writers against the follies and fripperies of the female and came to the conclusion that it was impossible to discuss and condemn modern women apart from modern men. Their follies were all "part and parcel of the follies of modern civilization." They also reflected "with great clearness the state of the heart and the imagination of men. When they present an ugly picture, therefore, we think it the part of wisdom for men to cast a glance at their own internal economy." This was of course what had happened to Osborne. But it suggested also that women existed only as images in men's minds and as "patient, sympathetic, submissive" creatures willing to model themselves upon those images. The entire question was to be revived by Henry James in a long novel of his middle years.

THE TWO GEORGES

TWO WOMEN WHO HAD BOTH CHOSEN TO CALL THEMSELVES GEORGE came to occupy a large place in Henry's life and not entirely because of their assumption of the masculine identification. George Eliot and George Sand figured prominently in Henry's little library in Quincy Street beside Browning, Balzac, Sainte-Beuve, Gautier, Taine and Goethe. Both represented for him the art of fiction practiced at its finest pitch even if at opposite poles. He had met the name of George Sand as a boy in Thackeray's *Paris Sketch Book* and had later felt that this English novelist failed to appreciate his trans-Channel confrère. He remembered also that one of

Margaret Fuller's first acts on arriving in Paris had been to bring her New England presence into the drawing room of the Lady of Nohant; the encounter apparently made a deeper impression on Margaret than on George. Henry spoke of George Sand as having an overwhelming glibness and as being a "great improvisatrice." She contributed to literature the "ardent forces of the heart." It was true that she often, in Henry's view, cheapened passion ("she handles it too much; she lets it too little alone"). She took too technical a view of it at times. As he outgrew her, he continued to admire her flowing style and increasingly complained of her lack of form. In his late essays he was fascinated by the revelations of her private life, while finding it difficult to justify the way in which she had paraded her affairs in print. He devoted to George Sand during all his writing years seven essays and reviews.

George Sand was an important influence and model during Henry's youthful scribbling. George Eliot became a prime influence during his young manhood, the appearance of her works coinciding with the years in which Henry was launching his own career. In the autumn of 1866, after reading "in ever so thrilled a state" the newly-published *Felix Holt* he contributed his first signed critical article, "The Novels of George Eliot," to the *Atlantic*. "It was by George Eliot's name," he wrote in his memoirs, "that I was to go on knowing, was never to cease to know, a great treasure of beauty and humanity, of applied and achieved art, a testimony, historic as well as aesthetic, to the deeper interest of the intricate English aspects." The emphasis undoubtedly belongs on the words "applied and achieved art." Her plots were forced and unsatisfactory; her endings clumsy and contrived; yet in *Felix Holt* he had found "so much power, so much brilliancy and so much discretion . . ." that she could be forgiven the tedium of her endless expositions. He was to admire *Daniel Deronda* and *Middlemarch** even more enthusiastically. George Eliot

. . . .

* An unsigned review of this novel in the *Galaxy* of March 1873 not hitherto identified is from the pen of Henry James.

offered much to a young man seriously concerned with the novel form, "a style, the secret of whose force is in the union of the tenderest and most abundant sympathies with a body of knowledge so ample and so active as to be absolutely free from pedantry."

It is in this essay, in its opening words, as in the case of his first book review, that Henry James shows us how he approached fiction when he was twenty-three. "The critic's first duty," he began, "in the presence of an author's collective works is to seek out some key to his method, some utterance of his literary convictions, some indication of his ruling theory. The amount of labor involved in an inquiry of this kind will depend very much upon the author." The writer of these words would some day write a story called "The Figure in the Carpet" and would some day collect his own works in conformity with a "ruling theory." George Eliot was an author who invited critical search for her method; and unlike Dickens and Thackeray she was "also a good deal of a philosopher; and it is to this union of the keenest observation with the ripest reflection, that her style owes its essential force." To George Eliot he devoted five essays or reviews between 1866 and 1878 the years of her greatest influence; but he did not return to her in his old age. His *Notes on Novelists* of 1914 has two papers on Balzac, one on Flaubert and one on Zola, three on George Sand; none on the English George.

In George Eliot the mind prevailed over passion; in George Sand passion prevailed over the mind. Both were voluble; both tended to moralize and philosophize to an inartistic degree, but George Eliot was "solid" and George Sand was "liquid"—and in his early writings it was the liquid Sand that proved inspiring; as he shed his early traces of romanticism, the last strong example of which was *The American*, George Eliot became an increasingly significant source of inspiration and by the writing of *The Portrait of a Lady* she had quite surpassed her French confidio. Both writers represented for Henry also aspects of femininity—the Gallic George, virtually a man, yet possessed of those qualities of soft self-assertiveness that Henry cautiously admired; the English George

possessing the feminine strength he had known from childhood in his mother, his grandmother, his aunt. He was to meet George Eliot, to meet and admire her; he was never to know George Sand save in the anecdotes of his friends in Paris—Flaubert, Goncourt, Pauline Viardot. *They*—the two Georges—never became for him Venuses or Dianas. If George Eliot, in spite of her assumed masculine name, had the true attributes of femininity, George Sand had the "true male inwardness" and for Henry much more masculinity than her many lovers. She was virtually a man, yet she was not—Henry observed—a gentleman!

THE TERRIBLE BURDEN

ONE DAY IN SEPTEMBER OF 1867 IN CAMBRIDGE, WHEN HENRY JAMES was twenty-four, he wrote a long letter to his friend, Perry, who was in Paris. It began in the characteristic vein of their correspondence. Since Perry was in France, Henry must write him in French and the opening sentences contain a brave show of subjunctives, *J'aurais bien mieux aimé que tu m'eusses parlé de toi, que tu m'eusses donné de tes nouvelles intimes.* Then he lapses into English. He lists his readings; he affirms that English literature is in reality a vast unexplored field "especially when we compare it to what the French is to the French." In a confiding mood he writes that "Deep in the timorous recesses of my being is a vague desire to do for our dear old English letters and writers *something* of what Sainte-Beuve and the best French critics have done for

theirs." He dismisses this promptly as an "arrogant hope." Yet "at the thought of a study of this kind, on a serious scale, and of possibly having the health and time to pursue it, my eyes fill with heavenly tears and my heart throbs with divine courage." He looks forward to Perry's return so that they may resume their old exchange of "feelings and ideas." And now the young man in Quincy Street suddenly drops the banter of their old friendship. The serious writer who was being published and noticed in New York and Boston literary circles begins to speak, and what he says is sufficiently remarkable. It is "by this constant exchange and comparison, by the wear and tear of living and talking and observing that works of art shape themselves into completeness." And then:

When I say that I should like to do as Sainte-Beuve has done, I don't mean that I should like to imitate him, or reproduce him in English: but only that I should like to acquire something of his intelligence and his patience and vigour. One feels—I feel at least, that he is a man of the past, of a dead generation; and that we young Americans are (without cant) men of the future. I feel that my only chance for success as a critic is to let all the breezes of the west blow through me at their will. We are Americans born—*il faut en prendre son parti.* I look upon it as a great blessing; and I think that to be an American is an excellent preparation for culture. We have exquisite qualities as a race, and it seems to me that we are ahead of the European races in the fact that more than either of them we can deal freely with forms of civilization not our own, can pick and choose and assimilate and in short (aesthetically &c) claim our property wherever we find it. To have no national stamp has hitherto been a regret and a drawback, but I think it not unlikely that American writers may yet indicate that a vast intellectual fusion and synthesis of the various National tendencies of the world is the condition of more important achievements than any we have seen. We must of course have something of our own —something distinctive and homogeneous—and I take it that we shall find it in our moral consciousness, our unprecedented spiritual lightness and vigour. In this sense at least we shall have a national

cachet.— I expect nothing great during your lifetime or mine perhaps; but my instincts quite agree with yours in looking to see
something original and beautiful disengage itself from our ceaseless fermentation and turmoil. You see I am willing to leave it a
matter of instinct. God speed the day.

He had had his vision during these solitary months in Cambridge, at the end of the long summer during which he had not
budged from the paternal home. With strange and remarkable pre-
science he had studied his native land and looked into himself
and seen the future: for it was he who was to deal "freely with
forms of civilization not our own"; he was to move out into that
world between worlds in which he had spent the happy years of
youth, a Janus turned both East and West, prepared to let "all the
breezes of the west blow through me at their will." The letter to
Perry could only have been the statement of a young cosmopolitan.
It was the view of a cultivated American, translated into cosmopolitan terms. Henry was determined from the first to be an American artist, and equally determined to discover what his native
land could offer his art. At the same time his ideal was that
"vast intellectual fusion and synthesis" which was to become the
melting-pot dream of later decades—the fruit of which puzzled
and perturbed Henry in his old age. What he could not foresee
in the Cambridge quiet of the 1860's was the great abyss that
would open up between the tight little eastern society, which was
the America of Henry James, and the flood-tide of immigration
and the growth of the industrial mammoth that followed the Civil
War.

Four years after writing this letter to Perry he wrote to Charles
Eliot Norton, "Looking about for myself I conclude that the
face of nature and civilization in this our country is to a certain
point a very sufficient literary field." He added, "But it will yield
its secrets only to a really *grasping* imagination. This I think Howells lacks. (Of course *I* don't!) To write well and worthily of
American things one needs even more than elsewhere to be a *mas-*

ter. But unfortunately one is less! . . ." And again to the same correspondent, "It's a complex fate, being an American, and one of the responsibilities it entails is fighting against a superstitious valuation of Europe."

There is an echo of this in the opening pages of *Roderick Hudson*. On the eve of his departure for Europe, Rowland exclaims, "It's a wretched business, this virtual quarrel of ours with our country, this everlasting impatience to get out of it. Is one's only safety in flight? This is an American day, an American landscape, an American atmosphere. It certainly has its merits, and some day when I am shivering with ague in classic Italy I shall accuse myself of having slighted them."

Henry was not to slight the America of his young manhood. The Cambridge years were filled with close and studious observation of the life around him. Van Wyck Brooks has told us that Henry admitted to being "at sea" about his native land. But Brooks was seeking to demonstrate that Henry James had no native land. What the novelist really said was that "It was a joke, polished with much use, that I was dreadfully at sea about my native land." The joke was not of Henry's making. It arose among those who could not understand that the novelist deliberately chose a cosmopolitan path as the one that came closest to his general experience and furnished him with the richest material for his fiction; a fundamental error of certain American critics has been to measure James with an exclusively national or a parochial ruler. Henry was at sea indeed when it came to the country of Bret Harte or Mark Twain. However, in New York or Boston or rural New England, where all his early stories are set, he was in safe anchorage. He did not attempt to write of Europe until he could see it with adult eyes. His first thirteen tales—those to which he signed his name—deal exclusively with his homeland. He confined himself to the people of his particular world in America, those who lived the leisured cultivated life of Newport and Boston. His characters were either rich young men, dilettantes, artists, doctors, lawyers, unhappy Civil War veterans from the mid-

dle class, young heiresses, and in one instance a young gentleman farmer. He believed then, as he did all his life, that the writer must create out of his intimate experience. He was to be accused in a later era of journalism of "turning his back" upon whole areas of American life—as if he could recreate them at will. Henry James was as incapable of writing of Howells's world, or Melville's, as Howells and Melville were of his. Those critics who suggested that Henry's feelings for things American, and in particular the New England scene, were derived from Hawthorne have, as is often the case, assumed that books played a greater role in his life than the use of his eyes and ears and imagination. Distinctly an urban dweller, a product of the streets and squares of many cities, he could speak for the cities of the East and evoke scenes from them with circumstantial detail. His first novel, *Watch and Ward*, was set in a city that is clearly Boston; later in the Balzac-Zola manner he "did" the city in a full-length work. The America and Americans he observed during the ten years between his adolescent return from Europe and his later journeys abroad remained with him all his life. Joined to his New York boyhood, his New England years had given him a firm grounding in his native land. He was alive to the virtues and shortcomings of his countrymen; he considered himself an American artist-in-the-making—with one important difference. Unlike some of his fellow-artists he brought to his observation the cultivated cosmopolitanism of his early years. He could not accept his Americanism lightly; he had seen the world sufficiently not to take it for granted. He was later to speak of it as a "terrible burden" which no European writer had to assume. An American, he wrote, had to deal "more or less, even if only by implication, with Europe; whereas no European is obliged to deal in the least with America. No one dreams of calling him less complete for not doing so. . . . The painter of manners who neglects America is not thereby incomplete as yet; but a hundred years hence—fifty years hence perhaps—he will doubtless be accounted so."

This was a further elaboration of the ideas he had expressed in

his letter to Perry and a statement of his own special problem. When he began his travels at twenty-six it was into a Europe already familiar to him; but he travelled also as a young man who had spent twenty-one years—including the formative years of his childhood—in the United States.

A SUBURBAN FRIENDSHIP

I

HE TALKED OF THESE QUESTIONS, OF AMERICA AND EUROPE AND OF his writing, with a new-found friend during these Cambridge years—a man seven years older than himself who admired his work and encouraged it and was himself a writer freshly returned from a stay in Italy. This was William Dean Howells, who had just moved to Cambridge to become the assistant editor of the *Atlantic Monthly.*

In later years the legend grew that it was Howells who gave Henry his start in the world of letters. It was, as with all legends, partly true. Henry himself contributed to it by writing an open letter on the occasion of Howells's seventy-fifth birthday saying, "You held out your open editorial hand to me at the time I began to write—and I allude especially to the summer of 1866— with a frankness and sweetness of hospitality that was really the making of me, the making of confidence that required help and sympathy and that I should otherwise, I think, have strayed and stumbled about a long time without acquiring. You showed me the way and opened me the door; you wrote to me, and confessed

yourself struck with me—I have never forgotten the beautiful thrill of *that*. You published me at once—and paid me, above all, with a dazzling promptitude; magnificently, I felt, and so that nothing since has ever quite come up to it . . . . you talked to me and listened to me—ever so patiently and genially and suggestively conversed and consorted with me. . . ."

Howells did not give Henry his start and in that very summer of 1866 Henry had found in the *Galaxy* a fourth journal ready to print him; but what he was saying in his generous tribute was that Howells was the first editor to take him seriously as a writer of fiction and to see that he had a future. When Howells assumed his post at the *Atlantic* two of Henry's stories had appeared in it and a third had been accepted. Howells remembered that the first Jamesian tale to reach his desk was "Poor Richard," late in 1866. "He was then writing also for other magazines; after that I did my best to keep him for the *Atlantic*," Howells recalled. Fields had asked Howells whether the story should be accepted and the new editor replied, "Yes and all the stories you can get from the writer." When Howells was dying in 1920 he began to set down his early recollections of Henry and the fragment he left starts with the words: "It is not strange that I cannot recall my first meeting with Henry James, or for that matter the second or third or specifically any after meeting. . . . All I can say is that we seemed presently to be always meeting, at his father's house and at mine, but in the kind Cambridge streets rather than those kind Cambridge houses which it seems to me I frequented more than he. We seem to have been presently always together, and always talking of methods of fiction, whether we walked the streets by day or night, or we sat together reading our stuff to each other. . . ."

Norton and Lowell at the *North American Review* were older men; they published Henry but could hardly become his intimates. Godkin and his staff were in New York and Henry's relationship to the *Nation*, while close, was essentially that of a reviewer who supplies his copy and is paid for it; his relationship with

the *Galaxy,* just begun, was formal. At the *Atlantic* J. T. Fields
had accepted Henry James as a promising young man to be encouraged among imposing Brahmins. Now, however, William Dean
Howells, himself a would-be novelist, full of the memories of his
Venetian years (where he had been American consul during
the Civil War, the reward for a campaign biography of Lincoln),
proved to be an editor who could also be a friend, moreover one
who was young enough and close enough to Henry's generation to
understand him and have deep faith in his art and his future.
"Talking of talks," Howells wrote in December 1866 to Edmund
Clarence Stedman, the New York banker-poet, "young Henry
James and I had a famous one last evening, two or three hours long,
in which we settled the true principles of literary art. He is a very
earnest fellow, and I think him extremely gifted—gifted enough
to do better than any one has yet done toward making us a real
American novel. We have in reserve from him a story for the
Atlantic which I'm sure you'll like." Happy time, when in three
hours they could settle the true principles of literary art! The
story was "Poor Richard," published in three numbers of the
Atlantic from June to August 1867. In August Howells wrote to
Norton that an adverse notice of the tale in the *Nation* made him
feel unsure of Henry's public. The notice seems not as sharp today
as it may have appeared then to the young aspirant in letters and
his editor. The *Nation* critic wondered whether a character as lout-
ish and belligerent as Richard would have "entertained a doubt as
to his inferiority" in the presence of the two Civil War officers
and the heroine. He also noted that sex in James's stories "is not
only refined but subtle—an aroma, as it were." He recognized,
however, Henry's fondness "for handling delicate shreds of feeling and motives in the intricate web of character." This prompted
Howells to observe to Norton that "I cannot doubt that James
has every element of success in fiction. But I suspect that he
must in a great degree create his audience"—a balanced and prophetic judgment. Yet Howells seemed to be taking the *Nation's*
criticism personally, since it reflected on his editorial opinion, and

he had been, perhaps, excessively enthusiastic. Later he spoke of the way in which Henry was at first "reluctantly accepted" by his readers. This was not entirely accurate. During this period Henry was noticed briefly—but decidedly noticed—on the strength of his few magazine appearances. If "Poor Richard" was criticized by the *Nation*, the same journal welcomed Henry James's next tale ("The Story of a Masterpiece") asserting with an enthusiasm akin to Howells's, that "within the somewhat narrow limits to which he confines himself Mr. James is . . . the best writer of short stories in America." This, for a young man with only six signed tales to his credit! "He is never commonplace," said the *Nation*, "never writes without knowing what he wants to do, and never has an incident or a character that is not in some way necessary to the production of such effects as he aims at." Howells himself, in an appreciation written in 1882, did recognize that Henry's "work was at once successful with all the magazines" and we may safely assume the magazines printed him, and asked for more, not for his as yet little known name, but for the tales he wrote.

II

The friendship between Howells and James, the one destined to become a distinguished editor and writer of fiction, and ultimately "dean" of American letters, the other America's cosmopolitan novelist and a remarkable innovator in fiction, lasted all their lives. It was a friendship both professional and intimate, filled with genuine affection on both sides. Their correspondence of almost half a century testifies to Howells's esteem from the first for his younger contemporary and an unswerving belief in his great literary powers; there is, in some of his later letters, pride in Henry James's achievement and a genuine humility and awareness of the narrower national limits of his own. They sent each other their novels and Henry always took pains to read and discuss Howells's work—and even on occasions to borrow suggestions from it. There was an interplay of influence between the two that in neither case was very significant, since their personalities so markedly differed.

Henry's strictures expressed always in the kindest terms his feeling of Howells's artistic limitations; he was candid, but in a gentle and generous way, and it is only in the letters to others, intimates of the Cambridge circle, that he allowed himself freer criticism.

"I sometimes wish . . . for something a little larger,—for a little more *ventilation*," he wrote to Howells in one instance while proclaiming that "the merit and the charm quite run away with the defect, and I have no desire but to praise, compliment and congratulate you!" When he read A *Hazard of New Fortunes* he wrote to his brother: "I have just been reading with wonder and admiration, Howells's last big novel, which I think so prodigiously good and able and so beyond what he at one time seemed in danger of reducing himself to, that I mean to write him a gushing letter about it not a day later than tomorrow. . . . His abundance and facility are my constant wonder and envy—or rather not perhaps, envy, inasmuch as he has purchased them by throwing the whole question of form, style and composition overboard into the deep sea—from which, on my side, I am perpetually trying to fish them up." On the following day he wrote his letter to Howells, "You are less *big* than Zola, but you are ever so much less clumsy and more really various, and moreover you and he don't see the same things—you have a wholly different consciousness—you see a totally different side of a different race. . . ." He then launched into this passage, anticipating a much later and finer imaging of the "house of fiction":

The novelist is a particular *window*, absolutely—and of worth in so far as he is one; and it's because you open so well and are hung so close over the street that I could hang out of it all day long. Your very value is that you choose your own street—heaven forbid I should have to choose it for you. If I should say I mortally dislike the people who pass in it, I should seem to be taking on myself that intolerable responsibility of selection which it is exactly such a luxury to be relieved of. Indeed I'm convinced that no reader above the rank of an idiot—this number is moderate, I admit—can really fail to take any view that's really *shown* them—any gift (of

subject) that's really given. The usual imbecility of the novel is that the showing and giving simply don't come off—the reader never touches the subject and the subject never touches the reader: the window is no window at all—but only childishly *finta,* like the ornaments of our beloved Italy—this is why as a triumph of *communication,* I hold the *Hazard* so rare and strong.

The praise is subtle and confined to that which Henry could honestly praise. He is saying, ever so gently, that the novel is limited, and implying that if it is a triumph of communication it was not necessarily a triumph of art. He had, much earlier (in 1870) expressed the same feeling, and in strong terms, to Grace Norton, writing after the appearance of Howells's *Their Wedding Journey:*

Poor Howells is certainly difficult to defend, if one takes a standpoint the least bit exalted; make any serious demands and it's all up with him. He presents, I confess, to my mind, a somewhat melancholy spectacle—in that his charming style and refined intentions are so poorly and meagerly served by our American atmosphere. There is no more inspiration in an American journey than *that!* Thro' thick and thin I continue however to enjoy him —or rather thro' thin and thinner. There is a little divine spark of fancy which never quite gives out. He has passed into the stage which I suppose is the eventual fate of all secondary and tertiary talents—worked off his slender primitive capital, found a place and a routine and an income, and now is destined to fade slowly and softly away in self-repetition and reconcilement to the commonplace. But he will always be a *writer*—small but genuine. There are not so many after all now going in English—to say nothing of American.

The letters Henry James wrote to Howells are large, full, literary, expressive of the busy and lively life he led abroad. They are filled with gossip, are business-like where editorial matters are concerned, and in later years make of Howells a counsel in publishing matters and a sympathetic adviser on questions of his literary

reputation. Some of the letters are slyly humorous and filled with prurient touches as if to tease his friend—the friend who was to sit ultimately for the portrait of Lewis Lambert Strether. It is difficult otherwise to explain the extent to which Henry James went out of his way to raise the very subjects which the *Atlantic* editor sought carefully to keep out of his magazine—and indeed his life. James is describing an afternoon at Gustave Flaubert's: "The other day Edmond de Goncourt (the best of them) said he had been lately working very well on his novel—he had got upon an episode that greatly interested him, and into which he was going very far." Flaubert inquired: "What is it?" Goncourt answered: "A whore-house *de province.*" To which Howells rejoined in his next letter he thanked God he wasn't a Frenchman.

In the following letter Henry returned to the charge. He had been visiting the supposedly illegitimate daughter of an English peer in Paris, a certain Baroness: "She lives in a queer old mouldy, musty rez-de-chaussée in the depths of the Faubourg St. Germain, is the greasiest and most audacious lion-huntress in all creation, and has two most extraordinary little French emancipated daughters. One of these, wearing a Spanish mantilla and got up apparently to dance the *cachacha,* presently asked me what I thought of *incest* as a subject for a novel—adding that it had against it that it was getting, in families, so terribly common."

We do not know whether Howells made any rejoinder on this occasion. Henry James, in still another letter, and with unconcealed delight, reported how a mother, after reading a novel by Howells, took elaborate precautions that it should not be read by her daughter. It seemed to James a pleasant irony that a novel by a writer scrupulously careful to keep his work "wholesome," who pleaded for happy endings and simple romantic tales from him, should be forbidden a *jeune fille.*

III

The friendship between James and Howells was never more intimate than during its early years when the two young men took

suburban walks on Sundays to Fresh Pond, talking of their art and
their ambitions, or when they sat, as they did one November day,
in the thin pale sunlight, on the edge of a hot-bed of violets at
the Botanical Gardens, Howells cheerfully punching his cane into
a sandy path while the talk followed a spontaneous and meandering course. Howells could talk about Italian writers and about
Italy and then refer back to his native Ohio; he had had a childhood in a log cabin and had gone to work in his father's print-
shop. Henry, the young patrician, could evoke the old New York,
and recount tales about his innumerable relatives and his European
boyhood. Howells remembered "a walk late in the night up and
down North Avenue, and of his devoting to our joint scrutiny the
character of remote branches of his family and the interest in
art. They were uncles and cousins of New York origin and of that
derivation which gave us their whole most interesting Celtic race."
If Howells talked of Hawthorne, whom he had met, Henry
talked of Balzac and of Sainte-Beuve whom he hadn't, but
whom he had closely read. And if Henry submitted to the *Atlantic* two rather Hawthorne-like tales we are led to suspect it was
to meet Howells's preferences at this time for the romance and
not necessarily because he had himself fallen under the American
novelist's influence.

I V

George Moore once remarked that Henry James went abroad and
read Turgenev while William Dean Howells stayed at home and
read Henry James. The remark was unkind, but it was not
without some measure of truth in the overlying thought of Henry
as a cosmopolitan and Howells as a provincial. Howells wanted
above all, during his early years, to become a Boston Brahmin. On
his first visit to the American Athens he had been treated with
marked respect by Lowell, Fields and Holmes; the memory of that
time, and of his talk with other Bostonians and the great Con-
cordians, was kept green all his life. He was later to reach toward realism and to flirt earnestly with socialism; yet his reach

had sharp limits and his flirtation was perhaps largely sentimental. Henry had more rigorous standards and more dazzling goals. The Brahmins revered by Howells were fallible humans—and sometimes rather boring—to Henry, who had known
some of them from his early years. If Howells reached from
Ohio to Boston, Henry was reaching from Boston to Europe. To
one of the Brahmins, Henry once tersely summed up his feelings about Howells's career. Five years after meeting him,
the young novelist could write—still from Quincy Street—to
Charles Eliot Norton: "Howells is now monarch absolute of the
Atlantic to the increase of his profit and comfort. His talent grows
constantly in fineness but hardly, I think, in range of application.
I remember your saying some time ago that in a couple of years
when he had read Sainte-Beuve &c. he would come to his best.
But the trouble is he never will read Sainte-Beuve, nor care to.
He has little intellectual curiosity, so here he stands with his admirable organ of style, like a poor man holding a diamond and
wondering how he can wear it. It's rather sad, I think, to see
Americans of the younger sort so unconscious and unambitious of
the commission to do the *best*. For myself the love of art and
letters grows steadily with my growth. . . ."

This was not only a candid evaluation of a literary friend: it
was the expression also of Henry's own consuming ambition and
passion—to do the *best*, to surpass himself, to grow, to escape from
the present into the future, to take as his models in the art he
practiced those who had in his time come as near attaining what
he deemed to be perfection. Henry was supremely confident that
when *he* would find himself holding the diamond of his style
and art he would know what to do with it.

A BRIEF ENCOUNTER

CHARLES DICKENS CAME TO BOSTON IN NOVEMBER 1867 TO BEGIN those readings of his works which were to be heard and acclaimed throughout America. On November 18, when the tickets were put on sale, Henry turned up at the box office at 9 A.M. to find nearly one thousand persons waiting. "I don't expect to hear him," he wrote William. He expected even less to meet him.

A few evenings later Charles Eliot Norton was host at Shady Hill to the visiting celebrity. It was a brilliant dinner party and the elder Henry James was among the guests. His son was invited to drop in later in the evening. The small boy who had hugged the carpet in Fourteenth Street while he listened to *David Copperfield*, was now twenty-four and about to set eyes on the author of that book.

Dickens stood there, a striking figure in conservative dinner attire, the sculptured beard, the handsome face, a "face of symmetry yet of formidable character," a chiselled mask. The great novelist looked at young Henry "with a straight inscrutability, a mercilessly *military* eye . . . an automatic hardness . . . a kind of economy of apprehension." It all took place in a moment in that famous house thronged with the elite of Cambridge and Boston. Henry was stopped in a doorway and quickly introduced; Dickens gave Henry a solitary stare; he said nothing and they didn't shake hands.

Many years later Henry mused that had they spoken to one another there would have been but an exchange of platitudes and a perfunctory handshake. Dickens was being lionized; he was tired and Henry's face was but one of many in Shady Hill. What had taken place instead was this fixed look, acute and penetrating, of this "mercilessly military eye" and the return of his look by the nervous young writer.

"I saw the master—nothing could be more evident—in the light

of an intense emotion, and I trembled, I remember in every limb." Emotion, however, did not blur Henry's recording eye. The "exquisitely complicated image" remained and all the more vivid for not having spoken. "How tremendously it had been laid upon young persons of our generation to feel Dickens, down to the soles of our shoes . . . no other debt in our time had been piled so high. . . ." And it was as "a slim and shaken vessel of feeling" that Henry stood before the Master, then near the end of his life. Henry's father remembered the novelist as "saintly" in appearance. His son found in him an "essential radiance."

These were the impressions Henry James read into that fixed moment and brief encounter. For one "single pulse of time" they had met—a novelist of the past, a young novelist of the future.

The Passionate Pilgrimage 1869=1870

DEPARTURE

IN LATER YEARS HENRY JAMES REMEMBERED HOW QUIET THE HOUSE had been when he called to say good-bye to Minny. She entered the old spacious parlor in the daytime stillness with her swift sliding step and her old free laugh. He was aware that she had been ill; he did not know how seriously: she was slight, erect, thin, almost transparent. He remembered ruefully later that he thought her delicate appearance "becoming."

The Henry James who, en route to Europe, journeyed in mid-February of 1869 to Pelham near New Rochelle to bid farewell to his cousin, was a quiet, rather sedate young man, going on twenty-six, of medium height, with a brownish beard, receding hair, piercing eye and shy manner. He spoke in a well-modulated voice, without hesitancy (and without the stammer apocryphally attributed to him). He was witty and warm, although possessed of a certain gravity beyond his years. His laughter was decidedly the laughter of a serious young man. He told Minny of his plans. First

he would go to England and then to the Continent, perhaps to winter in Paris or to push on southward to Italy where he had never been. They agreed it was "wholly detestable" that he should be voyaging off while she was staying behind. The doctors had talked to her about another climate. Rome had been mentioned. Perhaps the cousins would meet next winter in Rome. The idea charmed them.

She didn't speak of her illness. Henry did ask her whether she was getting enough sleep. "Sleep," she cried, "oh I don't sleep. *I've given it up.*" He remembered how she laughed at her little joke.

They talked of writers. Minny had come to feel a great affection for George Eliot. Did Harry intend to call on her? Would he give her Minny's love? She would like very much to see her. Henry recalled the toss of the head, the "bright extravagance of her envy" and the amount of laughter that contributed to "as free a disclosure of the handsome largeish teeth that made her mouth almost the main fact of her face." They parted gaily. Perhaps they would see each other soon abroad. He would write of his European progress.

"Harry came to see me before he sailed for Europe," Minny wrote to John Gray. "I'm very glad he has gone, though I don't expect to see him again for a good many years. I don't think he will come back for a long time, and I hope it will do him good and that he will enjoy himself—which he hasn't done for several years. . . ."

THE BANQUET OF INITIATION

CAMBRIDGE—AND AMERICA—WERE FINALLY BEHIND HIM. HE WAS TO have a new vision of Europe: the old, the boyhood memories had turned grey, like faded ink, and he was now making a fresh beginning. As he looked over the wintry sea from the deck of the S.S. *China*—it had put out from New York some ten days before, on February 17, 1869—he could see the "strange, dark lonely freshness" of the coast of Ireland, the homeland of his Albany grandfather. Then the black steamers were knocking about in the yellow Mersey under a low sky that almost touched their funnels. There was the promise of spring in the air and the promise also of new things, "the solemnity of an opening era." He was, in a sense, retracing ancestral footsteps, those of his grandfather and of his father; even more he was about to retrace the footsteps of a small boy who had seen and remembered so much and had dreamed he would one day return. Henry James was in Europe again.

I

He stepped ashore at Liverpool on a windy, cloudy, smoky day, Saturday, February 27. By the time he brought his luggage to the Adelphi Hotel in a hansom, it was two o'clock and he was hungry. In the deserted coffee-room he drank his tea and ate his boiled egg and toasted muffin, folding and refolding the crisp copy of the *Times*, much too excited to notice its contents. The damp dark light floated in from the steep street; a coal fire glowed in the room's semi-darkness; the waiter who hovered attentively about him was a familiar figure. He had met him in Dickens, in Thackeray, in Smollett. . . . He noted at once that there was a singular permanence to the impressions of his childhood: everything led him back into his own past. "The impressions of my boyhood return from my own past and swarm about my

soul," he wrote home a few hours after his arrival. Only ten years
had, in fact, elapsed since that autumn morning when he had
looked out of the window of the Hôtel des Trois Empereurs by
the Louvre and bade farewell from its balcony to the Second Empire and to Europe.

"The sense of change . . . lies with a most warm and comfortable weight on my soul," he further wrote. He slept deeply that
night, exhausted by his voyage, the excitement of arrival and the
afternoon in Liverpool. He had planned to go to Chester on
Sunday but he overslept. When he arose he found he had missed
the only train. The rain was coming down monotonously upon the
gloomy shut-up city and the prospect of spending the day in Liverpool was unattractive. Henry found that if he snatched a
hurried breakfast he could get the London train and this is what
he did. It was a slow Sunday train that stopped everywhere en
route. As it proceeded southward the weather lifted and Henry
studied the land from his window as best he could while a solic-
itous Englishman in the same compartment, discovering that he
was an American, volunteered information and counsel from which
the bored youthful traveller finally escaped by feigning sleep. This,
however, deprived him of the scenery. It was dusk when the train
pulled into Euston station and Henry engaged a four-wheeler into
which his luggage was piled. He apparently travelled with many
bundles since he purchased a trunk in London a day or two later.
As he rode through the town to Morley's Hotel in Trafalgar
Square, a hostelry recommended by his loquacious fellow-traveller,
he was struck by the "low black houses like so many rows of coal
scuttles and as inanimate" and the occasional flare of light from
the pubs. He found Morley's dingy enough although his later description tended to coat the dinginess with glamour. "What terrible
places are those English hotels!" he exclaimed in a letter to his
mother that evoked nostalgically the comforts of Boston's Parker
House. There was, however, a warm fire in the coffee-room of
Morley's Hotel when Henry James arrived, and the heavy mahogany furniture gleamed in its light. In his room the large four-

poster bed was lit up luridly by the bedroom candle, stuck in its deep basin. The shadows and silence made him think of the *Ingoldsby Legends*. To his mother he complained about the musty bedroom, the two-penny candle, the absence of gaslight. For the moment he felt homesick, as no doubt he was, although he may have been exaggerating for the benefit of Quincy Street. The mood passed quickly enough. He sallied forth early next morning, purchased a pair of gloves, went down to the City, probably to take care of his letter of credit, and "all history appeared to live again." As he passed under the then-standing Temple Bar and looked at the statue of Queen Anne on Ludgate Hill lines from *Esmond* came into his mind. He took a memorable walk along the Strand—it lived for him forever after, like the famous boyhood walk from the Louvre to the Luxembourg—and old pages out of *Punch*, old drawings out of the *Illustrated London News*, turned over as a boy in Fourteenth Street, came alive on all sides. He stopped at Mr. Rimmel's establishment and never quite forgot the scent of the particular hair-wash he bought that day from a slim, smiling young lady. He paused before the granite portico of Exeter Hall; he dallied before the shop windows resisting the temptation to buy everything. London, old and new, the city of boyhood memory and of history, and of mid-Victorian reality, assumed an air of magnificence, a grandiose tone it was ever to have for him in spite of its slums and squalor, its dirt and darkness. "The place sits on you, broods on you, stamps on you with the feet of its myriad bipeds and quadrupeds," he wrote to his sister. He imagined it as a great Goliath and this suggests that he must have thought of himself as a young David. He was to conceive of cities, and London in particular, as places to be besieged and conquered. He was to speak also of London as a great grey Babylon and to the end of his life, when he planned to write a great brooding book about it, it fascinated him as no other city in Europe. It was to become his home for twenty crowded years and a place of return for two decades after that. He was crushed at first under a sense of its magnitude, "its inconceivable

immensity." He was to see it as a "dreadful, delightful city,"
more delightful, however, than dreadful.

Charles Eliot Norton was in London with his wife and his sisters Grace and Jane. Norton introduced Henry to a young Englishman named Albert Rutson who worked in the Home Office.
Rutson told him there were furnished rooms available below those
he occupied himself, and introduced him to his landlord, Lazarus Fox, a pensioned retainer of the Rutson family. Within three
or four days of his arrival in London Henry had transported his
luggage from Morley's to No. 7 Half Moon Street just off Piccadilly. He had dark rooms on the ground floor decorated with
lithographs and wax flowers. He could hear the din of Piccadilly
at the end of the street and as he stared into the fire "a sudden horror of the whole place came over me, like a tiger-pounce
of homesickness." His rooms seemed "an impersonal black hole in
the huge general blackness." London appeared "hideous, vicious,
cruel and above all overwhelming." For a moment a grim fantasy
of decay and death came to him, "I would rather remain din-
nerless, would rather even starve than sally forth into the infernal
town, where the natural fate of an obscure stranger would be to
be trampled to death in Piccadilly and his carcass thrown into the
Thames." He discharged this sense of powerlessness in the face
of London into a letter to his mother, his feelings oscillating between lugubrious homesickness and the relish of his picturesque surroundings. He wished he were in Quincy Street "with my head
on mother's lap and my feet in Alice's!" He is "abjectly, fatally,
homesick"; however, he is soon lost in a description of his journey from Liverpool, the darkness of Morley's, the search for
rooms, his encounters with landladies, "hard-faced, garrulous, rav-
ening creatures encrusted with a totally indescribable greasy dingy
dowdiness!" and finally his discovery of Mr. Lazarus Fox. "My
landlord is a very finished specimen and I wish you could see
him. He is an old servant of some genteel family, who lets out
his three floors to gentlemen and waits upon them with the most
obsequious punctuality. He does everything for me—won't let me

raise a finger for myself—is butler, landlord, valet, guide, philosopher and friend all at once. I am completely comfortable, save that his tremendous respectability and officiousness are somewhat oppressive. Nevertheless, in this matter of lodgings, esteem me most happy and fortunate. . . ." Mr. Fox was to be immortalized in the opening pages of the unfinished memoir, *The Middle Years.*

Henry may have feared at first to venture out for dinner into the dark and forbidding streets of Victorian London but presently, at the recommendation of Mr. Fox, he found himself resorting with some regularity to the Albany—the name could not have been a happier one for the grandson of the first William James—a small eating-house in Piccadilly. It is incorporated into the opening pages of "A Passionate Pilgrim" where it figures as "The Red Lion." It had small compartments as narrow as horse-stalls and the feeders sat against the high straight backs of the wooden benches so close to one another that they seemed to be waving their knives and forks under their respective noses as they ate their mutton chops. It was a primitive place, full of life and aspects that reminded him of the London of Boswell or Smollett or even Hogarth. Every face in the establishment was a documentary scrap, every sound was strong to the ear and the scene that greeted him there was as definite as some of the Dutch paintings of low life.

Henry explored London vigorously from the first. A shipmate on the *China* had warmly urged him to go to Craven Street for lodgings. He was curious enough to inspect the quarter "for atmosphere" and obtained an abundance of it. The effect of Craven Street "was that it absolutely reeked, to my fond fancy, with associations born of the particular ancient piety embodied in one's private altar to Dickens . . . the whole Dickens procession marched up and down, the whole Dickens world looked out of its queer, quite sinister windows. . . ." It was the "socially sinister" Dickens and the "socially encouraging or confoundingly comic" who had significance for Henry here. Craven Street with its dead end on the Thames was packed "to blackness with accumulations of suf-

fered experience." The future author of *The Princess Casamassima*, relishing the picturesque and the sense of the past, could open his eyes wide as well to the sinister aspects of the great Babylon.

I I

The first phase of Henry's pilgrimage was in the fullest degree, as he put it, "a banquet of initiation." If his senses fed on London, he also discovered how sociable England could be when it is host to a cultivated young American provided with unusual credentials. With Norton's aid, great doors were swung open and great personalities proved readily accessible and willing to meet the young writer from America. "For one's self," he noted forty years later, "there all-conveniently had been doors that opened—opened into light and warmth and cheer, into good and charming relations." He recognized that this was not entirely the case for his young hero in *The Princess Casamassima* and that London had a general grimness from which he had been able to escape. The note of hospitality was struck with great promptness in his own lodging when young Rutson invited Henry to breakfast with him upstairs. There the American discovered a fellow-guest, the Hon. George Broderick, son of Lord Middleton, like Rutson bewhiskered in the Victorian fashion; both were well-turned out by their tailors; they were charming, interested, curious. They ate fried sole and marmalade and seemed to know more about American politics than Henry. They questioned him closely about Grant's new Cabinet— the President having taken office at the beginning of that year— and Henry was at a loss to identify its members and to offer any tid-bits of American political intelligence. He was distinctly more in his element when, two or three days after settling in his lodgings, Leslie Stephen, then thirty-seven and filled with memories of the hospitality he had received during his visits to Cambridge, formally called to invite him to lunch on the following day, March 7, a Sunday. They had met originally in the home of Mr. and Mrs. Fields, in Charles Street. Stephen was, in a sense, a colleague of Henry's, for he wrote a fortnightly London letter

for the *Nation*. Jane Norton also was a guest. In the afternoon Stephen took his American visitors by the London Underground to the zoo in Regent's Park. In the evening Henry dined with the Nortons and although tired out by the day's sociabilities went with them, again by Underground, to University College, to hear John Ruskin lecture on Greek Myths. Three days later he dines once more with the Nortons, and meets Miss Dickens, the novelist's only unmarried daughter. The next day is memorable. He breakfasts—still with the Nortons—and meets Aubrey de Vere, the Catholic poet, who tells good stories "in a light natural way." He rests at home for a few hours, then joins Norton in Bloomsbury and they go to call on William Morris. Henry is filled with curiosity: he has reviewed Morris's *The Life and Death of Jason* and *The Earthly Paradise* within the last year and a half and feels him to be a "supremely healthy writer" and "a noble and delightful poet." In the house in Queen's Square he finds Morris, "short, burly, corpulent," dressed carelessly, loud-voiced, with a "nervous restless manner" and a rather business-like way of speaking. He says no one thing that Henry can remember, yet all he utters shows good judgment. Henry examines his handiwork—tiles, medieval tapestry, altar cloths—all "quaint, archaic, pre-Raphaelite" and all exquisite. Above all he is enchanted by Morris's wife. "Oh, *ma chère*," he writes to Alice, "such a wife! *Je n'en reviens pas*—she haunts me still." She is a figure "cut out of a missal" or "out of one of Rossetti's or Hunt's pictures." And when such a figure puts on flesh and blood she becomes an "apparition of fearful and wonderful intensity." "Imagine," Henry tells Alice, "a tall lean woman in a long dress of some dead purple stuff, guiltless of hoops (or of anything else, I should say) with a mass of crisp black hair heaped into great wavy projections on each of her temples, a thin pale face, a pair of strange sad, deep, dark Swinburnian eyes, with great thick black oblique brows, joined in the middle and tucking themselves away under her hair, a mouth like the 'Oriana' in our illustrated Tennyson, a long neck, without any collar, and in lieu thereof some dozen strings of out-

landish beads—in fine complete." They stay to dinner. Then Mrs. Morris, suffering from a toothache, stretches out on the sofa with a handkerchief over her face while Morris reads an unpublished poem about Bellerophon from the second series of the *Earthly Paradise.* . . . "Morris reading in his flowing antique numbers a legend of prodigies and terrors . . . around us all the picturesque bric-à-brac of the apartment . . . and in the corner this dark silent medieval woman with her medieval toothache."

This little corner of the Pre-Raphaelite world was thus fixed in Henry's memory; later he glimpsed another corner, Rossetti's studio, in "the most delicious melancholy old house at Chelsea." He wrote John La Farge he found the painter personally unattractive—"I suppose he was horribly bored!" His pictures were "all large, fanciful portraits of women . . . narrow, special, monotonous, but with lots of beauty and power." His chief model, Henry noted, was Mrs. Morris. Henry also met during this time Edward Burne-Jones, destined later to become a warm friend.

A few days after meeting Morris, he dined with the great defender of the Pre-Raphaelites, John Ruskin: ". . . he has been scared back by the grim face of reality into the world of unreason and illusion," Henry wrote his mother, adding, "he wanders there without a compass and a guide—or any light save the fitful flashes of his beautiful genius." Decidedly the young Henry was not overawed by celebrities; his critical faculty, the note-taker and the evaluator, functioned sharply as he made his way from dinner table to dinner table. Again at Ruskin's, it was the womenfolk who interested him, Ruskin's two nieces, one a young Irish girl with "a rich virginal brogue" and the other a Scotch lass. Even more than the nieces, "I confess, cold-blooded villain that I am, that what I most enjoyed was a portrait by Titian—an old doge, a work of transcendent beauty and elegance, such as to give one a new sense of the meaning of art. . . ."

He dines, once more with the Nortons, and meets Frederic Harrison of the *Fortnightly Review.* He is always dining at the Nortons, not so much because of Norton himself, who tends to be

over-protective and quasi-paternal, but because the Norton women are friendly and congenial. During his first days in London, he calls on his father's old-time friend, Dr. Wilkinson, in the old, remembered St. John's Wood surroundings, and finds him a remarkable talker. For old-time's sake he journeys to Brighton to see Wilkinson's daughter, Mary, named after Mary James, now Mrs. Frank Mathews. She had been one of his playmates during his boyhood days in St. John's Wood. On a grey raw day he takes the penny steamer and rides on the Thames. He visits Hampton Court and Windsor, Richmond and Dulwich, he walks on Hampstead Heath and Putney Common, he inspects towers and temples and cathedrals and he strolls endlessly through the National Gallery. "I admire Raphael; I enjoy Rubens; but I passionately love Titian," he reports to William. His "Bacchus and Ariadne" is "one of the great facts" of the universe. One afternoon, as he studies the painting, he becomes aware that a little gentleman is talking vivaciously with another gentleman beside him—the little man with astonishing auburn hair "perched on a scarce perceptible body" whom Henry promptly recognizes (having had a picture of him in Quincy Street) as the author of *Atalanta in Calydon*. "I thrilled . . . with the prodigy of this circumstance that I should be admiring Titian in the same breath with Mr. Swinburne—that is in the same breath in which *he* admired Titian and in which I also admired *him*."

III

He was in the "best of health and spirits" he wrote to his mother after a month of this breathless London life. He was exaggerating somewhat to assuage maternal concern; in reality he had begun to be troubled by a recurrent and debilitating costiveness which troubled him throughout his stay in Europe. He had suffered from it in America, but he now attributed it to over-indulgence at the London eating-houses. In deference to his sluggish condition he went, in early April, to Malvern and took up residence in the therapeutic establishment of Dr. Raynor, a medical man who af-

fected a black velvet coat and wore an oily beard, but who inspired
confidence. Dr. Raynor's regimen consisted of a cold bath on rising,
a walk to "get up a reaction," breakfast at eight-thirty; another bath
at noon, followed by another reactionary walk. Dinner was at two,
and at five Henry took a running sitz bath. Tea was at seven and
an early bedtime was prescribed.

In the establishment Henry found himself in the company of a
group of plain, civil, amiable if rather inarticulate Britons who
read the *Telegraph* and the *Standard* by day and played cards
by night; among them were several Indian officers with yellow
faces and declining livers, a fox-hunting clergyman and a gentle-
manly and indifferent squire. The baths do not seem to have been
particularly helpful and Henry enjoyed, most of all, the walks
over the sloping pastures of the Malvern hills, "a compendium of
the general physiognomy of England." It was April and the whole
land had burst into spring.

For the rest, the suffering young man put into his pocket, as he
walked to get his "reactions," a rectangular sketch book and for the
first time since his Newport days with La Farge executed several
pencil sketches of hills and trees and spreading willows. He continued to sketch after leaving Malvern: there is a pleasant scene,
drawn with hasty semi-professional strokes, of English field and
stream and a distant Norman tower in which the austere chill of
early April is suggested. It is dated "Near Tewkesbury, Gloucester-
shire, April 8 P.M. '69." Another, drawn with some attention to
architectural detail, is marked "Old houses at Tewkesbury opposite Swan Inn where I supped." A letter to William completes the
picture: "I took tea in a dark little parlor in the old Inn . . . as
I consumed my bread and butter and Ale, tried to sketch in the
twilight one of the romantic, strangely tempered dwellings opposite."

Henry spent three comparatively sedentary weeks at Malvern
and then decided that what he really needed was "plain physical
movement." He wrote to his father that he believed "a certain
amount of regular lively travel would do me more good than any

urther treatment or further repose." He accordingly embarked on a tour of the England of valiant deeds in arms, the England of the old religion and the England of literature and scholarship. He visited Raglan Castle at Monmouth, Tintern Abbey and Chepstow; he went to Worcester by coach, to Gloucester and to Newport; he spent a day at Tewkesbury. He visited Salisbury and Ely, Blenheim and Winchester. At Oxford, bearing letters from Leslie Stephen and the Nortons, he dined in Hall at Christ Church and at Lincoln was the guest of the rector, a desiccated old scholar "torpid even to incivility with too much learning" and his young wife who was in riding habit and, Henry believed, "highly emancipated." Deeply stirred alike by their architecture, their quiet and their summer-term beauty, Henry wandered through the Oxford colleges experiencing great assaults of emotion that were to spill over into the vehement outbursts of Clement Searle in "A Passionate Pilgrim." "The whole place," he wrote William, "gives me a deeper sense of English life than anything yet." He lingered by New College's ancient wall; he spent a dreaming hour or two in St. John's spacious garden; he walked in Christ Church meadow; Magdalen's eight-spired tower was "the perfect prose of the Gothic"; the doorways of the colleges were monkish, the green quadrangles noble and hospitable. Oxford was "a kind of dim and sacred ideal of the Western intellect—a scholastic city, an appointed home of contemplation." Yet he found strange imagery for it—touched by a mildly erotic note; the plain walls of the street fronts suggested that the colleges were "seraglios of culture and leisure"—they "irritated" the fancy like the black harem-walls of Eastern towns. In the college gardens, Henry wrote, he wanted to lie on the grass "in the happy belief the world is all an English garden and time a fine old English afternoon."

IV

The little English tour lasted three weeks, after which Henry returned to London. Writing to Quincy Street he reported his improved health and mentioned, among other things, that the trip

had cost him £60—a large sum for a rather limited journey
The effect on the family was rather startling. William promptly
wrote on behalf of the elder Henry to say that "it seems a pity
to let such a sum go in a single escapade." Drawing upon his own
comparatively frugal experiences in Germany, he urged Henry to
proceed to that country where there was a "really classical and cosmopolitan literature, compared to which French and English both
seem in very important respects provincial." The proposal was
hardly to his brother's taste. Henry James had not gone abroad
without a plan: he wanted to travel, he wanted to learn more
about art, and he was determined to visit Italy. He hoped that
in the process his health would continue to mend. He answered William that doubtless Germany would be beneficial to him
but he had no desire to settle down and be a student; a life of
movement in Europe seemed to him the best prescription alike for
health and education. Nevertheless he was worried lest his parents
would think him improvident. He accordingly wrote a long and
rather troubled letter to his father, defending himself and giving
an accounting of his expenditures.

"To have you think that I am extravagant with these truly sacred funds sickens me to the heart and I hasten insofar as I may
to reassure you . . . I have now an impression amounting almost
to a conviction that if I were to travel steadily for a year I would
be a good part of a well man. . . . As to the expenses of my
journey, in telling that tale about the £60 I acted on gross misin-
formation. I . . . circulated for nearly three weeks and spent
less than £25, seeing a great deal on it. I am obliged, of course,
on account of the seats, to travel first class. My constant aim is to
economize and make my funds minister, not to my enjoyment—
which may take care of itself—it wasn't assuredly for that I came
hither—but to my plain physical improvement, for which alone I
live and move. . . . I can't bear to have you fancy I may
make light of your generosity."

Henry said he had spent during his eleven weeks in England
£120, distributed among five weeks in London, three at the ex-

ensive water-cure and three in travelling. It covered the purchase of considerable clothing and articles of permanent use, but "very little trivial, careless or random expenditure" except perhaps a large amount of cab-hire. "I have treated you to this financial budget," he added, "as a satisfaction to myself rather than because I suppose you expect it."

This letter does not seem wholly to have satisfied Henry's mother for shortly afterward, when Henry spoke of a trip to Scotland, he received a disapproving letter from her. "I was slightly disappointed," he wrote to William, "at mother's reply in her last to my remarks about going to Scotland and at her apparent failure to suspect that it was not as a spree but as part of an *absolute remedy* that I thought of the journey. . . . That she should have thought it necessary to place a veto on my proposition, nevertheless proves the necessity of my thus defining my situation."

He defined his situation as a need to lay the foundations for an education in the great works of painting and sculpture "which may be of future use to me." He also had to make the most of the opportunity to visit the great cities and historic places on the Continent. This was no time for him to settle down to reading and study. He was now twenty-six and there would be time enough for that later. "I shall hang on to a place till it has yielded me its last drop of life-blood," he said explaining his method of intensive study of each town he visited. "I promise you there shall be a method in my madness. In this way I hope to get a good deal for my money and to make it last a long time. How long I know not. When it is gone I shall come home," and he added, "a new man."

Henry told William he did not want him to read this letter to the family, but to use it as the basis for explaining his travel plans. "I feel," he reiterated, "that it is in my power to 'do' any place quietly, as thoroughly as it can be done. . . . I have established it as an Absolute Certainty that I can't sit and read and between sitting and standing I know of no middle state." He still had £867 in his letter of credit. "I want father and mother to

write and say that they understand and approve my representations. They cannot over-estimate my perfect determination to spend my money only as wisely as it was generously given and any future use I make of it will give me tenfold greater satisfaction for receiving beforehand some slight propulsion from them."

He added: "I have no right to concern myself with what lies *au delà* this season of idleness: my present business—strange destiny!—is simply to be idle. I shall have no plans but from month to month." Having thus called for a blessing of his plans, Henry James lost no time in carrying them out. He prepared to leave for Switzerland and Italy.

v

Henry James kept his promise to Minny Temple. "I was much interested in your account of George Eliot," she wrote him during the summer of 1869. This particular account has not survived. There is another, however, written for Henry's father, of May 10, 1869, which records the impression she made on him.

She is magnificently ugly—deliciously hideous. She has a low forehead, a dull grey eye, a vast pendulous nose, a huge mouth full of uneven teeth and a chin and jawbone *qui n'en finissent pas* . . . now in this vast ugliness resides a most powerful beauty which, in a very few minutes steals forth and charms the mind, so that you end as I ended, in falling in love with her. Yes behold me literally in love with this great horse-faced blue-stocking. I don't know in what the charm lies, but it is a thoroughly potent, an admirable physiognomy:—a delightful expression, a voice soft and rich as that of a counseling angel—a mingled sagacity and sweetness—a broad hint of a great underlying world of reserve, knowledge, pride and power—a great feminine dignity and character in these massively plain features—a hundred conflicting shades of consciousness and simpleness—shyness and frankness—graciousness and remote indifference—these are some of the more definite elements of her personality. Her manner is extremely good tho' rather too intense

and her speech, in the way of accent and syntax peculiarly agree-able. Altogether, she has a larger circumference than any woman I have ever seen.

He was to see her once more, ten years later, when he was less impressionable, but was still no less impressed. On this first occasion, although agitated over the illness of one of G. H. Lewes's sons, she nevertheless was cordial and communicative. She talked of a recent trip to the south of France, the mistral, Avignon, the frequency in those foreign parts of "evil faces; oh the evil faces." George Eliot, in her black silk dress and lace mantilla attached to her head with the low-falling thickness of her dark hair was "illustratively" great—there was grace in her anxiety that day and "a frank immediate appreciation of our presence." He counted it the "one marvel" of his stay in London—that he should have been admitted to her distinguished presence.

THE DISHEVELLED NYMPH

ENGLAND, HE WROTE HIS FAMILY, HAD BEEN "A GOOD MARRIED matron." Switzerland, where he spent the summer, was a "magnificent man." Italy, which he reached late in the autumn of 1869, he found to be a "beautiful dishevelled nymph." In due course he was to take up his residence with the matron; but at regular intervals all his life he went in pursuit of the dishevelled nymph.

I

In mid-May Henry James crossed the Channel to rediscover the Continent. Boulogne looked as if he had left it yesterday, only it seemed much smaller. The Grand Hôtel in Paris, where he stayed for a day while waiting for the train to Switzerland, was "a complication of terrors." He enjoyed the magnificence of the boulevards; they were too monumental and certainly, for Henry's Cambridge taste, over-lit at night. Too much "flare and glare." "*Napoléon a tué la nuit,*" he complained, adapting Hugo. Between noon and night Henry visited the Salon and strolled through the eternal Louvre. "Oh the tumult and the splendor," he exclaimed to his mother, "the headlong race for pleasure—and the stagnant gulf of misery to be seen in two great capitals like London and Paris. Mankind seems like the bedevilled herd of swine in the Bible, rushing headlong into the sea." Here spoke the voice of New England, through Henry, with a distant echo of the grandfatherly Calvinism, in formulations distinctly designed for maternal appreciation.

After this, Switzerland was a calm cool oasis. Geneva was still the city of the earlier decade. Henry took long walks over familiar boyhood paths, visiting Coppet with its memories of Madame de Staël and the Ferney of Voltaire. He walked to Vevey to call on the ubiquitous Nortons, who were staying there, and he renewed acquaintance with the Castle of Chillon to which Daisy Miller was to make her gay excursion a decade later. For a time he settled at Glion in a hotel-pension on the mountainside, above the castle. Finding himself fit and strong he began to tramp through Switzerland as he had done in his youth. "I feel," he wrote William who was still ailing at home, "as if every walk I take is a burning and shining light for your encouragement." This was on July 12, 1869 when he was at Scheidegg. A month later at Lucerne he was glowing with a sense of well-being. "The only thing worth now putting into words is just what I can't—the deep satisfaction in being able to do all this healthy trudging and climbing. It *is*—it *is* a pledge, a token of some future potency—Amen!"

His mother continued to caution him against extravagance, preaching economy alike in money and expenditure of physical resources. She now suggested that perhaps a winter in Paris, or even Germany, as William urged, might be more frugal (and sensible) than a winter of "recreation" in Italy. Mary James had a way of putting forward such suggestions to her sons, tentatively yet firmly, and arousing in them a conflict of obedience; having decided on one course Henry was put in the position of having to rebuff his mother. His firm letter of reply in this instance from Montreux is a detailed defense of his cherished project. "I duly noted your injunction to spend the summer quietly and economically. I hope to do both—or that is, to circulate in so far as I do, by the inexpensive vehicle of my own legs. . . . When you speak of your own increased expenses, etc., I feel very guilty and selfish in entertaining any projects which look in the least like extravagance. My beloved mother, if you but knew the purity of my motives . . . the only economy for me is to get thoroughly well and into such a state as that I can work. . . . A winter in Italy . . . will help me on further than anything else I know of. . . ." And he went on to say that in thinking of the proposed Italian sojourn as "an occasion not only of physical regeneration but of serious culture too (culture of the kind which alone I have now at 26 any time left for) I find the courage to maintain my proposition even in the face of your allusions to the need of economy at home. . . . My lovely mother, if ever I am restored to you sound and serviceable, you will find that you have not cast the pearls of your charity before a senseless beast, but before a creature with a soul to be grateful and a will to act. . . ."

Mary James, following her characteristic pattern, yielded completely when resisted. "Take the fullest liberty and enjoyment your tastes and inclinations crave, and we will promise heartily to foot the bill. . . . Italy will be just the place for you; and do not, I pray you, cramp yourself in any way to hinder your fullest enjoyment of it." She thus went from the extreme of preaching rigid economy to offering Henry *carte blanche*.

II

By mid-August, at Lucerne, he had had his fill of Switzerland. "What was Switzerland after all? Little else but brute nature, of which at home we have enough and to spare. What we seek in Europe is Nature refined and transmuted to art. In Switzerland what a pale historic setting; what a penury of relics and monuments! I pined for a cathedral or a gallery." Thus muses his narrator in a story written shortly afterwards which catalogues his life at Lucerne.

One morning, at the beginning of September, he marked his luggage Milan and took the steamboat at Lucerne. He approached Italy across the Alps, partly by coach and partly on foot. It was three years before the St. Gothard tunnel was carved through the mountain and almost forty before the Simplon. Henry crossed the granite bridge over the Reuss and the Devil's Bridge high on the long monotonous St. Gothard road. He tramped from Brieg over the Simplon up the Swiss side and down over the winding highway thirty-three miles to the border town of Isella and into Italy, the Italy of the Romantics, of the Renaissance, of the Pre-Raphaelites. "If I could only write as I might talk I should have no end of things to tell you about my last days in Switzerland and especially my descent of the Alps," he wrote William a few days later "—that mighty summer's day upon the Simplon when I communed with immensity and sniffed Italy from afar. This Italian tone of things which I then detected lies richly on my soul and gathers increasing weight. . . ."

From home there came a worried missive. "Since your last letter, darling Harry," wrote his mother, "I have had a new anxiety awakened in my too susceptible mind by thinking of you traversing alone those mountain solitudes. Of course I know you would not attempt any dizzy heights or any but well beaten tracks without a guide. But you might easily over-estimate your strength and sink down with sudden exhaustion. . . ." By the time Henry received this he was deep in Italy.

He felt he could never absorb and appropriate Italy as he had

appropriated London and Oxford, and indeed all England, where he had felt himself breathing the air of home. This was when his impressions were new and he had a sense still of strangeness in that land where the late summer lingered in the north and the soft landscape wrapped him in quiet enchantment. He could not surrender completely to the "Spirit of the South," but "I nevertheless *feel* it in all my pulses." And again ". . . How beautiful a thing this month in Italy has been, and how my brain swarms with pictures and my bosom with memories." He came to Maggiore and Como and paused at the Hôtel Belle-Ville at Cadenabbia on Como's shores: ". . . the pink villas gleaming through their shrubberies of orange and oleander, the mountains shimmering in the hazy light like so many breasts of doves, the constant presence of the melodious Italian voice." An Italian opera setting come to life!

From Cadenabbia Henry wrote a long and vivid letter to Alice describing his walk into Italy. Imbedded in its pages there is a brief remark about his art, provoked by his sister's praise of the three-part tale of "Gabrielle de Bergerac" which appeared that summer in the *Atlantic*. The story was laid in France before the French Revolution; it anticipated his rediscovery of Europe and now it struck him as "amusingly thin and watery—I mean as regards its treatment of the Past."

Since coming abroad and seeing relics, monuments, &c. I've got a strong sense of what a grim old deathly reality it was, and how little worth one's while it is to approach it with a pen unless your mind is *bourré* with facts on the subject—how little indeed it is worth while at all to treat it imaginatively. . . . The present and the immediate future seem to me the best province of fiction—the latter especially—the future to which all our actual modern tendencies and leanings seem to build a sort of material pathway.

He was never again to write directly of the past. What he did try to describe was the *sense* of the past possessed by men and women of the present.

III

He is in Milan, in the brooding heat, before Leonardo's "Last Supper." "I have looked at no other picture with an emotion equal to that which rose within me as this great creation of Leonardo slowly began to dawn upon my intelligence from the tragical twilight of its ruin." The soul of the "Cenacolo" nevertheless survived ruin. He is moved almost as much by Raphael's "Marriage of the Virgin" in the Brera. He goes to the Certosa of Pavia, the Carthusian monastery south of Milan; he will visit many monasteries, wherever he finds them, to capture the spirit of quiet and retreat within them, to sit in their cloister out of the sun and meditate. And then, unhurried, he turns the pages of Italy's early history . . . Brescia, Verona, Mantua, Padua, Vicenza, a chain of towns constituting his avenue to Venice, shabby, deserted, dreary, unclean, into which the sun pours fiercely, dead little towns yet how full of the past! How sentiment and passion had blossomed there! Henry James sat in the cafés and walked about with his Murray and his Baedeker—and in his pocket *La Chartreuse de Parme*. He is reading Stendhal for the first time, "a capital observer and a good deal of a thinker." In his later notes on Italian scenes he sprinkles such phrases as "a feast of facts à la Stendhal" and "innumerable anecdotes à la Stendhal. . . ." At Verona he sits in the Caffè Dante in the Piazza dei Signori eating ices and chatting with his neighbors: three nights running he comes here to linger until midnight experiencing the scene—the slender brick campanile, the white statue of Dante, the ancient palace . . . wherever he turns in Italy he finds "a vital principle of grace" whether it is in the smile of a chambermaid or the curve of an arch. The palaces are old and faded "but the ghost of a graceful aristocracy treads at your side and does the melancholy honours of the abode with a dignity that brooks no sarcasm." Art and piety here have been "blind, generous instincts." And at every step he feels "the aesthetic presence of the past" and he gathers "some lingering testimony to the exquisite vanity of ambition."

Romance—the romance of old faded things, of antiquity on

which had been superimposed the successive centuries—and Passion—such as he had found in George Sand and now in the Italy of Stendhal: this was what the special banquet of initiation in Italy meant for Henry James. It was as if this hot Italian sun and these dark shadows created by the venerable stones of old buildings alternately warmed and cooled his American blood, so that feeling could first run riot and then be poured into the crucible of the intellect. The young intellectual from Quincy Street had become quite suddenly a sentimental and impassioned traveller. The *Italienische Reise* of Henry James imbued him with what he could only call at the moment *"the Italian feeling."* It was he who italicized the words and he was to devote many pages later to explaining and interpreting the Italy of those early years. In the writings about it the word "passion" crops up at every turn, in letter, in travel impression, in story.

IV

He came into Venice toward the end of a mid-September day when the shadows began to lengthen and the light to glow. He caught the distant sea-smell, glimpsed the water, the domes, the spires, and then the brown-skinned white-shirted gondolier swept him through the water amid slimy brick, battered marble, rags, dirt, decay. It was not, however, Venice in its details, but Venice in its totality that fired his imagination. With Ruskin this time in his pocket, he walked or floated through the city. From this first moment it became a golden link in the chain of cities that comprised Henry James's life, and one has to read the pages consecrated to Venice in *The Wings of the Dove* to discover how enduringly the spirit of the place had entered his life and his art. Some of his finest pages were written here in old palaces, in rooms fronting on the Grand Canal, during long visits early and late. On this, his visit of discovery, he explored church and palace; and he discovered Tintoretto. Henry devoted hours to the contemplation of his two Crucifixions and to writing William long letters about him. Tintoretto *felt* pictorially "the great, beautiful,

terrible spectacle of human life very much as Shakespeare felt it poetically." The painter conceived his subject scenically; he was dramatic. He had boundless invention, passionate energy. "I'd give a great deal," he bursts out, "to be able to fling down a dozen of his pictures into prose of corresponding force and colour. . . ."

He was to note later that "it takes a great deal to make a successful American, but to make a happy Venetian takes only a handful of quick sensibility." He was quick to appreciate the plight of the Venetians. "The Venetian people have little to call their own —little more than the bare privilege of leading their lives in the most beautiful of towns. Their habitations are decayed; their taxes heavy; their pockets light; their opportunities few. . . ." Yet they could find compensations. They were on better terms with life than many people who had better advantages. "Not their misery, but the way they elude their misery, is what pleases the sentimental tourist." For the tourist the pleasures of the place were simple: fine Titians or Tintorettos, the ever-waiting windowless gloom of St. Mark's, the gondolas, the relaxed café life at Florian's in the Piazza. The mere use of one's eyes in Venice was happiness enough. Even the children, clamoring for coppers from the tourists, added to the tone, "the handsomest little brats in the world," furnished with eyes that could signify "the protest of nature against the meanness of fortune." A little American, straight-haired, pale-eyed, freckled, duly "darned and catechized" marching into a New England schoolroom was often seen and soon forgotten. These children, playing "on the lonely margin of a decaying world, in prelude to how bleak or to how dark a destiny" were remembered. Some of the impressions of Venice were early and some were late: the city offered Henry variety and richness and different aspects with the years. It was a melancholy city —in a sense the most beautiful of tombs. The Grand Canal, to which he devoted a long essay two decades after his first visit, had always the "supreme distinction of its tranquility" unless in-

deed in later years "rapid transit" in the form of little steam boats contributed to the ruin of the gondoliers.

· Henry's first stay in Venice lasted a fortnight. He frequented the cafés and studied the people; he went to the Lido—then a very natural place, with only a rough lane across the little island from the landing place to the beach—and dined on the wooden terrace, looking at the sea and thinking how much this resembled Easton's beach at Newport. Early in October he turned his footsteps to Florence. From Lombardy and Venetia to Tuscany—to that Tuscany whose landscape had figured in the parlor in Fourteenth Street—he travelled again by easy stages, to Ferrara, to the Parma of Stendhal, to Bologna and finally Firenze, in that time of the year when the sun is still hot, the evenings cool and the city's aspect softly jewelled in riverine and mountain setting. From the first it caught his fancy as no other city in Italy: the Tuscan palaces with their pure symmetry had for him the nobility of Greek architecture; there was less romantic shabbiness here than in the Lombardian and Venetian towns and when it did occur, as in the group of old houses on the north side of the Arno, between the Ponte Vecchio and the Ponte Santa Trinità it was, in the yellow light with mellow mouldering surfaces "the perfect felicity of picturesqueness." Tuscany had nine years before been united to the new kingdom of Italy and Florence had become its capital. Rome was still integrally Papal and the French troops of the Second Empire were its guards. Henry was in Italy during the last months of the great drama of the *Risorgimento*. The older, divided Italy, however, has a way of transcending the immediate political ferment and upheaval and facing unperturbed the parade of the centuries. In Florence, Henry spent his mornings at the Uffizi or the Pitti; he went on his regular walks; he explored the suburbs, the churches, the squares, the cafés, as in the other towns and cities. He had casual encounters with Americans, known and unknown, chance meetings such as were to furnish the point of departure for future stories: "Yesterday I met at the Uf-

fizi Miss Anna Vernon of Newport and her friend, Mrs. Carter, with whom I had some discourse; and on the same morning I fell in with a somewhat seedy and sickly American, who seemed to be doing the gallery with an awful minuteness, and who after some conversation proposed to come and see me. He called this morning and has just left; but he seems a vague and feeble brother and I anticipate no wondrous joy from his acquaintance." It was from Florence, after a number of such encounters, that Henry delivered himself, in the year of Mark Twain's *Innocents Abroad*, of his view of the same innocents. William had asked Henry how the English compared with the Americans and Henry replied, ". . . The Englishmen I have met not only kill, but bury in unfathomable depths, the Americans I have met. A set of people less framed to provoke national self-complacency than the latter it would be hard to imagine. There is but one word to use in regard to them—vulgar, vulgar, vulgar. Their ignorance—their stingy, defiant, grudging attitude towards everything European —their perpetual reference of all things to some American standard or precedent which exists only in their own unscrupulous wind-bags —and then our unhappy poverty of voice, of speech, and of physiognomy—these things glare at you hideously." This passage has often been quoted as evidence of Henry James's intolerant and snobbish attitude toward his fellow-countrymen in Europe. Yet placed beside the sentence which follows this outburst, the cry *vulgar, vulgar, vulgar* can be seen only as the strong reaction of a cultivated young American, to whom Europe was a deep and important experience, against those Americans who devote themselves, Mark Twain fashion, to a denigration of all that is foreign and strange and *different* from their own parochial horizons. Henry went on to say, "On the other hand, we seem a people of *character*, we seem to have energy, capacity and intellectual stuff in ample measure. What I have pointed at as our vices are the elements of the modern man with *culture* quite left out. It's the absolute and incredible lack of *culture* that strikes you in common travelling Americans."

Henry was to take up the story of the American abroad and play it out in all its variants. It was to remain, although he abandoned it in middle life, his greatest subject and in the end he was to return to it with a sense of relief. He was to feel, in the end, that there was no "possibility of contrast in the human lot so great as that encountered as we turn back and forth between the distinctively American and the distinctively European outlook." He was to feel just as strongly that this was *his* theme and that there could have been no other, given *his* experience. His work was to stress, however, in its totality, not the American deficiencies but the American virtues, and above all the innate nobility of the American character. As an artist and social satirist, James drew his Americans as he found them in Europe—and often the satire hurt. The hurt was deeply felt, but the ultimate meaning of James's tales was overlooked and he was often vilified alike for want of patriotism and disparagement of his fellow-citizens; his observations were regarded as arrogant and snobbish. In his very first story, written on his return from his European journey (it is set in Italy), Henry incorporated the views expressed in his letters concerning Americans. Mr. Evans, the absinthe-drinking father of the heroine of "Travelling Companions" was "in many ways an excellent representative American. Without taste, without culture or polish, he nevertheless produced an impression of substance in character, keenness in perception, and intensity in will, which effectually redeemed him from vulgarity. It often seemed to me, in fact, that his good-humored tolerance and easy morality, his rank self-confidence, his nervous decision and vivacity, his fearlessness of either gods or men, combined in proportions of which the union might have been very fairly termed aristocratic. . . ." Here is a foreshadowing of Christopher Newman and of Adam Verver. In those galleries and streets, cathedrals and cafés, along the well-beaten American-travelled nineteenth century paths in Europe, he met face to face the host of Americans, rich and poor, the struggling artists, the wandering dispatriates, the innocent young girls who were henceforward to walk across the pages of his fiction.

Henry James had found his great theme. But three years were to elapse before he was fully aware of it.

v

Early in October, in Florence, Henry's health, which had shown constant improvement, took a turn for the worse. It was again not the back-ache, but the condition which had led him earlier to Malvern.

On October 7, 1869 Henry wrote to William, then the newest of new M.D.'s, a long detailed letter which in the history of literature well may be the most elaborate account of the ailment extant, describing his symptoms in detail and appealing for guidance. A week later he began to ponder curtailing his trip and returning to Malvern to take the waters. In due course William's reply arrived, filled with medical generalizations and counsel. "It makes me sick," he wrote, "to think of your life being blighted by this hideous affliction." Writing to the younger brother, Robertson, William quite rightly assumed that Henry would improve. "I enclose you Harry's last letter, which please return. This devilish constipation of his seems the only trouble with him now, but I think it can be cured. He was entirely free from it at Malvern and afterwards in England and is only living from day to day in Italy before going back there."

For the time being, however, Henry had been reduced to a pathetic state. He dragged himself about Florence uncomfortable in body, unhappy in mind and deeply disturbed at the prospect of having to leave Italy in a renewed search for health. On October 26 he wrote William that his condition was "unbearable." He posted the letter and began an easy stroll; he walked through the Roman Gate, passed two rows of tenements and proceeded into the countryside. Three miles beyond the gate he came to a hillside; on its summit he perceived a Carthusian monastery resembling a medieval fortress and "lifting against the sky, around the bell-tower of its gorgeous chapel, a kind of coronet of clustered cells." It was but five minutes of uphill climb to gain its lower gate,

past a clamoring group of deformed beggars thrusting their stumps of limbs at him. He gained admission and inspected the great proportions of the church, designed by the primitive painter, Andrea Orcagna. On a later visit, as perhaps this one, he was struck by the contrast between the opulence of the church as a place of worship and the bareness of the monks' cells. . . . "The meaner the convent cell the richer the convent chapel. Out of poverty and solitude, inanition and cold, your honest friar may rise at his will into a supreme perception of luxury." He visited the subterranean oratories and the funeral vaults, he looked at dwellings of the monks in the great pillared quadrangles, lying half in the sun and half in the shade, with a tangled garden at the center. The little chambers were cold and musty; the view, beyond the Arno and the clustered towers of Florence, magnificent. As he conveyed his feelings to William, after his visit, in his second letter of the day to him, they show a great calm, the descent of an inner peace. In *Roderick Hudson*, Rowland has such an experience after a visit to a Franciscan monastery situated not far from this one. He goes into it in doubt and suffering and emerges cleansed in spirit. "On coming out," Henry wrote to his brother, "I swore to myself that while I had life in my body I wouldn't leave a country where adventures of that complexion are the common incidents of your daily constitutional: but that I would hurl myself upon Rome and fight it out on this line at the peril of my existence."

It was not difficult to leave his beloved Florence. The weather had turned cold and there was much rain. He took the train three days later and in the bleak dawn of October 30, 1869 he reached the Eternal City.

V I

The letter Henry James wrote to William that evening after his first solitary day in Papal Rome was an ecstatic outburst, a page of exuberant rhetoric, as if he had to inscribe the emotion of the moment for posterity—which indeed he did. If he was overdramatizing himself and striking an attitude (as in so many of

his letters home) this was understandable: the romantic spirit was strong in him, and to be in Rome was to visit History itself, to feel not only his own passion at the moment but the passions of the centuries. The letters home were written by a young man fully conscious of his literary powers. He could not resist "writing" a subject to the hilt the moment he put pen to paper. The letters were destined, moreover, for an invisible recipient who would read them later in the American setting—himself. "You mustn't let my letters bore you," he wrote home. "Don't read them if you don't feel like it—but keep them nevertheless. They will serve me in the future as a series of notes or observations—the only ones I shall have written." The letters, therefore, are to be read not only for their epistolary qualities: they constitute a working notebook, a repository of emotion and experience, stored up for the future. Written with intensity and under the immediate impress of the scene, they are long, vivid, reflective, a kind of continuing self-communion punctuated by bursts of appreciation and exclamations of enthusiasm. It was not surprising that the elder Henry sent them to Emerson, who read them approvingly, and that Norton read them to an approving Ruskin. On this evening in Rome Henry wrote:

At last—for the first time—I live! It beats everything: it leaves the Rome of your fancy—your education—nowhere. It makes Venice —Florence—Oxford—London—seem like little cities of pasteboard. I went reeling and moaning thro' the streets, in a fever of enjoyment. In the course of four or five hours I traversed almost the whole of Rome and got a glimpse of everything—the Forum, the Coliseum (stupendissimo!), the Pantheon, the Capitol, St. Peter's, the Column of Trajan, the Castle of St. Angelo—all the Piazzas and ruins and monuments. The effect is something indescribable. For the first time I know what the picturesque is. In St. Peter's I stayed some time. It's even beyond its reputation. It was filled with foreign ecclesiastics—great armies encamped in prayer on the marble plains of its pavement—an inexhaustible physiognomical study. To crown my day, on my way home, I met his Holiness in

person—driving in prodigious purple state—sitting dim within the shadows of his coach with two uplifted benedictory fingers—like some dusky Hindoo idol in the depths of its shrine. Even if I should leave Rome tonight I should feel that I have caught the keynote of its operation on the senses. I have looked along the grassy vista of the Appian Way and seen the topmost stone-work of the Coliseum sitting shrouded in the light of heaven, like the edge of an Alpine chain. I've trod the Forum and I have scaled the Capitol. I've seen the Tiber hurrying along, as swift and dirty as history! From the high tribune of a great chapel of St. Peter's I have heard in the papal choir a strange old man sing in a shrill unpleasant soprano. I've seen troops of little tonsured neophytes clad in scarlet, marching and countermarching and ducking and flopping, like poor little raw recruits for the heavenly host. In fine I've seen Rome, and I shall go to bed a wiser man than I last rose—yesterday morning. . . .

Henry was to revise his opinions and temper his first enthusiasm and to see Rome as a comparatively provincial city, even though a great symbol in Christendom, and to find in it many subtle pleasures beyond the mere spectacle of the accretions of the centuries and the pomp of the Church. That glimpse of Pius IX in his gilded coach, drawn by four black horses, remained with him and figures in *Roderick Hudson* as a clue by which we can determine the time-scheme of the novel. It was Henry's fortune to see Papal Rome almost in its last hours. Before another year was out the Patrimony of St. Peter—that is Rome and its environs—had shrunk to the domain of what is today Vatican City and the Pope's temporal power was curtailed as never before since the Middle Ages. The city Henry saw during this visit was still one of living Papal splendor—the Vatican draped in scarlet, the curfew rigidly enforced, the scarlet coaches of the Cardinals in the city's streets, the *monsignori* in their purple stockings followed by their solemn servants, the dominance of the two Papal newspapers, *Osservatore Romano* and *Voce della Verita*, and the traces everywhere that in this city material things were directed by Lords Spiritual and Divine

emanation. The great meeting of the Ecumenical Council was taking place at this very moment. It was to proclaim the dogma of
Papal Infallibility in a final attempt to solidify the Papacy within
its shrinking States. Henry was to see, at later stages, the gradual
secularization of Rome and while regretting acutely the loss of
some of the old color and ceremonial, he welcomed the reshaping
of the city, the new excavations, the installation of the monarchy
and a parliament. He felt them to be the inevitable and irreversible stages of Rome's flowing history.

Henry's health improved during the first weeks in the city, almost as if the stimulus it gave to his mind and his senses ministered as well to his physical well-being. He studiously visited all
sections of Rome, explored its churches and sculptures, its ragged
columns, its ancient stones; he found continued enjoyment in the
contemplation of the priests and the French troops upon whom
the Pope was leaning for support against the *Risorgimento* during
these critical months—troops soon to be diverted, at the first cannon
blast of the Franco-Prussian war, and to leave Rome open to the
final triumph of Italy's unifiers. Henry gave himself over to solitary rambles and laid the ground for his future visits, all much
longer than this one. He continued to read Stendhal. He made a
pious pilgrimage to the graves of Shelley and Keats; ever after,
when in Rome, he returned to the Protestant Cemetery to spend
some hours of quiet meditation where the ancient and modern
stones, in their setting of cypresses, shelter the dead pilgrims of
the Anglo-Saxon world. It was in this cemetery, a decade later,
that he was to set the final scene of *Daisy Miller*.

"I see no people, to speak of, or for that matter to speak to,"
he wrote home. Toward the end of his Roman stay, however, he
met some members of the American colony. In December he went
to Naples and wandered sadly among the excavations of Pompeii.
He found Naples to be a "barbarous" city but enjoyed its museum.
For Christmas he returned to Rome, having made up his mind by
this time that he would curtail his Italian journey. He was still
decidedly unwell. On December 27, the day before he left Rome, he

went to San Pietro to bid farewell to Michelangelo's statue of
Moses and decided that of all the artists who had wrought in
Italy he was the greatest. His energy, positiveness, courage, marked
him as a "real man of action in art." The *vigor* of the Moses,
and Michelangelo's willingness to "let it stand, in the interest of
life and health and movement, as his *best* and his only possible"
had a powerful appeal for Henry at this moment. For one whose
ambition it was to be a man of action in art, the figure of Moses,
leader of men, engraved in stone, could speak eloquently. In describing him to William, however, and stressing his "health and
movement" he was to a degree accentuating his own wish for similar health and strength—and power—while meeting William on
his critical ground. Indeed the ensuing passage sounds much more
like his brother than himself.

I'm sick unto death of priests and churches. Their "picturesqueness" ends by making me want to go strongly into political economy or the New England school system. I conceived at Naples a
ten-fold deeper loathing than ever of the hideous heritage of the
past, and felt for a moment as if I should like to devote my life to
laying railroads and erecting blocks of stores on the most classic
and romantic sites. The age has a long row to hoe.

The day after his view of the Moses he took the train for
Assisi and had there "a deep delicious bath of medievalism." He
went on to Perugia and Siena and thence to Florence to which he
bade a fond farewell—of much greater intensity than he had
thought possible. He experienced at this moment an emotional
crisis, so profound that some years later it welled out of his pen as
he sat writing a book of travels about France. Into *A Little Tour in
France* Henry incorporated a direct passage of personal reminiscence
which began with his saying, as he came to write of Avignon,
that he had been there before. "I shall not soon forget the first
[visit], on which a particular emotion set an indelible stamp. I was
creeping northward in 1870, after four months spent, for the first
time, in Italy. It was the middle of January, and I had found

myself unexpectedly forced to return to England for the rest of
the winter. It was an insufferable disappointment; I was wretched
and broken-hearted. Italy appeared to me at that time so much
better than anything else in the world, that to rise from table in
the middle of the feast was a prospect of being hungry for the
rest of my days. . . . In this state of mind I arrived at Avignon,
which under a bright, hard winter sun was tingling—fairly spinning—with the *mistral*. . . ."

A contemporary record of his feelings is preserved in a letter
to his father written when he reached Genoa. "The whole affair,"
he said, speaking of his decision to leave Italy, "was brutally and
doggedly carried through by a certain base creature called
Prudence, acting in the interest of a certain base organ which shall
be nameless. The angel within me sate by with trembling fluttering wings watching these two brutes at their work. And oh! how
that angel longs to spread these wings into the celestial blue of
freedom and waft himself back to the city of his heart. . . . Last
night I spent—so to speak—in tears." The city of his heart was
Florence.

Thus Henry's plans were abruptly altered by his ill-health which
again seems to have been a function of intense inner malaise. Only
a few weeks before he had been day-dreaming of staying in
Italy until March and then going for the summer to Paris, Nor-
mandy, Brittany and perhaps thereafter on a little tour of the Low
Countries and the Rhine. He had even contemplated spending the
following winter in Dresden, where William had been two years before. Now he turned his face resolutely northward, from the
warm south to the winter sleet and drizzle of England. He was
deeply depressed. He called his journey a "tragical pilgrimage."
He regarded his decision as an act of courage, "the deliberate,
cold-blooded, conscious, turning of my back on Italy." It required
courage indeed to turn one's back upon a dishevelled nymph!

MINNY TEMPLE

THE DREAM THAT THEY—HENRY AND MINNY—MIGHT MEET IN ROME
had been a dream indeed. The months during which Henry had
been discovering Europe and writing letters home that reflected
new experiences and the growth of his imagination were dark
months for Minny. Of this Henry appears to have been unaware.
He continued to have hopes of meeting her. Twice in September
of 1869 he asked his mother: "What of Minny Temple's coming
to Italy?" "Is Minny coming abroad?" The record of his cousin's
illness is preserved in the letters which she wrote to John Chipman Gray and which, late in life, he turned over to the novelist.
They were incorporated by him into the final chapter of *Notes
of a Son and Brother*, without, however, mention of Gray's name.
Whether Henry, with his penchant during those final years for
revision not only of his own works but the writings of his father
and of William, "doctored" Minny's letters as well we shall never
know. According to his literary executor he destroyed the originals.
Of Minny's letters to himself he kept four which she wrote to
him during these months. His letters to Minny—and we know that
he wrote to her—do not appear to have survived.

I

In the weeks that elapsed after Henry's departure for Europe
Minny was having increasingly frequent lung hemorrhages. She had
lived her life with a restless intensity that did not abate even
in her lowest moments and the doctors in those days knew little
that could help. They prescribed quiet to that dancing spirit and
she went to bed, at Pelham, at Newport or in Philadelphia,
wherever she might be among her numerous relatives. Then, when
she felt better, she would start anew a cycle of visits, sleigh rides,
concerts, dances—followed by an inevitable relapse. Her letters to
Gray speak of "my old enemy hemorrhage" and she tallies them

for him: she had had "seven big ones" on one occasion and several smaller. "I can't stop them. . . ." The voice is unresigned, helpless, yet full of courage. "I mean to beat them yet." She speaks freely of death, laughs at it with the free laughter of her twenty-three years. The hemorrhages stop. She lays plans to see *Faust*. The doctor orders her back to bed. Music excites her too much. She is in New York. The doctor packs her back to Pelham. He listens to her lungs. He tells her they are sound. "Either sound lungs are a very dangerous thing to have, or there is a foul conspiracy on foot to oppress me," writes Minny from her bed. She rebelliously accepts the regimen of "gruel and silence." There has come a moment when she has no choice.

11

Her letters to Henry James are written with the same candor as those to Gray, although they are briefer and contain a considerable amount of family gossip absent from the others. "I have had no more interesting news so far, to give you but of my repeated illnesses, so I thought I would spare you," she writes from Newport in June of 1869. "My darling Harry," she writes, and parenthesizes: "You don't mind if I am a little affectionate now that you are so far away, do you?" She tells him that his last letter "reached me while I was in the very act of having the third hemorrhage of that day, and it quite consoles me, for them." She adds, "I still continue in my evil courses which, however, don't seem to have killed me, yet." She had journeyed from Pelham to Newport to visit her aunt and to see Frank and Lizzie Boott. She plans to visit the Jameses in Quincy Street: "I shall miss you, my dear, but I am most happy to know that you are well and enjoying yourself. If you were not my cousin I would write and ask you to marry me and take me with you, but as it is, it wouldn't do. I will console myself, however, with the thought, that in that case you might not accept my offer, which would be much worse than it is now." Had he seen George Eliot? "Kiss her for me. But from all accounts, I don't believe that is exactly what one wishes

to do to her. If I were, by hook or by crook, to spend next winter, with friends, in Rome, should I see you, at all?" And so she continues, in a half flirtatious tone, with a slightly forced euphoria and an abundance of misplaced commas. At moments it is the prattling of a little girl counselling Henry not to be homesick, inquiring about his health, giving him gossip of her sisters. She signs herself "always your loving cousin Mary Temple."

Two months later, at Pelham, she writes of her younger sister's engagement, the birth of a baby to Kitty, her older sister, and her continuing dream of going to Rome. "Think, my dear, of the pleasure we would have together in Rome. I am crazy at the mere thought. It would be a strange step and a sudden for me to take. . . . I would give anything to have a winter in Italy. We must trust in Heaven and wait patiently." She doesn't mail this letter until a week later when she adds, "The evening I wrote you I was enchanted with the project, but the next morning I was disenchanted. I am really not strong enough to go abroad with even the kindest friends. I have been ill nearly all the week with a kind of pleurisy, which makes me clearly perceive that it would never do for me to be ill away from home, on the bounty of strangers for my nursing, See'st thou?" And she pleasantly purrs, "My dearest Harry, what a charming tale is 'Gabrielle de Bergerac,' just as pretty as ever it can be. I am proud of you, my dear, as well as fond—have you any special objections?"

During the summer of 1869 Henry's mother, writing to him from Pomfret, contrasted Lizzie Boott with Minny, showing a marked preference for the European-bred Miss Boott: "What a striking instance she is of what a careful and thorough education can accomplish, perhaps I should add under the most favorable circumstances. Of course she never could have been formed as she is in America. . . . Look at Minny Temple in contrast with her. Minny has all the tastes and capabilities naturally in a high degree, and look at the difference. Minny writes that she gets up at 6 o'clock every morning and takes a lesson in drawing. Perhaps she is beginning to work out her own salvation."

Mary James was chatting off the top of her head. The "admirably produced" Lizzie was precisely the kind of Americano-European girl that Henry could convert into the delicate Pansy Osmond—and the name he gave her completely describes her; but Minny's heroic qualities and intensities totally escaped his mother. Minny wasn't working out her salvation at this particular moment: she was trying quite simply to *live,* even if the process meant early rising for the sake of art—although we suspect that it was not exclusively for art's sake that Minny was up at six. She was spending sleepless nights. In those weeks Minny was living at a feverish pitch that seemed to be a final endeavor to defy her fate. "I have a cough nearly all the time . . ." she writes Gray. Yet she continues her rounds of visits. Her last letter to Henry is dated from Pelham, November 7, 1869. She had spent some days in Quincy Street and read some of Henry's letters to William and to his father. "To think that you should be ill and depressed so far away, just when I was congratulating myself that you, at all events, were well and happy, if nobody else was. Well, my dearest Harry, we all have our troubles in this world—I only hope that yours are counterbalanced by some true happiness, which Heaven sends most of us, thro' some means or other. I think the best comes thro' a blind hanging on to some conviction, never mind what, that God has put deepest into our souls, and the comforting love of a few chosen friends. . . ."

She goes on to describe her Cambridge visit and talks much of John Gray who had come to see her at Pelham during a period of pouring rain and shown much awkwardness in kissing her sister's baby: ". . . he is a most noble gentleman in spite of his not knowing how to kiss!" Upon reflection she adds, "The foregoing has a depraved sound. But I do indeed like him much—better as I know him better."

There was a possibility that she might go to California "soft air and mild climate and fruits and flowers" and on this thought of San Francisco she adds: "Think of me over the continent—

"When shall we meet again,
Dearest and best,
Thou going Easterly
I, to the West? as the song saith. It will be fun when we
do meet again."

In Cambridge, she had lunched twice with Lizzie Boott and
talked with John Gray, T. S. Perry, Wendell Holmes and Fanny
Dixwell whom Holmes was to marry; and she had much light
banter with William James, whom she deeply admired. On December 5 William wrote to Henry, "M. Temple was here for a week,
a fortnight since. She was delightful in all respects, and although
very thin, very cheerful." He went on to describe her as "a
most honest little phenomenon" and to say that she was "more
devoid of 'meanness' of anything petty in her character, than anyone I know, perhaps, either male or female. . . ."

Henry had written to Minny that gondolas reminded him of
her (the "sliding step?") and she wrote, "My dear, I hope you
may henceforth *live* in gondolas, since gondalas sometimes make
you think of me—so 'keep a doin' of it' if it comes 'natural.'
. . . I feel much better now-a-days. Good-bye, dear Henry—
'words is wanting' to tell you all the affection and sympathy I
feel for you. Take care of yourself, write soon. God bless you.
Your loving cousin, Mary Temple."

III

Affectionate these letters are. They are a compound of feeling and
pleasant inconsequential chatter, the letters of a cousin who had
known Henry from her earliest years. Decidedly they are not love
letters. The letters to Gray are; longer and more detailed, filled
with much discussion of the why of life, they are the communications of a serious young lady to a serious young man: ". . . if
morality and virtue were the test of a Christian, certainly Christ
would never have likened the kingdom of heaven to a little

child, in whose heart is no struggle, no conscious battle between right and wrong, but only unthinking love and trust." She wonders whether she is "hopelessly frivolous and trifling" or does this mean that she really doesn't *believe*, "that I have still a doubt in my mind whether religion *is* the one exclusive thing to live for, as Christ taught us, or whether it will prove to be only *one* of the influences, though a great one, which educate the human race and help it along in that culture which Matthew Arnold thinks the most desirable thing in the world? In fine is it the meaning and end of our lives, or only a moral principle bearing a certain part in our development—?" She goes to hear Phillips Brooks preach and doesn't find an answer. He didn't say anything new or startling "though I believe I did have a secret hope that he was going to expound to me the old beliefs with a clearness that would convince me for ever and banish doubt." He didn't touch the real difficulties at all. "I wonder what he really does believe or think about it all," Minny muses, "and whether he knows the reaction that comes to me about Thursday, after the enthusiasm and confidence made by his eloquence and earnestness on Sunday. Tomorrow will be Saturday, and I shall be glad when Sunday comes to wind me up again."

The time was coming when no amount of winding would help. The "old consolatory remark, 'Patience, neighbour, and shuffle the cards,' ought to impart a little hope to me, I suppose; but it's a long time since I've had any trumps in my hands, and you know that with the best luck the game always tired me. . . ." It was now near the end of January 1870 and Minny was exhausted. There had been a plan to go to California which had fallen through and she was depressed. And she couldn't sleep. "Oh yes," she said to herself, and wrote it to John Gray, "here it is again; another day of doubting and worrying, hoping and fearing has begun." She describes this as the "demon of the Why, Whence, Whither?" The doctors are giving her morphine in the hope that it will help her sleep. It only makes her ill. "I am sometimes

tempted to take a drop of 'pison' to put me to sleep in earnest," she confesses.

"I had a long letter yesterday from Harry James at Florence—enjoying Italy but homesick," she writes to Gray. The letter was apparently written during Henry's brief pause there as he was England-bound. In the middle of February Minny left Pelham for Manhattan in a state of great fatigue and weakness to consult Dr. Metcalfe, an important specialist. She stayed with a cousin who urged her to allow her physician, a Dr. Taylor, to examine her. Dr. Taylor had a brutal bedside manner. He sounded Minny's lungs and she quoted him to Gray as saying to her solemnly: "My dear young lady, your right lung is diseased; all your hemorrhages have come from there. It must have been bad for at least a year before they began. You must go to Europe as soon as possible."

Minny then asked the doctor "for the very worst view he had conscientiously to take," but didn't mean definitely to inquire "how long I should live." The doctor, however, understood her question in that sense and she was unprepared for his "two or three years." "Well, Doctor," Minny replied, "even if my right lung were all gone I should make a stand with my left . . ." and promptly fainted away. Dr. Taylor revived her and assured her that perhaps her case was not so bad as all that and left. "His grammar was bad," Minny reported to Gray, "and he made himself generally objectionable."

Dr. Metcalfe brought re-assurance the next day. He told Minny her right lung was weaker than her left, which was quite sound and that the hemorrhages had kept it from actual disease. He said that if she kept up her general health she might fully recover. He had known, he said, a case ten times worse get entirely well. He recommended a trip to Europe; "so this last is what I am to do with my cousin Mrs. Post if I am not dead before June. . . ."

She sat on the piazza at Pelham bundled up on this February day scribbling her long letter to John Gray in pencil. ". . . If I

begin to be indifferent to what happens I shall go down the hill
fast. I have fortunately, through my mother's father, enough Irish
blood in me rather to enjoy a good fight.

"I feel the greatest longing for summer or spring; I should
like it to be always spring for the rest of my life. . . ."

IV

After Henry James had his last look at Florence he travelled
with an aching heart to Genoa where, on January 14, 1870 he
wrote a long, affectionate and philosophical letter to his father, telling him he wasn't sure whether he was in a position to assess his
notions "with regard to the amelioration of society." His year
abroad had convinced him, however, of the "transitory organization
of the actual social body. The only respectable state of mind,"
he added, "is to constantly express one's perfect dissatisfaction with
it." His father had apologized for sermonizing his son. Henry rejoined, "Don't be afraid of treating me to a little philosophy. I
treat myself to lots." And he went on to tell him of his regret
at leaving Italy. Three days later he was at the Hotel de Grande
Bretagne in Mentone. From there he went the following day by
carriage to Nice. He visited Monte Carlo and watched the play
at the gaming tables; for a while he toyed with the idea of stak-
ing a napoleon "for that first time which is always so highly profitable."

Discretion—and the maternal frugality—triumphed; he turned instead to study the "nobler face of the blue ocean." He enjoyed
the French cooking and was deeply happy over the play of light
and color along the Riviera. Aboard the train from Nice to
Marseille he fell in with an English consumptive and earned his
gratitude by showing him kind attention. When he reached Arles
there was a howling mistral; Avignon caught his fancy, but seemed
pretty tame after Italy. On January 27 he was in Paris. He went
to see *Frou Frou* with Desclée at the Gymnase and for the first
time he visited the Théâtre Français where he saw Molière. One
doesn't know Molière, he wrote his mother, until one has seen

him done by Regnier, Got and Coquelin; nor Augier without Mlle. Favart. He spent hours at the Louvre, he dined modestly, he returned evenings to the Théâtre Français and read late into the night by the fire in his hotel. He would have liked to linger in Paris—"I should have learned *bien des choses* at the Théâtre Français." However, his goal was England. He recrossed the Channel via Boulogne and went to the Charing Cross Hotel where he promptly re-acclimatized himself by dining in the coffee-room off roast beef, Brussels sprouts and a pint of beer.

On February 5 in a letter from London he gave his mother an accounting of his year's expenditures and although it was quite clear that he had made discreet use of the funds at his disposal he felt the need to justify the course he had taken. He had been in Europe almost eleven months and had drawn $1,895 of the $3,000 in gold his father had put at his disposal. He had not been extravagant; perhaps too many hansoms, but he had pampered himself in this respect because of poor health. Apparently only poor health could serve as a sufficient justification in Mary James's eyes for such travels as Henry had undertaken. He told his mother he wasn't a good economist and that he had purchased only a few clothes and half a dozen books.*

"My being unwell," he explained, "has kept me constantly from attempting in any degree to rough it. I have lived at the best hotels and done trips in the most comfortable way." Nevertheless $1,895 seemed to him a large sum. Everything would depend now how things would go at Malvern. If he didn't feel better he would return home. Even if he improved, he was inclined to return in the autumn. He would not be disappointed at the curtailment of his grand tour; he had on the whole had a "magnificent holiday."

. . . .

* At least two of these were still in his library at the time of his death: Jules Zeller's *Entretiens sur l'Histoire* (Paris, 1869) in which he inscribed his name and the date Florence, October 1869, and Charles de Brosses, *Lettres Familières* (2 vols.; Paris, 1869) in which he also signed his name adding, "Rome, Nov. 1869."

Eight days later he was at Malvern, living in a dingy bedroom and writing a long letter to William summing up his Italian journey. He was convinced that Florence "has really entered into my life and is destined to operate there as a motive, a prompter, an inspirer of some sort." (This it did; for here he began, three years later, his first important novel.) He still liked England —the fields were vivid in their rain-dampened green and "ah! that watery sky, greatest of England's glories! so high and vast and various, so many-lighted and many-shadowed, so full of poety and motion. . . ."

v

Three more weeks flew by and he was again writing to William from Malvern. He was obtaining plenty of "gentle emotions from the scenery." He had found no intellectual companionship, however, among his fellow-patients at the thermal establishment. The women, particularly, struck him as plain, stiff, tasteless in "their dowdy beads and their lindsey woolsey trains."

"Nay, this is peevish and brutal," he added. "Personally (with all their faults) they are well enough. I revolt from their dreary deathly want of—what shall I call it?—Clover Hooper has it— intellectual grace—Minny Temple has it—moral spontaneity."

The name of Minny, and the present tense, slipped easily from his pen as he wrote this letter in his rapid hand. The date of the letter was March 8, 1870. What Henry could not know was that the time had come to write in the past tense. On this very day Minny's tired, sick lungs had drawn their last breath in the quiet house in Pelham where little more than a year before Henry had said the good-bye to her that was destined indeed to be their last good-bye.

THE WINGS OF THE DOVE

From Henry James's notebook—twenty-four years after the death of Minny Temple:

34 De Vere Gardens, W. November 3rd, 1894

Isn't perhaps something to be made of the idea that came to me some time ago and that I have not hitherto made any note of— the little idea of the situation of some young creature (it seems to me preferably a woman, but of this I'm not sure), who, at 20, on the threshold of a life that has seemed boundless, is suddenly condemned to death (by consumption, heart-disease, or whatever) by the voice of the physician? She learns that she has but a short time to live, and she rebels, she is terrified, she cries out in her anguish, her tragic young despair. She is in love with life, her dreams of it have been immense, and she clings to it with passion, with supplication. 'I don't want to die—I won't, I won't, oh, let me live; oh, save me!' . . . If she only could live just a little; just a little more —just a little longer. . . .

I

The heroine—the "very heroine of our common scene"—was dead at twenty-four and Henry, contemplating the cold green landscape of Malvern through his tears, found himself trying to face the hard, irreversible truth. Minny was "*dead*—silent—absent forever . . . While I sit spinning my sentences she is dead. . . ." He received the news on March 26 from his mother and replied to her on the same day. At moments his letter is almost a soliloquy, interrupted by a sharp cry of grief, and then the grief is submerged in a flow of memories and of self-solace—relief that Minny had not lived to suffer; in that light her death was "the happiest fact of her career."

"I have been spending the morning letting the awakened swarm

of old recollections and associations flow into my mind—almost *enjoying* the exquisite pain they provoke," he wrote. He experienced a feeling of "absolute balm in the thought of poor Minny and *rest*—rest and immortal absence." Life on a footing of illness and invalidism would have been impossible for that disengaged and dancing flame.

It had come as a sudden sharp shock. "Your last mention of her condition had been very far from preparing me for this. Minny seemed such a breathing immortal reality that the mere statement of her death conveys little meaning." He scribbled the thoughts as they came to him. "Oh dearest Mother! oh poor struggling suffering *dying* creature!" He wanted all the details of her death, the last hours, the funeral, "any gossip that comes to your head. . . . I have been raking up all my recent memories of her and her rare personality seems to shine out with absolute defiant reality. Immortal peace to her memory!"

When he had written himself out, he took a long walk and gradually the thought of her disappearance became familiar. He wished they could have met in Europe; he would have liked to tell her many things, to take up the talk where they had left off at Pelham. "Poor Minny! how much she was not to see!" He strolled across the fields; the landscape assented stolidly enough to death: ". . . this vast indifferent England which she fancied she would have liked. Perhaps!" Minny was "a plant of pure American growth," however; there was no telling what Europe would have meant for her.

He returned to his room and picked up his pen again. The writer in him soliloquized best pen in hand. He had written in the first part of his letter. "It comes home to me with irresistible power, the sense of how much I knew her and how much I loved her." He now added: "It is no surprise to me to find that I felt for her an affection as deep as the foundations of my being, for I always knew it." *Dear bright little Minny* his mother had written. He answered: "God bless you dear Mother, for the

words. . . . I am melted down to such an ocean of love that you may be sure you all come in for your share."

II

The letter to Mary James, written in the first moments of grief, reflects his immediate feelings. The eloquent letter he wrote three days later to William is long, self-conscious, rambling and repetitive, the fruit of reflection and expressive of inner contradictions. Over and over its refrain is that Minny can now be translated from reality into an image of the mind. He had written his mother: "Twenty years hence—what a pure eloquent vision she will be" and now he reiterated, as if talking to Minny, "Twenty years hence we shall be living with your love and longing with your eagerness and suffering with your patience." Minny now lived "as a steady unfaltering luminary in the mind rather than as a flickering wasting earth-stifled lamp. . . ." And again, "her image will preside in my intellect," and still again, "the more I think of her the more perfectly satisfied I am to have her translated from this changing realm of fact to the steady realm of thought. There she may bloom into a beauty more radiant than our dull eyes will avail to contemplate," and yet again, "I could shed tears of joy far more copious than any tears of sorrow when I think of her feverish earthly lot exchanged for this serene promotion into pure fellowship with our memories, thoughts and fancies."

From this his mood swings to "a little decent passionless grief —a little rummage in our little store of wisdom—a sigh of relief —and we begin to live for ourselves again." Minny alive was a creature of flesh and blood to be loved; and also, for Henry, a threat, as women were; Minny dead was an idea, a thought, a bright flame of memory, a statue—Diana!—to be loved and to be worshipped in complete safety "embalmed forever in all our hearts and lives." She had been "a sort of experiment of nature . . . a mere subject without an object . . . the helpless victim and toy of her own intelligence."

The letter to William culminates in a passage describing what Minny had meant to Henry James—"she *represented*, in a manner, in my life several of the elements or phases of life at large—her own sex, to begin with, but even more *Youth*, with which owing to my invalidism, I always felt in rather indirect relation." Everyone, he said, was supposed to have been more or less in love with Minny . . . "others may answer for themselves: I never was." It may be that Henry was making a fine distinction here; he had written to his mother that he loved Minny; this was different from being *in love* with her. One might love a cousin without being in love with her. He tells William:

Among the sad reflections that her death provokes for me, there is none sadder than this view of the gradual change and reversal of our relations: I slowly crawling from weakness and inaction and suffering into strength and health and hope: she sinking out of brightness and youth into decline and death. It's almost as if she had passed away—as far as I am concerned—from having served her purpose, that of standing well within the world, inviting and inviting me onward by all the bright intensity of her example. She never knew how sick and disordered a creature I was and I always felt that she knew me at my worst. I always looked forward with a certain eagerness to the day when I should have regained my natural lead, and our friendship on my part, at least, might become more active and masculine. This I have especially felt during the powerful experience of the past year.

At the end of his letter he repeats: "I can't put away the thought that just as I am beginning life, she has ended it."

III

This thought is the key to Henry's feelings at the moment of Minny's death. What he had observed from his earliest years and later recorded in his fiction had now become in his mind (for so he articulated it) a part of his own life—"the gradual change and reversal of our relations." But what *had* been his relation to

Minny? He had not been engaged to her as De Grey was to Margaret in the tale he had written two years earlier; nor had he been her avowed lover, like poor Richard, who had shouted his passion to Gertrude on the banks of the river. What mystic strength was he endowing himself with, that fed on Minny's weakness and grew ever greater? what transparent mental link had he forged with the image of his cousin to arrive at the equation that her loss was his gain? It was almost as if, in his mind, he had already imagined himself betrothed to her or even married. He was drawing up the eternal balance sheet of the love-death as he had observed it, in which either the man or the woman, or both, were victims of a love relationship. While Richard had recovered from his typhoid fever, Gertrude had begun to waste away; in the story of De Grey the equation was reversible—one or the other had to die.

He said that twenty years hence Minny would be "a pure eloquent vision." She began to figure in Henry's short stories and novels long before the day when, a quarter of a century later, he made his first notebook entry of the theme that became *The Wings of the Dove*. Seven years after Minny's death Henry wrote a curious tale that reads as if it stemmed directly from the letter to William on the death of his cousin. The story bears the title of "Longstaff's Marriage." The heroine is named Diana—Diana Belfield—and she is as beautiful as the chaste huntress, with a "tall, light figure . . . a nobly poised head . . . frank quick glance . . . and rapid gliding step." She has had many suitors; like the wakeful huntress she is "passionately single, fiercely virginal." Travelling abroad with her faithful companion, Agatha Gosling, she winters at Nice and there daily on the promenade she finds herself being observed by a handsome young Englishman whose strongly masculine name she discovers to be Reginald Longstaff. He sits for a long time in the sun, a book in his pocket, staring at the sea— when he is not staring at Diana. Agatha believes that one of Longstaff's lungs is "affected" and he is in Nice for his health. He is clearly a worshipper of Diana—but from a safe distance. His reti-

cence is complete. He makes no effort to speak to her or to be introduced to her. The ladies fall into the habit of speaking of him as "poor Mr. Longstaff." "No one, indeed, knew, with certainty, that he was consumptive . . . but unless he were ill, why should he make such a mystery of it?" Agatha wonders why he doesn't ask to be introduced. One day, however, he does summon the courage to speak to her. He tells her he is a dying man and in the ensuing conversation Agatha becomes conscious that "what he meant was simply that he admired her companion so much that he was afraid of her. . . ." He explains that because of his invalidism "to speak to her of what I felt seemed only to open the lid of a grave in her face. . . ." He adds that he knows he will not recover and asks Agatha to tell Diana after he is gone how much he loved her.

Shortly after this interview Longstaff's serving man comes to announce that his master is dying, not of consumption but of love. Agatha urges Diana to go to see him, out of pity. "What is Mr. Longstaff to me?" replies the chaste Diana. When a second urgent request is received, however, she yields. She finds Longstaff in bed, as white as the sheets, and gravely ill. He makes an extraordinary proposal: nothing less than a death-bed marriage so that Diana may inherit his possessions, "lands, houses, a great many beautiful things." In exchange he would have "a few hours in which to lie and think of my happiness."

Diana is not unmoved by his sad mien, his deathly pallor, his plea. However, she comes out with a down-to-earth reflection: "Suppose, after all, he should get well." Longstaff, overhearing this, moans softly and turns his face to the wall. Diana leaves. "If he could die with it," she observes coldly, "he could die without it." From that moment, however, she is uneasy and restless. She returns to America.

Two years pass and she summons Agatha to her. "Will you come abroad with me again? I am very ill." Later she tells her, "I believe I am dying. . . ." They wander across Europe and Agatha Gosling observes the changes in her companion. "The beautiful

statue had grown human and taken on some of the imper-
fections of humanity." One day in Rome, in St. Peter's, Diana
glimpses a healthy and completely recovered Longstaff. "So you
were right," Agatha tells Diana. "He would, after all, have got
well." Diana replies: "I am right now, but I was wrong then. He
got well because I refused him. I gave him a hurt that cured
him." Later Agatha meets Longstaff and discovers that he too attributes his cure to the "miracle of wounded pride." He is clearly
no longer interested in Diana. She, however, is now in love with
him and is dying. She sends for him. He agrees to marry her on
her death-bed. Unlike Longstaff, she does not recover. Love—and
marriage—have been fatal to her. "She loved you," says Agatha,
"more than she believed you could now love her; and it seemed
to her that, when she had had her moment of happiness, to leave
you at liberty was the tenderest way she could show it." The
words *to leave you at liberty* come very close to Henry's words to
William that Minny had passed away almost as if she had ful-
filled her purpose—that of inviting him onward into the world.

The story was published in *Scribner's Monthly* in August 1878
a month after "Daisy Miller" had appeared in the *Cornhill Magazine*. It is decidedly not in the happy manner of *Daisy* although it
is told with all the narrative charm Henry had mastered by this
time. Weak in substance and art, it is strong in biographical content since in it James worked into story form the very ideas expressed or implicit in the letters written immediately after Minny's
death. He had felt that there had been a reversal of his and
Minny's relationship; he recovered and Minny died, and this is
the story of Longstaff and Diana. What is striking in the tale is that
Longstaff is afraid to avow his love in the first instance and
that fear is a component of his illness. His later rationalization is
that hurt pride contributed to his recovery: actually what did was
the removal of the source of his great, brooding, disastrous anxiety.
From the moment that Diana rejected him—from the moment that
she made it clear the relationship must remain that of a man to a
statue—Longstaff no longer felt himself threatened. He was suffer-

ing, indeed, from the Jamesian malady to which we have already alluded, which the novelist unwittingly summed up in the names in his notebook, *Ledward, Bedward, Dedward.* . . . So Henry's reiterated expression in his letter to William, stated in four different ways—that Minny had become a memory, a thought instead of a fact, an image, "a steady unfaltering luminary in the mind"—seemed in reality an expression of relief that Minny had permanently been converted into an invisible statue, an object to be serenely contemplated, appreciated and even loved—through the opaque glass of memory; and this without the uncomfortable feeling that he ought, in the process of becoming "more active and masculine," to do something about his feelings. Henry and Longstaff were one. And Minny's death, much as it brought deep personal grief and a sense of irreparable loss, brought also, in this curious buried fashion, a concealed emotional relief. Years later Henry was to re-embody the same situation in an even more morbid tale than "Longstaff's Marriage"—"Maud-Evelyn," in which a "hero" named Marmaduke, renounces marriage in order to accept an imaginary marriage to a girl who has died; the dead girl's parents think of him as the man she would have married had she lived. He humors them and he more than humors himself; for a flesh-and-blood wife he has substituted a ghost. The dead Dedrick girl shapes and controls his life. Fear-ridden, shut in, he escapes his fears and finds an easy security in this fancied espousal to a woman who will never be a threat to him. He achieves the status of a widower with even less difficulty than Longstaff. The two tales, separated by a quarter of a century, are corollary to one another; in reality they tell the same story.

I V

The ending of Henry James's long letter to William about Minny Temple is a summing up of all his feelings, expressed and re-expressed in a kind of Shakespearian last tribute over the tomb of an unattainable Juliet or Ophelia: "Farewell to all that she was!

How much this was, and how sweet it was! How it comes back to one, the charm and essential grace of her early years. We shall all have known something! How it teaches, absolutely, tenderness and wonder to the mind. But it's all locked away, incorruptibly, within the crystal walls of the past. And there is my youth—and anything of yours you please and welcome! turning to gold in her bright keeping. In exchange, for you, dearest Minny, we'll all keep your future. . . ."

The crystal walls of the past. Minny alive had been a constant reminder to Henry of his inarticulateness and his fear to assert himself. Minny gradually sinking into decline could renew his strength. Dead, Minny was Henry's, within the crystal walls of his mind. He could write—and it is almost in a tone of triumph— "She has gone where there is neither marrying nor giving in marriage! no illusion and no disillusion—no sleepless nights and no ebbing strength." In these balanced parallels—marrying and giving in marriage, illusion and disillusion, sleepless nights and ebbing strength—marriage and decline again are wrapped together, ledward-bedward-dedward fashion. He did not have to marry Minny and risk the awful consequences—and no one else could, neither John Gray, nor William, nor Wendell, none of the clever young men who surrounded her at Conway or in the ballrooms of New York. Minny was now permanently his, the creature of his dreams.

She became, nine years after her death, the heroine of *The Portrait of a Lady*. The hero of that scene, Ralph Touchett, dies of consumption (again a reversal of roles) but not before he has watched Isabel—whose last name is Archer and so has a kinship with the Archeress Diana—play out the drama of her life and make a mess of it. "Poor Minny! how much she was not to see!" Henry had written to his mother. To Grace Norton he elaborated this thought and set down in 1870 what was to become the core of his novel of 1880: "She was a divinely restless spirit— essentially one of the 'irreconcilables'; and if she had lived to

great age, I think it would have been as the victim and plaything of her constant and generous dreams and dissatisfactions."

In the novel Henry gave his heroine a chance to see the world and live out her dreams and dissatisfactions. Isabel goes from Albany to England, to Italy, and sees all that Minny might have seen; she has much of the happiness Minny might have had, is surrounded by a group of lovers strangely parallel to the lovers in "Poor Richard," becomes the stepmother of Pansy Osmond (sketched from Minny's friend Lizzie Boot) and is the victim of her own bright intensities. Surrounded by the three lovers, one disqualified by invalidism, she picks a fourth and ruins her life.

In the years between *The Portrait* and *The Wings of the Dove* there was a curious story, a pot-boiler, written for a newspaper syndicate and therefore intentionally sensationalized by James, entitled "Georgina's Reasons" in which there figures a girl named Mildred or Milly Theory who dies of consumption, and her sister Kate. Milly Theory is a pale shadow of the future Milly Theale and Kate in no way resembles Kate Croy of *The Wings*. (That a Kate should be placed beside the two Millys is not surprising, for Minny's older sister was Katherine, commonly known as Kitty.) Again Minny's ghostly figure had passed across Henry's desk and she came back finally at the turn of the century to be converted into the ultimate flame-like creature of his fiction. The theme of *The Wings* was the reverse of that of *The Portrait*. The earlier novel had grown from the speculation. "What sort of life would Minny have had?" The later novel was the fictional rendering of her actual ordeal, the real frustration and tragedy—the death of a young woman who wants to live.

". . . Death, at the last, was dreadful to her; she would have given anything to live." And when Milly Theale, the "dove," has folded her wings, Kate Croy and Morton Densher confront one another. Milly's money makes possible at last their long-deterred marriage. Kate, however, is no longer sure of Densher.

"Your word of honour that you're not in love with her memory."

"Oh—her memory!" Densher exclaims.

Kate makes a high gesture. "Ah don't speak of it as if you couldn't be. . . . *Her memory's your love. You want no other.*"

So it was with Minny Temple and Henry James.

RETURN

HENRY RECROSSED THE ATLANTIC IN THE SPRING OF 1870 EAGER TO be home. Fifteen months had elapsed since his visit to Pelham, the most crowded and dramatic of his life. Minny had been laid to rest next to her father and mother in Albany Rural Cemetery and Henry seems to have observed the prescription of his letters: a little decent grief, "a sigh of relief—and we begin to live for ourselves again." The hallowed memories had no relation to the continuing reality; and reality for him was the determination to recover his health completely and become a great American novelist.

In the first days at Malvern after receiving the news of Minny's death he had had a bad relapse in health. The back-ache returned and he rushed to London to consult a specialist. He was told that he had indulged excessively in hip baths and given himself "a sort of inflammation" in the kidney region. Dressing the balance between remaining abroad and returning home he decided that the most economical road to recovery lay through Quincy Street. In London a meeting with his Aunt Kate, who had been travelling abroad, provoked an acute fit of homesickness. They sailed together on April 30, on the *Scotia*.

By the time he reached Cambridge—on May 10—he was so much improved that the comparatively new Dr. William James, who examined him, pronounced him "tough and stout" although he still found tenderness in the kidney region. Writing to Robertson, William gave a full report on Henry and remarked, "His constipation meanwhile has been reduced to very manageable limits and will probably give him no more serious trouble. He . . . seems in every way a different being from what he used to be."

For the moment Henry sought some point of re-attachment to the old scenes. He had a sense of lost time and of pressure to get back to his writing. A few days after his return, in a letter to Grace Norton, who was still abroad, he proceeded to recreate Harvard into an Italian scene. "Here I am—here I have been for the last ten days—the last ten years. It's very hot: the window is open before me: opposite thro' the thin trees I see the scarlet walls of the president's *palazzo*. Beyond, the noble grey mass—the lovely outlines, of the library: and above this the soaring *campanile* of the wooden church on the *piazza*. In the distance I hear the carpenters hammering at the great edifice in process of erection in the college yard—and in sweet accordance the tinkle of the horse-cars. Oh how the May-wind feels like August. But never mind: I am to go into town this P.M. and I shall get a charming breeze in the cars crossing the bridge. . . . Howells is lecturing very pleasantly on Italian literature. I go to the lecture room in Boylston hall; and sit with my eyes closed, listening to the sweet Italian names and allusions and trying to fancy that the window behind me opens out into Florence. But Florence is within and not without."

He goes on to ponder his course. "I wish I were able to tell you . . . what, now that I have got America again, I am going to do with it. Like it enormously *sans doute:* they say there is nothing like beginning with a little aversion. My fear is that mine is too old to end in a grand passion. But America is American: that is incontestable, and consistency is a jewel. I wish I could tell you how characteristic everything strikes me as being—every-

thing from the vast white sky—to the stiff sparse individual blades of grass."

Two days later he went to lunch at Shady Hill. Cambridge was in the fullest beauty of the spring. "The grass was all golden with buttercups—the trees all silver with apple blossoms, the sky a glorious storm of light, the air a perfect hurricane of zephyrs. We sat (Miss C. Hooper, Miss Boott &c) on a verandah a long time immensely enjoying the fun. But oh my dear Grace it was ghostly. For me the breeze was heavy with whispering spirits. Down in that glade to the right three women were wading thro' the long grass and a child picking the buttercups. One of them was you, the others Jane and Susan—the child Eliot. Mesdemoiselles Hooper and Boott talked of Boston, I thought of Florence. I wanted to go down to you in the glade and we should play it was the Villa Landor. Susan would enact Miss Landor. But the genius of my beloved country—in the person of Miss Hooper—detained me. I don't know indeed whether I most wanted you to be there or to be myself in Florence. Or rather I do very well know and I am quite ashamed of my fancy of robbing that delightful scene of its simple American beauty. I wished you all there for an hour, enjoying your own. . . ."

For Henry the year in Europe had worked its spell and he could announce to Grace Norton, "When I next go to Italy it will be not for months but years." In the meantime there were contrasts and comparisons to be made between the Old World and the New, tales to write that were the fruit of his journeys, and the question of his career. He had tasted enough of Europe to want to see much more of it: ill-health and the money anxieties of Quincy Street had interrupted his course. What was to follow now was a period of careful exploration of New England and then a renewed and longer experience of Europe. It was William James who in a letter to Robertson peered questioningly into Henry's future:

"I fear his taste of Europe will prevent his ever getting thoroughly reconciled to this country and I imagine that he will

end, when he becomes self-supporting, by spending most of his time there. Certainly with his artistic temperament and literary occupations, I should not blame him for the choice."

When he was writing the closing words of *Notes of a Son and Brother*, almost half a century later, Henry James said that he and William felt the death of Minny Temple to be "the end of our youth." Shortly afterwards, however, he qualified this in the opening words of *The Middle Years:* "We are never old, that is we never cease easily to be young, for *all* life at the same time." And he went on to liken youth to a continuing "reluctant march into the enemy country, the country of the general lost freshness."

If in 1870 one phase of his youth seemed at an end, another was about to begin; there was still a great fund of freshness that had not yet been lost. By trial, by error, by the happy accidents of nature and the long ordeal of discipline, the artist had been formed, a quiet, pondering, sovereign being, with a great, strange, passionate gift of expression wedded to the gift of observation and insight. "Mysterious and incontrollable (even to oneself) is the growth of one's mind," he wrote to William. "Little by little, I trust, my abilities will catch up with my ambitions."

They were catching up more rapidly than he believed. He was ready now to test to the full the literary resources of his country before he would again test those of Europe. The fledgling years, the untried years, were at an end. The long ordeal of the war, the struggle for health, Minny's death "the whole infinitude" of pain, "door within door" had been experienced. "I have in my own fashion learned the lesson that life is effort, unremittingly repeated," Henry wrote to Norton. Now, before him, stretched the broad new decades he was to call his "middle years."

NOTES

Henry James wrote the story of his boyhood and youth in A *Small Boy and Others* (1913) and *Notes of a Son and Brother* (1914) and left a brief fragment of what would have been a third volume, *The Middle Years*, posthumously published in 1917. These remarkable volumes have been indispensable guides in the writing of this book. James, however, was looking back at the small boy and the adolescent across half a century; and it has been my task to review and evaluate his memories while supplementing them with the biographical details now available. Autobiography is written out of experience, memory, emotion; biography is a re-living and re-examination of someone else's experience, and this distinction had to be borne in mind constantly.

The greatest single collection of documents for a biography of Henry James is to be found at Harvard University, in the Houghton Library. I was given access to much of this material by the late Henry James, of New York, literary executor of his father, William

James, and his uncle, Henry, before it was presented to Harvard. I have continued to have access to it and to the new materials which have enlarged this collection to make it a vast repository of the history of a great American family. I am indebted to the President and Fellows of Harvard College for the privilege of continued access to this priceless collection as well as to corollary materials in the other collections of the Houghton Library. William A. Jackson, the librarian, has shown me many kindnesses over many years; and I am indebted to Carolyn E. Jakeman, of his staff, for generous assistance.

No work on Henry James during the past half century has been written that has not been indebted to the bibliography compiled by Le Roy Phillips in 1906 and extensively revised in 1930. Mr. Phillips preserved and recorded much that might have been lost to us and his work has been the foundation stone of all Jamesian studies. I am grateful to him not only for his invaluable book but for a tolerably long friendship during which he made available to me all his bibliographical files.

My debt to others who have aided me in my work is acknowledged in the Introduction to this volume and in the Notes on my sources given below.

I have used the initials of the members of the James family, HJ Sr, Mrs. HJ Sr, CBJ, HJ, WJ, AJ, RJ.

Letters listed in these notes without any other indication are in the James Collection of the Houghton Library.

Abbreviations for certain key works are as follows:

Lubbock: Percy Lubbock, *The Letters of HJ* (New York, 1920).
WJ *Letters: The Letters of* WJ edited by his son Henry (Boston, 1920).
Perry: R. B. Perry, *The Thought and Character of* WJ, 2 vols. (Boston, 1935).
Notebooks: F. O. Matthiessen and K. B. Murdock, *Notebooks of HJ* (New York, 1947).
JF: F. O. Matthiessen, *The James Family* (New York, 1947).
Phillips: Le Roy Phillips, *A Bibliography of the Writings of HJ* (New York, 1930).

Harlow: Virginia Harlow, *Thomas Sergeant Perry* (Durham, N. C., 1951).
SBO: *A Small Boy and Others* (New York, 1913).
NSB: *Notes of a Son and Brother* (New York, 1914).

BOOK ONE: *Interrogation of the Past*

The Spectral Eye: Ms family letters from 1816 to 1824 referring to William James of Albany (1771-1832); wills of William James and CBJ; the will of William of Albany was broken by decree of 30 Dec. 1836 and as a result of litigation properties in Syracuse were partitioned by the courts which resulted in the allotment of certain parcels of real estate to HJ Sr. See "James Townsend and Abba his wife, and Augustus James and Elizabeth his wife *vs* James McBride and Hannah his wife, William James and others" (*In Chancery*, Albany 1844 and 1846) with documents pertaining thereto annexed. The partition decree was handed down in 1846. The HJ Sr allotment is listed on pp. 57-60. The court documents were bound into a volume labelled "The Syracuse Partition Suit" which is in the Houghton Library together with miscellaneous genealogical material; Hastings, Katherine B., *William James of Albany N.Y. and His Descendants*, reprinted from the New York Genealogical and Biographical Record, Vol. LV (1924); WJ *Letters* I, 1-19.

HJ Sr (1811-1882): *Lectures and Miscellanies* (New York, 1852); *The Nature of Evil* (New York, 1855); *Substance and Shadow* (Boston, 1863); *The Secret of Swedenborg* (Boston, 1869); WJ, ed., *The Literary Remains of Henry James* (Boston, 1885), 123-91; NSB, Chaps. V, VI; Warren, Austin, *The Elder Henry James* (New York, 1934); Grattan, C. Hartley, *The Three Jameses* (New York, 1932); Perry, Chaps. I-VIII; JF, 3-59; Young, F. H., *The Philosophy of Henry James Sr.* (New York, 1951); Howells, W. D., *Literary Friends and Acquaintances* (New York, 1900).

Vastation: HJ Sr, *Society the Redeemed Form of Man* (Boston, 1879), 43-54, 70-74; NSB, 173 *et seq*; Walsh, Rev. William, *A Record and Sketch of Hugh Walsh's Family* (Newburgh, N. Y., 1903); *Correspondence of Carlyle and Emerson* (Boston, 1883), I, 308; II, 38, 83, 252; SBO, 233; HJ Sr to Thoreau, 12 May 1843, in Morgan Library, New York; I am indebted to Dan H. Laurence for establishing the exact location of the birthplace by research in the New York City Hall of Records.

Keystone of the Arch: NSB, 268, 178 *et seq*; *Notebooks*, 39-41; Mrs. HJ Sr to Mrs. J. J. Garth Wilkinson, 29 Nov. 1846; Miss Florence Pertz, granddaughter of Dr. Wilkinson and a friend of HJ's last years, made available to me the James letters to members of her family. The collection subsequently was added to the material at Harvard; Mrs. HJ Sr to WJ, 10 June, 21 Nov. 1867, 23 Jan. 1874; to HJ, 21 Jan., 25 May, 1 July, 12 Sept. 1873; AJ, *Journal* (New York, 1934), 112, 130 *et seq*; Emerson, E. W., *Early Years of the Saturday Club* (1918), 328; Ogden, Rollo, *Life and Letters of E. L. Godkin* (New York, 1907), II, 117-18; Harlow, 18; WJ *Letters*, 9.

Mere Junior: HJ to WJ Jr, 19 May 1913; Lubbock, II, 314-15; Mrs. HJ Sr to HJ, 4 Aug. 1873; HJ to unidentified autograph hunter, 12 Feb. 1882, communicated to the author by Earl Daniels; WJ *Letters,* 21; Lubbock, I, 69; *Favorite Fairy Tales,* The Childhood Choice of Representative Men and Women (New York, 1907).

Notes on a Nightmare: SBO, Chap. XXV; *Notebooks,* 367-68; Harlow, 262-63; NSB, 60.

BOOK TWO: *Scenes from a Boyhood*

The Two Squares: SBO, 17, 53-54; HJ Sr to CBJ, undated letter, Windsor [1844]; HJ, *The American Scene,* 87-89.

A Flavor of Peaches: WJ *Letters,* I, 4-6; Hastings, *op. cit.*; SBO, 70. Catharine (with an "a") is the form used in speaking of Catharine Barber James in most records and in WJ's edition of HJ Sr's *Literary Remains,* although HJ spelled the name Catherine.

58 West Fourteenth Street: Dan H. Laurence established some of the details concerning this house by researches kindly conducted on my behalf in the New York City Hall of Records; SBO, 63, 177; NSB, 203-07; HJ, "George Du Maurier" in *Partial Portraits.*

Picture and Scene: SBO, 3, 76, 182-86, 267.

An Initiation: SBO, 76-78.

The Dickens Imprint: SBO, 117-18.

A Small Boy at the Theatre: SBO, 78-80, 101-20, 154-71.

. . . *And Others:* SBO, Chaps. I, IV, XI, XXVIII; Hastings, *op. cit.*

BOOK THREE: *The Nostalgic Cup*

Theory of Education: NSB, Chap. III; Harlow, 268-69; SBO, Chaps. XV, XVI; Perry, Chap. IX. In a number of instances I have corrected names and places mentioned by HJ, basing my information on New York City directories of the time.

The Thames and the Seine: HJ Sr to Emerson, NSB, 183; cf. Perry, I, 59; HJ Sr to Dr. Wilkinson, 9 Sept. 1851; HJ, Preface to Vol. XIII, N. Y. Edition, xix-xx; HJ Sr to CBJ, 11 July 1855; SBO, 281-85; HJ Sr to CBJ, 13 Aug. 1855; HJ Sr letters to *Tribune,* 3, 8, 22 Sept. 1855; 15, 16 Jan.; 7 Feb.; 17 Mar.; 26 Aug.; 12, 16 Sept.; 1 Oct. 1856; Dan H. Laurence sent me the advertisement in the London *Times* inserted by HJ Sr; I am indebted to Simon Nowell-Smith for the correct spelling of Thomson's name. In a letter from HJ to Robert Thomson, 21 Dec. [?1880] owned by Mr. Nowell-Smith, HJ wrote "Dear Mr. Thompson" and then scratched out the "p"; SBO, Chaps. XXI-XXVII, XXIX; HJ Sr to Mrs. Charles A. Dana, 26 Mar. 1856; HJ Sr to

CBJ, 23 July, 10 Sept., 15 Oct. 1857; HJ Sr to Rev. William James, 28 Oct. 1857; to Anna H. Barker, 2 Nov. and 25 Dec. 1857; Mrs. HJ Sr to CBJ, 24 Dec. 1857.

Newport Idyll: HJ Sr to Fanny MacDaniel, 15 Aug. 1858; to Sam Ward, 18 Sept. [1859]; HJ (nephew) record of talk with his uncle in an unpublished note in possession of his widow; Harlow 239, 245, 344; NSB, Chap. IV; HJ, "Newport" in *Portraits of Places;* "The Sense of Newport" in *The American Scene.*

The Rhône and the Rhine: HJ, "Swiss Notes" in *Transatlantic Sketches;* Harlow, 239-64; NSB, Chaps. I-III; HJ to Mrs. HJ Sr, Bonn, "Tuesday evening" [Aug. 1860].

Palette and Pen: Anna Hunter, "Kay Street During My Life" (Newport Historical Society Bulletin No. 83); the deed for purchase of land and later sale of the Spring Street property is in the City Hall records, Newport; Maud Howe Elliott, *Three Generations* (Boston, 1923), and *This Was My Newport* (Cambridge, 1944); Cortissoz, Royal, *John La Farge* (Boston, 1921) 117-19; LaFarge, John, S. J., "Henry James's Letters to the LaFarges'," *New England Quarterly,* XXII, No. 2 (June 1949), 173-92; Mackaye, Percy, *Epoch, The Life of Steele Mackaye* (New York, 1927), Chaps. II and III; Robinson, Edwin Arlington, *Letters of Thomas Sergeant Perry* (New York, 1929); Morse, John T., *Thomas Sergeant Perry* (Boston, 1929).

BOOK FOUR: *The Vast Visitation*

An Obscure Hurt: Quotations from T. S. Perry's diaries are printed here with the kind permission of his daughter, Miss Margaret Perry, and were generously supplied by Virginia Harlow, Perry's biographer; HJ Sr, *The Social Significance of Our Institutions* (Boston, 1861); NSB, Chap. IX; I am indebted to Herbert O. Brigham, librarian of the Newport Historical Society, for supplying the records of the Newport Fire Department; Newport *Mercury,* 2 Nov. 1861; Newport *Daily News,* 29 Oct. 1861; Lubbock, I, 89, 317, 406-07; Gosse, Edmund, "Henry James" in *Aspects and Impressions* (New York, 1922); *Notebooks,* 320; HJ, "Mr. and Mrs. J. T. Fields," *Atlantic Monthly,* July 1915; Spender, Stephen, *The Destructive Element* (London, 1935), 36-37; JF, 247; Spiller, Thorp, Johnson, Canby, eds., *Literary History of the United States* (New York, 1948), II, 1040; Trilling, Lionel, *The Liberal Imagination* (New York, 1950), 169; *Hound & Horn,* HJ issue, April 1934; William McCann allowed me to draw upon his extensive knowledge of the history of the Civil War for certain details in this chapter; Rosenzweig, Saul, "The Ghost of Henry James," in *Character and Personality* (Dec. 1943), examines HJ's first signed story "The Story of a Year," which dealt with the Civil War, in the light of HJ Sr's amputation and HJ's "obscure hurt." Dr. Rosenzweig was the first to draw attention to HJ's belief that his hurt would be of long duration. The essay is an insightful study, by means of thematic apperception,

of some of the forces which shaped HJ's personality; it is inevitably limited by the minimum biographical data which the writer used.

The Younger Brothers: NSB, Chaps. IX, XI; Mary James Vaux, of Bryn Mawr, daughter of Robertson James, generously made available her family papers which had been used by Anna Robeson Burr in the editing of Alice James: Her Brothers, Her Journal (New York, 1934); Hawthorne, Edith Garrigue, The Memoirs of Julian Hawthorne (New York, 1938), 120-22; WJ, "Robert Gould Shaw" in Memories and Studies (New York, 1917); HJ to Viscount Wolseley, 7 Dec. 1903.

A Particular Divergence: NSB, Chaps. IX, X; Harlow, 260; although HJ speaks of "John" May in NSB, 328, T. S. Perry identified him as "Joe"; HJ, "Emerson," in Partial Portraits, HJ, "James Russell Lowell" in Essays in London.

Ashburton Place: NSB, Chap. XII; HJ, essay on Mr. and Mrs. Fields, op. cit.; HJ, Preface to Roderick Hudson, Vol. I, N. Y. Edition, ix-xii; Norton, Sara and Howe, M. A. DeWolfe, Letters of Charles Eliot Norton, 2 vols. (Boston, 1913); The North American Review letters from HJ to Norton in the Houghton Library are not originals, but hand-copied, apparently from the originals. It is from these that I have quoted in this chapter; HJ to Norton, 9 Aug., 15 Oct., 11 Nov., 1 Dec. 1864; 29 May, 31 July, 11 Sept., 13 Oct., 28 Nov. 1865; 28 Feb. 1866; Cheney, Ednah D., Louisa May Alcott (Boston, 1899); I am indebted to Mrs. John Hall Wheelock for discovering among her grandmother's letters to her father the letter which enabled me to identify HJ's unsigned story; Edna Kenton, in her preface to Eight Uncollected Tales of Henry James (1950), analyzes the terms, ideas and techniques in HJ's early work foreshadowing his later fully-developed art; Harlow, 275; Ogden, Rollo, op. cit.; NSB, 424-26.

Heroine of the Scene: HJ to T. B. Aldrich, 13 Feb. [1884]: HJ promises to write The Princess Casamassima for the next year, 1885, but writes it "1865" throughout; Notebooks, 319-20; NSB, 76, 412-56, 460-64; Howe, Mark DeWolfe, "The Letters of Henry James to Mr. Justice Holmes," Yale Review, XXXVIII (Spring 1949), 410-33 (the two letters from Jefferson, N. H., dated [1865] should be of [1868]); HJ to Norton, 31 July 1865; Tilton, Eleanor M., Amiable Autocrat, A Biography of Dr. Oliver Wendell Holmes (New York, 1947); Bowen, Catherine Drinker, Yankee From Olympus, Justice Holmes and His Family (Boston, 1945); Howe, Julia Ward, Reminiscences (Boston, 1899).

BOOK FIVE: A Cambridge Life

The Silver Mirror: Notebooks, 35-36.

Jacob and Esau: Genesis, 25-28; Notebooks, 320; WJ Letters, I, 84-86; HJ to WJ, 10 May, 21 May [1867]; Mrs. HJ Sr to WJ, 27 May, 10 June 1867;

WJ to HJ, 26 Sept. 1867; WJ to Norton, 3 Sept. 1864; HJ to WJ, 21 May
[1867]; Harlow, 277-88; Perry, I, 241, 245-46, 250-51, 261-73.

Venus and Diana: HJ to Katherine Temple, 28 July 1868; HJ's letters to
Grace and Jane Norton, Theodora Sedgwick, Frances Morse, Elizabeth and
Francis Boott, are preserved in the Houghton Library; Edna Kenton collected
(1950) "The Story of a Year," "The Story of a Masterpiece" and "Osborne's
Revenge" in *Eight Uncollected Tales;* Saint-Victor, Paul de, *Hommes et
Dieux* (Paris, 1867): the essay on the Venus de Milo constitutes the first
chapter. The translation is mine, and the copy with the HJ inscription is in
my possession, as well as a second copy, also owned by HJ.

The Two Georges: HJ's writings on George Sand and George Eliot are listed
in Phillips with the exception of the unsigned review of *Middlemarch,* which I
identified in the *Galaxy* of March 1873 from a letter, HJ to Mrs. HJ Sr, 17
Feb. [1873] in which HJ spoke of having reviewed the novel for the *Nation;*
they had, however, given the book to another reviewer and sent HJ's review to
the *Galaxy* without consulting him. He told Mrs. HJ Sr he would have preferred to give it to Howells for the *Atlantic.* Further confirmation is contained
in HJ Sr to HJ, 18 Mar. [1873] informing him that *Galaxy* had sent pay-
ment for the review.

The Terrible Burden: Harlow, 282-86; *Notebooks* 24.

A Surburban Friendship: Lubbock, II, 221-26; HJ's correspondence with
the editors of the *Galaxy,* W. C. and F. B. Church, is preserved in the New
York Public Library; Howells, Mildred, *Life in Letters of William Dean
Howells* (New York, 1928), 116-18, 394-99; W. D. Howells to HJ 2 Jan.
1870; HJ to WJ, 16 May 1890; to W. D. Howells, 17 May 1890; to Grace
Norton, 27 Nov. 1870; to W. D. Howells, 3 Feb., 28 May [1876]; to Norton,
9 Aug. 1871; Howells, W. D., "Henry James, Jr." *Century,* n.s. III (Nov.
1882), 25-29.

A Brief Encounter: NSB, 253-56; Perry, I, 251; Howe, M. A. DeWolfe,
Memories of a Hostess (Boston, 1922).

BOOK SIX: *The Passionate Pilgrimage*

Departure: NSB, 467-70.

The Banquet of Initiation: HJ, "London" in *Essays in London;* HJ, *The
Middle Years,* Chaps. I-IV; although HJ speaks at the beginning of *The
Middle Years* of arriving in Liverpool in March 1869, his ship docked at noon
Feb. 27, a Saturday, as two letters written that day show, HJ to his parents
and a letter to Catherine Walsh; HJ to Mrs. HJ Sr, 2 March 1869 in JF,
253-55; Lubbock, I, 15-21; 1869: HJ to Grace Norton, 6 April; to WJ, 8 April;
WJ to HJ, 23 April; HJ to WJ, 26 April; to HJ Sr, 10 May; to WJ, 20 May.

The Dishevelled Nymph: HJ to parents, 10 Sept. 1869; to Mrs. HJ Sr, JF
258; to John La Farge, 20 June, 21 Sept. 1869 (in *New England Quarterly,
op cit.* 176-78); to Mrs. HJ Sr, JF, 256; Mrs. HJ Sr to HJ, JF, 258; HJ to AJ,

31 Aug. 1869; Mrs. HJ Sr, to HJ, 21 Sept. 1869; HJ, *Italian Hours*, 1909, assembled most of his writings about Italy, early and late; Lubbock, I, 21-25; HJ, A *Little Tour in France*, Chap. XXXIII.

Minny Temple: NSB, Chap. XIII. The Jameses were never consistent in spelling her name, varying between Minnie and Minny. I have chosen the latter since it is in this form that HJ wrote her name at the time of her death; Minny Temple's letters to HJ are of 3 June, 15 Aug., 22 Aug. and 7 Nov. 1869. These were published by Robert C. LeClair, in "Henry James and Minny Temple," *American Literature*, XXI No. 1 (March 1949), 35-48, but there are several errors in their transcription; Mrs. HJ Sr to HJ, 24 July 1869, JF, 258-59; HJ to HJ Sr, 14 Jan. 1870; to AJ, 25 Jan.; to Mrs. HJ Sr, 5 Feb.; to WJ, 13 Feb; Lubbock, I, 26; HJ's letter to his mother on Minny's death of 26 Mar. 1870 was published in *American Literature*, by LeClair, *op.cit.* 38-41 but wrongly dated 29 Mar.; HJ to WJ, 29 Mar., JF, 259-63.

The Wings of the Dove: Notebooks, 169; HJ to Grace Norton, 1 April 1870.

Return: WJ to RJ, 2 Jan. 1870 from a letter in the papers of Mary James Vaux; HJ to Grace Norton, 20 May 1870.

Index

345

HENRY   JAMES

1843=187

DATE DUE

#47-0108 Peel Off Pressure Sensitive